Praise for the previous edition of *How Rude!*®

A "Book for the Teen Age"—**New York Public Library**

A "Quick Pick" selection—**American Library Association**

A "Read, America!" Classic selection

"This is one fast-paced, fun-to-read book that covers the basics of good behavior for teens. But before you dismiss it with a roll of your eyes and a huge yawn (now that's rude!), just one look at the table of contents will convince you that this isn't your grandma's guidebook. This is a wonderfully hip and humorous, easy read!"—*College Bound* Magazine

"Covers everything from table manners to hygiene, handling friendship problems politely, thank-you notes, flaming online, and manners around the house."—*KLIATT*

"From its intriguing title to the tongue-in-cheek ideas for dealing with many kinds of situations, readers will find this manual humorous, nonthreatening, entertaining, and educational. You will return to it again and again."—*School Library Journal*

"*How Rude!* offers surprisingly simple ways for teens to respond to and interact with people to get the best results in today's world. It shows that if we'd all follow a few simple, common-sense rules, the world would be a far better place."—*Youthworker*

HOW RUDE!®

The Teen Guide to Good Manners, Proper Behavior, and Not Grossing People Out

ALEX J. PACKER, PH.D.

free spirit
PUBLISHING®

Library of Congress Cataloging-in-Publication
Packer, Alex J.
     How rude! : the teen guide to good manners, proper behavior, and not grossing people out /
by Alex J. Packer, Ph.D. — Revised and updated edition.
          pages cm
     Includes bibliographical references and index.
     ISBN 978-1-57542-454-5 — ISBN 1-57542-454-1 1. Etiquette for children and teenagers. I. Title.
     BJ1857.C5P33 2014
     395.1'23—dc23
                                                                                      2014001602

ISBN: 978-1-57542-454-5

Reading Level High School–Adult; Interest Level Ages 13 & Up; Fountas & Pinnell Guided Reading Level Z+

Edited by Pamela Espeland and Darsi Dreyer
Cover and interior design by Tasha Kenyon
Illustrations by Jeff Tolbert

10 9 8 7 6 5 4 3 2
Printed in the United States of America
B10951114

Free Spirit Publishing Inc.
Minneapolis, MN
(612) 338-2068
help4kids@freespirit.com
www.freespirit.com

Free Spirit offers competitive pricing.
Contact edsales@freespirit.com for pricing information on multiple quantity purchases.

Dedication

For Janet . . .
. . . who, except for call waiting, is impeccably polite.

Acknowledgments

Even if it weren't the polite thing to do, I would still want to thank the following individuals whose advice, support, and expertise were essential to the creation and/or revision of this book.

Joel Anderson, Melissa Banta, Susan Banta, Tim Braine, Angel Colón, Patricia Colón, Adrienne Covington, Shelley Cross, Ida Del Vecchio, Launa Ellison, Bruce Embry, Keith Evans, the teachers of FCD Educational Services, Betsy Gabler, Jay Gabler, Richard V. Goodwin, Eric Grunebaum, Stephen Gustin, Sue Hallowell, Jan Hassan, Ross Herbertson, John Houchin, Aaron Hubbard, Norman Jenkins, Sharon Johnson, Paul Jordan, Midge Kimball, Suzanne Laberge, Alejandro Lobo, Reina O'Hale, John Packard, Janet Packer, Brian Ogden, Sandi Pei, Nancy Robinson, Amy Rotenberg, Mark Rotenberg, Efrem Seeger, Maurice Soulis, Renee Soulis, Charles L. Terry III, Desirae Vasquez, Craig Vezina, and Ned Vizzini, who left us so much, and left us too soon, for their advice, encouragement, and help in distributing surveys;

The hundreds of teenagers, parents, counselors, and educators who participated in my surveys;

Mindy Anderson, Jay Gabler, Ollie Hallowell, Ollie Hallowell Productions, John Houchin, Jonah Klevesahl, Monica Longe, Greg Nadeau, Kerri Nadeau, Max Nadeau, Ellen Paquet, Gabrielle Scott, Jill Thunborg, Teja Upadhyaya, David Waterman, Zoë Wentzel, Jessica Wilber, and the Free Spirit Teen Advisory Council for reading and commenting on the manuscript;

Toyla Ashe, Adriana Banta, Gabrielle Banta, Max Banta, Sophia Banta, Alex Herdman, and Patrick Kinsey for their invaluable advice—without rolling any eyeballs—on teenage computer, smartphone, and social media use and terminology. (Example: Me: "Do you guys use the expression 'booting up'?" Blank stares. "You know, when you turn on your computers." Blank stares. "Well, what word do you use for when you turn on your tablets or smartphones?" Pause. "We never turn them off." "Oh.")

Kim Armstrong, formerly with the Killington Ski Resort in Killington, Vermont, for her help with slopeside courtesies;

The dudes at the legendary Maximus Skatepark in Cambridge, Massachusetts, for their thoughts on and demonstrations of skateboard etiquette;

The Inline Club of Boston for tips on skating etiquette;

Arthur Kinsman, former director of public, government and community relations, American Automobile Association, Massachusetts, for AAA safety advice and rules of the road;

Daniel Vest and the Gay and Lesbian Alliance Against Defamation (GLAAD) for suggestions and research data relating to bigotry and homophobia;

Debbie Fiore at the Federation for Children with Special Needs; Brad Pearson, advocate, Massachusetts Office on Disability; Jody Williams, abuse prevention project coordinator, Commonwealth of Massachusetts Disabled Persons Protection Commission; and the Massachusetts Association for the Blind for providing information on interacting with people with disabilities;

The Authors Guild for their tireless efforts on behalf of writers;

My agents Gail Ross and Howard Yoon of the Ross Yoon Agency for their advice, support, and generosity;

Darsi Dreyer, Lauren Ernt, Sara Hartman, Steven Hauge, Heidi Hogg, Tasha Kenyon, Lisa Leonard, Julie Smith, Anastasia Scott, Elizabeth Verdick, and the staff of Free Spirit Publishing for their enthusiasm, responsiveness, and unswerving professionalism;

Judy Galbraith, president of Free Spirit Publishing, for her courage and imagination as a publisher, and her encouragement and good humor as a friend;

Pamela Espeland for her brilliance and creativity as an editor; for putting up with my authorial moods and bad jokes; for keeping me within the bounds of good taste (or at least trying to); and for the respect and repartee that made the process of creating the first edition of the book so stimulating and enjoyable;

And finally, I wish to thank the countless individuals whose ill-mannered, disgusting, boorish, vulgar, selfish, and arrogant behaviors kept me inspired and motivated throughout the course of this project.

Contents

List of Reproducible Pages

Preface

I wrote the first edition of *How Rude!* in the mid-1990s. This period was known as the Stone Age. You may have studied it in school. Life was primitive then. Teenagers didn't have cell phones. Most families didn't have computers. Fewer than one in six households were connected to the Internet.

If something went viral you gave it an antibiotic.

There was no YouTube. No Facebook. No Google.

No tweeting. No trending. No texting. (I *told* you it was primitive.)

Harry Potter hadn't even gotten into Hogwarts.

Yes, it was a long time ago in a galaxy far, far away. But in many ways it was a Golden Age. Government worked. (Well, kinda worked.) There was ice in the Arctic. You could take a flight without an electronic strip search.

Life was good back then. But rudeness was in the air. Go for a walk and you were likely to be run over by a skateboarder, deafened by a "boom box," or snarled at by a sales clerk. Ill-mannered adults were everywhere. And they were failing in their responsibility to pass along good manners to the next generation.

If adults weren't going to teach proper behavior, I would have to do it. So I decided to write a manners book for teens. I felt that my own flawless behavior, expertise in psychology, and demented sense of humor would make me the perfect Etiquette Guru to the Youth of America.

And thus, I began to write the book. Not a boring book about curtsies and raised pinkies that you might use to squash a bug but wouldn't be caught dead reading. No, I wanted to write a practical book that addressed the real lives of real teens and offered advice on:

- braces and bigotry
- barfing and belching
- backpack attacks
- locker room lapses
- cafeteria courtesies
- classroom coping
- dealing with bullying, rude adults, and total idiots
- picking noses
- popping zits
- giving gifts
- joining cliques

- breaking up
- breaking down
- making friends
- making enemies
- making out
- dodging dancing
- dumping dates
- artful listening
- clever conversing
- rowdy roommates
- pervy dogs
- bossy parents
- nasty blogs
- carefree carpools
- covert yawns
- super greetings
- stinky johns

So, my book came out and the rest, as they say, is history. Thousands of schools. Millions of teens and families. All basking in the bountiful benefits of best behavior. Knowing that treating people with kindness and respect is not only the *right* thing to do, but the smart thing to do: Good manners are good for *you*.

My work is done, I thought. I will leave the world a better place.

Fat chance.

Fast-forward to today. People are crankier than ever. You've got spoiled celebrities and vile politicians. Road rage and radio rants. Civility has sunk to new lows. Some days you go to school and it feels like you're a Hunger Games tribute.

Yup, the world has changed since I wrote the original *How Rude!* The biggest changes have to do with technology and communication. Today, kids come out of the womb wearing earbuds. Texting teens walk into trees. Parents yell "no electronics at the table." Ask people about their "significant other" and they'll show you their smartphone.

With all these changes I knew I had to revise the whole book, updating it for the 21st century. Here's just some of what's new in the new and improved *How Rude!*

New surveys. For the original *How Rude!* I asked teens, parents, and teachers for their ideas on manners—good and bad. I had to read each paper-and-pencil survey manually, first question to last, counting thousands of little hash marks, to record answers and score questions. For the new *How Rude!* I created three *online* surveys for parents, teachers, and teens. This time around I had computers to analyze data and calculate statistics, revealing what teens and adults really think about one another's behavior. What's the rudest thing anyone's ever done to you? If someone's rude is it okay to be rude back? Is sexting bad manners? You'll find answers to these and many other questions in the new *How Rude!*

Facebook etiquette. Parents who want to friend you? Drama queens who Facebook their meltdowns? Friends who bombard you with updates and post your photo without permission? Classmates who spread nasty gossip and rumors? In this brand-new section you'll discover polite ways to deal with Facebook *faux pas*. You'll find 24 Facebook Do's and Don'ts suggested by genuine teens. There's also a "Code of Facebook Etiquette for Parents" that you can show to you know who.

Tips for texting. According to my latest surveys, what really bothers teens is when they spend time with friends—who spend that time texting. Or, as one teen put it, "If you're with me, be with *me*." And you know what the #1 adult complaint about teen behavior is? Teens using electronic devices at inappropriate times. With so many teens texting and messaging, it's a whole new way of relating that's ripe for rudeness. So you'll find in the new *How Rude!* the latest tips for knowing when (and when not) to text; when (and when not) to use abbreviations, emoticons, and Internet slang; how to deal with textaholic friends; and much, much more.

Twittiquette. It's amazing how much pollution 140 characters can create. With so many people tweeting their every thought and move, the Land of Twitter is awash in litter. If you're a Twitter heavy hitter, you need to know the latest rules of the road for traveling down Tweet Street. Sweet.

Cyberbullying. Think of it as bullying to the power of 10. Thanks to social media and the Internet, an act of bullying that might once have been witnessed by five people can now be witnessed by 5,000,000! And it can be done anonymously and last forever. The new *How Rude!* contains advice on how to handle cyberbullying—whether you're a target, a bystander, or a perpetrator.

Airport protocols. Back in the 1990s, if you went to the airport to take a flight you'd scream for security if some stranger started pawing all over you. Today, post 9/11, it *is* security pawing all over you. So here's an updated guide for airport etiquette and friendly flying.

Hugging. Hugging is the new handshake. With more and more teens catching a clinch, it's time to lay out some new rules for the etiquette of embracing.

These are just some of the bigger changes in the new *How Rude!* But there are a lot of smaller changes as well. Some topics—like video store manners and fighting over the newspaper—were so last century they had to go.

Other topics needed makeovers to reflect new terms, new technologies, and the advancement of knowledge: In with voicemail, out with answering machines. Hello iPod, good-bye Walkman. You'll find new advice for online invitations, helping sick friends, talking to computers, the best way to sneeze—and much more!

The building blocks of good manners—respect, empathy, kindness, and consideration—never change. But times do. And when times change, manners change. If you're going to keep your edge, you've got to stay on top of these changes. You need to master Politeness Two-Point-O. This book will help you do just that.

MINDING MANNERS

Nobody's Polite Anymore, Why Should I Be?

This is a book about manners. If that makes you feel like throwing up, at least say "Excuse me" before rushing to the bathroom.* You have every reason to feel queasy upon hearing the word *manners*. For it is under the guise of teaching manners that young people are subjected to a blizzard of rudely imparted criticisms. When adults do it, they call it "correcting." When you do it, they call it "being fresh."

"Use your fork."
"Don't talk with your mouth full."
"Sit up straight."
"Look at me when I'm talking."
"Don't interrupt."

If the idea of learning good manners makes you feel like a dog being trotted off to obedience school, this is understandable. But if you turn your back on manners, you end up hurting yourself. This is because having good manners involves a lot more than knowing not to drink from the toilet bowl. It means knowing how to handle yourself in your life and relationships. And people who know how to handle themselves come out on top. They get what they want, feel good about themselves, and enjoy life to the fullest.

*SEE "RALPHING" FOR MORE ON THE ETIQUETTE OF UPCHUCKING.

This book will show you how to become a master of the art—and game—of proper social behavior. It will answer real questions from teenagers across America—such as:

"Is Miss Manners dead yet?"
Good gracious, no. She lives in Passaic with two cats and a doily.

"Do you have to extend your pinkie when drinking from a teacup?"
This practice is no longer necessary. But under NO circumstances should you extend your middle finger!

You'll find out things you've always wanted to know:

- Why do adults get mad when you text?
- How do you tell people they have spinach in their teeth?
- How much should you tip the pizza guy?
- Why should you be nice to people you don't like?
- Who came up with these ridiculous rules, and why are we expected to follow them?

You'll learn how to:

- deal with idiots
- react to bigoted remarks
- respond to adults who make rude comments
- tell someone his fly is open
- be the perfect host so your parents will beg you to have more friends over

You'll know just what to do when:

- people spread nasty rumors about you
- a dog nuzzles at your crotch in public
- two of your friends aren't talking to each other
- your aunt gives you handkerchiefs for the sixth birthday in a row
- a friend pressures you to take drugs

You'll discover:

- the 14 Do's and Don'ts of Toiletiquette
- the best way to ask someone out
- surefire strategies for getting invited back wherever you want
- secrets of dressing for tactical advantage

- the most effective ways to put rude people in their place
- proper techniques for spitting, scratching, sneezing, yawning, coughing, hiccupping, nose-picking, and zit-popping

You'll be cool, calm, and collected when a friend:

- asks you if she's ugly
- goes out with your ex-boyfriend
- comes to you with a serious problem
- wins the prize you were supposed to get

You'll find out how to:

- ace a job interview
- react when a friend tells you he's gay
- impress admissions officers when applying to schools
- broach the subject of condoms in a relationship
- respond to teachers who pick on you in class

By now, you may be thinking *Holy Napkin Ring! I never knew manners could be such a source of power, pleasure, and self-confidence.* Or you may still find it heretical to embrace the etiquettical. You're thinking *Manners, shmanners. Nobody's polite anymore, why should I be?* Thank you for asking.

Why Good Manners Are Good for You

Here are 10 reasons why it's to your advantage to have good manners:

1. **Good manners put people at ease.** People at ease are more likely to agree to your requests.

2. **Good manners impress people.** People who are impressed by your behavior are more likely to treat you with respect.

3. **Good manners build self-esteem.** Teenagers with self-esteem are more likely to get what they want out of life.

4. **Good manners are attractive.** Kids with *savoir-faire** are more likely to have the friends and relationships they want.

5. **Good manners allow people to live and work together without unnecessary friction.** This makes your everyday world more pleasant.

*A FANCY FRENCH TERM FOR "KNOW-HOW"—THE ABILITY TO SAY OR DO THE RIGHT OR GRACEFUL THING IN SOCIAL SITUATIONS.

6. **Good manners can save your skin.** Teenagers who know what to do if they accidentally dis the wrong person are less likely to get into fights or dicey situations.

7. **Good manners are rare.** Young people who have them sparkle like diamonds and immediately get elevated status in the eyes of adults.

8. **Good manners make you feel good.** You can hold your head high, knowing that you're doing your part to stop humanity's slide into the cesspool of incivility.

9. **Good manners make others feel good.** You can help create a world in which people treat one another with care, respect, and compassion.

10. **Good manners don't cost anything.** You can have the BEST for free.

Most teens want to learn proper etiquette and behavior. In fact, 99 percent of the teenagers I asked in my survey on manners agree with the statement "It's important to have good manners." Why do they think so?

"It's a way of respecting yourself."

"People will like you better."

"The way you act is the way you get treated."

"If nobody was polite, the world would fall apart."

"I want to make good first impressions with people."

"Being polite feels better than being rude."

Some teens agreed that good manners were important, but advised moderation:

"There is a time and a place for everything."

"I don't think you should become a perfectionist."

"Over the top can be too much."

True, we wouldn't want to have *too much* of a good thing. But having the *right amount* of manners can work to your advantage. How? Here are the Top Five ways in which being polite has paid off for the teens who responded to my survey:

1. Got a job.

2. Got something I wanted from my parents.

3. Got compliments and respect.

4. Got in good with someone I liked.

5. Got help from teachers.

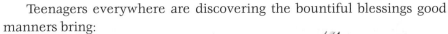

Teenagers everywhere are discovering the bountiful blessings good manners bring:

> *"By letting someone go ahead of me, they got the bird doodoo on their head instead of me."*

> *"I was really polite so my mom saw how responsible I could be so she let me have a dog."*

> *"I got to have a sleepover."*

> *"I got my allowance raised."*

> *"My family compliments me."*

> *"Teachers respect me more."*

> *"Good manners do a lot to ensure prompt service in restaurants."*

> *"When I was meeting a distant aunt at a family reunion, I was very polite and she was so impressed she gave me a $100 bill."*

"After you."

> *"I gained the respect of my friends' parents through my good manners at the dinner table."*

> *"I have been hired for different jobs because adults are looking for kids with good manners and don't think they exist."*

> *"Because I am always polite and respectful, I avoid some of the misfortunes of adolescents, such as getting into fights."*

If this doesn't convince you of the advantages that come to those with good manners, listen to what teens said when I asked them to describe a time when NOT using good manners hurt them:

> *"I got suspended."*

> *"I got a bad reputation."*

> *"I got grounded."*

> *"I was rude to my foster mom, and that made her want me to leave. At the time I didn't care, but now I wish I had cared."*

> *"I said something that hurt someone's feelings when they found out."*

> *"I was talking with my mouth full and later my friend told his other friends behind my back."*

> *"I lost respect from my teachers by insulting them."*

> *"Once I wanted my parents to do something and I started yelling and then they said 'We would have let you, but not anymore because you are yelling.'"*

"I got into a fight in eighth grade. I was beaten to a pulp."

"We used to spend every Christmas with my aunt. I was always a nasty, bored, annoying brat. When she died, I lost out in her $1,000,000 will."

You can see how important it is to have good manners. This book is going to show you how to get them and use them. Now that you've begun to read it, you won't want to put it down. You'll hole up in your room for the next four days until you've read it from cover to cover. But don't feel you have to. The book is designed so you can dip in and out of it—a question here, a question there. You can use the Contents to find chapters and the Index to find topics that are of most immediate interest to you. Meanwhile, a little background will help set the stage.

What, Exactly, Are Manners?

Manners are the customs and traditions of a society that govern how people treat one another and behave in social situations. Manners are meant to smooth the rough edges of human nature. They maintain order, promote societal values, and foster positive human interactions. Imagine the chaos and hurt we would experience if everybody did whatever they wanted, whenever they wanted, without any regard for the feelings or interests of others.

Etiquette—the sets of rules that give expression to manners—can vary from culture to culture. In Japan, you would remove your shoes before entering someone's house. If you did this in the United States, people would give you strange looks and hold their noses. In some Asian and Middle Eastern countries, belching and smacking your lips is a way to compliment the chef. In the United States, it's a way to get sent to your room. It's important to know the manners of the culture in which you're operating. Otherwise, an innocent, friendly gesture could cause offense or embarrassment.*

Here are some interesting things about etiquette:

- It's alive. It changes as societies change. For example, children in Western countries no longer bow or curtsy when presented to adults. Women today do things—drive, pick up the tab, wear bikinis—that would have been scandalous in days of yore. Sometimes, changing attitudes, styles, and technologies render some forms of etiquette extinct (such as how a lady should enter a horse-drawn carriage) while new ones emerge (such as how to use a cell phone).

*SEE "BODY LANGUAGE AROUND THE WORLD," PAGE 37.

- Etiquette is context-sensitive. For example, within every culture are many subcultures—surfers, bikers, teenagers, business executives, senators, musicians, women, men, adults, children, minorities, etc. These subcultures usually have their own rules that dictate, for example, who has the right-of-way when catching a wave, where to sit at a board meeting, what to bring to a sleepover, how to treat the opposing team at a home game. The manners men and women use in same-sex groups may differ from those they use in mixed settings. Similarly, teenagers have forms of greeting, address, and speech that are perfectly appropriate amongst themselves but not with adults, or are acceptable in a locker room but not in an assembly. People with good manners are sensitive to context and know how to adapt their behavior accordingly.

- Etiquette, like steering a car, requires constant adjustment. For example, it might be considered good manners to treat a friend in a restaurant. Your dinner guest may protest. You insist. Your guest continues to protest. At a certain point, it might be more polite for you to relinquish the check and let your guest pay. (See? Good manners can be profitable.)

One thing you'll hear frequently is that the purpose of manners is to make people feel comfortable. That's very true. But sometimes—and here's where being polite can be so much fun—the purpose of manners is to make people *uncomfortable!* For example, when somebody makes a racial slur. Or allows their children to run wild in your living room. Or invades your private life. Being courteous doesn't mean letting people walk all over you. Sometimes, those who are unkind and inconsiderate need to be put in their place—politely, of course.

A Brief History of Manners

Manners go back thousands of years. For a long time, humans were hunter-gatherers. They had to forage for food to keep from starving. This took a lot of energy and kept them on the road quite a bit. Around 9000 BCE, a new age of agriculture dawned in the Near East. People learned how to plant crops and farm. This led to a more stable existence, since food could be stored. As people began to eat communally, rituals evolved for the preparation and sharing of meals. These were then passed from one generation to the next.

The first known "etiquette scroll" was written around 2500 BCE. It was called *The Instructions of Ptahhotep* (after its Egyptian author), and it contained all sorts of advice for getting along with others and moving up in the world. For example, it was considered rude to unwrap mummies or spray-paint pyramids. This book was so widely read that many religious scholars believe its influence can be found in the Bible.

Over the centuries, manners continued to evolve. For example, prior to the 11th century, people in Europe ate with their fingers. A well-bred person used only three fingers—the thumb, the index, and the middle finger. You can imagine parents of that era saying "Ethelred, how many times do I have to tell you?! Don't stick your whole hand into your food!"

The evolution of table manners can be quite fascinating. For example, when forks were first used for eating in Tuscany in the 11th century, they were condemned by the clergy. This was because food was seen as a gift from God. Only the human hand, another of God's creations, was fit to touch it. ("Ethelred, use your fingers, not your fork!")

Stone knives were first made 1,500,000 years ago by *Homo erectus* for slaughtering animals. By the Middle Ages, most men never left home without their knives, which were hung at the waist so they could be quickly drawn to kill an enemy or slice a steak. One of the biggest etiquette problems of the 17th century was that men would use the pointed ends of their knives to pick their teeth at the table. According to legend, this so disgusted the Duc de Richelieu that he had all the points filed off the table knives in his chateau, thus creating the blunt-tipped table knife we use today.

Modern etiquette books came into full flower in 13th-century Europe. They were written to instruct the upper classes on how to behave when invited to the royal court. These books contained such gems as:

> When you blow your nose or cough,
> turn round so that nothing falls on the table.

> Refrain from falling upon the dish like a swine while eating,
> snorting disgustingly, and smacking the lips.

Possibly the most influential etiquette book of all time was written in 1530 CE by Erasmus, a classical scholar who lived in Rotterdam. He believed that good manners were most easily acquired in childhood. His book, *On Civility in Children,* became a huge best seller and was required reading for kids throughout Europe for over two centuries. Here are some of the things he advised:

> Turn away when spitting lest your saliva fall on someone.

> Do not move back and forth in your chair. Whoever does that gives the
> impression of constantly breaking or trying to break wind.

You should not offer your handkerchief to anyone unless it has been freshly washed. Nor is it seemly, after wiping your nose, to spread out your handkerchief and peer into it as if pearls and rubies might have fallen out of your head.

If you look at old etiquette books, you can see that some manners have remained constant over the centuries ("Don't spit on anyone"), while others continue to evolve in response to changing technologies, economic forces, and societal attitudes.

Aren't Manners Sexist?

They certainly are. Why should men have to remove their hats indoors while women get to keep theirs on? It's not fair!

Manners reflect the values, beliefs, and traditions of a society. These include attitudes toward social caste, age, sexuality, and the proper place of women, men, and children. Over the centuries, many cultures have viewed women as weaker and in greater need of protection than men. This doesn't mean that all the men sat around a campfire toasting marshmallows one afternoon 15,000 years ago and said "How can we discriminate against women?" Sex roles developed out of necessity; it made more sense for men to go out to slaughter wild boars while women stayed home and had babies.

As history marched on, rules of chivalry developed. These rules governed the behavior of men toward women. The rules were based on principles of medieval knighthood, such as honor, bravery, protecting the weak, and not standing outside in your armor during a lightning storm. Thus, a gallant gentleman always treated the fairer (that is, "weaker") sex with deference and respect. He would stand when a lady entered or left a room, defend her honor, hold doors, tip his hat, and offer his cloak.

Gradually, these rules of etiquette gave birth to many of the gender-based manners that ushered in the 20th century. For example, a gentleman would offer his seat to a lady, carry the luggage, pay the bill, drive the car, earn the money, and run the roost. Women were forbidden by custom and law from doing all sorts of things. In fact, women in the United States couldn't even vote until 1920.

Happily, times have changed, and the role of women in the United States (and many other countries) has been transformed over the past decades. Women now hold office, run corporations, drive buses, preach sermons, remove organs, fly planes, and drop bombs. Girls can ask boys for dates. Enlightened people no longer believe that women are "weak" and "inferior."

Society is often resistant to change, and even rights that have been won after years of struggle (for example, women's rights, voting rights, gay rights) can come under renewed attack by those who wish to turn back the clock. Manners are even slower to change because they are passed from older to younger generations. We are now in a period of great flux in terms of defining proper behavior for and between men and women. Attitudes and actions that were once considered polite are now considered rude or anachronistic.

By today's standards, certain rules of etiquette are sexist in that they are based on untrue and discriminatory presumptions about the nature and role of women (and men). But manners, by definition, should not, and need not, be sexist. Kindness knows no gender.

Now that you know a bit about where manners come from, let's turn to our very first questions, sent in by genuine American teenagers.

Dear Alex

"Aren't manners just for snobs and rich people?"

Not at all. Snobs, by definition, have bad manners. This is because snobs, in their attitudes and behavior, make people feel inferior and unschooled. This is the height of rudeness! If others put you down for using the wrong fork, *they're* the ones with terrible manners.

As far as rich people go, good manners are the one thing money can't buy. All you have to do is take one look around you to realize that rudeness is an equal opportunity annoyer. Thus, manners are a great equalizing force in society.

It's true that some rules of etiquette are more likely to be practiced by the affluent (for example, tipping the wine steward or setting a formal dinner table). And that the rich, because they have money, can get away with bad manners in ways that others can't. But a nose being picked at the dinner table is disgusting—whether its owner is rich or poor.

Dear Alex

"Why are manners so important? Isn't it what's inside a person that counts?"

Certainly, but nobody's going to stick around long enough to know the "real you" if being in your presence grosses them out.

THE SURVEY SAYS . . .

When I asked teenagers "What's the rudest thing anyone's ever done to you?" here's what they said:

"SOMEONE . . .

lifted me completely into the air by my underwear.

ignored me when I was talking to them.

farted in my face while we wrestled.

told me I was fat and needed to go on a diet.

spread rumors about me."

"My sister chewed up her food and spit it on the table."

"My brother always makes me feel stupid in front of other people."

"A kid with purple hair flicked me off."

"SOMEONE . . .

stabbed me in the back.

slammed my arm in my locker.

smacked me in the face in front of a big crowd.

bullied me to the point of crying.

told me that I will never amount to anything."

"A store clerk completely ignored me."

"A friend told a secret about me when I told him not to."

"My brother chews with his mouth open all the time to bug me (he's 16). He walks into my bedroom without knocking, and he defends my mom while she talks down to me."

"SOMEONE . . .

pulled my pants down.

hung up on me.

accused me of something I didn't do.

put down my thoughts because they are different.

pretended to be my friend."

"My brother took something of mine, hid it, and wouldn't give it back when I needed it."

"I was spit on and cursed at."

"This boy kept coming up to me and saying 'Chinese, Japanese.' Finally I just told him I was Korean and he left me alone."

"SOMEONE . . .

went through my personal things.

embarrassed me in front of my friends.

made me wait.

tried to trip me as I walked by.

excluded me from a party for no reason other than seeing me suffer."

"My friend said a few times 'I have a dad and you don't' because my parents don't live together."

"My boyfriend dumped me because I wouldn't have sex with him."

"My mom went through my journal."

"My best friend lied to me and said she was grounded when we had plans. Later I discovered she was out with her boyfriend."

"For the sake of looking cool in public, a person has pretended not to know me."

"I bought concert tickets for a girl who was meeting me at the show. She never thanked me for the tickets, so that made me a little upset because I went through a lot of trouble to get them. Then she showed up an hour and a half late. I couldn't go in because then she wouldn't have been able to get in. Afterward, she didn't meet me at the car until an hour after the concert was over, so we were stuck in the parking lot for two hours."

"The rudest thing anyone's ever done to me? I'm not sure. But rude? Texting other people when we're hanging out, being late and not apologizing, not saying thank you, asking to borrow money and not paying me back, making fun of me after being asked to stop, not replying to emails, talking about me behind my back, and so forth. Mostly little things that add up."

Which Manners Are Most Important?

Here, according to my survey, are the Top 20 Good Manners parents*
would like you, their children, to practice:

1. Say "Please," "Thank you," "You're welcome," "May I . . . ?" and
   "Excuse me."

2. Write thank-you notes.

3. Look people in the eye.

4. Clean up after yourself.

5. Respect adults.

6. Don't interrupt. Wait for your turn to speak.

7. Treat people as you would like to be treated.

8. Use good table manners (wait to begin; chew with your mouth
   closed; stay at the table until the last person is finished eating; etc.).

9. Give people a firm handshake.

10. Have compassion toward others.

11. Be thoughtful about opening doors and offering your seat.

12. Respond when spoken to.

13. Listen when others speak.

14. Show special consideration to guests.

15. Say "yes" rather than "yeah."

16. Don't say hurtful things.

17. Think before you speak.

18. Respect the property of others.

19. Respect the privacy of others.

20. Use cell phones and personal devices in appropriate ways at
    appropriate times.

Here's what teachers* said when I asked them "What manners-related
behaviors most impress you in students?"

1. Saying "Please" and "Thank you."

2. Thoughtful listening and questioning.

3. Asking for help in a polite manner.

4. Kindness and understanding toward peers and adults.

5. Free yet thoughtful expression of their views.

6. Saying they're sorry and meaning it.

7. Thanking me for teaching or helping them understand.

8. Paying attention.

9. Taking pride in their appearance.

10. Holding a door or being otherwise considerate.

11. A spirit of generosity and gratitude.

12. Keeping phones off and out of sight.

13. Helping or defending students who are being picked on.

14. Helping someone who is left out.

15. Respectful tone of address to each other and adults.

16. Positive attitude toward learning.

17. Coming to class with an open mind.

18. Raising a hand to speak.

19. Offering to help one another or a teacher without being asked.

20. Smiling and making eye contact.

Dear Alex

"Why should kids respect adults?"

So adults will learn how to respect kids.

Having Manners vs. Being Fake

Some people equate "having manners" with "being fake." But why think of it this way when you could perceive it as "being tactful," "being kind," or "being clever"? "Being real" can hurt people's feelings, provoke fights, and work against your best interests. "Being fake" can preserve relationships, engender respect, and help others feel good about you and themselves. Here are some examples of "being real" and "being fake." Which would you rather hear?*

*ALSO SEE PAGES 376–380 FOR A DISCUSSION OF WHEN AND WHETHER HONESTY IS THE BEST POLICY.

Being "Real"

"I wouldn't go out with you if you were the last person on earth."

"This is so ugly I'm going to use it as a rag."

"You are the most boring drone I've ever met. I'm outta here!"

"We wiped the floor with you, you bunch of losers."

"You're a good-for-nothing idiot who's never going to amount to anything."

Being "Fake"

"I'm sorry, but I already have plans for that night."

"Aunt Jane, thank you so much for the shirt."

"Excuse me, but I'd better be going. I've got a lot of homework to do."

"You had some bad luck, but you played a good game."

"I know that you have the potential to do anything you want if you work hard and use your talents."

Real Fake

Dear Alex

"Manners restrict our emotions and make us act differently than we would without them. Why not just act natural?"

Human beings are a complex species. They can be selfish, violent, and aggressive; they can be generous, compassionate, and nurturing. These traits are all natural. If people just did what they felt like doing, if they acted solely according to their own desires and self-interest, life would be violent and chaotic. This is because any "society"—be it a family, a football team, a business, or a nation—must operate according to certain shared "rules" if its members are to live and work in harmony and get anything done. These rules go by many names: laws, values, expectations, goals, corporate policies, game plans—and manners.

At first glance, these rules may seem confining because they inhibit "natural" tendencies. But, on closer examination, you'll find that these rules, rather than restrict personal freedom, create it! Think about it.

If there were no rules, how could anyone play baseball? If there were no traffic regulations, how could anyone drive? If there were no laws, how could people be secure in their own homes? And, if there were no manners, how could we get along without constantly fighting or hurting each other's feelings? Would you really want to live in a world in which there were no constraints on what people could do and say?

There's a certain romanticism associated with the "natural" human animal. But given a choice between a society that values grabbing and harassing, and one that values asking and respecting; given a choice between living with people who are greedy, insensitive, and unkind, and those who are generous, empathetic, and supportive; given a choice between neighbors who are noisy, destructive, and antisocial, and those who are quiet, helpful, and friendly; given a choice between an evening of bickering and belching, and one of fine food and conversation—which would you prefer?

Dear Alex

"Why do you have to be nice to ignorant jerks?"

Because you never know when one of them might be a Hollywood talent agent.

Dear Alex

"How can you have manners without people thinking you're weird?"

The only people who think manners are weird are those without any. Who cares what they think?

Is It Ever Okay Not to Have Manners?

Yes. Manners waivers are granted to:

- those who are too young to know better
- those with physical or mental illnesses that prevent them from having the necessary self-awareness or control
- those who are responding to an emergency (firefighters need not say "Excuse me" as they brush past bystanders blocking their path)
- those who are victims of crime (introductions are not necessary when being mugged)

- those who are alone and unobserved and whose actions have no adverse consequences for others (it's okay to eat whipped cream from the can in the privacy of your bedroom)
- those who are in the company of others, but who agree amongst themselves to suspend certain manners—as long as doing so does not have adverse consequences for anyone (it's okay to burp loudly while watching football and eating junk food with your friends)

THE SURVEY SAYS . . .

When I asked teenagers "What's the rudest thing you ever did to anyone?" here's what they said:

"Borrowed a formal dress for a dance and forgot to return it for five months."
"Walked past a person I knew because I couldn't remember his name."
"Told a friend I was sick and went to another friend's house."

"Canceled a date to a dance a couple days before."
"Kicked some kids because I was mad at them."
"Made this girl fall while she was running down the hall."
"Bumped someone and told them to apologize."

"Talked about someone behind their back."
"Called someone 'four-eyes.'"
"Wrote a nasty note to my best friend because she was totally ignoring me."
"I once put a stinky sock in someone's mouth."

"Threw a glass of water in my sister's face."
"Stared at a handicapped person."
"Called someone a fag."
"Made fun of someone only to be part of the group."

"I led a boy on but then stopped talking to him because I found someone else."
"I told someone she might be really pretty if she lost a lot of weight and you could see her features."
"I invited someone to meet me somewhere and didn't show up on purpose."

"Laughed when someone got hurt."

"Flipped the bird to a teacher."

"Texted my friends while at the dinner table."

"Repeated a secret."

"Chewed up my food and opened my mouth to show everyone."

"I snubbed a couple of childhood friends for a different group of newer friends."

"I told my mother that I hated her, told her I wished I was someone else's kid, and slammed the door in her face."

"I honestly don't do rude things. That sounds like a lie or possibly like I'm living in a fantasy world, but my parents raised me correctly and I applaud them for that."

Dear Alex

"If someone's rude to you, is it okay to be rude back?"

Here's what the teenagers I surveyed said:

Yes 32%

No 68%

And here are some reasons they gave:

"Yes, it's okay to be rude back because . . ."

"It gives them a taste of their own medicine."

"Everyone will think you're weak if you don't."

"It's good to stand up for yourself."

"There's no other choice but to be rude."

In fact, there *is* another choice: You can choose not to be rude back. But before we get into that choice, let's hear from some teenagers who said:

"It depends . . ."

"If the person is another student or peer, I feel that being rude back is justified. However, one should never be rude to a teacher, parent, or other adult in charge."

"I almost always let an occasional rudeness go. But if a person is rude all the time, telling them off or embarrassing them will sometimes make them stop and respect me."

"It depends on the situation. It's important to be patient and mature even with difficult people. However, if someone's really just being a jerk I think it's okay to tell them to shut up."

Finally, let's hear from teenagers who said:

"No, it's not okay to be rude back because . . ."

"Then they'll be rude again and then you'll be rude and it'll just go in a circle."

"Why lower yourself to their childish standards?"

"You should set a good example. People will feel weird if they're the only ones being rude."

"You might regret it later."

"It can feel as good as a comeback when you deliberately say something positive in response to a rude comment."

"Two wrongs don't make a right. But three rights make a left."

What's your opinion? Do two rudes make a right? Before you decide, read on.

If you respond to rudeness with more rudeness . . .

* you may offend someone who had no intention of being rude
* you may get into a fight
* you may end up in trouble yourself
* you add to the general level of rudeness in the world
* you miss the opportunity to educate or enlighten
* you let others control you—you let them set the agenda and the tone of the interaction

When you use good manners to respond to rudeness . . .

* you stand the best chance of stopping the behavior
* you stand the best chance of getting what you want
* you stand the best chance of winning others over to your cause
* you serve notice that people can't walk all over you
* you maintain your own dignity
* you set an example that may change the behavior of others

Dear Alex

"What's the best way to respond to rudeness?"

Actually, there are *two* ways.

1. **Ignore it.** Let's say you're standing in a long checkout line that extends into the aisle. Someone barges through with his cart

and runs over your foot. He doesn't say "Excuse me." He doesn't apologize. He just keeps going.

You could yell "You stupid idiot! Why don't you watch where you're going?" Or you could ignore it. Which is better?

If you yell, you'll be letting some ill-mannered stranger pull your strings. You'll probably be seen as rude and foul-mouthed yourself. And you could easily get into an ugly argument or a fight.

If you ignore the barbaric buffoon, your toe will still hurt. But you'll have the satisfaction of knowing that you possess good manners and self-control. And your restraint will likely arouse the sympathy of spectators.

2. Be polite. Some people equate politeness with weakness. They think it's cool to be rude. Nothing could be further from the truth.

Politeness isn't a sign of weakness. It's a sign of *strength*. It's an incredibly powerful tool that can gain you respect, protect your rights, stop rude people in their tracks, and even make adults apologize. It can turn almost any situation to your advantage.

If politeness is so effective, you may wonder why more people don't practice it. The reason is, it's an acquired skill. It takes thoughtfulness, patience, empathy, and even a bit of cleverness. And, as you may have noticed, these commodities are in short supply these days. But that's to your advantage. Your politeness will stand out all the more.

You'll discover throughout this book how to use politeness to put others at ease and to stand up for yourself in virtually any situation. In general, though, the best way to respond politely to rudeness is with one of the following two tactics:

TACTIC #1: Assume that the Rude One is well-intentioned and would never knowingly cause offense. This is the secret for getting rude people to stop their behavior and/or apologize. "Accusatory phrasing" puts them on the defensive. "Benefit-of-the-doubt" phrasing gives them a face-saving way out. Examples:

Accusatory Phrasing and Likely Response	**Benefit-of-the-Doubt Phrasing and Likely Response**
A. *You say:* "No cuts. End of the line, buttface!"	**A. *You say:*** "Excuse me, it's a little confusing, but the line actually begins back there."
He says: "@%!#&!"	***He says:*** "Oh, sorry. I didn't see it."

Analysis: This response accuses the Rude One of trying to cut into line. He probably is. But the remark, rather than sending him packing, turns the incident into a battle of egos.

Analysis: If the Rude One truly didn't notice the line, your polite response is a pleasant way of steering him in the right direction. If he did try to pull a fast one, giving him the benefit of the doubt provides a face-saving way for him to slink off.

Accusatory Phrasing and Likely Response

B. *You say:* "What d'ya think you're doing? That's only for handicapped people. You can't park there."
She says: "@%!#&!"

Benefit-of-the-Doubt Phrasing and Likely Response

B. *You say:* "I beg your pardon, the paint is so dull that you may not have noticed that's a handicapped space."
She says: "Actually, I did notice. My handicap isn't visible. But thank you for caring about these parking spots."

Analysis: Once again, an "in-your-face" attack is likely to result in a "you-can't-tell-me-what-to-do" response.

Analysis: Another good reason to give people the benefit of the doubt is that sometimes they deserve it. Maybe it's *your* assumption rather than *their* behavior that needs correcting.

TACTIC #2: Ask the Rude One to indulge your sensitivity rather than stop being a boor. This strategy is based on human nature. People don't like to be scolded or told what to do. But most people are willing to *modify* their behavior in response to a *reasonable* request.

Stop-Your-Boorishness Phrasing and Likely Response

A. *You say:* "Shut up! How do you expect anyone to hear what's going on? If you want to talk during the movie, go outside!"
They say: "@%!#&!"
Analysis: When chastised, a lot of people lash out. Even if they know you're right, their hurt pride puts them on the defensive.

Please-Indulge-Me Phrasing and Likely Response

A. *You say:* "Excuse me, but it's hard for me to hear in movie theaters. Would you mind not talking?"
They say: "Sorry."
Analysis: Talkers are more likely to quiet down if they feel they're doing a favor rather than "giving in."

Stop-Your-Boorishness Phrasing and Likely Response

B. You say: "Grandma, mind your own business! What makes you think you can tell me I can't go skiing with my friends?"

She says: "What a way to talk to your grandmother! I just don't want you to injure yourself."

Analysis: Your grandma is hurt and upset. Your relationship has been damaged.

Please-Indulge-Me Phrasing and Likely Response

B. You say: "Grandma, I'd feel terrible if I thought your visit was going to be spoiled worrying about me. Mom and Dad wouldn't have gone to Greece if they didn't trust me. They let me go skiing all the time."

She says: "I just worry so. You know how grandmas are."

Analysis: You're far more likely to retain your freedom if you empathize with your grandma's concern rather than reject it.

THE SURVEY SAYS . . .

Here are two questions I asked parents—and the results:

1. Do you think *adults* today are more polite, less polite, or the same as when you were growing up?

MORE POLITE 3%
LESS POLITE 74%
THE SAME 23%

2. Do you think *children* today are more polite, less polite, or the same as when you were growing up?

MORE POLITE 6%
LESS POLITE 75%
THE SAME 19%

Ask your parents what *they* think!

Why Don't People Have Manners Anymore?

There are a lot of different ideas as to why this is. Here's what the parents in my survey said when I asked them why they think *adults* today are less polite than those of a generation ago:

"Unfortunately, people seem to think that politeness is a sign of weakness."

"Reality shows present bad manners as entertainment."

"We are a demanding, privileged, entitled society, and our communication with each other reflects that spoiled attitude."

"A lot of it has to do with the advance of technology. People are no longer having face-to-face conversations—they text, call, email, and IM. This has resulted in a generation of people buried in their devices and not caring about extending basic courtesies."

"There's a lot more stress today. I think we're all in the fast lane and just don't take the time to help or acknowledge each other."

"America is a melting pot of cultures with varying ideas of manners. Rudeness is accepted under the name of 'diversity.'"

"We have become much more of a 'me' centered society than a 'we' centered society."

"Society has less respect for authority. The traditions that upheld manners and respect are crumbling."

"The dream has been lost. People in general feel powerless so it creates hostility."

And here's why the parents in my survey think *children* today are less polite than those of a generation ago:

"Television."

"Exposure to vulgarity in mass media."

"The proliferation of electronic devices as well as society in general being more casual and putting less importance on politeness."

"Manners are not stressed in the home or reinforced in school."

"Children today see so many public figures, such as sports stars, actors, and politicians, behaving rudely that they think bad manners are fashionable."

"Parents have become lazy in teaching their children appropriate behavior. A lot of parents would rather be their child's friend than their parent."

"Peer pressure."

"Children are given more freedom and less supervision."

"Too many activities, not enough family time."

"With social media, reality TV, a divided nation (haves vs. have-nots; political parties; ethnic, gender, cultural differences, etc.), young people see rude, unkind social behaviors modeled."

In other words, adults seem to think that rudeness in kids is the result of changing societal conditions, bad influences in the media, and the failure of adults to teach proper etiquette and behavior. So now we know that it's not necessarily your fault if you have bad manners. But if you grow up and pass them on to *your* children, then whose fault are *their* bad manners?

Chapter Quiz

1. *You're excused from having to have good manners as long as:*

   a) you can't stand the person

   b) you just ate a gallon of baked beans

   c) you're in a bad mood

   d) you're dead

2. *If kids are rude, it's because:*

   a) they weren't taught good manners at home

   b) they're imitating ill-mannered movie stars and sports heroes

   c) they think politeness is uncool

   d) they're having a bad hair day

3. *Parents can best teach their children good manners by:*

   a) hitting them when they misbehave

   b) responding to rudeness with "Can't you do anything right, you moron?"

   c) coming to the dinner table in their underwear

   d) setting a good example

4. *It's okay to be rude back if:*

   a) you're bigger than the other person

   b) your girlfriend or boyfriend is watching

   c) you enjoy being pummeled into dog meat

   d) you don't know any better

2

SOCIAL INTERACTIONS 101

The Rituals of Relating

Unless you're a hermit, a castaway, or a monk who has taken a vow of silence, you experience many social interactions each day. Some are brief and anonymous, such as holding a door for a stranger or giving money to a sales clerk. Others are intimate and meaningful, such as consoling a friend or confiding in a parent. Yet they all have one thing in common: They are acted out according to certain rules and expectations for behavior. These rules and expectations govern everything from gift giving to eating, job hunting to babysitting, greeting people to meeting people. Your ability to "play the game" will help you feel confident, and others feel comfortable, in virtually any situation.

An Introduction to Introductions

Like it or not, first impressions count. You can make a lifetime of good first impressions by learning how to give and receive introductions.

Introducing Yourself

This is the simplest introduction. All you have to do is remember your own name. At school or parties, or when others have neglected to introduce you, look the person you want to meet in the eye, smile, extend your right hand, and say "Hi, I'm _____." If the person doesn't respond with his or her name, you can continue with "And you're . . . ?"*

Introducing Others

Let's start with the adult world, where things tend to be a bit more formal. If you're making the introduction, simply say "Mother, I'd like to present my friend, Sticky Fingers." It's not necessary to add "Sticky, this is my mother." Life is too short for such double-talk.

You may also use such phrases as "Mother, I'd like to introduce Sticky," or, if you're in a hurry, "Mom, this is Sticky."

If you think that the people might know each other but you're not sure, you can turn your introduction into a question: "Mother, have you met Sticky?"

Sometimes kids and parents have different last names. In which case you would say, after presenting Sticky to your mom, "Sticky, this is my mother, Mrs. Her-Last-Name." That way, he'll know not to call her Mrs. Your-Last-Name.

Piece of cake.

But how do you know *who* to present to *whom*? Here's the rule: You present the person of "lesser" status to the person of "greater" status. You address the person of "greater" status by saying his or her name first:

"Your Highness, I'd like to present Simon the Stableboy."

"Warden, I'd like to introduce my cellmate, Lucky."

"Professor Glockenspiel, this is my poodle, Puddles."

Since *who* outranks *whom* can be as confusing as knowing *when* to say *which*, the following chart will help you keep things straight.

"Greater" Status	**"Lesser" Status**
Adults	Children
Teachers	Students
Longtime friends	New friends
Females	Males
Relatives	Non-relatives
Bosses	Employees
The Queen of England	The town dogcatcher

***FOR WAYS TO GET A CONVERSATION GOING SEE PAGES 353–357.**

Please don't have a fit about this status thing. It doesn't mean that royals are better than commoners, women are better than men, or adults are better than children. It's just the way things are done. And don't worry about making a mistake. If you present whoever to whomever when whomever should have been presented to whoever, few people will notice, since they'll be delighted that you made any introduction at all. And your own status will be tops in everyone's eyes.

When you make an introduction, try to include a little information about the person you're introducing. Otherwise, the people you've just introduced may stare at their feet with nothing to say.

You can try things like:

"Grandma, this is my friend Harry Houdini. He does magic tricks."

"Ms. Grier, I'd like to present my sister Charlotte. She has the lead in the school play."

"Dad, this is Ron Gomez. He's on the swim team with me."

You can see how these introductory add-ons provide openings for further conversation. Be discreet, though. The idea is to offer an enticing tidbit of information, not to reveal any secrets.

Introducing Couples

Couples come in many varieties: gay, straight, married, unmarried, engaged, conjoined. They may refer to themselves as each other's spouse, partner, paramour, husband, wife, girlfriend, boyfriend, significant other, insignificant other, etc. To avoid giving someone foot-in-mouth disease, it's helpful when introducing a couple to use titles or other descriptors to provide a clue as to the nature of their relationship. For example:

"Mom, I'd like to introduce my swim coach, Chlorine Williams, and her fiancé, Rocky Poole."

or

"Dad, this is my French teacher, Madame Floofee, and her brother, Louis Quatorze."

or

"Theo, I'd like you to meet Juan and Juanita Rodriguez, they're our next-door neighbors."

Now, it could be that Juan and Juanita are a married couple, but they could also be siblings, or father and daughter, or grandmother and grandson. You'll have to make a judgment call as to whether their relationship will be obvious based on their age, looks, and behavior. If in doubt (let's say Juan looks like he's 85 and Juanita looks like she just graduated from high school), you can expand on the introduction by saying, "This is Juan

Rodriguez and his wife Juanita, they're our next-door neighbors," or "This is my neighbor Juan Rodriguez and his granddaughter, Juanita."

Married couples don't always share the same last name, so you need to be vigilant as to how they wish to be introduced. If you're not sure, ask them. That way, when introducing your gastroenterologist to your best friend, you would know to say:

"Bongo, have you met Ted Sharpe and his wife, Dr. Penny Sillan?"

Sometimes you might introduce two people as a couple because they share a common denominator, i.e., they're tag team wrestlers: *"Grandma, I'd like to introduce Bubba and Bulldog, this year's WWE champs."* Or partners in crime: *"Grandma, I'd like to present my favorite bank robbers, Bonnie Parker and Clyde Barrow."* Or ice cream purveyors: *"Mom, Dad, have you met Ben and Jerry?"*

Dear Alex
"How do you introduce a same-sex couple?"

Exactly the same way you'd introduce a heterosexual couple. First, pay attention to the words they use. If you've known the couple for a while you're likely to have observed them introducing themselves or referring to each other in conversation. For example, if Gertrude calls Alice her "partner," you'd be on safe ground using the same term when introducing them as a couple: *"Jamie, I'd like to introduce Gertrude Stein and her partner, Alice Toklas."*

If you're not sure what they like to be called, ask: "How do you like to be introduced?" Or, if you're with just one of them you could ask: "How do you refer to each other?" They will appreciate your thoughtfulness in wanting to use the same terms they do. Based on their answer you will know whether to introduce them as husbands, wives, life partners, boyfriends, girlfriends, civil unionists, or spice (plural of spouse).

In a heterosexual marriage, the male spouse is referred to as a husband. The female spouse is called a wife. This holds true for same-sex marriages unless the couple prefers a different nomenclature for their relationship. So you would say:

"Georgia, I'd like you to meet my yoga instructor, Lucy McPretzel, and her wife, Lizzy Borden."

or

"Billy-Bob, let me present my troop leader, Bruce Wayne, and his husband, Dick Grayson."

Dear Alex

"How do you introduce people if you've forgotten their names?"

With difficulty. "Dr. Femur, I'd like you to meet . . . er, ah, um, uh . . . " is inadequate as an introduction. But we all forget names sometimes. Since it's worse to make *no* introduction, you have three choices when memory fails you:

1. be up-front

2. bluff

3. cheat

Being up-front means coming clean about your mental lapse. You begin the introduction ("Dad, this is a friend from math class"), then turn to your friend and say "I'm so sorry, I've forgotten your name." At this point, your friend will supply her name.

If you're introducing yourself, you can say "Hi, we've met before, but I'm afraid I've forgotten your name. I'm _____."

What if you're introducing two people to each other and you've forgotten *both* of their names? The up-front approach would be "I'm sorry. I'm so terrible with names I'd forget my own if it wasn't sewn into my underwear. Do you think you could introduce yourselves?"

With the bluffing method, you hope to avoid detection by getting those people whose names you've forgotten to introduce themselves. Begin by looking warmly at both people. Then say "Do you two know each other?" If the bluff works, they reply "No" and introduce themselves. If it doesn't, they say "No" and turn to you with expectant looks on their faces. Uh-oh!

If you've forgotten just one person's name, turn to him and say "Have you met Mrs. Dickens? She was my eighth-grade English teacher." With any luck, he'll reply "No, I haven't had the pleasure. Hi, I'm Nicholas Nickleby."

You can even use the bluff technique when introducing yourself to someone whose name you've forgotten. Smile, stick out your hand, and say "Hi. It's good to see you again. I'm _____." Then hope that person will respond with her name.

Cheating isn't nice, but sometimes it's necessary. Assume a frantic air and invent an emergency: "Oh, dear, I think the dog just ate my gerbil." Then say "Could you please introduce yourselves?" as you rush from the room.

Group Introductions

Situations may arise that call for group introductions. For example, let's say your cousin joins you and some friends for a movie. If the group is small (five people or fewer), you can introduce him to everyone. If the group is large, individual introductions will take forever and you'll miss the movie. At times like these, it's perfectly acceptable to make an efficient group presentation: "Hey, everybody, this is my cousin Alfredo Fettucine. He's visiting from Rome."

Alfredo can smile and say "Hi." The rest of you can smile and say "Hey" or "How's it goin'?" Physical gestures are also acceptable—a wave, a friendly salute, a tip of the baseball cap—anything that makes Alfredo feel welcome. Handshakes and standing up (if you are sitting down) are unnecessary in such informal situations. Individual members of the group should introduce themselves to Alfredo as they talk with him.

Dear Alex

"Why do people shake hands?"

The earliest hieroglyphic record of a handshake (in Egypt in 2800 BCE) suggests that this was how a god transferred power to a king. A similar image appears on Michelangelo's Sistine Chapel ceiling, which shows God reaching for Adam's hand. And it reappears in the movie *E.T.,* when Elliott and E.T. touch fingertips.

Another possible reason for the handshake goes back to the days when strangers approached each other with suspicion. Men would brandish their daggers in their right hands until determining that no threat existed. At that point, they would sheath their daggers and hold out their right hands as a gesture of friendship and goodwill. (This helps to explain why women didn't shake hands until fairly recently.)

Today, people shake hands because it's a custom. Many sports teams, peer groups, and fraternal organizations use secret or special handshakes. Such greetings originated during the Middle Ages as a way to confirm the identities of messengers and spies. Special handshakes are perfectly appropriate within peer groups, as long as they're not used to make others feel excluded.

Handshaking is a good example of how customs can vary from country to country. In the United States, children are taught to give a firm handshake: "Don't be a limp fish!" In other countries, such as China, Japan, Turkey, and the Arabic-speaking Middle East, a weaker handshake is preferred and a powerful grip would be considered rude. Some

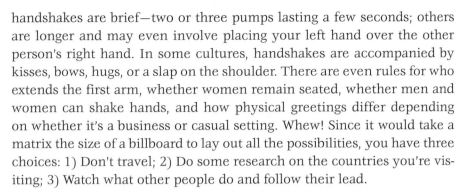

handshakes are brief—two or three pumps lasting a few seconds; others are longer and may even involve placing your left hand over the other person's right hand. In some cultures, handshakes are accompanied by kisses, bows, hugs, or a slap on the shoulder. There are even rules for who extends the first arm, whether women remain seated, whether men and women can shake hands, and how physical greetings differ depending on whether it's a business or casual setting. Whew! Since it would take a matrix the size of a billboard to lay out all the possibilities, you have three choices: 1) Don't travel; 2) Do some research on the countries you're visiting; 3) Watch what other people do and follow their lead.

The Secret Handshake of
Those Who Survived Third Period Biology

Being Introduced

What should you do when you're being introduced? Follow these five steps:

1. **Assume the position.** If you're not already standing, stand up. Use good posture. Don't fidget or pace.

2. **Make eye contact.** Give people a friendly, welcoming look. Don't stare into space or study your shoes.

3. **Shake hands.** Exert enough pressure so they know they're shaking a hand, not an overcooked piece of linguine. A confident, steady grip sends the message that you're a confident, steady person.

4. **Express a greeting.** You can't go wrong with "How do you do?" A warm "Hello" or "Pleased to meet you" are suitable substitutes. Save "Yo," "Hey," "Hi," "Howdy," "Whazzup," "How's it goin'," and trending salutation fads for really informal settings or people around your

age. For extra credit, spice up your greeting with "I've really been looking forward to meeting you" or "My sister has told me so much about you."

5. **Converse.** If the introducer did his job, he gave you a clue about the person to whom you were introduced. Follow up with related questions and/or comments. For example, if a friend introduced you to one of his teammates, you might say "What position do you play?" or "What are practices like?" or "How do you think the team will do this season?" Try to avoid questions that can be answered with a simple yes or no.

You could ask a student who's new to your school "How do you like our town so far?" or "What courses are you taking?" or "What was your last school like?" or "What clubs are you thinking of joining?"

This isn't exactly the Oxford Debating Union. But it is a warm, friendly, well-intentioned way to put people at ease. If you keep at it, you'll soon discover interests and experiences you have in common. And if the person turns out to be a bore, there are ways to exit the conversation without being rude.*

Starting a conversation may feel awkward at first. Just remember that most people like to talk about themselves. They will be grateful for your attention and efforts to keep things going smoothly.

Bonus Tip: When you're being introduced, be alert to the possibility that the introducer may have forgotten your name. If she hesitates or asks if you know the other person, don't call her bluff. Help her out the way you'd want to be helped. Leap in with "Hi, I'm _____."

And that's about it for introductions. Any questions?

"What do you say if you're introduced to someone who's gay?"
"How do you do?"

"What do you say if you're introduced to someone you can't stand?"
"How do you do?"

"What do you say if you're introduced to triplets?"
"How do you do?" "How do you do?" "How do you do?"

*SEE PAGES 366–368.

Dear Alex

"Is it okay to call adults by their first names?"

Only if they ask you to. Otherwise it's "Doctor," "Mister," "Mrs.," "Miss," or "Ms." followed by their last names, of course.

Dear Alex

"What do you do when you shake a person's hand and he won't let go?"

Give the person's hand one final, authoritative squeeze. Then withdraw your hand while warmly intensifying eye and verbal contact. This shows that it's his hand, not his company, from which you wish to remove yourself.

Dear Alex

"I'm going to a new school, so I don't know a lot of people. I have this one friend and every time we walk down the hall people come up to talk to her. I don't know what to do. Do I say hello to these people if I don't know them? Do I say good-bye? Can I say good-bye if I haven't said hello? Help! I HATE standing around feeling stupid."

If your friend's hallway hailings are conducted in passing (i.e., at full, reduced, or momentarily suspended pace), no introductions are required. The speed of the exchange should spare you from feeling stupid.

If, however, bodies stop and information is exchanged, you have three choices:

1. **Meditate yourself** into a state of distant yet friendly contentment (daydream, hum, stare peacefully into the distance) so your friend won't feel uncomfortable and you won't feel stupid.

2. **Excuse yourself**, as in "I'm going to my locker for a sec. Be right back."

3. **Introduce yourself**, as in "I don't think we've met. I'm _____." Others should respond in kind, and before you know it, you'll be having a conversation. At the end, say "Good-bye," "Later," or "Ciao." From this point on, you can greet them and chat with them in the hall, just like your friend.

It's really your friend's obligation to introduce you, but she may not be aware of that. Help her out with a gentle suggestion: "Since I'm new and all, I'd really appreciate it if you could introduce me to people you know whenever you get the chance."

Hugs

All across the USA and in many parts of the world, today's teens are hugging as a form of greeting. While hugs have always been a way to express love, friendship, support, and consolation, more and more teenagers use hugs interchangeably with handshakes.

There are many different types of hugs. Loose hugs and tight hugs. Short hugs and long hugs. Half hugs and back-slap hugs. Most teens practice your basic friendly hug: The hugger advances toward the huggee with open arms at which point the huggee reciprocates by opening his or her arms, thus presenting a clear path for final approach. Depending on the length and history of the relationship, the embrace may be brief and light, signifying "Hi, great to see ya," or longer and squeezier, conveying a more meaningful nonverbal message.

Hugs are a lot like social kisses (see page 35), except more circular. While they typically occur between people who already know each other, you might hug someone you've never met if he or she is a relative, an intimate of your circle of friends, someone you've heard a great deal about, or someone you have already gotten to know as an online friend.

Hugs have become gender-neutral. They can occur between girls, boys, or a boy and a girl. You can even have group hugs, sometimes referred to as football huddles.

While most teens embrace hugs, some teens are hug-averse. This could be for any number of reasons. You need to watch for signs suggesting a reluctance to hug and be respectful of the person's boundaries.

Hugging has, as you might expect, upset many adults and school administrators. Some schools have instituted bans on hugging, envisioning a total breakdown of discipline and decorum if teens are allowed to arm-wrap each other. This has led to protests with rebellious students offering free hugs and chanting, "Hugs not shrugs!"

One principal feared that a greet-and-grab culture could lead to "needless hugging." This, if unchecked, could cause hug-jams in the hallways, especially between lunch and fifth period. A more enlightened principal chose not to outlaw these snuggly displays of affection but, rather, impose a three-second cuddle curfew. Uncouple one second late, young lady, and it's off to detention for you! Of course, this meant that all hall monitors had to be armed with stopwatches.

Yes, the wanton and spontaneous expression of warmth threatens the well-being of adolescents everywhere. Go down this slippery slope and before you know it, teens will be—sharing pencils! But I think it's worth the risk and hereby grant get-out-of-detention-free passes to any teen harassed for hugging.

Dear Alex

"If two boys hug, does it mean they're gay?"

If a boy and a girl hug, does it mean they're straight?

The Social Kiss

The use of one's lips as an act of greeting is known as a *social kiss*. The use of one's lips as an act of intimacy is known as *making out*. Our concern here is with the former.

It's important to master the intricacies of social kissing, because the consequences of not doing so include locked braces, banged foreheads, and the silly feeling you get when the cheek you thought you were about to kiss turns out to be a nose.

The social kiss is body language for "It's so wonderful to see you again." You use it with people you've already met, rarely or never with those you're meeting for the first time. There are only two targets for the properly delivered social kiss:

1. the lips

2. the cheek

Kisses to other destinations are either misdeliveries or indications that something else is going on. What makes social kisses tricky is the fact that sometimes the participants make different assumptions about the destination. If you head for the lips and the recipient turns her cheek, you'll end up with an ear. Thus, the art of social kissing involves paying attention to nonverbal cues—good practice for more intimate relationships later in life.

In the United States, social kissing has traditionally occurred between males and females (lips or cheeks) or between females (cheeks), but not between males. Sometimes males hug each other in greeting. These aren't really hugs, though. They're more like extended hearty backslaps intended to show how macho they are. Males who are comfortable with their masculinity and sexual orientation have no problem giving other males real hugs. In fact, there's no reason why men shouldn't be able to give each other social kisses. In Europe, the Middle East, Latin America, and many other cultures, men and teenage boys do this all the time.

The person of "greater" status* is the one who signals what kind of kiss it will be. Between men and women, this is always the woman. If she

*FOR A REMINDER OF WHO HAS "GREATER" AND
"LESSER" STATUS AND WHY, SEE PAGE 26.

presents her face straight on, she is saying "Lip Kiss, please." Your gentle peck should follow. If she turns her head to the left, it's "Cheek Kiss." Permission is granted for you to enter her cheek zone and await further nonverbal instructions.

These will come in the form of:

1. a peck on your cheek (signaling a full-fledged Cheek Kiss)

2. a nuzzle on your cheek (a Cheek-Bump Non-Kiss)

3. a smacking sound near your ear (an Air Kiss)

You must be so alert that your response (made a mere microsecond later) seems simultaneous. If you can do this, you will have accomplished a perfect social kiss.

But wait . . . there's more! At this point, the person of "greater" status selects one of the following options:

1. breaking contact after one kiss (the Basic Social Kiss)

2. repeating the procedure with the other cheek (the Basic European Social Kiss)

3. continuing with another right-cheek/left-cheek kiss, nuzzle, or air kiss for a total of four (the Advanced European Social Kiss)

Social kisses are sometimes accompanied by a hug-lite. These minimalist embraces are perfect for those times when you want to express affection without crushing your clothes.

Lip Kiss with Hug-Lite

Basic Social Air Kiss

Basic European Cheek-Bump Non-Kiss

Misdelivered Social Kiss

BODY LANGUAGE AROUND THE WORLD

Gestures considered friendly in one land might be offensive in another. For example, in Australia, an enthusiastic thumbs-up sign doesn't mean "All right!" It means "Up yours!" It's wise to learn a little about other countries before you visit them—or when you're making friends with people from other cultures—so you don't end up flat on your back for giving someone a "compliment."

Here are more ways in which rituals of greeting and friendship vary:

- Latinos, Asians, and people in Middle Eastern and Mediterranean countries consider same-sex hand-holding or arm-linking a sign of friendship. They would be amazed to learn that these gestures may be interpreted in the United States as signs that the couple is gay.

- Japanese people bow as a form of greeting. They disapprove of public displays of affection—even between husbands and wives.

- People in Sri Lanka, India, Bangladesh, and Thailand greet each other by placing their hands in a prayerlike position in front of their chins and nodding their heads.

- Most Middle Easterners refrain from body contact when greeting members of the opposite sex. But men and women often kiss and embrace when meeting those of the same sex.

- Most people in France, Italy, Spain, and other Mediterranean countries kiss each other on both cheeks in greeting.

- Because many Asians believe that a person's soul resides in the head, the U.S. custom of patting a child's head is seen as threatening.

- In the United States, people are taught to look each other in the eye when speaking. Children in many Asian, Latin American, and Caribbean countries are taught that it's respectful to avoid eye contact. In the United States' culturally diverse schools, teachers may misinterpret a child's avoidance of eye contact as a mark of disrespect when, in fact, it's the opposite. In some urban schools, direct eye contact between teenagers is considered a form of dissing and has led to fights.

Giving and Receiving Gifts

You'd think it would be easy to give people gifts, and even easier to receive them. Wrong! Here's how to avoid the most common mistakes:

Gracious Giving

Choose the gift carefully. Everyone says it's the thought that counts, but some thoughts count more than others. If you give a 10-pound box of Godiva chocolate truffles to a friend who's dieting, or a smartphone case to someone who doesn't have a smartphone, you haven't been paying attention. When your choice reflects careful consideration, you give a little something in addition to the gift.

Remove the price tag. But if the price is on the gift and can't be removed without damaging the gift or the packaging (for example, the price of a book is often printed on the inside of the dust jacket), leave it. Otherwise it might be hard for the receiver to return the gift. And if he thinks the book you paid a dollar for at Buck-a-Book cost $45, that's not *your* fault.

Wrap the gift. Tradition calls for beautiful paper, ribbons, and bows. Creativity allows for aluminum foil, cloth, yarn, dried macaroni, collages, rubber stamps, etc. Your handmade giftwrap becomes part of the gift.

Include a card. How else will the person know who the gift is from, especially if it arrives in the mail along with a dozen more? Or ends up in a pile upstairs while the Big Birthday Blow-Out Bash is happening downstairs? Your card can be short and simple. You don't even have to use complete sentences.

> { *For Aunt Dotty, with hugs on your birthday*
> *Your loving nephew, Caspar* }

If your gift is meant as a thank you for someone's hospitality or thoughtfulness, that doesn't excuse you from having to write a thank-you note.[*] In fact, your gift will be much more impressive if it isn't seen as "payment" for services rendered, but rather as something that happened to tag along with your written thanks.

Give with confidence. Don't undercut your generosity by saying:

"I know you won't like this."

"This is a dumb present."

"I couldn't spend very much."

"I didn't know what to get you."

"You probably already have one of these."

[*]FOR MORE ON THANK-YOU NOTES, SEE PAGES 43–45.

Instead, adopt a modest smile, hand the gift to its recipient, and say:

"Happy birthday!"

"Congratulations!"

"This is for you."

"I hope you like it."

With gifts of clothing, if the box or label indicates where the item was purchased, the recipient will know where to exchange it if need be. If it's not obvious where you bought it, it's fine to say "I hope I got the right size. If it doesn't fit, let me know, and I can tell you where I got it."

Dear Alex

"My boyfriend (actually he's my ex-boyfriend now) gave me a necklace for my birthday. It cost over $300. My parents made me give it back. They said boys his age (15) shouldn't give girls my age (15) such expensive presents. I don't see why not. It was his money."

Your boyfriend's gift was thoughtful and generous. But it was also inappropriate, which is why your parents made you return it. Appropriateness is determined by a combination of four criteria: *selection, timing, proportion,* and *taste.*

1. **Selection** refers to the *relationship* between the gift and the receiver. The following gifts would *not* be appropriate:

   - a case of expensive champagne for a recovering alcoholic
   - a DVD of a silent movie for a person who is blind
   - the complete works of Shakespeare in a leather-bound edition for someone who really, really hates Shakespeare

   These are all fine things to give—just not to everyone. Since a necklace is a lovely gift for a young man to bestow upon a young woman, your boyfriend's *selection* was entirely appropriate.

2. **Timing** refers to the *when* of a gift. A beautiful tie presented to your favorite teacher *after* he writes 28 college recommendations for you is a gift. The same tie presented *before* he writes them is a bribe. Since a birthday is a wonderful occasion for gift-giving, your boyfriend's *timing* was excellent.

3. **Proportion** refers to the *magnitude* of the gift. This is a delicate way of saying how much it cost—in effort, money, or both. Did it cost too much or not enough? Determining the answer isn't easy, but luckily there's a formula you can use for this purpose:

$$P = \frac{V}{NR} \times \frac{AG}{AR} \times \frac{FRG}{FRR} \times \frac{3xy}{\pi}$$

In this equation, *proportional appropriateness* (P) is a function of the *value* (V) of the gift divided by the *nature of the relationship* (NR) times the *age of the giver* (AG) over the *age of the receiver* (AR) multiplied by the *financial resources of the giver* (FRG) divided by the *financial resources of the receiver* (FRR) times 3xy, where x equals *service or kindness previously rendered* and y equals *unspoken or unintended messages,* divided by pi.*

According to the formula, the following gifts would *not* be appropriate in terms of proportion:

- a bag of chips as a graduation present from your parents
- a private jet as a graduation present from your parents
- a $300 necklace from a 15-year-old boyfriend

Your boyfriend goofed in the area of *proportion.* Expensive presents can cause embarrassment, resentment, discomfort, and/or confusion in relationships. They may be intended (or felt) as attempts to control or manipulate; they may place unspoken demands on the receiver, or require too much sacrifice from the giver.

Proportion is also related to context—the circumstances in which the gift-giving occurs. Your parents might have let you keep the necklace if your boyfriend had just won $13 million in the lottery, or if you were both 18 and had dated all through high school. But teenagers can go through relationships very quickly, and expensive gifts can complicate things. It's hard to be dumped; it's devastating to be dumped the day after giving someone a $300 necklace.

4. **Taste** is the final measure of appropriateness. That silk tie you gave your teacher? An excellent choice, but not if it was printed all over with the words "SCHOOL IS FOR FOOLS." Since taste is highly personal, mistakes are easy to make. Be sure you know the receiver well before giving a gift with questionable humor value.

Even though your parents made you return your now ex-boyfriend's gift, I hope they will think kindly of him. After all, he only made a simple error of proportion. And your ex-boyfriend should think kindly of your parents. He may have lost you, but at least he has the necklace back.

*LEMON MERINGUE.

Righteous Receiving

There are only two ways to receive a present:

1. with great pleasure

2. with greater pleasure

Response #1 is for gifts you *don't* particularly like. It involves a warm smile, a look of delight and surprise, and expressions of gratitude such as:

"Thank you so much."

"I'm going to enjoy reading it."

"This will look so nice in my room."

"I'll sure stay warm in these."

For gifts you *do* like, use response #2. Wear an ear-to-ear grin. Let your jaw fall open and your eyes bug out. Remain speechless for a second or two as words fail you. Run around the room a few times. Do cartwheels. Say "I can't believe it" and "Oh, wow!" over and over while you try to regain control of your conscious mind. Then let loose a torrent of thanks:

"This is S-O-O-O-O fabulous!"

"I've wanted one of these forever and ever!"

"This is the greatest present!"

"I've never seen one this beautiful in my whole life!"

"Thank you! Thank you! Thank you!"

For the grand finale, shower the giver with hugs and kisses.

You'll notice that these responses do more than just convey gratitude. *They make the person who gave you the present feel like giving you another one.* This is a lovely by-product of the proper expression of thanks.

Now that you know what to do, here's what *not* to do:

Don't ask how much something cost. This is always a serious breach of etiquette.

Don't complain about gifts you receive. As in:

"Not another stupid wallet."

"Nobody wears these."

"Why'd you get me this?"

"I already have one."

This may be difficult, particularly if you were expecting a car and ended up with an Etch-A-Sketch. But sometimes, for the sake of the greater good, you have to pretend. (Think of the last time you faked being sick in order to stay home from school.) So, even if you're disappointed, act pleased and grateful because:

1. it's bad manners to deliberately hurt someone else's feelings

2. your behavior encourages the person to give you another present, thus giving her a chance to get it right the next time

Don't ask for presents. Parents and other gift-givers don't like to hear:

"Can I have one of those?"

"Buy me that!"

"What are you going to get me?"

So, how do you let them know what you want?

Nobody said you couldn't share your hopes and dreams. If you're passing a bike store, it's okay to point and say wistfully to your dad "Someday, when I've saved up enough money, I'm going to buy one just like that." Or to confide to your mom "Isn't that sweater gorgeous? I wish I had one like it." This isn't begging. This is parent-child communication.

It's also okay if your parents happen to overhear you telling a friend that you'd give anything to have a Bizarro Madboy X-90 Pro Skateboard with a Skullbone Black-Blood Deck, Zirconium Glow-in-the-Dark Forged-Base Trucks, and Tube Tech Turbo-Core Retro Space Wheels. And you're certainly entitled to circle items in catalogs, or cut out ads, and keep them in your bedroom for handy reference where they might be discovered by parents who wander by.

For those of you who are interested in parent psychology, here's why this indirect approach works: When grown-ups give a gift, they like to feel that they're surprising you rather than filling an order. By subtle hints instead of outright asking, you can give them the opportunity to show how attentive and sensitive they are. You put icing on the cake of this method when you respond to the gift with:

"How did you ever know I wanted one of these?"

Your parents will smile, feel clever, and say "Oh, we have our ways." And you can smile inside and feel clever, too.

Dear Alex

"Is it okay to return or give away a present you don't like?"

It depends on what it is, who gave it to you, the particulars of the gift, the likelihood that the giver will ever find out, and your reason for returning it.

It's fine to exchange things that you already have, such as books or CDs. No one would consider it rude to return clothing that doesn't fit or things you're allergic to. If you get tons of gifts all at once (for example, for a Bat Mitzvah or graduation) and end up with 11 sweaters and 43 bottles of perfume, it's okay to pare things down a bit.

The main thing you want to do is avoid hurting anyone's feelings. If one of those sweaters was handmade, you shouldn't give it away, even if you'll never wear it. The same goes for art people create especially for you, or items they consider very special or sentimental. You may just have to hang Aunt Fanny's hideous (er, lovely) paint-by-numbers portrait of Elvis when she comes for her annual visit, and then stick it back in the basement for the rest of the year.

Don't tell people you returned their gifts unless they ask. And then phrase your reply as gently as possible:

"I absolutely adored your going-away present, but since I'm moving to Hawaii I just don't know how often I'll get a chance to use a snowblower, so I exchanged it for a surfboard and now I'll think of you and your kindness every time I catch a wave."

Thank-You Notes

The reason teenagers have such a hard time writing thank-you notes is because they start off with the wrong attitude. They think of it as a *chore* instead of an *opportunity* to make the gift-giver feel wonderful. People who feel wonderful are more likely to keep giving you gifts than those who don't. Here's how to write terrific thank-you notes:

TRUE STORIES

FROM THE
MANNERS FRONTIER

Writer's Cramp
Sometimes it's safe to recycle gifts on to other victims (er, recipients) after a number of years have passed. But be careful!

I was browsing through a used bookstore one day and discovered a book that I had written. I picked it up to see if anyone had highlighted passages or otherwise mutilated it. And there, on the title page, was an inscription, in my handwriting, to the person to whom I had given it years earlier!

If you're not sure whether to write a thank-you note, write one. It's better to overthank than underthank. Notes are obligatory for all gifts received by mail, FedEx, or Pony Express, whether for a birthday, graduation, Bar or Bat Mitzvah, confirmation, Christmas, Hanukkah, Kwanzaa, etc. You should also write notes for services rendered, hospitality provided, and thoughtfulnesses extended. Generally, it's not necessary to write notes for presents given in person and for which you have already thanked the person verbally. But think of the mileage you could get out of a follow-up note!

Written thanks aren't required every time a courtesy is extended, but might be in order after a period of time has passed. For example, let's say a friend's mother drives your team to sports practice twice a week for an entire school year. She never fails to have some munchies in the car for everybody's enjoyment. Your verbal thanks each time are sufficient. But if you send her a note in June to recognize the cumulative value of her chauffeur service, she'll think you're the greatest. The same goes for a teacher who has meant a lot to you over the year.

Write immediately. Thank-you notes get exponentially more difficult to write with each day that passes. By the second day, they are *four* times harder to write. By the third day, they are *nine* times harder, and if you wait 12 days, they are *144* times harder to write!

Write by hand. Use personal note stationery or attractive cards (the ones that are blank inside). However, if your handwriting is absolutely atrocious, it's better to send a laser-printed, personally signed letter than none at all.

Consider alternative forms of communication. I know that for some of you the thought of a hand-written note makes you break out in a cold sweat. So, despite the fact that writing by hand carries on a centuries-old tradition as the sine qua non (look it up) of thank yous, today's nifty digital world presents grateful teens with other acceptable methods (no-point-denying-the-march-of-technology) for conveying thanks.

- Send a warm and thoughtful text message.
- Send a warm and thoughtful email.
- Send a warm and thoughtful private message.
- Send a digital thank you from one of those websites with animated cards for different occasions. Be sure to include a personal note.

Never begin with "Thank you for . . . ." Start with some news, a recollection of the event or visit, a reaffirmation of your friendship, or other charming chitchat.

For example, you've just spent a wonderful two weeks with the Gump family (distant cousins on your mother's side) at their California seaside condo. You might write:

Dear Mr. and Mrs. Gump,

I'm back here in Iowa, safe and sound. School started three days ago, and it already seems as if I've been back for three months. I can't believe it was just last week that I left the sunny shores of the Pacific for the long flight back home. I can't tell you how much I enjoyed my visit . . .

Continue by mentioning the places they took you to, the memories you'll always cherish, the delicious dinners, etc. Then, and only then, thank them for their thoughtfulness and generosity to you. Express the hope that you and your parents can one day host their kid for a stay in America's heartland. You'll bring smiles to the faces of the Gumps, make a fine impression, and guarantee that you'll have a standing invitation to return for more surf, sun, and fun.

Always mention the gift by name. If I give somebody a wedding present and I get a letter back that simply thanks me for my "wonderful and generous gift," I know it's a form letter they cranked out. Even if it's handwritten. Make the effort to refer to the gift in some way:

> *"All my friends are jealous of my new talking sneakers."*
>
> *"You must have read my mind to know I wanted a garlic press."*
>
> *"I'm absolutely thrilled with my Chia pet."*

Always mention special moments. If the gift was one of hospitality, you must send a note, even if you thanked your hosts during the visit. When you write, don't just say "Thanks for letting me stay with you." Let your hosts know the things that made the visit so special: falling into the river, being eaten alive by mosquitoes, having your picture taken with Mickey Mouse.

Tell how you're going to spend the money. If someone gives you the big green, mention what you plan to do with it. If you have no idea, make something up:

> *"I'm planning to buy some guitar strings that I've been wanting for ages."*
>
> *"I'm saving for a car, and this will really help me with that goal."*

Don't spoil your thanks with a bummer. Not every gift will be to your liking. Sometimes this is nobody's fault. Avoid saying things that let gift-givers know their efforts were unappreciated or pointless:

> *"I lost it the first time I took it to school."*
>
> *"It hit a tree and broke."*
>
> *"I got hives so my mom made me throw it out."*

Compliments

A compliment is a gift. The fact that it's verbal rather than material doesn't change a thing. If someone gives you a compliment, the proper way to receive it is by saying "Thank you." If you're really bowled over, you can add "You're very kind to say so."

Many people, however, deny, deflect, or deflate the compliments they are handed:

If someone says . . .	They reply . . .
"What a beautiful dress!"	"Oh, it's just a little nothing I picked up on sale" OR "I look terrible in it."

If someone says . . .	They reply . . .
"You played beautifully!"	"I was totally out of tune" OR "Yo-Yo was so much better."

People do this because they have low self-esteem and can't imagine why anyone would compliment them. This comes from not receiving enough compliments.

Negating a compliment implies that the person giving it doesn't know what he's talking about. That's a rude way to respond to someone who's just said something nice about you.

Occasionally, you'll receive a compliment from someone you've just beaten at something. If your win was a squeaker or the result of subjective judging, accept the compliment with modest grace:

"I feel really lucky they picked me. Any of us could have won."

If the compliment comes from someone you wiped the floor with, try to say something nice:

"You put up a stiff fight."

"You had a bad day, but I saw you yesterday against Brewster High and you played great."

Won't people know you're just trying to make them feel better? Probably. And won't they still feel lousy that they lost? Probably. But at least they will have the comfort of your empathy. You will have been a nice human being. That counts for a lot.

Giving compliments can be just as hard as receiving them, especially if you're disappointed or upset. It's not easy to congratulate the classmate whose experiment just won first prize over yours at the Science Fair, or the teammate who beat you out for a starting position. But these compliments are the most valuable, precisely because they are hard to give. They will mean a lot to the other person, who may (believe it or not) be feeling guilty and uncomfortable about having won. And they will also mean a lot to *you*, because you'll know that you can behave nobly even though you feel like smooshing a banana cream pie in the person's face.

There are a few pitfalls to watch for when handing out accolades:

Don't compliment one person by putting down another person.

Wrong	*Right*
"You kiss so much better than Sean."	"I love the way you kiss."
"It's wonderful having someone on the team who doesn't drop the ball the way Chris does."	"It's great having you on the team."

Don't tarnish your applause with envy or bitterness.

Wrong	*Right*
"Congratulations on winning the scholarship. At least *you'll* be able to go to college."	"Congratulations! You worked so hard!"
"You were great at the audition. But I don't see why I didn't get the part."	"Congratulations on getting the part. You'll make a great cat!"

Don't pollute your praise with criticism.

Wrong	*Right*
"You look so nice I didn't recognize you."	"You look really nice."
"You were great today. It's about time you scored."	"Great goal. You were terrific out there."

Don't undercut your compliment with nosiness.

Wrong	*Right*
"That's a gorgeous jacket. How on earth could you afford it?"	"Nice jacket!"
"Congratulations on your job. Who'd you have to bribe to get it?"	"Your new job sounds terrific!"

Applying for a Job

Sooner or later, most teenagers are motivated to get a job. This is due to a basic human drive called *wanting more money*. In order to get work, you'll need a social security number, which you probably already have. Depending on the job and your age, you may need to show a work permit, immigration papers if you're not a U.S. citizen, or even a statement from your doctor saying you're in good health. You can find out about this sort of stuff from your school, your state Labor Department, or potential employers.

It's nice to earn money. It's even nicer to earn it for doing something you like. So, before you go out looking for any old job, think of what you really enjoy. What fires you up? What do you want to learn? What are you good at? Fixing cars? Gardening? Music? Swimming? Babysitting? Biomolecular chromosome splitting?

Once you've identified your skills and interests, it's time to start looking. Finding a job can be difficult, particularly for younger teenagers. You may have more success creating your own job. Start a business. Provide a service. Depending on where you live, there may be a real demand for lawn and garden care, snow shoveling, dog walking, window washing, gutter cleaning, or babysitting. You might establish a grocery buying and delivery service, or run errands for people who are very busy or very lazy. You could go to people's homes or places of business and wash and wax their cars. A lot of people take vacations during the summer and could use someone responsible to water plants, care for pets, and look after the house while they're away. You could run a repair or sewing service for people like me who'll lose a button on a shirt and never wear it again. You could organize parties, a summer camp, or play groups for kids; do cooking and catering; do laundry and ironing. You could run a computer consulting service.

Have business cards printed. Put up flyers. Place an online ad. Set up a website or Facebook page. Get letters of recommendation from people you've worked for to show to prospective customers. If you provide a necessary service, price it fairly, and don't fall asleep on the job, you'll build an income and a client base. Those clients will tell their friends and, before you know it, you'll have work coming out your ears. You might even have to hire someone to help you!

If you want to work for someone else instead of yourself, brainstorm people and places you could approach. Look on job websites. Network. Ask your parents and siblings; ask your friends and their parents; ask your teachers, coaches, and school counselors. Don't be afraid to contact people who are doing what you want to do and ask them for advice. Most adults enjoy helping polite and appreciative young people who are interested in exploring or entering their field of work. Call businesses and shops to see if they have positions available. Keep your eyes peeled for signs in storefronts. Check out bulletin boards at the supermarket, the laundromat, the public library. See if your school has a job placement service. Place your own ad. Use Facebook, online discussion groups, and email to get the word out.

Many positions are seasonal (such as camp counselors, lifeguards, and ski lift operators). Find out when these types of places do their hiring. Show your interest early. Get a jump on everybody else. Don't be a pest, but if you stay in touch and let it be known that you're really serious about a job, your perseverance may work to your advantage.

You might need to put together a *résumé*—a written summary of your skills and experience that you can send to places where you'd like a job. You can also leave copies of your résumé with people who interview you. Your résumé should include:

- your name, address, and phone number
- your email address

- the schools you've attended and degrees you've attained (for example, a high school diploma with honors in chair tilting)

- descriptions of any jobs you've held, and what your responsibilities and accomplishments were

- any honors or prizes you've received

- any activities, interests, and courses you've taken that relate to the type of work you hope to find

You may want to include the names and phone numbers of people who have agreed to tell potential employers how great you are. These are called *references*. They should not be confused with parents or other relatives whose opinions might be biased. Be sure to get permission before you list someone as a reference.

Your résumé should be flawless. As in perfect. That is to say, no misteaks. It should represent the quality, care, exactitude, and smart appearance you would bring to the job. It is your stand-in. In the computer age, there is no excuse for a sloppy résumé. And believe me, when employers are looking through hundreds of résumés, they want an excuse to throw out as many as they can. You can find more information about preparing a résumé from your school guidance or career office, the public library, or online resources.

Once you've got a résumé and have identified where you'd like to work, you're ready to seek an interview. Some places, like fast-food joints and convenience stores, usually don't require you to make an appointment. You can just walk in, ask to see the manager, and say that you'd like to apply for a job. You'll be handed an application and asked if you want fries with that. The manager may interview you then and there, or ask you to come back at another time. Be sure you look nice when you make these preliminary rounds. If you make a crummy first impression, the manager may just tell you that there aren't any openings.

Other places require you to schedule an appointment for an interview. Call them up. Tell the person who answers the phone that you'd like to apply for a job. You'll either be told what to do or transferred to the personnel office.

You can also send a query letter. This is what I did when I was a lad of 14. I wanted a summer job working for an architect. I drafted a letter in which I spoke of my love of architecture, my desire to become an architect, drawings I'd done, places I'd traveled to, courses I'd taken, and what a hardworking, responsible, all-around great kid I was. I concluded by saying that I would call to schedule an interview.

I sent off 20 perfect letters to 20 architectural firms—and didn't get a job; there were too many college and graduate students applying. But most of the architects complimented me on my letter and invited me to visit their offices. I took some great tours, met some fascinating people, and ate some yummy donuts. Several architects said that I could come back anytime to hang out, use their libraries, and pick up tips on drawing and lettering from the people who worked there. Soon, some of the architects were giving me little projects to do, like drawing bricks and leaves.

This brings to mind one of the major challenges in job-hunting: A lot of places say "Sorry. We only hire people with experience." *But how do you get experience if nobody will hire you without it?* One way is to volunteer where you want to work. A place that can't hire you might still be willing to take you on as an unpaid intern or apprentice. That way, you get experience and on-the-job training. If you make a good impression, you could be first in line for a paying job at some later date.

In fact, that's what happened to me. When I was 15, I wrote another 20 letters. Only this time, I was able to truthfully* say that I had worked for architects. (The fact that I didn't get paid for my work was none of their business.) I was able to name-drop local architects I knew, and to use them as references. And, sure enough, the next summer I got a job. And the summer after that, I got a job with the same firm in their Tokyo, Japan, office! The rest, as they say, is history. One thing led to another, and before I could say Frank Lloyd Wright, I became . . . a developmental psychologist and writer of books for teenagers?!

At the Interview

Let's say you've set up an interview. This is your chance to show in word and deed that YOU are the person for the job. Here are some pointers to keep in mind:

Be punctual. Coming late does not a good impression make. Leave enough time to get where you're going. Allow for the possibility of a traffic jam, or trouble finding the right building. If you see that you're going to be late, try to call the interviewer. This shows consideration and responsibility. When you get to your appointment, be sure to apologize. If it was your fault, admit it:

"I'm terribly sorry about being late. I got lost. I should have allowed more time."

This shows that you're mature enough to accept responsibility rather than make excuses. On the other hand, if being late wasn't your fault, apologize and explain what happened:

"A barge hit the bridge, and traffic had to detour 30 miles around Lake Looney. I'm sorry, I hope this hasn't upset your schedule too much."

*SEE "BE HONEST BUT NOT STUPID" ON PAGE 54.

A reasonable person will understand and won't hold your lateness against you.

Once you get where you're going, let the receptionist know who you are, who you're seeing, and the time of your appointment. He or she will probably tell you to have a seat. Try not to fidget, tap, or pace while waiting. You never know who might be watching. If other people are waiting, it's fine to engage in small talk:

"Have you worked for a landscaping company before? I think the opening here is because the last person fell into the wood chipper. I hear they force you to work 14 hours a day. Chain saws make you go deaf, did you know that?"

At worst, you'll have a pleasant conversation. And if you're lucky, the person will say "Excuse me" and head for the door. One less competitor for the job!

Dress appropriately. Wear clothes that are neat, clean, pressed, and nonodoriferous. A good rule of thumb is to put on something a little snazzier than what you'd normally wear on the job. Interviewing for a lifeguard position? Don't go in your Speedo. Wear nice shorts and a T-shirt or polo shirt. A job in construction, lawn care, or manual labor? A *good* pair of jeans, a work shirt, and boots or sneakers (laced and tied). If you're applying to work in a store or an office, boys should wear khakis or dress slacks (no jeans), a nice shirt (no T-shirts or tank tops), and presentable footgear (loafers, boat shoes, dress shoes). If it's a fancy store or a very "establishment" business (such as a bank or a law firm), boys should wear a tie and jacket or even a suit. Girls would dress correspondingly: nice shorts, slacks, or skirts and tops for informal positions such as camp counseling, babysitting, or manual labor; a nice skirt or dress pants and blouse for office and service jobs; a businessy dress or suit for the pinstripe and Perrier establishment crowd.

Whatever position you're applying for, you should be well-groomed and well-coiffed. That means no dirty fingernails, no milk mustaches, no green food particles between your teeth. Hair should be combed, brushed, and under a semblance of control. Boys should be clean shaven. If you happen to be a 14-year-old with a beard, keep it neat and trimmed. Avoid the five-day stubble look. Girls should use makeup in moderation. Both boys and girls should use scent in moderation (if at all), and avoid wearing clothes that are too tight or sexually provocative: No bare midriffs or pants worn halfway to your knees.

"But that's the style!"

"I'm not going to be some phony."

"Why can't I wear sneakers?"

"I don't have a suit."

"I want them to know the real me."

Tip: Let them hire you first. Then they can get to know the *real* you. What we're really talking about here is avoiding extremes. You want your appearance to say "I have a sense of what's appropriate; I care about how I look; I care about the impression I make." When you work for someone else, you represent that person or business. You are their link to customers or clients, and the quality of *your* work reflects *their* competence. Employers need to know that you can be trusted with their image and reputation. They need to know that you'll behave appropriately and responsibly on their behalf. The way you present yourself at a job interview shows whether you know how to do so on *your* behalf.

Of course, there are exceptions to every rule. If you're auditioning for a role as a skinhead punk in a movie, you might come looking like a skinhead punk. If you're hoping to get a job playing drums in a band, you might help your chances by looking the part. It's probably a fair statement to say that people in the art, music, entertainment, fashion, and computer/software/Internet/video gaming fields tend to be more casual, individualistic, and diverse in how they dress than people in service industries or the worlds of business and finance.

The main idea is to use your good judgment—that thing your parents are always telling you to have more of. If you think it's okay to wear a T-shirt to an interview, just don't wear one with a picture or phrase that's going to offend anyone. If you don't own or can't borrow any dress clothes, dress casually, but show that you have a sense of style and appropriateness.

"Yeah, I applied for a job here, but they won't hire me. I don't get it."

Come prepared. Bring any documents or information you might need to show. This could include your résumé, proof of age or citizenship, social security number, certifications, etc. If you have examples of your own work that relate to the position, bring them along, too. For example, if you're applying for a job in a photography store, you could show the interviewer some photographs you've taken.

Turn off your cell phone and other devices. Nothing is more annoying to an interviewer than hearing the applicant's cell phone suddenly start blaring away. No, wait, there is something more annoying: ANSWERING the cell phone! Make sure yours is silenced.

"Wait a sec. I've got a phone call."

Mind your manners. An interview is one occasion where the sorry state of the world today works to your advantage. Use your best manners, and you'll set yourself apart from the unkempt competition who will grunt, mumble, and fidget their way through the meeting.

When the interviewer comes to greet you, stand up straight. Smile. Shake hands (firm grip). Look the interviewer in the eye. Be confident, even if your stomach's churning and your legs feel like jelly. Use your acting skills. Take deep breaths. Say "How do you do." Follow the interviewer to wherever your meeting is going to take place. Once you get there, she will tell you to take a seat. (Don't ask "Where should I take it?") If the interviewer doesn't cue you to sit but just sits down herself, take the seat opposite her. Sit up straight in the chair. Don't slump or stretch out. Try not to tap, bounce, drum, bite your nails, pick your skin, or crack your knuckles. Use "Sir" and "Ma'am." Don't chew gum, blow bubbles, spit tobacco, or smoke.

You may be asked if you'd like some coffee, water, or soda. While it's fine to accept, before doing so, think whether you want to risk spilling it all over yourself. Since there's a chance of doing so, or creating unnecessary work for your interviewer, my inclination is to always decline. Of course, if you're applying for a position in a bakery or candy factory and you get offered a treat, this rule can be bent.

Be poised. Some interviewers may try to provoke you or throw you a curveball. They want to see how you react to stress. I can remember an interview during my teen years. The interviewer was asking all these rapid-fire questions about where I went to school and my courses and grades and extracurricular activities and what I had done previous summers and what I wanted to do with my life and all of a sudden he asked "What's 19 times 15?" Without missing a beat, I said "78" (I was always very good at math), and continued to talk about my hopes and dreams for the future. From this experience, I learned to expect the unexpected at interviews and to carry a pocket calculator.

Be honest but not stupid. Don't lie about your qualifications or experience. Prospective employers can easily check these things by contacting your references or previous employers. At the same time, don't be honest to a fault.

Let's say an interviewer asks "Why do you want to work here?" If you say "Because my stupid parents are forcing me to get a job," you're not going to help your cause. Tell a different truth. Say "Because I like children and being outdoors, and I've heard good things about your camp."

Getting a job can be an uphill battle. You need to persuade an employer to hire *you* over everyone else. Telling him what he wants to hear is part of the game. And what he wants to hear is that you're gung ho, responsible, and interested in the work.

Be digitally discreet. It is now standard practice for employers to check out job applicants online. They'll Google your name, look for you on Facebook, see what you've tweeted. Keep that in mind as you create your online persona.

Be enthusiastic. An interviewer is going to ask you questions. Give more than one-word answers. Without being hyper, show that you're excited about the opportunity. This suggests you might be energetic on the job, which is something employers like.

Suppose the interviewer says "So you want to work in a ski store?" Say "Yeah" and she'll show you to the door.

Say "You bet!" and she might sit up and take notice.

Say "Boy, would I ever! I got my first pair of skis when I was three and I've been schussing down the double diamonds ever since" and she may offer you the job.

Have questions ready. Many interviewers will ask if you have any questions. Even if most of your questions have already been answered, try to come up with a few more. This shows that you're a thoughtful person who wants to evaluate the fit of the position. You could ask about the nature of your duties, the future plans of the company, the type of customer or client you'd be working with, opportunities for training and growth, the pay and benefits of the job (wait 'til the end to ask this), etc.

Send a thank-you note. When the interview is over, thank the interviewer for her time and willingness to see you. If the interview was very quick and impersonal—say, for a job in a fast-food restaurant—your verbal appreciation is ample. If, however, the interviewer spent a considerable amount of time with you, or the position was with an office or store that really appeals to you, send a thank-you note. Let her know how much you appreciated the opportunity to meet. Repeat how eager you are to work there. Even if you don't get the job, your letter will make a positive impression. And it just might improve your chances for the next job that opens up there.

Dear Alex

"I've had my eyebrow, lip, and nose pierced. Is it all right to wear my rings to a job interview?"

Not unless you're applying for a job in a piercing parlor. Numerous metal objects poked through your flesh will not make the interviewer think how great you'd be in the job. It will make him think *eee-youch!!!*

Dear Alex

"I'm a 14-year-old girl and I babysit a lot for this one family. I like the kids, but every time I come over the mom always asks me to do the laundry or clean up from their dinner or something like that. I don't think housework should be part of my job, but I don't know how to tell her."

Housework should not be part of a babysitter's job unless:

1. the babysitter agrees to it and/or is paid extra

2. the work is directly related to childcare activities (for example, cleaning up the kitchen after giving the kids or yourself a snack, vacuuming the family room after a popcorn fight)

It's always tricky for employees to set limits for what they will and won't do, and even more so when the employee is a kid and the employer is an adult. But, since a good babysitter is worth her weight in gold, you're at a definite advantage. Simply say to the mother "I really enjoy babysitting for your family, but I don't feel housework should be part of my responsibilities. Of course, I'll clean up any messes we make while I'm babysitting." If you're willing to do extra work for extra pay, you can mention this and see what the mother says.

Since healthy relationships between parents and babysitters are crucial to the functioning of society, here's a summary of each party's responsibilities:

The parents should:

- drive you to and from the job as needed
- maintain adequate snacking supplies
- keep the television, DVR, and DVD player in working order
- leave emergency telephone numbers and information as to their whereabouts
- return at the agreed-upon hour
- provide instructions for feeding, medicating, and/or handling the children ("Johnny won't go to sleep unless Mr. Penguin faces north")
- inform their children that they must be good
- pay at the time services are rendered
- if they want to stay on your A-list, round off to the next highest hour or half-hour (as in three hours and forty minutes of babysitting = four hours of pay)

You should:

- approach your job as if it were one of the most awesome responsibilities a person could be entrusted with (because it is)
- give your full time and attention to the children you're sitting for
- make sure you ask for any information the parents may have forgotten to provide
- keep the phone line free so the parents can call you (they should have your cell phone number, too)
- admit no one into the house unless this has been cleared beforehand
- report significant problems or milestones ("Junior swallowed your wedding ring")
- if you want to stay on your employer's A-list, always do a little something extra that shows initiative and thoughtfulness—bake some cookies with the kids, wash the last few dishes that the parents left in the sink, help a child clean up her room or write a thank-you note

People with Disabilities

One of the greatest challenges that people with disabilities face is dealing with the manners-impaired. These "well-intentioned" folks will talk about a person with a disability as if she weren't there:

"Can she walk?"

"Will she grow?"

They'll pry into areas that are none of their business:

"Were you born that way?"

"Can you have sex?"

They'll treat the person as an object of pity or praise, not as a human being with needs and feelings no different than their own.

Many people feel uncomfortable around people with disabilities because they don't know how to act—or react. Or they may not know how or whether to help. Or they may view the person's disability through their own perspective. A sighted person meets a person who is blind, imagines not being able to see, and feels a sense of loss, tragedy, and fear. Or a person who can walk sees a person who uses a wheelchair and feels immobile and claustrophobic. These feelings color the interaction, even though the person with the disability probably doesn't feel anything like that. The essence of good manners is the ability to put others at ease *regardless of one's own discomfort.*

In the sincere hope that you'll never be manners-impaired when relating to people with disabilities, here are some do's and taboos*:

- Don't assume that one disability implies another. There's no need to shout at a person who is blind or speak slowly to someone in a wheelchair. Also, don't make decisions and assumptions as to what people with disabilities can or can't do. They know better than you. Let them decide.

- Always address people with disabilities directly. Look them in the eye. Just because they may have a parent, friend, or nurse with them doesn't mean they can't speak for themselves. Never refer to them in the third person in their presence ("Would he mind if I took him for a walk?" "Can she swim?").

- When talking to a person who is deaf or hard of hearing, turn toward him so he can read your lips. Try to speak in a quiet location. Make sure there is light on your face. Unless asked to do so, don't

*FOR STRAIGHTFORWARD, SENSITIVE WORDS AND PHRASES TO USE, CHECK OUT "GUIDELINES: HOW TO WRITE AND REPORT ABOUT PEOPLE WITH DISABILITIES," (LAWRENCE, KS: THE RESEARCH AND TRAINING CENTER ON INDEPENDENT LIVING, 2013). FOR A PRINTED COPY CONTACT RTC/IL AT (785) 864-4095 OR RTCIL.ORG/GUIDELINES.SHTML.

speak unusually slowly or loudly or overpronounce words. If an interpreter is present, face the person who is hard of hearing, not the interpreter.

- Never take a person's cane or crutches. If you're going to be seated for a while, you can ask "Would you like me to set these over here while we eat?"

- Always ask before helping. If you saw someone struggling to carry a lot of luggage, you wouldn't just grab the bags out of her hands. You'd ask if she could use some assistance. The same thing applies when you encounter people with disabilities. Don't start steering them across the street as if they were grocery carts. Say "Would you like to take my arm?" or "May I help in any way?"

- Don't pry. People with disabilities don't owe anyone a medical report. It's rude to ask about the source, duration, symptoms, prognosis, or limitations of their condition.

- If you're in the company of a friend with a disability, third parties (such as waiters, sales clerks, or acquaintances of yours) might address you rather than your friend. If this happens, don't respond or make eye contact. This will encourage them to speak directly to your friend.

- Be patient when interacting with people who have a speech disorder. Give your full attention. Don't finish their sentences for them. Don't pretend that you understand what they're saying if you really don't. Say "I'm sorry, I didn't get that" or "You went where?" or "What was that number again?"

- Never touch a person with a disability without permission. This is an invasion of his or her personal space. (So is leaning on a wheelchair.) Similarly, never pet or call to a service animal such as a guide dog without the owner's permission. This could distract the animal and/or interfere with its training.

- If you're asked for directions by a person with a disability, consider the terrain, weather, locations of ramps/stairs/curb-cuts, and any other physical obstacles that could make travel difficult.

- Don't use euphemisms to describe disabilities. Disability groups object to terms such as "handicapable," "mentally different," "physically inconvenienced," and "physically challenged." These terms reinforce the idea that disabilities can't be dealt with up front.

- Use respectful terminology. Don't define people by their disabilities. And always put the person first, not the disability. For example, say "My friend who is deaf," not "My deaf friend."

Unacceptable	Preferred
generic labels like "the blind," "the deaf"	people who are blind; people who are deaf
a cripple	a person who is physically disabled
a retard	a person with an intellectual disability
an epileptic	a person with epilepsy; a person with a seizure disorder
a spastic	a person with a motor disorder
a vegetable	a person with a brain injury
an HIV victim; an AIDS victim	a person with HIV; a person with AIDS
a mongoloid	a person with Down syndrome
a cerebral palsy victim	a person who has cerebral palsy
a person afflicted by multiple sclerosis	a person who has multiple sclerosis
a person who suffers from muscular dystrophy	a person who has muscular dystrophy
a person who is confined to a wheelchair	a person who uses a wheelchair
an autistic person	a person with autism

Dear Alex

"What should you do if you see someone in a wheelchair? I know it's polite to help, but I've heard that people with disabilities don't want to be helped and might get mad if you try."

Start by thinking of a person in a wheelchair simply as a *person*. Then, if you think she might like or need some help, offer your assistance. It will either be accepted or declined. End of story. Never push or move people in wheelchairs without permission. In most cases, they are fully capable of getting where they want on their own.

When speaking to people who use wheelchairs, try to position yourself at their eye level. Find a chair, sit down and face them, or, if you're standing, bend at the waist. But don't squat or kneel. This might come across as condescending. Never grab onto or lean against someone's wheelchair. And don't ask them to hold things in their lap for you.

Dear Alex

"I use a wheelchair. You won't believe how many times total strangers just start pushing me. How do I tell them I don't need their help?"

It's a wonder that people who would never dream of swooping strangers into their arms and carrying them across the street feel at liberty to propel people in wheelchairs into motion. Tell the eager beaver "Thank you, but I don't need any assistance." And then, if you feel like it, do a few 360s, pop a wheelie or two, and scorch on outta there.

Dear Alex

"There's this blind girl who started coming to a youth center in my neighborhood. I want to be friendly, but I'm scared I'll do something dumb or not know what to say."

Say "Hi. Welcome to the center. My name is _____. What's yours?" And then start a conversation, just as you would with any new acquaintance. You're approaching her not because she's blind, but because it's polite to welcome and get to know any new person. Ask about her interests and activities, where she lives, where she goes to school, etc. She's probably just like any other teenager—eager to have friends, talk, go places, and do things. The fact that she can't see presents her with challenges most kids don't face. But it doesn't *define* her. (That's why it's best to think or speak of her as a girl *who is blind* rather than a "blind girl.") So don't focus on her being blind as an initial topic of conversation unless she brings it up. As you build a friendship and begin to do things together, the subject may come up naturally.

If she uses a guide dog, don't pet it without her permission. If you go walking together, stand on the side of her away from the dog. Don't pull her by the hand or steer her by the shoulders. Offer her your elbow. If she chooses to take it, let her set the pace. If you approach an obstacle or hazard, don't just shout "Look out!" Instead, give her specific information: "There's a big mound of dog doo-doo and four really steep steps."

Identify yourself each time you see your new friend until you're positive that she recognizes your voice. If you're ever in a group conversation with her and somebody leaves, let her know. That way, she won't talk to a person who's no longer there. It's also fine to tell her things you see that she might find helpful or amusing:

"They're all laughing because Mrs. Finderstock just made a face."

"Jaleel shaved his head."

"Mr. Dripps looks so mad I think he's going to explode."

"That new guy is S-O-O-O cute!"

Don't worry about using words like "see," "watch," and "look." A blind person won't be offended if you say "See what I mean?" or "I hear the math sub is tough. You better watch out for her." But do avoid expressions that use disabilities as insults. For example, don't say "Whatsa matter, are you blind?!" to a person who steps on your toe. Or "You retard!" to someone who makes a mistake.

Dear Alex

"The other day, I was introduced to someone who was missing his right hand. I went to shake hands, and I felt pretty embarrassed when I realized there was nothing to shake. What should I have done?"

The next time you meet him, let him take the lead. Anyone whose hand is unavailable, whether temporarily or permanently, is likely to have encountered this situation before. He may extend his left hand (which you may shake with either your left or right hand); he may extend a prosthetic hand for you to shake (not *too* vigorously, though); or he may extend no hand at all, in which case your interaction will be verbal. Take your cue from his behavior.

Dear Alex

"I was badly burned in a car accident. Wherever I go, people either stare at my face or avoid looking at it entirely. If I walk into a room, the conversation sometimes stops, or kids start whispering. It's bad enough what happened without having to be reminded of it every minute of the day. I don't want to be rude, but I think those people are being rude to me. What should I do?"

First, recognize that you don't owe anybody an explanation. Even though some people are likely to be curious, uncomfortable, and/or insensitive in your presence, you're not responsible for their social disabilities. But you can choose to respond in any of several ways:

1. **Ignore rude reactions.** Simply go about your business. In time, conversation will resume. Whispering will stop. And people will look beyond your skin to see the fine person inside.

2. **Intensify your social correctness.** Introduce yourself. Get the conversation going again. Your naturalness may make others feel self-conscious about their lapse in manners, and they will get with the program.

3. **Break the ice.** When you enter a room, *you* know that people are wondering what happened to you. And *they* know that you know. It becomes one of those situations in which everybody's *thinking* about the same thing but nobody wants to *say* anything about it.

It's not your obligation to satisfy people's curiosity or to compensate for their poor social skills. But there may be certain occasions when you feel comfortable about speaking out. You can do this in one of two ways, depending on which feels right to you. For example, you might simply say "I was burned in a car accident." Or you might take a light, humorous tone and say "Don't worry, it's not contagious." Either way, you're alleviating the awkwardness by bringing what's on people's minds out into the open. And either way, you're being *very* generous.

People will probably respond with embarrassed expressions of apology ("Sorry, I didn't mean—" or "It's none of my—"). In which case, you can say "Oh, that's okay." Then change the subject to something you want to talk about.

Dear Alex

"I have a birth defect that affects my coordination. People, even strangers, ask things like 'What's wrong with you?' or 'How did you get that way?' Is it okay to be rude back?"

No. But it *is* okay to make them squirm. Strangers merit no reply. You may, however, slowly turn your head toward your interrogator, give him a hard look a nanosecond short of a stare, and slowly look away. He'll get the message.

If someone asks "What's wrong with you?" you can smile and say "There's nothing *wrong* with me. Why? Is there something wrong with you?"

You can also ignore the question. Respond to any prying inquiry by saying "Do you think the Yankees will win the pennant?"

Another way to answer intrusive questions is by saying "I'm sorry, but I don't discuss such things with people I don't know."

Some people may ask about your disability because they want to get to know you better. (As opposed to those who simply want to satisfy their own curiosity.) You'll probably sense when a question indicates sincere interest, and you'll feel more comfortable answering it.

Chapter Quiz

1. *You're hosting a party when you notice that two of the guests, whose names you've forgotten, are standing awkwardly next to each other. Do you:*

a) yell across the room "If you're going to look so glum, you're going to have to leave"

b) introduce them using any old names you can think up

c) approach them and say "It's great to see you. Do you know each other? I've got to check the food, but why don't you two introduce yourselves?"

2. *The proper social kiss is designed to:*

a) wipe a milk mustache off on someone's cheek

b) help you get to first base

c) express affection between friends

3. *It's your birthday. Your aunt has just given you the most hideous shirt you've ever seen in your life. Do you:*

a) blow your nose in it

b) ask "How much did this horror set you back?"

c) beam, give your auntie a kiss, and say "Thank you so much! I can't wait to show this to all my friends."

4. *You've just finished a job interview for a position in a pet store. The owner rises, signaling that the interview is over. Do you:*

a) put your feet up on the desk and say "What's the rush, bossman?"

b) ask if the parrot knows any swear words

c) get up, shake hands, and thank the owner for his time

5. *You're skateboarding to school when you see a woman who is blind waiting to cross a busy street. The proper thing to do is:*

a) push her into the traffic

b) slam into her and yell "Why doncha watch where you're going?"

c) stop and say "Excuse me, can I give you a hand?"

3

UNCOMMON COURTESIES

Saving the Earth from a Manners Meltdown

In your mind's eye, step back from your daily world of family, school, Facebook, and friends; forget about homework, chores, and YouTube; let go of all the little worries and hassles that crowd your consciousness. Zoom away from the planet. See Earth as a tiny dot, people as grains of sand. Travel through space to the edge of the universe, climb up on the wall, and have yourself a think about the state of the world.

War. Starvation. Poverty. Disease. Drugs. Murder. Terrorism. Tofu.

Think about the rudeness you encounter every day. From classmates. Teachers. Parents. Store clerks. Brothers and sisters. People on the bus. Strangers in the subway. Think about the rude things *you* do every day.*

Think about reality TV shows that present cruelty as entertainment.

Think about kids being shot for an iPod.

Think about bumper stickers that beg people to be kind to one another.

Now that you're in a cheery mood, think about this: Is it possible that human beings, at this very moment, are headed for extinction? Will greed, selfishness, and ignorance turn our species into an evolutionary laughingstock? Or will generosity, kindness, and respect prevail? Will

*OKAY, EVERY *OTHER* DAY.

we do ourselves proud? Or will we die out, leaving nothing behind but golden arches and toxic waste?

The answer can be summed up in one word: *Beats me.* But I can tell you what the deciding factor will be: *Manners.*

The survival of the human race depends on everyone minding their manners. Manners allow people to live and work together in harmony, to go about the daily business of life without constant friction or fighting.

It is in the anonymous, everyday interactions of modern life that manners have most broken down. On sidewalks. In stores. At movie theaters. On the highways. Anonymity breeds rudeness. It's easier to give the finger to a stranger than to someone you know. It's easier to bully someone online than face-to-face.

North America is not the only region experiencing a manners meltdown. Many cultures around the globe are facing similar epidemics of impoliteness. French drivers tell pedestrians who refuse to get out of their way what they can do with their baguettes. In Singapore, you can be flogged for chewing gum or spitting in public. In China, according to a Reuters news report, rudeness by employees who serve the public has gotten so bad that 50 phrases are now banned in such places as post offices, airports, train stations, hospitals, and stores. Among them are:

"Ask someone else."

"If you're not buying, what are you looking at?"

"Don't you see I'm busy?"

"What do you have ears for?"

Of course, here in the United States, we would never deal with rudeness by banning it. We'd set up a congressional committee to study it. And it would become the discussion flavor-of-the-week on all the talk shows ("I Threw a Pie at My Sister's Boyfriend," "Men Who Pick Their Noses in Public and the Women Who Love Them").

Unfortunately, nothing is going to change if we leave the sorry state of manners in the hands of adults. If adults were behaving themselves and teaching manners to their offspring as they should, we wouldn't be in this mess. So it's up to you. Do you want to inherit a rude, ugly world? Or do you want to do your part to restore kindness, consideration, and proper behavior to our society?

The place to start is in that anonymous public sphere. If every teenager does his or her part—if we can all use good manners *with people we don't even know*—we can all attend concerts, get from A to B, and step out into the Real World without being jostled and sworn at. Remember, the future of the human race depends on it.

THE SURVEY SAYS . . .

Here, according to my survey of adults, are the 25 Rudest Things Teenagers Do in Public:

1. Use obscene language in loud voices.

2. Spit, burp, and belch.

3. Display too much affection.

4. Smoke where it's prohibited.

5. Pick their noses.

6. Not say "Please" or "Thank you" to salespeople.

7. Talk back to their parents.

8. Mutter insults or wisecracks at people walking by.

9. Fill all the seating in a public place and not offer it to senior citizens.

10. Litter.

11. Ridicule or behave inconsiderately toward people with disabilities or elderly people on public transportation.

12. Tease small children.

13. Use their cell phones in inappropriate places.

14. Flip the bird.

15. Walk five abreast on a sidewalk or in a narrow corridor.

16. Text while adults are talking to them.

17. Are loud, obnoxious, and rowdy in movies and stores.

18. Push and shove each other with no respect for others around them.

19. Let doors close in other people's faces (on purpose or accidentally).

20. Not observe boundaries regarding personal space.

21. Make fun of others.

22. Engage in conversation while serving the public (for example, cashier chatting with bagger during rush-hour shopping).

23. Write on other people's property.

24. Embarrass, insult, or bully one another.

25. Wear clothes with pants or tops that show way too much.

Bodies in Motion

Have you noticed that bodies in motion tend to collide? Or that doors were not designed to admit 15 people simultaneously? Of course you have, as you've gotten shoved, knocked, and gouged while walking down a school corridor or bus aisle. Take heart! Here's what you need to know to travel through life without getting your toes stepped on.

The Ups and Downs of Elevator Behavior

The *ifs, ands,* and *butts* of elevator etiquette are:

- *If* the call button is already pushed, don't re-push it. Multiple pushings will not make the elevator come any faster. In fact, the elevator may get so irritated that it decides to skip your floor.

- *If* you're entering an elevator, allow those exiting to step off first.

- *If* the elevator is crowded, people closest to the door should exit first.

- *If* the elevator isn't crowded, it's considered polite for males to let women and girls leave first (and enter first).

- *If* you stink or you're only going a floor or two, consider the stairs. You'll avoid the stares of your fellow passengers who are silently judging and cursing you. And, it's great exercise.

- *If* there are other people in the elevator, position yourself so as to provide maximum personal space to your fellow passengers. This takes great skill and constant fine tuning as people get on and off.

Proper Elevator Positioning (PEP)

- *If* you're getting off at one of the highest floors, stand farthest from the door. Always stand facing the door (although I admit it would be kind of funny to face the rear of the elevator).

- *If* you're in front of the door but it's not your floor, stand aside as best you can. Or take a walk on the wild side: Step out for a moment to let people off, then dart back in before the door closes again.

- *If* you need to get off and people are blocking the way, say "Excuse me" and gently move toward the front. This should not be confused with pushing, shoving, or elbowing.

- *If* you're standing by the control panel, you're the designated driver. Press the "Open Door," "Close Door," and floor buttons to assist the efficient flow of traffic. It's fine to accept tips.

- *And* whatever you do, don't stare, fart, push all the buttons, or pinch anyone's *butt*.

Sandwiched on the Subway

The protocol for subways is similar to that for elevators, and the same rules apply with regard to entering and exiting: Don't block the doors, stand aside, and let people get off before you get on.

While five-course formal subway dining is to be discouraged, a soda or non-smelly, non-messy snack may be consumed discreetly. Just be sure you don't smack your lips, leave crumbs, or spill anything. (Be aware that some subway systems prohibit eating and/or drinking entirely.)

Reading is a long-established tradition on subways. Looking over someone's shoulder is acceptable; breathing down the person's neck is not.

Trash must be carried off the train and deposited in a receptacle. Leaving a newspaper neatly on the seat, however, is not littering. It is sharing.

If you really want to be an uber-underground connoisseur, make sure you don't adopt any of the following personas (these apply to bus riders, too!):

The Sprawler: Keep your knees together. Nobody wants to see your legs spread apart like a chicken wishbone, preventing people from sitting in the seats next to you. And no lying down unless you're dead.

The Pole Hugger: Don't molest the pole with your whole body. Hang on with one hand so that other riders can steady themselves, too.

The Seat Hoarder: Always offer your seat to anyone who is pregnant, elderly, disabled, or just looks like they need it more than you do. This creates good karma that will come around to reward you.

The Noise Polluter: Keep conversations to a reasonable volume. Same with listening to music. What sounds like music to you comes out of your headphones as metallic scratching to your neighbors.

The Gymnast: Those are not chin-up bars. They're for holding onto so you don't lose your balance.

The Door Hog: Have you noticed how people bunch up around the doors? Move into the car so everyone has more room. And if you have to stand by the door, don't lean on it. You never know when it might accidentally open.

The Groomer: The subway is not the place to catch up on flossing, fingernail clipping, nail polishing, ear cleaning, or eyelash curling. Save those tasks for home.

The Disease Spreader: Coughing and sneezing without covering your nose and mouth. Yiccch! Or grabbing the pole with mucus-coated hands. Double yiccch! This would be a good time to remind you to wash your hands after riding the subway and other public conveyances.

Escalators and Slidewalks

The etiquette for escalators is simple:

- Don't crowd or push. Some people are understandably nervous on stairs that move by themselves. You wouldn't want to cause anyone to lose his balance and get sucked into that little crack at the top or bottom.

- Stand right. Pass left. Escalators are essentially divided highways, with two lanes in each direction. Standers should occupy the right lane so sprinters can get by on the left. If someone is blocking the passing lane, it's not polite to tailgate or go "BEEEP! BEEEP! Outta the way!" A brief "Excuse me" is sufficient.

- When you get off the escalator, move away from the landing. This is not the place to stop to text a friend or contemplate your navel. You wouldn't want to cause a chain reaction of rear-end collisions as the person behind you bumps into you, and the person behind him bumps into him and so on and so forth until there is major carnage on the escalator.

- Tie your shoes, pull up your pants, keep your tongue in your mouth, and gather together your waist-length hair. Escalators love to eat anything loose and flowing.

The same rules apply to slidewalks.

Public Buses

Bus riding is fraught with tension and danger: crowded aisles, not enough seats, traffic jams, fumes, people with packages, people with children, people who are late, people who are lost, people who forgot to put on their deodorant, people who are two seconds away from a megaspew. These are the building blocks of bad manners. To maintain some level of civilization, everybody's cooperation is required. Here's all you need to know to bus with the best:

- Let people off before you get on.

- Have your money or pass ready so you don't hold up the line.

- If the bus is crowded, don't take up more than your fair share of space by spreading your belongings and/or body parts over several seats. Check that you're not in a seat reserved for the elderly or people with disabilities.

- If you have to stand, move to the rear. If everybody crowds into two square feet at the front because one person is blocking the aisle, a cattle prod works wonders. If you don't have one handy, a simple "Excuse me, could I get by?" or "Could you please move down?" should suffice.

- When it's time to get off, there's no need to ring the bell more than once. You're not a clock striking twelve. And when you do alight, it's nice to thank the driver. Especially if you see him or her every day.

- According to tradition, ladies get on first so men can catch them if they fall backwards. Similarly, men get off first so they can turn and offer assistance to disembarking females. (Why it was once assumed that women were prone to falling on and off of buses is a mystery.)

- Finally, don't misspell the plural of bus. It's *buses,* not *busses,* no matter what the signs say. And, as you'll soon discover (if you haven't already), the two are very different.

Dear Alex

"Sometimes I'm on a bus and the person next to me will try to start a conversation. I don't want to be rude, but my parents have told me to never talk to strangers. What should I do?"

This is a bit of a dilemma. If all people are strangers until you get to know them, and if you can't talk to people you don't know, then how will you ever get to know anyone? Bus drivers could start making introductions, but that's not likely to happen. So here's what I suggest: Talk to your parents about their prohibition. It may be in need of updating. It certainly makes sense not to talk to strangers if you're a seven-year-old kid taking the bus by yourself and some weird guy offers you candy. But if you're a teenager in a nice, safe place with lots of people around—like a public bus, a waiting room, or an airplane—it would be a shame to slam the door on the many interesting souls whose paths you will cross. I mean, just think of the friendships, marriages, and business deals that all began with one stranger saying to another "Excuse me, but I couldn't help noticing the book you're reading."

If someone persists in having a conversation against your wishes, you can move to another seat (ideally, one close to the driver or another adult). Or say "I'm sorry, I don't mean to be rude, but I have a test tomorrow and I need to use this time to think about my answers."

By the same token, if you're the initiator of the conversation, be alert to signs that your overtures are unwanted. If they are, pipe down.

Offering Someone Your Seat

This doesn't mean *giving up* your behind. It means *getting off* your behind. Few gestures are so easy, so appreciated, and so underutilized as this one. If you're in a crowded waiting room, or you're traveling on a bus, subway, or train, offer your seat to someone who could use it more than you. This could be a person who's elderly, injured, disabled, pregnant, loaded down with tons of packages, or carrying a baby. It could be a little kid who has a hard time standing, or a running back with a broken leg. It doesn't matter whether they're old or young, big or small, male or female. All that matters is that you notice the need and offer to help.

If they're adults, you might simply say "Ma'am, would you care to sit down?" or "Sir, would you like a seat?" For people your age or younger, you can dispense with "Sir" and "Ma'am," but avoid "Hey, you!"

People may thank you and decline your kind offer, in which case you'll feel great because you asked (*and* got to keep your seat), and they'll feel great because of your thoughtfulness.

Giving up your seat can be tough. There will be days when you'll be the one who's exhausted, sore from practice, or lugging a bag of books. At those times, you'll just have to make a judgment call as to whose need is greater, yours or the other person's. But here's a situation where having the right attitude can help. When you find yourself thinking:

Why do I have to give up my seat? Why doesn't someone else do it for a change? It's not fair. I'm tired and I got here first!

try thinking:

I sure am glad I don't have a hard time walking, or a broken collarbone, or a thousand things to carry, or a screaming kid in a stroller.

Dear Alex

"Do I really have to call adults 'Sir' and 'Ma'am'?"

You don't *have* to, but there are reasons why you may *want* to. Addressing adults with "Sir" and "Ma'am" is a near-extinct custom in the United States. While this is bad news for society as a whole, it's good news for you: Simply by using these little words, you can reap fabulous rewards with virtually no effort! Any teenager who says "Yes, Ma'am" or "No, Sir" or "Excuse me, Ma'am" is automatically given a halo and a badge of honor by the adult so addressed. These are redeemable for many wonderful things: respect, trust, privileges, jobs, unsought-for gifts, and, best of all, the sense of confidence and self-worth you get when you know your behavior is appreciated and admired by others. Try it and see for yourself.

Carpooling Protocols

Unless you're a city kid who gets around by public transportation, or a country kid who travels by mule, chances are you're a frequent carpooler. The idea behind carpools is that parents trade off misery. Actually, many parents like to drive carpool. It's how they learn all the neighborhood gossip and check out their children's friends. Since your mobility depends on staying in the good graces of these saints who moonlight as chauffeurs, here are some tips for being a tip-top traveler. Follow them, and adults will beg for the opportunity to drive you around.

Watch for your ride. This not only spares someone from having to come to your door, it spares the neighbors from being honked at daily at 7:00 AM.

Be on time. Don't make everyone else late just because you are. Rather than keep anyone waiting, finish your muffin, your homework, and your toilette* in the car.

Don't be a no-show. If you won't be gracing the carpool with your presence, send advance word. This ensures that the carpool will neither wait for you in vain nor show up at your door for naught.

Don't stick your head out the sunroof. In the event of a sudden stop, the sunroof could fly forward and decapitate you. This would not only cause your head to go on without you, but could also lead to a nasty lawsuit that would make things quite tense in the carpool.

Wear your seat belt (both in the front- and backseat). Seat belts save lives, and yours is worth saving.

Don't make a mess in the car. While the discreet watercress sandwich is permissible, anything that drips, stains, or drops crumbs upon seats or seatmates is not.

TRUE STORIES
FROM THE MANNERS FRONTIER

Re: A Pizza

Once, when I had stopped to turn into my driveway after picking up a pizza, someone plowed into the rear of my little sports car at about 60 miles per hour. My life was saved because I was wearing a seat belt.

The pizza was not so fortunate. All the toppings flew off, and when I opened the box I found a soggy mess of mushed cheese and mutilated pepperonis. To add insult to injury, my insurance company would not reimburse me for the cost of the pizza.

The moral of this story is: *Always check to see if your automobile policy includes pizza coverage.*

---

*THIS MOST CERTAINLY DOES NOT MEAN THAT YOU SHOULD GO TO THE BATHROOM IN SOMEONE ELSE'S SUV. ONE'S *TOILETTE* IS "THE ACT OR PROCESS OF DRESSING OR GROOMING ONESELF."

No fighting. Physical or verbal fighting can result in the driver pulling to the side of the road to wait. This is one of life's most awkward moments. The passengers sit in sheepish silence, or worse, say things like "She started it!" To avoid such embarrassment, squelch your squabbles.

Take your belongings. Most carpools have two phases. Phase One is the dropping off of children. Phase Two is the dropping off of everything they left behind. Try to remember your possessions. Abandoned backpacks, homework, volcano models, and tuna sandwiches have been known to disappear forever into the great beyond beneath the backseat.

Avoid making startling noises. If you suddenly scream "LOOK OUT!" the driver will assume you're speaking to her rather than to Rumi Taylor, whose jar of nail polish is about to spill. Sudden movements should also be avoided.

Always thank the driver. Adults who drive children around a lot are at high risk of developing a medical condition known as Carpool Tunnel Syndrome. Its symptoms include a sore butt, fatigue, feeling unappreciated, and nightmares in which the rest of one's life is spent behind the wheel of a car full of noisy teenagers. Sufferers typically report that they have hallucinations of school parking lots, shopping malls, skating rinks, soccer fields, and freeways at rush hour.

There's no known treatment for this affliction. But it can be prevented if carpool passengers offer the driver their sincere thanks each and every time they alight from the car. Do this even if the driver happens to be your parent. Also, the child who brings the driver an occasional flower or cupcake will never lack for a ride.

Dear Alex

"I'm in a lot of different carpools. There's one mother who's always late picking us up from hockey practice. I wouldn't mind, except I have to get to a job and this makes me late, which gets me in trouble with my boss. What can I do?"

You might say something like this:

> "Mrs. O'Malley, I want to thank you for driving me all these times, but I'm afraid I'm going to have to drop out of the carpool. You see, I have a job, and I'm just not getting there on time, and this is causing problems for me at work."

Notice that you're not blaming her for being late. You're simply presenting a set of facts. If she's perceptive, she'll put two and two together and come up with something like this:

> "Oh, dear, I'd hate to lose your company. Let me see if I can pick you all up earlier."

If she isn't perceptive and doesn't put two and two together, you'll have to make alternate arrangements or try to change your hours at work. Lack of punctuality is one of the most common and offensive forms of rudeness. People who are perpetually late always have explanations:

> "Traffic was so bad." (Then you should have left earlier.)

> "I had to stop at the cleaners." (You could have done that afterward.)

> "The phone rang." (You didn't have to answer it.)

> "I just lost track of the time." (Then pay better attention.)

What they fail to realize is that an explanation isn't the same as an excuse. Lateness is rude because it implies that "my time is more valuable than your time," and it often sets up a chain of lateness that can affect others for hours or days to come. Lateness is excusable only when it results from events beyond one's control or unforeseen circumstances that are truly worthy of being given a higher priority. The fact that one person is doing another a favor doesn't absolve her of the responsibility for being on time.

It's very difficult for a child or teenager to call an adult on being late. The best way to do it is indirectly. If your piano teacher always runs behind schedule, you could say:

> "Mr. Liszt, would it be easier for you if I came at 4:30 instead of 4:00? I noticed that you always give people extra time, and this way you wouldn't have to worry about keeping me waiting."

Notice how skillfully you cloak your message. You credit your teacher for being generous with his time and for feeling bad about keeping people waiting. But what you're really saying is "I hate having to sit around twiddling my thumbs every time I come for a lesson."

Another way to deal with the lateness of adults is by asking your parents to intervene on your behalf. Finally, always have a book, a sketchpad, some homework, a video game, a smartphone, or an MP3 player with you. That way, you can at least make use of the time you spend waiting.

If it's peers who are always late, you can be more assertive. Warn repeat offenders that a new policy is in effect by saying:

"Please be sure you get here on time. We're going to leave at 8:30 sharp, and I'd feel terrible if we had to go without you."

If they don't arrive by the appointed hour, give them a tiny grace period and then leave. Let them experience the consequences of their tardiness. If you're consistent, they'll shape up.

Banning Backpack Attacks

With all the focus on keeping guns and knives out of children's hands, it's amazing how little attention has been paid to the most dangerous weapon of all—backpacks. The Health Information Clearinghouse for Children Using Packs (HICCUP) estimates that more people are injured each year in backpack attacks than from biking, boarding, and blading combined. Most of those assaulted were minding their own business when someone turned or pushed past them and BAM!

Most perpetrators are unaware of the destruction they cause, which is scant comfort to the victims of this violence. But satchel savagery has got to stop! And it can—with a little help from you and your friends.

There are several things you can do to keep your canvas out of someone's kisser. If you're running, recognize that your purse, pack, or bag will be bouncing wildly to and fro. Allow extra clearance around objects, human or otherwise, that you pass.

If you're in a crowded setting like a bus or sidewalk, pretend that you're driving a car. Good drivers know exactly how much space their car occupies. This is useful information if you don't want to make a habit of clobbering pedestrians and clipping parked cars. Get to know how much space you occupy. A small backpack or shoulder bag may add as much as a foot to your upper body depth. A large backpack with a sleeping bag, bed roll, pick ax, and satellite dish may add several feet to your girth. Calculate your clearance before you pass fellow travelers on the road of life. If it's going to be tight, say "Excuse me, I don't want to hit you with my pack" as you squeeze by. And then, as your pack L.L. Beans them, which it inevitably will, they will at least be comforted by your good manners.

Fear of Flying

Flying can be stressful. Bouncing through bad weather has a way of making people think they're going to miss their connection, hurl their lunch, or die. Throw in jet lag, lack of in-flight food, a few screaming babies, and smokers having to go *two whole hours* (or longer) without a cigarette, and you've got a recipe for frayed nerves and bad manners.

Air travel used to be an elegant, civilized mode of transportation, but not anymore. Barefoot, half-dressed, and foul-smelling passengers have presented themselves at the gate for boarding. Alleged adults have been arrested or thrown off flights for having temper tantrums when told to turn off electronic devices. There have been food fights, pilot meltdowns, princesses attacking flight attendants, actors urinating in the aisle, and even an inebriated banker flying from Buenos Aires to New York who—let's see, how shall we put this—defecated on a food trolley.

With all the stress of flying, here's how you can do your part to restore some civility to the once friendly skies.

my attention was drawn to the brothers S. by a loud snorting sound. One of them, to the great amusement of his sibling, was blowing his nose into the barf bag. This was followed by a game of who could flip his reading light on and off faster.

We are not talking five-year-olds here. We are talking 25-year-olds. My nausea was complete when, right after dinner, one of the brothers removed his shirt (allowing me to count the 38 layers of his stomach) and lay down across five seats to go to sleep. Yes, all night I could listen to him snoring and watch his hairy belly rise and fall. My only comfort was the thought that the French, who are a bit more fastidious about these things, might deny him and his family entry into their country based on aesthetic grounds.

Alas, they didn't, and my faith in the French was severely shaken as I watched the brothers Slobola pass through customs, giggling, snorting, and saying "Bone-jure, bone-jure" to each other.

Before Boarding

Believe it or not, you used to be able to just stroll through an airport to the plane—no IDs, no metal detectors, no carry-on prohibitions, no pat-downs, no strip searches. I know, how boring. But that all changed with 9/11. Now, we've got airport security. This doesn't mean they give you a soft little blankie to snuggle with. It means they check out your whole—and I do mean *whole*—body for no-nos like guns, knives, and explosives. The latest technology can actually see through your clothes. While that might give the exhibitionists among you a thrill, it gives most people a chill. There are a few things you can do to speed yourself and fellow passengers through security:

Know the guidelines. Familiarize yourself with what can and can't be packed in carry-on luggage, or carried on your person. Before you walk through the scanner, you'll want to remove belts, buckles, hair barrettes, metal snaps and buttons, cuff links, rings, watches, coins, phones, piercings, replacement hips, rebar—anything with metal.

Be friendly. Gate security agents are not known for their warmth or sense of humor. So humor them. Be pleasant and cooperative and don't do anything to draw attention to yourself. If they take a disliking to you, they can pull you aside into a private room and question and search you until long after your plane has left.

Plan for easy access. You're going to have to remove certain items from your carry-on luggage such as laptops and toiletries in plastic bags before placing them on the X-ray belt. Pack these so they can be easily reached without having to take 10 minutes to search your backpack. Wear foot gear that is easy to take off. Avoid shoes with 40 yards of laces to undo, or boots that require an army of helpers to pry off of your feet.

Follow instructions. The security agent will point you toward a scanner. The old-fashioned scanners just require you to walk through without bumping into anything. Newer ones may require you to stand still while they look through your clothes to see if you're carrying a machete or bazooka. This is not the time to mime hula-hooping or practice your karate moves. You may elect or be asked to submit to a pat-down in which the agent will paw all over you in search of weapons. Try not to laugh if you're ticklish. And don't call the agent a perv.

Watch for urban sprawl. Unless there are tons of empty seats or you're waiting at an unoccupied gate, keep your personal sphere to one seat. It's so annoying when people take three seats for themselves and their belongings, leaving other passengers with no place to sit.

Think ahead. Before boarding, anticipate what you'll want to keep at your seat. This way, you can stow your carry-on bags quickly and efficiently, and 200 people won't have to wait while you stand in the aisle deciding which magazines, devices, or snacks you'll want during the flight.

Keep cool. Delays go with flying. At those times, you're a captive. There's nothing you can do about a) the weather; b) the missing copilot; or c) the equipment failure that is keeping you from departing on time. So, stay calm. Practice deep breathing. Take out a book. Take out your tablet or phone. If you need to speak with the gate agent, be as friendly and empathetic as you possibly can. They are being screamed at by everyone else. If you're kind and respectful, you're more likely to get their help and a primo seat.

Boarding

Have your documents ready. You'll need to show your boarding pass and possibly other documents. Have them out and ready. You don't want to hold up the line while you search the 83 pockets on your backpack for your passport.

Don't block the gate. Have you ever noticed how people stand near the entrance to the jet bridge well before boarding is called? Since most airlines board people by groups, this won't get you on any faster. In fact, it will slow things down as passengers boarding before you have to run an obstacle course to get on the plane.

Carry on. Planes have only so much space. So there's no point in carrying on tons of carry-ons. The rules airlines have created really do make sense in terms of fairness and sharing (otherwise known as good manners). Put your small items under the seat in front of you, your one large item in the overhead bin (wheels first), and wait until everyone has boarded and stowed their gear before putting coats up above. If you place something in an overhead compartment, stow it securely so it doesn't topple onto the next person who opens the door. Try not to squash other packages;

items carried into the cabin are often fragile, and you may inadvertently crush an ancient Etruscan vase destined for the Metropolitan Museum of Art. Never force a suitcase into the overhead bin. I saw someone do this. They broke the latch on the bin, and the entire flight was delayed an hour while maintenance fixed it.

Up in the Air

Don't throw up on your neighbor. Use the airsickness (a.k.a. barf) bag. If you're feeling queasy, take deep breaths. Aim the little fresh-air nozzle at your face. Pretend that you're lying on a calm, sunny beach.

Recline slowly. However much comfort the person reclining gets is equal to the discomfort the person being reclined upon suffers. If you recline your seat back, do it slowly so the person behind you doesn't suddenly get a tray table in the jaw. Keep in mind that if your seat is fully reclined, the person behind you doesn't have room to use a laptop or DVD player. (**Tip:** If you sit in an emergency exit row, the backs of the seats in front of you won't recline all the way for reasons of safety. This gives you a bit more room.)

Tap not. Try not to tap, kick, or knee gouge the seat in front of you. If a child is kicking your seatback, depending on her age you can: a) turn around and make a scary face; b) ask her to stop; or c) turn to the parent and say, "I know how tough it is to travel with small children, but I'm trying to sleep, which is hard to do when my seat is being kicked." A little empathy goes a long way.

Armrest skirmishes. This tiny piece of real estate has triggered countless airborne turf wars. It's probably due to some evolutionary instinct to grab territory as one's own. The basic rule is 50-50. You each get half of the arm rest. Truly courteous fliers often take pity on the occupant of the middle seat and allow him the use of both armrests as a consolation prize for having to endure such discomfort for the entire flight. If your neighbor is being piggy about the armrest you can gently press against his arm to push him back onto his side. Since most people don't want to play armsies with their seatmates, they will move their arm.

Getting out of your seat. If you're sitting at an inside seat and want to get out, say "Excuse me, may I please get by?" Your neighbor will then either get up and stand in the aisle or remain seated. People who do the latter usually make a futile effort to occupy less space. This is a signal that means *Okay, you can step over me, but please don't crush my toes or land in my lap.* Restrain yourself from getting up 11 times an hour or when beverages are being served. (**Tip:** Make sure you don't grab the seatback in front of you to pull yourself up. This can cause the hapless occupant of said seat to suffer whiplash, spill her coffee, or wake up from a deep sleep.)

Rush hour in the cabin bathrooms. This is not the time to count your freckles or braid your hair. Schedule major grooming tasks for off-peak periods.

Toilet training. NEVER flush an airplane toilet if you're sitting on it. The suction is so great that you could easily be drawn into the toilet and expelled over Kansas.

Be nice. Flight attendants have demanding jobs. Try not to keep asking "Are we there yet?" "How much longer?" "What time is it?" "Did you hear that noise?" "Are the wings going to fall off?" Avoid pushing the call button every two minutes to ask for 1) a soda, 2) pretzels, 3) another soda, 4) a towelette, 5) aspirin, 6) a deck of cards, 7) a pillow, 8) another soda, and/or 9) a pair of Junior Captain's Wings. Issue your requests when the attendants come to serve you, or during quiet times when they're not serving others.

Disputes over reading lights and window shades have led to countless airborne etiquette atrocities. Here are some suggestions for nonviolent compromise when interests conflict:

- If a movie is being shown, lower your window shade. Even if you've seen the movie and want to look at the pretty clouds, one unshaded window can make it difficult for others to watch the film (which is already difficult on those tiny screens). If the flight is long enough for a movie, there'll be time to look out the window after it's finished.

- If you want to read, it's fine to turn your reading lamp on during a movie or at night when others are trying to sleep. Once you're through, remember to turn it off so it doesn't needlessly shine in someone else's eyes.

Playing with toys. Electronic devices are a great way to make time pass. You start a video game in New Jersey and before you know it, you're crossing the Rockies. It's considerate to turn the volume off on video games so your neighbors don't have to hear the pings and pongs, bangs and bombs, and screeches and screams of play. Also, keep in mind that your screen is visible to those nearby so you shouldn't have anything stronger than PG-13 on it. And, of course, wear headphones if your device is producing any sound.

Flights of the Future

Blah-blah-blah. Heaven help you if you're seated next to a compulsive talker. These are the folks who can keep up a monologue (they think it's a conversation) for six hours straight. After an hour of nonstop blather you'll have an earache, a headache, and an acute desire to jump out of the plane at 30,000 feet. Now, there's nothing wrong with having a conversation with your seatmate. He or she may be an interesting person. But there's also nothing wrong with wanting to be left alone. You can use body language and props to convey your desire to create an impenetrable personal bubble around yourself. Wear headphones; focus on your smartphone or gaming device; bury your face in a book. If these don't work, you may have to say to your neighbor, "It's been nice meeting you. But I'd like to spend a little time now reading/resting/watching the movie." If the person STILL persists in talking, you can throw them out of the airplane.

Blah-blah-blah-blah-blah-blah-blah-blah-blah-blah. Can you imagine being subjected to a seatmate blabbing away on her cell phone at full volume for five hours while you're trying to rest?! I'm telling you, phone calls in the sky will lead to in-flight insurrections and airborne altercations—riots and rumbles, battles and brawls. And I will be leading the charge. Well, actually not, since I have to set a good example. But if anyone next to me starts talking on a cell phone I will simply start talking. To myself. Out loud. Let's see how she likes *that!*

Food-to-go. Now that airlines no longer serve free meals on most flights, you are invited to bring on board your own nourishment. Grab whatever grub you like, but make sure it isn't messy or smelly. Your neighbors won't appreciate stinky cheese, funky fish, or odiferous curries.

No joke. This is *really* serious, so PAY CLOSE ATTENTION: Never, *ever* joke about bombs, guns, terrorists, or hijacking at or near airports or aboard airplanes. First, such jokes are usually rude and unfunny. Second, they can get you yanked out of line or off the plane, or arrested.

Back on the Ground

Getting off. Etiquette says you file out row by row from the front. This means, don't jump out of your seat to try to race ahead of as many passengers as you can. You may gain 20 seconds, but you'll still have to wait 30 minutes for your luggage. Grab your carry-on bag from the bin as quickly as you can. If you're not prepared to exit, don't block the aisle. Let others go by.

Inside the terminal. When you leave the jet bridge and enter the terminal, keep moving so you're not blocking the path for those passengers behind you.

At the carousel. Why is it that everyone wants to stand within five feet of where the luggage drops onto the carousel? Move down a bit. You won't be jostled and you'll have a more pleasant experience as you wait longer for your luggage than your flight took. However tempted you are, please refrain from riding round and round on the carousel.

The Ins and Outs of Doorway Decorum

As you enter and leave libraries, schools, restaurants, stores, terminals, and various other public buildings, you may notice obstacles that have been placed in your path. These are called *doors*. They needn't pose a problem to you or others if you adhere to the following basic guidelines:

- When you approach a pull door, look to see if there are any people about to enter or leave who might have difficulty opening it on their own. If you see someone in a wheelchair, or pushing a stroller, or on crutches, or laden with packages or babies, it's very gracious to step aside and hold the door open for him or her.

- If there's someone on your heels who appears nondisabled and unburdened, you needn't hold the door. But do keep it open so he or she can grab it after you've passed through. (Otherwise, it's like being in the woods and letting a branch swing back and smack somebody in the face.)

- Where automatic electric-eye doors are concerned, it isn't necessary to leap in front of others, place yourself in the sensor beam, and say "Please, allow me."

Revolving doors were invented for people who are never quite sure whether they're coming or going. These dizzifying doorways are fraught with danger. So stay alert, or you could emerge from the spin cycle with your foot on the sidewalk and your head in the lobby.

- Revolving doors should never be rotated at more than a moderate walking speed. The object is to enter or leave a building, not to launch someone into space. If you happen to be going around with an elderly person or a three-year-old on a sit-down strike, the polite thing to do is reduce speed to the slowest common denominator. Use your cell phone to cancel the afternoon's appointments.

- In the olden days, this was the traditional male-female protocol: If the door was already in motion, the woman entered first. The male followed in the next compartment and, with a light touch of his powerful hand, kept the door spinning. If the door was not moving, the man got in first. He used his fabulous muscle power to get it going while the lady stepped into the compartment behind. Today it's considered proper for the pusher to be either male or female, depending on who's in possession of more strength and/or gallantry on a given day.

- Except for parents with small children and couples in perfect harmony, it's one person per compartment. Two tend to tangle, and woe to anyone who falls down.

- Otherwise well-behaved children are permitted, twice a year, to spin round and round and miss their exit, provided they establish a lookout who will warn them at the first sign of an approaching passenger.

Self-Propelled

Having looked at protocols for public transportation, let us now turn our attention to personal transportation systems—skates, bicycles, skateboards, skis, snowboards, and feet.

The main courtesy you can offer as a self-propelled person is *not to run into anybody.* This means watching where you're going. And yielding to those with the right-of-way. On a sidewalk, the right-of-way belongs to those who are walking. (Note that it's called a side*walk*, not a side*blade*, -*bike*, or -*board*.) If you're jogging or cruising along a sidewalk on anything that rolls, it's your job to control your speed and course so you don't knock anybody down or scare them to death.*

*SIMILARLY, SOMEONE ON FOOT SHOULD YIELD THE RIGHT-OF-WAY TO SKIERS ON A SLOPE OR SKATEBOARDERS IN A SKATEPARK.

Following are more courtesy pointers for the self-propelled:

Inline Skating

Faster than a speeding bullet. Able to leap tall buildings in a single bound. Superman? Nah. You—on your inline skates.

Blading has swept the world. And that means that every year tens of thousands of skaters are stitched, set, realigned, patched, and put back together again in hospital emergency rooms. Since nothing can spoil an outing more than two broken wrists, a snapped femur, and eight crushed ribs, here are some inline skating tips that will keep you in the pink:

- Take some lessons. Practice before you set out in search of crowded or tricky skating venues. Learn how to start, turn, cruise, and stop. *Especially* learn how to stop. It's rude to barrel into innocent bystanders.

- Don't be caught dead without a helmet. (The majority of inline skating fatalities involve skaters who weren't wearing helmets.) Always wear guards on your wrists, elbows, knees, and other body parts you'd like to keep intact. For night skating, wear reflective gear, safety lamps, twinkling Christmas lights, etc.

- Yield the right-of-way. If you must skate on a sidewalk, it's your responsibility to maintain control at all times so as not to knock pedestrians into next week.

- Keep to the right. Don't sway from side to side and hog the entire path. If you want to pass someone, look behind you before pulling into the passing lane. Then check to make sure there's no oncoming traffic. Don't suddenly zoom past the skater you're overtaking. Say "On your left" as you approach.

- Adjust your speed to path conditions. Slow down if it's crowded. Slow down for small children clogging your artery. Slow down for gravel, oil, tar, grass clippings, leaf piles, water, and large objects blocking your way. Otherwise you're liable to go sprawling, and it's rude to obstruct the trail with your splayed body.

- If you see a dog to the far *right* of the path and a human to the far *left* of the path (or vice versa), it's likely that the two are connected by a leash. Prepare to leap, limbo, or leave the path.

- Watch out for hazards. History has shown that inline skaters were not meant to roll over steel grates, bumpy manhole covers, roadkill, tree limbs, or human limbs.

- If you need to stop or rest, pull off the path. (Would you stop your car in the middle of a superhighway to check your map?)

- If you wear headphones, keep the volume very low. You need to be able to hear people say "On your left" or "Look out! A truck is heading your way!"

- Refrain from carrying objects that will interfere with your balance or the safe passage of others.

- Be very careful if skating on a street. Skate in the direction of the traffic. Unless you enjoy getting whomped in the stomach, be on the lookout for car doors that open into your path.

- Use your turn signals.

Bicycling

Bicyclists should follow the same rules as inline skaters: wear a helmet, use safety lights at night, yield to pedestrians, ride with the traffic, watch out for car doors, dogs, and other hazards of the road, be alert to dangerous pavement conditions, check for oncoming or overtaking traffic when riding on bike paths, etc. In addition:

- Don't park your bike where others will trip over it. It's natural to want to lock your bike where you can keep an eye on it or where you think it will be safest. But don't block steps, stoops, sidewalks, entrances, or railings.

- Follow all traffic laws. If you want drivers to watch out for and respect your presence on the road, it's only fair that you follow the rules of the road, too: obey stoplights, use hand signals, and don't go the wrong way down one-way streets.

Skateboarding

If there was ever a sport that belongs to the young, it's skateboarding. (Have you ever seen a 70-year-old stick a nollie five-O heelflip? Me neither.) So it was with great excitement that I plunged into the culture of youth to inquire about the protocols of skateboarding.

The basic principle skateboarders follow is this: *Chill*. Central to chilling is the avoidance of collisions. Toward that end, these remarkable young men and women on their flying machines exhibit extraordinary vigilance and courtesy. They wait patiently while their compatriots execute frontside 50-50 fakie heelflips. They take turns and don't cut in line. They stand far from coping so they don't get in the way of someone doing a trick. They learn the traffic patterns and cross the skatepark with care. They give the right-of-way to those who are airborne. They yell "board" if a riderless board is flying through the air. They know their limits and don't attempt tricks far beyond their capabilities. They say "sorry" if they accidentally run into somebody or take someone else's turn. They sit and rest away from the action so they don't block the rails, ledges, and ramps for others. They applaud their peers with shouts, whistles, or board taps when they finally land a trick they've been practicing. They gently correct and encourage the "little guys" since everyone was once a beginner. And if a fellow enthusiast should monopolize the ramps, they don't get angry. They lay down some mellow vibes and say "Hey, dude."

I take off my helmet to these wholesome boarders. I believe that every community in America should provide skateboard parks for its young citizens. But until they do, kids on skateboards will have to skate "street" and use public sidewalks and plazas. And they will want to observe the following rules:

- Yield the right-of-way to pedestrians.
- Leave graciously if told to get lost by an owner or guard.
- Don't ollie up a park bench if someone is sitting on it.
- Don't grind or backside lipslide on a handrail if someone is holding on to it.

The skateboarding community was so well-chilled in their receptivity to my queries that I can't wait to do further research in this domain. I already know what my first question will be: *Why don't more girls skateboard?*

Skiing and Snowboarding

Skiing is my favorite sport. I love the feeling of snot icicles hanging from my nose. And the thrill of careening down a 78-degree incline with my shades so fogged I can't see the forest for the tree I just ran into. And the sheer joy of standing on a mountaintop with the windchill at minus 166 degrees. It does wonders for my confidence to swoop down a slope as three-year-olds ski circles around me. And then it's on to the lodge, where the rich aromas of mulled cider, crackling logs, and sweat-drenched socks waft through the air.

TRUE STORIES
FROM THE
MANNERS FRONTIER

Totally Rad
I spied a pleasant-looking lad skating fast and gnarly down the street.

"Excuse me, young sir," I said. "May I interrupt your switch-stance frontside kickflip long enough to ask you a question?"

"Sure, dude."

"Could you please enlighten me as to the rules of skateboarding?"

"Rooooools?" he replied.

"Quite. Do's and don'ts. Common courtesies. Codes of behavior. No-no's. That is to say—rules."

"Rooooools?"

Perhaps I needed to approach a skater with a more extensive vocabulary. Out of the corner of my eye, I detected a fast-moving, knee-padded youth.

"Excuse me," I said.

"Dude?"

"Yes, young sir, and might I congratulate you on that totally rad nollie noseblunt slide?"

"Dude?" **CONTINUED ›››**

"Could you be so kind as to tell me, what might a skateboarder have to do to be considered rude?"

"Dude?"

"Rude?"

"Rude? Dude?"

Oh, dear. I wasn't making much headway with this concept. I decided on a new plan of attack. I would talk to the manager of my neighborhood skatepark. Surely a commercial establishment for skateboard enthusiasts would post a proper code of conduct.

I entered a warehouse in which was housed a mountain range of ramps, funboxes, and railings, as well as a regiment of whirling, airborne youth. As I watched these healthy striplings execute feats of physical prowess and derring-do, I was consumed with one thought: *How do their pants stay on?*

I located the service counter. A shaved-headed personage in his late teens approached me.

"Hey, dude," he said.

"Dude," I replied.

We then proceeded to have a lengthy conversation in which the bald dude elucidated the protocols of the skateboarding subculture. I will summarize them here: *Don't run into anybody.*

To make sure that we all have a pleasant time on the slopes, here are a dozen ski tips:

1. **Remember that skiing and snowboarding are dangerous sports that require your full attention if you don't want somebody's pole up your nose.** The trail map for a famous resort in Vermont lists some of the hazards that are part of the sport's challenge: "Snow, ice, moguls, spines, rolls, jumps, snowmaking mounds, shear drop-offs, bare ground, rocks, roots, stumps, trees, lift towers, ruts, bumps, snowmaking equipment, grooming vehicles, snowmobiles, [and] power poles." To this I would add "grizzly bears and out-of-control teenagers on snowboards." Stay alert for changing weather and terrain conditions.

2. **Ski or snowboard only on designated trails, slopes, glades, and zones.** In some states, if you ski off of designated areas, you're liable for all search and rescue expenses. A bill of $278,549 could put a crimp in your ski budget for next season.

3. **Never ski or snowboard alone.** This is a no-brainer. Should you make an unscheduled departure from the trail, or injure yourself in a fall, you want to have a friend who knows where you are and can go for help. While woodpeckers are good company, they can't summon the ski patrol.

4. **Know how to read the trail markings.** Those double black diamonds don't mean "This Way to a Poker Game." They mean you're about to descend an advanced expert trail. A rope across a trail means the trail is closed, which means don't go down it.

5. **Learn how to ride the lift before trying to get on.** Ask a friend or the lift operator for instructions. Most lift operators would rather slow the lift to help you than stop it to untangle you from the bars.

6. **Don't drop anything from the lift.** Many trails go under or alongside ski lifts. It's rude to drop a soda can or boot on the people below. On a related note: Stow your trash properly. The pristine beauty of nature is part of the joy of skiing. Look for a slopeside trash receptacle.

7. **Maintain control.** Quite a few fearless teenagers begin their skiing or snowboarding careers by pointing themselves downhill and shoving off. Quite a few end up in ski resort hospitals. Don't ski beyond your ability to stop, turn, and avoid people and objects.

8. **Yield the right-of-way to people ahead of you.** If you pass other skiers, give them a wide berth. If the trail is narrow, or the skiers you're overtaking are schussing from side to side, say "On your left" or "On your right" prior to passing. Don't say "Through your legs."

9. **Never stop on a trail and obstruct it.** Skiers don't like to catch air over a crest and find another skier in the way. Be sure you're visible from above. Move to the edge for extended pit stops.

10. **When you enter a trail or start downhill, look uphill.** Those skiers already comin' 'round the mountain have the right-of-way.

11. **Don't forget to use straps or other devices to prevent your skis or snowboard from continuing downhill without you.** Unless you enjoy taking long and slippery hikes back to the lodge.

12. **Stop when you're tired.** Accidents are more likely to happen when skiers are weary and muscles are exhausted. Head for the lodge. Between food, beverages, video games, more food, movies, saunas, blazing hearths, hot tubs, and ski bums and bummettes, you should find all sorts of things to keep you occupied.

And finally: Always wear your jammies to pipe jams.

On Foot

You wouldn't believe what a perilous place a sidewalk can be. So you don't get arrested for reckless reconnoitering, here are some protocols for polite promenading:

Sidewalk conventions. You wouldn't park your car in the middle of the street. By the same reasoning, don't park yourself in the middle of the sidewalk to have a conversation. Step to the edge. Don't force others to detour off the walk or pass between you.

Sidewalk snowplows. Sidewalks, like stairways, are two-way. That means each direction is entitled to no more than one-half its width. If there's no one coming the other way, then five of you can walk abreast. But if people *are* coming the other way, don't run them off the road. (Not only is this rude, it's intimidating.) Retreat to your lanes and let other walkers by.

Sidewalk shuffles. These are the mortifying maneuvers that occur when you're on a collision course with somebody and, to avoid them at the last minute, you go to your right just as they go to their left, and you counter-correct but so do they, and the two of you spend most of the afternoon shuffling back and forth unable to get by each other. Not only is this a total waste of time; it also makes you feel like an idiot.

The way to avoid sidewalk shuffles is to pretend you're a jet aircraft. Two planes speeding toward each other don't wait until the last moment to take evasive action. If there's even a chance that they might collide, one of them immediately changes course. So, if you and another person are walking toward each other with even the slightest possibility of inter-section, make a sharp correction by changing lanes early on. Usually, this means moving to your right.

Sidewalk chicken. In sidewalk shuffles, you end up in somebody's face because of inattention, or a failure to walk defensively and anticipate the moves of other pedestrians. No ill will was intended, and both parties feel equally moronic. In sidewalk chicken, you walk down the sidewalk as if you own it. This means YOU DON'T MOVE FOR NOBODY! Not one inch. But that's okay. Because everyone else will be chicken and get out of your way.

You can always tell when you've passed one of these sidewalk marauders, because they're the ones who bang their shoulders or jackets or bags or purses into you. They're the ones who make you step off the curb, scrunch against a building, or turn sideways to avoid getting crunched. They're the ones with the look that says *What do you think you're doing on my sidewalk, you little warthog?* Unfortunately, there's not much you can do about them. But you can silently thank them as they run you off the road. For it's people like this who remind us how unattractive bad manners really are.

Pushing buttons. By all means, push the button that stops traffic at an intersection so you may cross the street safely. But if you do push it, WAIT FOR THE "WALK" SIGNAL! Don't push the button as insurance in case you can't jaywalk, and then waltz across the street at the first opportunity. It's not fair to make traffic come to a standstill while you're already halfway down the block.

Dear Alex

"Aren't men supposed to walk on the outside of women?"

No. Walking on women is never proper. There is, however, a tradition of men walking on the outside of the *sidewalk* when escorting women down the street. In olden days, this offered the woman some protection against slop from above and slush from below.* Today, however, we have dry cleaning. And we recognize that the greatest sources of muck are no longer windows and roadways but politicians and reality shows. Young men who aspire to be gentlemen can do no wrong by walking on the street side of a lady. I mean, you gotta walk someplace. But true gentlemen have the sensitivity to accept the reciprocation of such thoughtful protection from the women of their acquaintance.

> *IN THE DAYS BEFORE INDOOR PLUMBING, PEOPLE RELIEVED THEMSELVES DURING THE NIGHT IN CHAMBER POTS, WHICH THEY THEN DUMPED OUT THEIR WINDOWS IN THE MORNING. (I'M NOT MAKING THIS UP!)

Baby carriages. Sidewalks usually have strollers on them. And strollers usually have babies in them. And people with babies are usually stressed out. Why? Try diapers, crying, being up all night, teething, screaming, wiping up spills, more diapers, and other joys of parenting.

You can do two things to help harried parents with babies in strollers: First, hold doors open for them. Second, offer to help carry the stroller up and down steps and stairs. Just make sure you have a firm, two-handed grip, or the stroller could tip upside down. While this would be a good lesson in gravity for the baby, it wouldn't go over well with the parent.

Behind the Wheel

If someone made a graph of parental worry, it would look something like this.

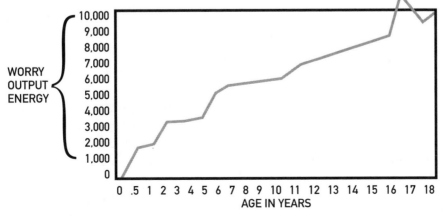

You can see that although parental worrying increases with the child's age, it does not do so in a straight line. Rather, it rises in fits (as in "Mom's having a hissy") and starts ("You can start by showing some responsibility"). Worrywartologists (scientists who study the protective instincts of parents) have determined that each jump in WOE (Worry Output Energy) can be traced to an increase in the child's mobility.

Thus, the surge around four months occurs when the infant is able to turn over and move around in her crib. Up to this point, parents only had to worry about their child being attacked by her teddy bear in the middle of the night. Soon the child will be able to crawl. This triggers worries such as:

What if she crawls under the sofa and won't come out?

What if I step on her?

Once the child learns to walk, new worries surface:

What if she climbs the stairs?

What if she goes into the street?

What if she tracks mud across the kitchen floor?

Worry increases in quantum leaps as the child becomes skateboard mobile:

What if she smashes her kneecap?

inline-skate mobile:

What if she breaks her wrists?

bike mobile:

What if she cracks her head open?

and auto-mobile:

What if she DENTS THE CAR?

The minute you get your driver's license, parental anxiety goes off the charts. Your parents will worry that their insurance premiums will skyrocket; that you'll get stopped for speeding, run someone over, or have an accident; that you'll text and drive, you'll drink and drive, your friends will drink and drive, or other drivers will drink and drive; that you'll be hurt, maimed, disabled, or killed. Most of all, they'll worry that you'll spend too much time in the backseat, and you won't be looking for quarters.

Their worries are not groundless. The risk of being in a car accident is higher for 16- to 19-year-olds than it is for any other age group. Motor vehicle accidents are the #1 killer of teenagers, with the risk of a car crash being highest during the first year a teenager is able to drive.

What you must remember is that your driving puts your parents' two most precious possessions—you and their car—together in the same place at the same time. Your parents' love for you, combined with your love for vehicular independence, makes teenage driving an emotionally charged arena for disputes. These can be minimized if you follow certain rules of the etiquette road:

Negotiate up-front. Before you get your license, impress your parents with your maturity (always a good thing to do when the issue is your driving). Ask them how they'd like to handle such issues as insurance, gas, maintenance, reserving the car, whether you can take the car when they aren't around, etc.

Don't litter. Clean up all candy wrappers, food, paper bags, and soda cans that you and your friends bring into the car.

Take good care of the car. Maybe a Taurus minivan isn't your dream car, but it's better than no car. Without being asked, give it a wash and a vacuum from time to time. Check the tires and fluid levels. Wax it twice a year.

Turn your driving into a family asset. Help your parents realize the benefits that accrue from your new mobility. Offer to do errands in the car that your parents would normally have to do—and make good on your offer.

Give your parents gas. When people hop into a car, they are often in a hurry. They need to get to work, pick someone up, catch a plane. It's very annoying to get into a car (especially if it's your own) and discover that the previous driver left a thimbleful of fuel in the tank. Never return the car empty. Fill 'er up. Make an agreement with your parents about who pays. For example, if you use most of a tank for your personal driving, you should pay to fill it. If you use most of a tank for a combination of personal driving and errands for your parents, you can split the costs. If your folks do most of the driving, tell them you'll happily keep the tank topped if they'll keep your funds from running on empty.

Turn off the radio. Parents are fragile creatures with sensitive ears. They don't like to turn the key and get blasted out of their seat by a thousand decibels of post-punk techno-crunk when they were expecting the sweet purr of the engine.

Return the dial to your parents' radio station. A lot of parents listen to just one favorite station when driving. For some reason, they find it annoying to have to bump those digitals all the way from 106.3 back to 89.7, or change those satellite channels from 777 to 7. You can avoid this

rude shock to their system, which could result in a rude shock to *your* system, by restoring the dial to the station to which it was tuned.

Return the seat to your parents' position. Tiny moms dislike getting into the driver's seat after their 6'4" sons have pushed it all the way back. And 6'4" moms dislike smashing their knees on the steering wheel after their tiny teens have pushed the seat all the way up. If your car has memory buttons for different seat positions, then each time you leave it, reset the seat to the preferred position of the person likely to drive the car next. If your car doesn't have presets, return the seat to the approximate position you found it in.

Finally: When your parents agree to let you drive—and especially when they agree to let you drive the family car—they are assuming that you are mature enough to handle it. Don't disappoint them. In fact, you should probably make a special effort to act *more* mature at home. This will help reassure them that you won't drive like all those rude, impatient, and dangerous so-called ADULTS on the highway.

"What do you MEAN I'm too immature to use the car?!?!?!?"

On the Road

Once you get behind the wheel, new rules come into effect. The rules of the road. Or, in other words, the rules of the jungle. For that's what it's like out there.

You should see what goes on in Boston, home of baked beans and steamed motorists. This city boasts the rudest drivers on the face of the planet. To the typical Boston driver, green means "Twice the speed limit." Yellow means "Pedal to the metal!" And red means "Outta my way, you moron!" Boston motorists are trained from birth to add the words *this means everyone but me* to road signs. Thus, we have:

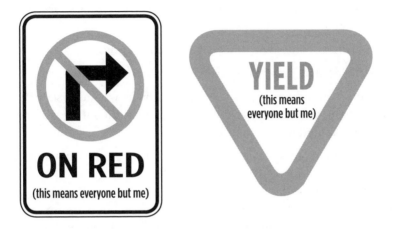

If a Boston driver runs you over in a crosswalk, he (or she) will get out of the car, rush back, and give you the finger. One motorist was shot dead for having the effrontery to beep at the inattentive driver in front of him. Naturally, the police are very concerned about the lawless barbarism on the Beantown byways. This is why they spend all their time handing out parking tickets.

Some of the rudest behavior *Homo sapiens* is capable of occurs behind the wheel of a car. There's no stopping the "ME FIRST!" mentality when it's reinforced by 4,000 pounds of steel. People feel anonymous and protected when driving. They do things they wouldn't dare to do if they were in a face-to-face encounter with another human being.

Take tailgating, for example. Motorists think nothing of roaring down the highway at 80 miles per hour two inches behind the car in front of them. But they wouldn't dream of walking down the sidewalk two inches behind another pedestrian.

Or how about honking. If some poor guy doesn't burn rubber within .000001 seconds of the light turning green, the Very Important Person behind him blasts him out of his seat with a **HONK!!!!**

Can you imagine being in line to buy concert tickets and having the person behind you scream in your ear:

"GET GOING, FUNGUS BRAIN! CAN'T YOU SEE THE LINE'S MOVED?!"

There are three reasons why it's essential for you to master the finer points of proper driving etiquette:

1. so your parents will trust you with the car

2. so you'll be a safe driver

3. so you won't get shot by a motorist you've ticked off

Here are some common (and commonsense) courtesies to abide by when behind the wheel:

- Don't run anyone over. This is very bad manners.

- Stop for pedestrians in crosswalks. Never aim for them.

- Refrain from tailgating. This is dangerous as well as discourteous. And, in the event of an accident, the person tailgating is almost always deemed to be at fault.

- On multilane freeways, use the right-hand lane for cruising, the left-hand lane for passing. Don't hog the passing lane. This is one of the rudest, most dangerous and egocentric things a driver can do. In Europe, nobody would dream of doing this. A car going slowly in the passing lane would be eaten for lunch and spit out by a Ferrari doing 150 m.p.h. But here in the United States, people dawdle along at 40 and refuse to pull over, causing accidents, strokes, anxiety attacks, arguments, traffic jams, acid rain, and just about everything else bad you can imagine.

- Yield the right-of-way when you don't have it.

- Yield the right-of-way when you *do* have it but that truck bearing down looks awfully serious.

- When honking to prevent an accident, lay on the horn as if your life depended on it.

- When honking to tell an inattentive driver that the light has changed, use a gentle, friendly chirp.

- Don't take up two spots in a parking lot. If your car is that new or fancy, park in a far corner.

- Avoid opening your car door into the vehicle parked next to you. Nobody likes to come back to their car and find a new gouge in it.

- If you hit a parked car, leave a note with your name and phone number. This is one of the most noble things a human can do. Imagine how you would feel if you returned to your car and found a dent. Now imagine how you'd feel if you also found a note assuming responsibility. (And, besides, with so many surveillance cameras around, your transgression may have been recorded.)

- Keep the sound system volume low enough to hear other cars, emergency vehicles, etc. When you pull up to a light, the people in the car next to yours should not experience sonic booms within their chest cavities.

- Learn everything you can about defensive driving techniques and driving in snow or wet weather. These safety tips will keep you alive so you can continue to be a courteous driver.

- In heavy traffic, wave someone in who'd otherwise be stuck forever. You'll get where you're going .002 seconds later than you otherwise would have, but the look of amazement on the person's face, as well as the warm glow in your heart, will more than make up for it.

- Always wear your seat belt. Insist that your passengers do, too (including in the backseat).

- Use your turn signals.

- Never, ever drink and drive.

- Never, ever text and drive.

Public Events

As an avid culture hound, you no doubt frequent the opera, the theater, the symphony, the sports stadium, the movie house, and the concert hall or arena. Proper conduct varies with the entertainment. For example, at certain rock concerts it's appropriate to dive from the stage or pass one member of the audience over the heads of others. This would not be acceptable behavior at a lecture on Greek mythology. Conversely, many of these cultural offerings have a lot more in common than you would think. For example, both hockey and opera feature violent acts committed by well-padded individuals wearing strange headgear. Of course, hockey players use sticks instead of swords to draw blood.

You need to be on your toes when you go out to catch some culture. It just wouldn't do to heckle the harpsichordist or tell the conductor he needs glasses. Following are some more public performance protocol guidelines:

At the Symphony, Theater, and Opera

People attending the opera or theater tend to take these events quite seriously. You would, too, if you had paid $150 a ticket. Thus, the standards of conduct are somewhat more rigorous than those for a mud-wrestling match.

First, arrive on time. A stream of latecomers is distracting to those who are already seated, as well as to the performers themselves. In fact, many places refuse to seat latecomers until a natural break in the program—so you may miss even more of the show just waiting to be let in.

At the end of the event, people often have to hurry to catch a train, get to the garage before it closes, relieve the babysitter, relieve themselves, or finish their homework. Thus, contrary to what some people think, it is not rude to leave as soon as the show is over. This is defined as the moment the curtain falls, or the final piece on the program has concluded. The event may continue for quite some time with curtain calls, standing ovations, rhythmic clapping, and/or encores. If you wish to leave right away, say "Excuse me" as you pass.

If, for some reason, you must leave before the conclusion of the performance, try to do so at intermission, between acts, when the music has stopped, or, as a last resort, during a moment of particularly frenzied stage activity or spontaneous applause, when the audience and performers are likely to be distracted. If you're about to be sick, these rules are suspended. You are permitted to quietly race for the exit. Throwing up off the balcony interferes with the enjoyment of more concertgoers than does leaving early.

Spontaneous laughter, applause, and gasps of surprise are welcome at the theater and opera. Talking is not. Neither is texting (the light is a distraction); food or drink; the kicking of seats; the blocking of anyone's view; nor tapping, bouncing, drumming, strumming, or humming. If you are two years old and feel a good cry coming on, excuse yourself and go to the lobby.

Applause

One of the joys of live concerts and plays is the rapport that develops between audience and performer. Protocols have developed for how audiences communicate their delight and esteem. Although these vary with the event, in general a balance is sought between allowing the audience to express its appreciation as these moments occur and allowing the performers to carry on.* Of course, audiences may want to convey something other than approval. We'll get to that in a moment.

The most strict rules of applause apply to performances of classical music: orchestral and chamber works; concerti, sonati, rotini—you know, all those pieces that were written by men in wigs. The main rule when attending these concerts is *never applaud between movements*.

*FOR A GOOD EXAMPLE OF HOW OBNOXIOUS INCESSANT APPLAUSE CAN BE, WATCH THE PRESIDENT'S STATE OF THE UNION ADDRESS SOMETIME.

This doesn't refer to anyone's digestive schedule. Rather, it refers to those divisions within a piece of music that are noted on the program: e.g., allegro, largo, adagio, pesto. Each time the playing stops, another movement has passed, so to speak. The tempo, and often the key, will change.

Between movements, the conductor should keep the baton raised. At the end of the piece, he or she will lower it. Sometimes, composers make one movement sound like several to try to trick concertgoers into applauding at the wrong spot. Sometimes, you may zombie out and lose count. If you're in doubt as to when to applaud, wait for others. They may be wrong, but at least you won't be the one who started it.

It is also appropriate to clap when a guest soloist walks out onto the stage. It is never appropriate to clap if she falls off the stage.

At the end of the concert, assuming you're still there, you have numerous options for showing your appreciation. You can clap—mildly or enthusiastically. (In Europe, people usually clap in unison.) You can stand as you applaud. This is known as a *standing ovation*.* You can shout "Encore!" This is concert-speak for "More, more!" You can also shout "Bravo!" This is Italian for "well done," unless you're referring to a steak.

If you want to get technical, you can shout "Bravo" for male artists and "Brava" for female artists. People in the audience may look at you like you're nuts, but at least you'll have the satisfaction of knowing you're correct.

At jazz concerts, individual musicians usually rotate solos. You can applaud after each improvisation—even if the piece is still being played by the others. It is also acceptable to applaud when jazz and pop artists begin playing songs they have made famous.

Standards for audience behavior at rock concerts vary with the group and the venue. Many bands bring their own culture, and audiences go to these events knowing that dancing in the aisles, swooning at the stage, or crashing into each other is acceptable and expected. At some concerts, audience members light candles or raise glowing cell phones and sway as if they were tipsy waves of grain holding a wake on some Nebraska wheat field.

Now you know what to do if a performance was terrific. But what if it was terrible? At the opera, or at the premiere of a composer's new work, tradition allows robust booing when it's over. (Of course, if it was *that* terrible, why are you still there?) Booing should be used with great discretion; this centuries-old custom should not be devalued by overuse.

The more typical response to a lackluster show is lukewarm applause. Unless the performance was so hideous that you're sitting in stunned

*DUH.

silence, immobilized by disgust, it's only polite to acknowledge the performers' efforts. And, in fact, responsibility for the failure may reside with the composer or director, not with the performers. So dole out your applause as you would a tip in a restaurant:[*]

- none if you feel angry and/or insulted
- a little if you're displeased
- a standard amount if you're satisfied
- an extravagant measure if you're thrilled

At the Movies

A lot of folks don't go to movies anymore. They're fed up with people who crinkle wrappers, crunch food, leave trash, kick and tap, block the view, put their feet up on seats, and text and talk through the whole picture.[**]

It's a shame that so many people have been chased away from theaters by the rudeness of others. Seeing a film on the Big Screen is one of life's great pleasures. At the cinema, good manners mean good viewing. Here's how to maximize everyone's enjoyment, including your own:

Silence your devices. Nobody wants the magic spell of the movies shattered by ringing cell phones or you've-got-a-message notifications.

Try not to sit in front of others. It's much better if everyone is spread out. If you need to go in or out and people are blocking the way, say "Excuse me" and scoot sideways past them, keeping the front of your body parallel to the screen. You'll need one "Excuse me" for each person you pass. If someone wants to get by you, you can either stand (this is what men are expected to do when women wish to get by) or turn both your knees in the direction in which they are traveling.

Don't dance in the aisles or squirt water at your fellow moviegoers (unless you're watching *The Rocky Horror Picture Show*).

And especially:
DON'T TALK!!!!!!!!!!!!

Few things are more annoying than people who keep up a running commentary during the whole show. Especially if they've already seen the picture. It really enhances your moviegoing pleasure to hear such gems as "In a minute he's gonna get shot" and "That's not really the detective" and "They won't fall in love because she's going to die"—like, thank

*FOR MORE ON THE TOPIC OF TIPPING, SEE PAGES 308–312.
**NOT TO MENTION HIGH TICKET PRICES AND WALLS SO FLIMSY
YOU HEAR THE SOUND FROM 10 OTHER MOVIES.

you very much why don't you just tell me how the whole thing ends and I'll leave now.

If someone's talking disturbs you, you have several choices. A sharp, no nonsense "Ssssshhh!" delivered at the first sign of trouble often nips it in the bud. This approach is especially useful when the perpetrators are unknown or sitting far away from you. Plus, it serves notice to those who haven't talked yet—but were going to—that this is a serious showing.

If the offenders are seated to your rear, a determined steady gaze in their direction can be effective in lighting the lamp of self-awareness that leads people to shut their traps. (Some might call this staring—but it's not, since we all know that it's rude to stare.)

You can also say something like "Could you please be quiet? I can't hear the movie when people are talking." A lot of people, though, if they are rude enough to talk in the first place, will ignore your request. (Which—and how sad that we must be grateful for such things—is at least better than dumping a tub of popcorn over your head.) If you get no satisfaction (or you'd rather not confront the person in the first place), you can either change your seat or go tell the manager. It's his or her job to ensure that people in the theater don't disturb others.

Take your trash with you when you leave. If the person before you had done this, the bottoms of your sneakers wouldn't be glued to the floor with orange soda.

Try not to tap or kick the seat in front of you. Even if the nearest people are six seats away, they'll still feel your fidgeting.

Eat quietly. If God had intended people to have picnics at the movies, he would have installed tables and ants in the theater. Nothing is more annoying than someone chomping and smacking their way through a seven-course dinner during a movie. If you must unwrap

TRUE STORIES
FROM THE MANNERS FRONTIER

Shut Up!

Make sure that your efforts to quiet somebody don't create an even greater disturbance. I was at a theater where this couple up front kept talking loudly.

"Shut up!" yelled someone in the back.

"You shut up!" the guy in the front replied.

"&#%@!" yelled the fellow in the back. (This was a very high-level conversation.)

Then the woman up front started shouting to her boyfriend about the guy who told them to shut up. "If he doesn't like it, he can just leave. Who the &#%!@ does he think he is?"

"He's just some %@#!& who's gonna get the &!$@! beat outta him."

"All of you shut the &#%!@ up!" Just what we needed. Another voice of calm and reason.

Pretty soon, half the audience was screaming "Shut up!" as well as suggesting anatomical acts individuals could commit upon themselves. It was quite an uproar. I hadn't seen such rowdiness since the French Revolution. **CONTINUED** ›››

Fortunately, it was a terrible movie, so this rare glimpse into how far we've come as a species was actually more entertaining than what was on the screen.

Still, it ruined the moviegoing experience for me. My only consolation was the free pass to another showing I received after my polite request to the manager.

If anything interferes with your enjoyment of the show, most theater managers will give you a complimentary pass so you can come back at another time. If your request is reasonable and refused, ask the manager for his or her name and explain that you'll be writing to the owner of the theater. If the manager refuses to give you his or her name, mention this fact when you write and note the time and day of the showing you attended. Corporations, too, must sometimes be reminded of their manners.

Requests for free passes should not be made while the final credits are rolling. Unless a disturbance or equipment failure occurs late in the show, asking at such a time makes it appear as if you're pulling a con. And while I know you'd never do such a thing, the manager doesn't.

something, at least do it quickly. People think that if they take five minutes to s-l-o-w-l-y unwrap foil, it's less annoying than if they do one quick, loud jerk. Well, they're WRONG!! It's MORE annoying!! It's a THOUSAND TIMES more annoying!!

And finally:
When you leave the theater, don't give away the ending to people waiting in line.

Dear Alex
"Why aren't you supposed to text at a movie? It doesn't make any noise."

People go to the movies to disappear. They want to leave the cold, cruel world behind and lose themselves for two hours in an alternate reality where nothing matters anymore except the big screen, and possibly the person sitting next to them whose hand seems to be creeping increasingly closer to theirs. When you text, your phone lights up. This annoys the people close to you and shoots up a column of light that anyone sitting behind you can see. Thanks to you, they have now been brought crashing down from their fantasy world, and all the stressful things they managed to forget come racing back to mind. Bummer.

Sporting Events

It may seem ludicrous to be concerned with your own manners while the people you came to see are gouging out each other's eyes and spitting at umpires. Nonetheless, there are standards for sporting events. At least for the spectators. Here are some do's and don'ts:

- DO stand while the National Anthem is being played. But DON'T feel you have to sing. (Indeed, this may be an act of courtesy to your neighbors.)

- DO yell, stomp, and whistle. But DON'T do it in anybody's ear.

- DO insult the players and referees. But DON'T use personal slurs.

- DO come late, leave early, and get up to go buy a hotdog. But DON'T pass in front of anyone without excusing yourself.

- DO bring a glove to baseball games. But DON'T catch fly balls that have not been hit into the stands.

- DON'T spill refreshments on others.

- DON'T pat anyone on the fanny. Only football, baseball, and basketball players can do this to each other.

- DON'T block anyone's view.

- DON'T make waves. Unless everybody's doing the wave.

- DON'T throw snowballs at the opposing team.

Some sporting events, such as tennis or golf matches, have a tradition of expecting spectators to remain quiet. These tend to be competitions where a great deal of concentration is required, or where the stands or galleries are close to the action. If you attend one of these, don't talk or move about in such a way as to distract the athletes. For some sports, special rules apply.

- *Tennis:* Don't race onto the court to get a souvenir ball.

- *Golf:* Don't yell "Miss!" just as the golfer begins his swing.

- *Diving:* When the diver does her run-up, don't say in a stage whisper "She's going to do a belly flop."

- *Swimming:* Don't snicker at how tight the men's swimsuits are.

- *Auto racing:* If your candy wrapper blows onto the track, don't chase after it.

- *Steeplechases:* Don't string wires across the course.

- *Baseball:* Don't use a mirror to flash the sun into the eyes of an outfielder who's about to catch a fly ball.

Waiting in Line

Nobody likes to wait in line. But lines are a fair system for giving people access to events or services in the order of their arrival. And waiting politely and patiently is better than a free-for-all slugfest.

Cutting in line is no fair, yet people try to do it all the time. You've probably seen some of the techniques they use—or attempted a few yourself:

The Unconscious Merge. As the line moves, you nonchalantly walk alongside it. When it halts, you continue for a few steps and then stop. You repeat this process until you have moved way ahead. You then start looking for a nonassertive individual who is unlikely to challenge you when the actual butt-in occurs.

The Puzzled Where-Am-I Merge. This approach is similar to the unconscious merge, except you affect a perplexed attitude, as if you can't quite imagine what you're doing here and why you're lined up with all of these strangers. You scour your surroundings for clues. You search your pockets. You squinch up your face in bewilderment. And, finally, you sigh, give up, and cut in.

The Entitled Intrusion. At least this approach is honest. You just go to the head of the line and aggressively cut in. You're home free unless someone challenges you.

The Find-a-Friend Ploy. You scope out the line for people you know. As soon as you see a good friend, like that kid you once sat next to at lunch five years ago and haven't seen since, you say "Hey, how's it goin'?" and launch into an extended conversation. And since it would be rude to break it off, you continue to accompany this person right up to the ticket window.

The Don't-I-Know-You Gambit. This is what you do when the Find-a-Friend Ploy fizzles. Pick out a stranger. Act as if you know her. Start a conversation. Continue as above.

Those who cut in line succeed because most people would rather not confront them. But you're not going to confront them. You're going to *help* them. Because, obviously, they are lost. They can't find the end of the line!

"Excuse me," you'll say. "The end of the line is around the corner." Amateurs may be sufficiently humbled to slink to the end of the line. More brazen buttinskis may ignore you or say "I was here." In that case, there's safety in numbers. Engage the interest of those around you. "Excuse me," you can say to them. "I was trying to show this person [at this point you can address the person, as in 'I'm sorry, I don't know your name'] where the end of the line is. Is that it back there? I wouldn't want to point him in the wrong direction."

If you can get at least half a dozen people behind you interested in this question, the intruder will usually give up. He may try out his wares further along the line, but you'll have done your duty in trying to uphold the inherent fairness of the system. (You could also report the person to the manager, bouncer, guard, or anyone else in a position of authority.)

The gray area in queuing up has to do with holding places. If five people hold a spot for one who's off parking the car, that's fair. But if one person lets five in, and then one of those five admits a few more friends, and then one of *them* . . . . You get the picture. Suddenly, you're 30th in line instead of 10th.

Dear Alex

"What do you do when you're in a store and the clerk serves everyone else before you? This happens because I'm a kid, I think."

Customers should be served in the order of their arrival. If the clerk simply ignores you, say "Could you please help me?" If the clerk serves others in your stead, say "Excuse me, I believe I was next." If the clerk continues to overlook you, find the manager and report the incident. Politely describe what happened and explain that you won't continue to patronize the store if this reflects their policy toward younger customers.

If the situation is a free-for-all with everybody clamoring for service, the clerk may not know whose turn it is. You'll need to be assertive. To the next customer who tries to jump ahead, say "I'm sorry. You must not have noticed me waiting here in all the confusion. But I believe I'm next."

Pollution Prevention

Litter

Littering is a trashy thing to do. It messes up our environment and makes things ugly and unsanitary. It's dangerous—like when you step on broken glass at the beach or slip on a banana peel.* And it's ecologically unsound. Trash should be recycled; otherwise we'll run out of precious natural resources. Your grandchildren will never see a tree or know the joy of holding an aluminum can in their hands. Animals will choke on Styrofoam, since they don't know the Heimlich maneuver.

> *WHICH A FRIEND OF MINE ACTUALLY DID, AND HE BROKE HIS ARM IN A ZILLION PLACES AND HAD TO HAVE SURGERY AND BE IN A CAST FOR ABOUT SIX YEARS.

In addition to obvious things like candy wrappers, fast-food containers, cans, bottles, paper bags, and the entire Slobola family, litter includes such items as gum, peach pits, and cigarette butts. Even biodegradables such as toilet paper and watermelon rinds are considered litter if you leave them in somebody else's yard.

TRUE STORIES

The Brothers Slobola, Part Two*

Speaking of animals, let's return briefly to the Slobolas, that loathsome family introduced earlier in this chapter.

While waiting for our flight to Paris, they all spread out on the floor of the lounge at the gate and stuffed themselves, having bought one of everything at the airport food court. When it came time to board the plane, they wiped their sticky hands across their meat-juice-covered faces and got up. And then Slobola junior, with a self-conscious little smirk, jauntily KICKED the trash under the seats. He acted as if he thought he was the coolest *Homo erectus* ever to stand on two legs. Meanwhile, there were 48 trash receptacles within three feet of him.

*SEE PAGES 77–78 FOR PART ONE OF THE SAGA OF THE BROTHERS SLOBOLA.

Littering is a perfect example of how one person's abdication of responsibility can affect others. The good news is, it could end tomorrow if we all cleaned up after ourselves.

Visual Pollution

There are those who insist that graffiti is a form of urban art, and that people have the right to express themselves. It's true that graffiti can be artistically significant, and it's also true that self-expression is a good thing. But what if one person's "art" defaces another person's property? How would you feel if you came back to your room one day and found graffiti all over your walls, posters, and furniture? Spray painting someone's building, bridge, or car without permission is vandalism, even if you're the Michelangelo of the aerosol can.

Noise Pollution

Few inventions have done more than headphones to preserve peaceful relations between teenagers and adults. Parents no longer have to yell "Turn that noise down!" a hundred times a day. On the other hand, their kids rarely come when called.

The rules for polite use of personal, portable listening devices are few but essential:

- Remove your earbuds or headphones when speaking to someone. Show that you're giving your full attention to the conversation. This also eliminates the need to shout so you can hear yourself.

- If someone wearing headphones addresses you, mouth your response silently. He'll think the problem is on his end and will remove the headphones, which is what he should have done in the first place.

- In public places, keep the volume low enough so only you can hear it. If you're nuking your brain, it probably means that people at the other end of the bus can also hear your music. Only instead of the pleasant sounds you're enjoying, they're hearing a scratchy metallic noise comparable to fingernails scraping across a chalkboard.

- If you listen to music when walking downtown, riding a bike, jogging, skating, or strolling along train tracks, keep the volume very, very low. Make sure you can hear approaching traffic or someone shouting a warning. If you get run over by a truck or hit by a train, you'll make a mess that others will have to clean up, and that's bad manners.

- Don't wear your headphones while driving a car. Not only is this dangerous, in some states it's illegal.

Health Tip: There's another good reason for keeping the volume low on your listening device: Research shows* that listening to loud music on portable devices can cause noise-induced hearing loss in teens. That's right, as portable music gadgets increased in popularity, so did teenage hearing loss. In fact, it's estimated that 1 in 5 adolescents now suffers some degree of impaired hearing. This type of hearing loss occurs pain-lessly, gradually, and unknowingly, but you can minimize the chance this will happen to you:

- **Lower the volume.** I said, **LOWER THE VOLUME!** (Under 85 decibels.) Many teens listen at full volume (100 or more decibels) on their devices. This is equivalent to having a chainsaw or motorcycle engine blasting into your ears. If the volume is set so that only you can hear it, chances are it's a safe level that is unlikely to damage your hearing.

- **Wear headphones instead of earbuds.** Headphones are better at reducing background noise so you can hear the music at a lower volume. And they don't laser quite as much sound energy into your ear.

- **Take a 15-minute silence break every hour.** Nonstop listening increases the risk of permanent damage to the sensory cells of the inner ear.

*ONLY ETIQUETTE ADVISORS WITH A PH.D. CAN USE THIS EXPRESSION.

Dear Alex

"Is it rude to wear headphones in public?"

When you wear headphones, you're putting up a wall. It's a way of retreating into a private world—and letting other people know you've gone there. If you're on a bus, train, or plane, if you're jogging or working out, if you're studying in a library—places where no communication is required of you—it's perfectly fine to commune with your tune. Keep in mind, though, that your music, if the volume is loud, is heard by those near you as tinny, unnerving, annoying noise. Therefore, if you are listening in public, the polite thing is to always keep the volume low enough so that only you can hear it.

If you're transacting business (ordering fast food; checking out of a store; doing banking), or someone asks you a question, remove both your earbuds. People in the flesh always count more than gadgets and you want to give them your full attention.

Air Pollution

You've heard all about the health effects of smoking. You know that smoking is an addictive habit that will turn your teeth brown, stain your fingers, foul your breath, stink up your clothes, consume your allowance, sicken those around you, and ultimately kill you. You're aware that smoking causes lung cancer, throat cancer, esophageal cancer, and emphysema. You realize that most people who smoke wish they could stop, and that the recruitment of fresh, young teenage smokers by cigarette manufacturers is cynically and dishonestly nurtured by executives who care more about your money than your life. So there's no need to discuss any of these issues here. Besides, this is a book about etiquette, not health.

It used to be that only men smoked, and unwritten laws governed when and where they could light up. For example, in Northern Europe of the 19th century, it was never proper to smoke in the company of ladies, including one's wife. No gentleman would smoke a pipe in the street or a cigarette in the street during daylight hours. Smoking was not permitted in any public place where ladies might be present, such as a racecourse, restaurant, church, flower show, or theater.

In the words of Thomas Tegg, who lived during the 19th century:

> The tobacco smoker in public is the most selfish animal imaginable;
> he perseveres in contaminating the pure and fragrant air, careless
> whom he annoys, and is but the fitting inmate of a tavern. Smoking
> in the streets, or in a theater is only practiced by shop-boys,
> pseudo-fashionables, and the "swell-mob."

Prior to meeting a lady, a gentleman who had been smoking was expected to change his clothes to avoid offending her with the smell of stale tobacco. (This is why men wore "smoking jackets.") At dinner parties, men would retire after the meal to the library to smoke, while women had coffee in the parlor.

Thus, there was a natural segregation of smokers and nonsmokers. Over time, it became acceptable for men to smoke in the presence of women, provided they asked permission first. In the 20th century, as the status of women in society began to change, more women began to smoke, thus achieving equal access to cancer. Once smoking became a mixed-company activity, smokers were in the majority, and the tradition of asking before lighting up began to die out. If nonsmokers didn't like it, too bad.

Today, we know much more about the harmful effects of smoking. The newly recognized dangers of secondhand smoke have led nonsmokers to demand smoke-free environments. Some smokers claim that this is an assault on their right to smoke. Nonsense. Virtually all rights are limited at the point at which exercising them harms others. Because smoking is still a legal activity, adults have the right to smoke—but not if it irritates other people's eyes, nose, or lungs. The law increasingly recognizes these limitations on smokers' rights, and this has led to new regulations that prohibit smoking in many buildings and public areas.

The etiquette of smoking is based on mutual respect. Smokers have the right to hasten their death. They don't have the right to inflict their smoke on others. Nonsmokers have the right to smoke-free environments. They don't have the right to behave rudely toward smokers.

Dear Alex

"What's the best way to ask someone whose smoke is bothering you to stop smoking?"

Simply say "Excuse me, but your smoke is bothering me. Would you mind putting out your cigarette?" Note that this wording embodies the principles for responding to rudeness:

- convey the assumption that the person would never knowingly wish to cause offense
- own the problem as your sensitivity
- allow the offender to see compliance as doing you a favor, as opposed to knuckling under

---

Dear Alex

"I was having lunch at an outdoor café and the woman next to me was smoking. It was blowing straight into my face. I asked if she could please put out her cigarette, but she refused, saying she was outdoors and could smoke if she wanted. Was she right?"

Yes and no. If the outdoor seating area was divided into smoking and nonsmoking areas, she was within her rights to smoke as long as she was seated in the smoking section. A polite response to your request would have been "I'm sorry my smoke is bothering you, but this is the smoking section. I think those tables over there are nonsmoking." If, however, there was no nonsmoking section, the courteous response would have been for her to put out her cigarette.

When smokers and nonsmokers both claim their rights on neutral turf, the decision must go in the favor of the nonsmoker. After all, nobody likes it when smoke gets in your fries.

Dear Alex

"My friend and her parents came to dinner at my house. My friend's father asked if he could smoke, and my mother said no. I was so embarrassed I could have died. Isn't it rude to tell a guest he can't smoke?"

Not if you do it politely. Let's assume that your mom said something like "I'm terribly sorry, but we maintain a nonsmoking home," not "Don't you dare light that filthy thing in here." She might have added "Please feel free to step out onto the patio." Guests are usually allowed to break a few minor house rules. But that immunity ends at the point where the behavior is offensive, illegal, dangerous, or smoky.

Dear Alex

"Sometimes I go over to a friend's house and his parents smoke. I have asthma, and the smoke really bothers me. Would it be polite to ask them not to smoke?"

This is a very complicated question. It involves the rights of smokers vs. those of nonsmokers; the prerogatives of hosts vs. the privileges of guests; and the perks of age vs. the example that adults should set for kids. It even involves the issue of whether exceptions to etiquette can be made on the grounds of health.

In general, it's not proper for a young person visiting the home of a friend to ask the friend's parents to change their behavior. After all, it's *their* home. But smoke is smoke, and the fact that you have asthma grants you a certain latitude. You have four choices, listed from worst to best:

1. Don't go to the house of that particular friend.

2. Go there, but stay out of rooms where the parents are smoking.

3. If you must be in the same room with the parents, say to them "Please forgive me for even mentioning this, it's so rude of me, but I have asthma and smoke makes it very hard for me to breathe. Do you think you could please put out your cigarettes?" They might be so impressed with your manners and courage that they will comply.

4. Tell your friend about your asthma and how smoke bothers you. Maybe he'll volunteer to ask his parents not to smoke around you. If he doesn't volunteer, ask him. If he makes the request in private, nobody loses face, and his parents may decide to adjust their behavior when you come to visit.

Dear Alex

"How do you know if other people mind your smoking?"

You know if they ask you to stop. Other clues include coughing loudly, holding their noses, and keeling over. In any case, the polite thing to do is to assume that it bothers people and put out your cigarette without groaning, making faces, or muttering. On second thought, **WHAT ARE YOU DOING SMOKING IN THE FIRST PLACE?!**

Dear Alex

"I was in a public place where smoking was prohibited and someone was smoking. I pointed to the 'No Smoking' sign and asked politely if they would stop. They refused and were very rude to me. What can I do the next time that happens?"

If smokers extinguished their smoking materials when asked to do so, we wouldn't need laws, signs, fines, and separate sections in public places. But they don't, so we do. Now that popular support has shifted in favor of nonsmokers, it's they who often forget the basic principles of etiquette, treating smokers like moral delinquents. It's time for everybody to take a deep breath of pure, fresh air, relax, and recognize that the world is large enough to accommodate smokers and nonsmokers alike.

If your polite request to put out a cigarette is ignored, you can:

1. Move away from the smoker. The rudeness may escalate into something uglier if you persist in challenging him or her.

2. Call the situation to the attention of someone in authority—a manager, police officer, security guard, usher, maitre d', etc. Make it that person's responsibility to enforce the law.

Teens About Town

At the Supermarket

Many people seem unaware of the major distinction between restaurants and grocery stores. In the former, one dines and then pays; in the latter, one pays and then dines. It's bad behavior to help oneself to grapes, nuts, cookies, and salad bar ingredients while strolling the aisles, unless the store is handing out free samples. Here are a few more market manner musts:

Don't stand with the freezer doors open. The reason freezer doors are made out of glass (as opposed to brick) is so people can see through them. There's no need to stand for 10 minutes with the doors wide open while you decide whether you want fudge ripple or marble fudge. And then, when you close the doors, they fog up, causing the *next* person to have to open them to look.

Drive carefully. The second most dangerous place in the world to drive is a supermarket parking lot. What's the first most dangerous place? The supermarket itself. You've got little kids running wild with carts, senior citizens poking along at .00001 miles per hour, teenagers careening around corners, and people leaving their carts in the aisles. Follow these rules of the road for optimal market maneuvering:

- Don't tailgate. Always leave at least a watermelon's length between you and the cart in front. This will prevent those horrible rear-end collisions.

- Pull to the side of the aisle when stopping. There's no need to cause a traffic jam while you squeeze a cantaloupe.

- Keep to the right except when passing. If everyone followed this highway protocol, there would be fewer head-on collisions in the cereal aisle.

- Know your cart. Things can get very confusing if you pull away from the pickles with someone else's cart and shopping list.

- Keep personal belongings with you. Never leave your purse, backpack, or baby unattended in a cart. They might not be there when you get back.

Honor the express lane. Can we all count to 12? Apparently not, judging by the number of express lane violators who pull up with 15, 20, or more items in their cart. Abide by the express lane rules. Twelve means 12 (oh, okay, I might let you in with 13).

Have your money ready. Many shoppers seem totally surprised when the clerk says "That'll be 43 dollars and 12 cents." How else to explain the fact that they wait until that moment to burrow in their bag for their purse, their purse for their wallet, their wallet for their money. At this point they s-l-o-w-l-y pull out their bills, s-l-o-w-l-y put them in order, s-l-o-w-l-y peel off the few they need, s-l-o-w-l-y dig back into their bag for change, s-l-o-w-l-y count out their coins, only to say, "Ooops, I'm a little short. Guess I'll have to put back the succotash." Naturally, this all takes place in the express lane. Do your part to avoid traffic jams and frayed tempers: Have your Saver's Card, coupons, credit card, speedy pay app, and/or cash ready. If you're writing a check, fill out everything except the amount while your groceries are being rung up.

At the Fast-Food Restaurant

If you frequent fast-food emporia, the last thing you need to do is commit a burger blunder. So let's ketchup with the latest in express eating etiquette:

- Know what you want before you get to the head of the line.

- If you're ordering as a group, get your act together so everyone can order quickly.

- Greet the person at the counter with a friendly "hi."

- Remove your headphones if you're listening to music.

- Don't talk on your cell phone while ordering. Two conversations at once are confusing for everybody.

- If there's going to be a wait for your food, stand aside so those behind you can order.

- Have your money ready.

- Try to avoid paying with large bills or tons of change. This turns *fast* food into *slow* food for those behind you.

- Be kind to the environment. Take only as many condiment packets and napkins as you need.

- Remember that children are likely to be present, and they will be watching and idolizing cool teenagers such as yourself. Adjust your language and behavior accordingly.

- Clear your table when you're through.

- Never try to move a chair that's bolted to the floor.

- Smile when you eat a happy meal.

At the Library

Here are some things to keep in mind when you visit Bookland:

1. **Sssssshhhh!** This doesn't mean that as long as you whisper you can talk to your heart's content. It means that if you absolutely *must* talk, do it as quietly as you can. Even whispers are distracting to people who are trying to read or study. Most libraries have lobbies, lounges, or reference areas where it's okay to talk in a regular voice or even use a cell phone. But if you really want to talk, go someplace else.

2. **Don't reshelve books yourself.** If you take a book down and put it back in the wrong place, it could be lost forever. This happens quite often in libraries. You misshelve a book, the next person goes to look for it, the book is missing, the librarian says "According to the computer, it's in," but nobody can find it since it's three shelves up and two shelves over from where it's supposed to be. Use the to-be-reshelved carts.

3. **No food or drink.** Nobody wants to pick up a book smeared with chocolate or drenched in soda. So stash your snack in your pack.

4. **Keep the volume low.** If you're listening to music using headphones, make sure it's inaudible to your neighbors.

Asking for the Time

From time to time (especially if you're separated from your electronic devices), you'll find yourself in need of the time. It's perfectly fine to ask a stranger what time it is; just don't grab his wrist and look for yourself. Simply say "Excuse me, Sir (or Ma'am), do you have the time?" Most people under the age of six will say "Yes" and stand there with a stupid grin on their face. Those over the age of six will give you the time. Those over the age of 60 will be so impressed that a teenager actually addressed them as "Sir" or "Ma'am" that they'll probably hand over their Rolex.

Chapter Quiz

1. *An elderly woman wearing sneakers hobbles onto a crowded bus and stands in front of where you're sitting. As the bus lurches along its route, she struggles to keep from falling. Do you:*

a) stretch out your feet and try to trip her

b) say in a loud voice "Boy, it sure is great to be sitting down!"

c) offer her your seat

2. *One of the parents who drives your carpool insists that everyone wear seat belts. Do you:*

a) let the air out of her tires

b) spill a carton of sour milk on the carpet

c) thank her for caring enough to protect you

3. *You're skateboarding in a public square. You can stay within the bounds of propriety as long as you:*

a) frontside bluntslide American cars only

b) yell "On your fingers!" before grinding a handrail

c) add "Is Not" to the "Skateboarding Prohibited" sign

4. *You're at the symphony when you suddenly feel like throwing up. Do you:*

a) heave to the beat

b) ask the lady next to you if you can borrow her purse

c) exit as quickly and quietly as you can

5. *You and your best friend are doing the food shopping for your family. It's fine to play basketball with the produce as long as:*

a) your hands are clean

b) oranges are four for a dollar

c) you don't dribble the tomatoes

4

FAMILY LIFE AND STRIFE

Creating the Civilized Home

Belonging to a family means that you have a place where you can be yourself—even your worst self. You can brag, cry, and complain. You can be silly and moody, dreamy and weird. You can break a promise, tell a fib, slam a door, and shout "I wish I was never born!"—secure in the knowledge that your parents will still love you. This is because, in the context of family, we don't call such behavior "rudeness." We call it "growing up." And as long as you make progress along the road to maturity, your mistakes, tantrums, and occasional hurtfulness will be forgiven.

Somehow, though, this greater leeway for error and expression has spawned the strange notion that people don't have to be polite to each other at home. So we hear:

"I hate you."
"I wish you were dead."
"You can't make me."
"Yeah, right."
"Whatever."

And:

"You look like a tramp."
"Why did I ever have kids?"
"You're a selfish, spoiled brat."

THE SURVEY SAYS . . .

Here, according to my survey of adults, are the 25 Rudest Things Teens Do at Home:

1. Interrupt conversations.
2. Not say "Please" or "Thank you."
3. Text, check Facebook, or answer their cell phone during conversations, meals, and other inappropriate times.
4. Throw backpacks and jackets on the floor when they come home.
5. Talk back.
6. Use vulgar language.
7. Behave unkindly to siblings; annoy each other on purpose.
8. Are discourteous on the telephone.
9. Don't say "hello," "good morning," "good-bye."
10. Whine.
11. Leave a mess for others to clean up.
12. Ignore their parents' requests.
13. Not respond when spoken to.
14. Play video games with so much absorption that they ignore everything else.
15. Not appreciate the value of money.
16. Wait to be asked to help rather than jumping in to help.
17. Not use appropriate table manners.
18. Chew with their mouth open.
19. Walk away from the dinner table without clearing their dishes.
20. Call people names.
21. Burp and pass gas.
22. Use disrespectful tone of voice.
23. Insist that parents take care of their problems, even when parents have said they're too busy at the moment.
24. Treat adults as peers.
25. Not do their chores without repeated prompting.

Why do people behave so rudely to those they care about most? Probably because they can. If you're rude to an employer, you'll get fired. If you're rude to a boyfriend or girlfriend, you'll get dumped. If you're rude to your parents, they'll still be your parents in the morning.

Part of the problem has to do with the concept of "company manners." This implies that there are two sets of behaviors: one for show, and one for family. The one for show is the "phony" you—because it's polite and refined. The one for family is the "real" you—because it's sloppy and gross. But where did we get the idea that if we scrape away the surface to discover our "real" selves, we find disgusting slobs?

It's okay to relax our standards a bit when company isn't around. But we should strive for increased *informality* rather than increased *inconsideration*. In other words, it's okay to bring the ketchup bottle to the table, but it's not okay to ask for it without saying "please." It's okay to tell jokes and be silly, but it's not okay to belch, burp, and stick straws up your nose.

You spend more time with your parents and siblings than just about anyone else. Home should be the place where you feel safe and loved, relaxed and accepted. It should be the place where you know you'll be treated with kindness and understanding. It should be the place where you practice your best, rather than worst, manners.

Family Manners

Most families have domestic personnel who provide children with services such as cooking, cleaning, laundry, security, recreation, transportation, tutoring, and moral instruction. These staff persons are generally referred to as "Mom" and "Dad." Here's how to be on good terms with yours, along with other family members:

Acknowledge their presence. This doesn't mean you have to say "Hi, how are you? Lovely day! What's new?" each time you run into a room where a family member is present. And it doesn't mean you should interrupt someone in deep concentration. But it's nice, particularly in the morning when you're overjoyed to see that your parents and siblings didn't disappear during the night, to say "Good morning." Similarly, "Good night" is a pleasant way to end the day. And if, in between, your paths should cross, it's fine to engage family members in conversations that show you care about them and their lives.

Notice their moods. If your own moods go up and down faster than a speeding yo-yo, then you understand that sometimes people need to be left alone. And that sometimes they need to be kept company, or given a hand. Be alert to your parents' and siblings' moods. If they seem upset, say "You seem kind of sad/upset/stressed out today" and ask if there's anything you can do to help. If they want to talk, they will. And if they don't, they will still appreciate your kind sensitivity.

Watch your timing. If your brother just broke up with his girlfriend, it's not a good time to tease him. If your mother just got a raise, it's an excellent time to mention that class trip to Spain you've been hoping to go on. Adjust your requests and behavior to the emotions and needs of others. This is not only a cornerstone of politeness, but also a way to increase the chances that your requests will be granted.

Talk to them. Just because they brought you into this world, nursed you, fed you, wiped you, clothed you, consoled you, and devoted umpteen thousands of hours and dollars toward your upbringing, your parents have this bizarre notion that they're entitled to know what's going on in your life. This is why the following typical parent-child conversation annoys them:

Parent: *"What did you do in school today?"*

Child: *"Nothin'."*

Parent: *"Who was that you were talking with?"*

Child: *"Nobody."*

Parent: *"What are your plans for this evening?"*

Child: *"I dunno."*

Parent: *"Are you thinking of going to the game?"*

Child: *"Whatever."*

One of the most polite things you can do for your parents is *talk to them.* This may already happen in your family. Your parents may be the first people you think of when you have news to share and problems to sort out. If so, keep it up. You're probably enjoying the rewards of a loving, supportive relationship. If, however, you're muter than a sulking clam, it's likely that your parents feel hurt and ignored.

You shouldn't have to divulge your innermost secrets or provide résumés of your boyfriends or girlfriends. Simply engage in the kind of chitchat that says "Hello. I know you're here. Since we live in the same house, let's at least make our time together as positive as we can, even if we're not sharing much of our inner lives." You can do this in two ways:

1. Volunteer information about what went on at school, what you're thinking, how you're feeling. It doesn't have to be deeply personal—just stuff about classes, teachers, other kids, plans, reactions to current events, etc.

2. Ask questions of your parents. Remember, this is the secret to being a good conversationalist. Ask them about their work and friends. Ask them about their childhood. Where did they grow up? What kind of schools did they go to? What kind of students were they? How did they spend their time as kids? What did they worry about? How did they get along with their own parents? How did your mom and dad meet? The list is endless. In fact, one well-chosen question such as "Dad, what was it like growing up on military bases and moving all the time?" can keep your father talking for half an hour. And when he's through, he won't notice that he was doing all the talking. He'll appreciate your interest and feel a warm glow from having spent some time with you.

Bring things up before they become problems. Many of the petty irritations of family life can be avoided by thinking ahead. Don't wait until the last minute to ask to borrow the car, or to tell your mom you volunteered her to bake 400 brownies for the cast party. In fact, don't *ever* volunteer a parent to do *anything* without checking first.

Let your parents know where you are. The #1 qualification for being a parent is the ability to worry. If your parents expect you home from school at 3:00 every day, they will be in full worry mode by 3:30 if you haven't shown up. And then, when you appear at 5:00, instead of acting grateful that you weren't mugged, abducted, or run over, they'll bite your head off.

Establish a reasonable framework with your parents for the boundaries of your freedom. Depending on your age, your trustworthiness, and where you live, this may mean that within certain limits you can come and go as you please. Or it may mean that you must leave a note or a phone or text message so your parents know where you are. Taking these minimal steps to reduce parental anxiety doesn't mean you're a baby or untrustworthy. It means that you're courteous.

Smile on occasion. There's nothing like a scowling teenager to cast a pall over the home front. Granted, adolescence has its dark and gloomy days, but if you're fed, clothed, housed, and generally treated fairly well, why not show your appreciation by wearing a pleasant expression? This doesn't mean you have to grin like a monkey 12 hours a day, or that you should walk around with a fake smile plastered across your face. But your parents will notice (and appreciate in return) a happy, friendly demeanor.

Tip: If you've been in a permanent pout for the past few years, start slowly. Too obvious a show of cheerfulness will only raise your parents' suspicions and make them wonder what you're up to.

Pick up after yourself. Parents HATE IT when kids drop their belongings all over the house. If you're ever kidnapped, by all means try to leave a trail. Otherwise, close doors, shut drawers, wipe off, pick up, put away, take back, and clear off as required.

"Have you seen Chris?"

"Try the kitchen."

Do things without being asked. Your election to the Courteous Kids Hall of Fame will be guaranteed if you notice a need and fill it.

Say "Mom, let me hold that for you." Or "Dad, do you want me to get the blade sharpened?" If a faucet is running, turn it off. If car windows are open in the rain, close them. If the trash is overflowing, tie up and remove the bag and replace it with a new one. These thoughtful gestures will do wonders to enhance your standing at home.

Dear Alex

"Should parents barge into their kids' rooms without knocking?"

Not unless flames and cries of "Help!" are coming from within. Respecting the privacy of others is one of the most basic concepts of polite behavior. Once children reach the age when they want privacy, parents should knock and wait for a "Come in" before

TRUE STORIES
FROM THE MANNERS FRONTIER

Arrrgh!

I was once backing a very large school bus out of a very small parking lot. A student of mine found this very amusing as he perched on a nearby brick wall. He found it even more amusing when I crumpled the door of a teacher's brand-new car.

While I didn't wish to displace my anger and embarrassment onto this innocent observer, I was curious enough to inquire of him, "Why didn't you tell me I was about to hit her car?"

"Because you didn't ask," he replied.

entering their rooms. After all, your parents wouldn't want *you* barging into *their* room without being invited. As in:

Dear Alex

"The other day, I walked into my parents' bedroom and they were having sex. I left right away, but I know they saw me. Nobody's said anything about it since. I don't know what to do."

It can be quite a shock to witness parents' lovemaking. To think that they're still doing it at their age! Fortunately, the rule of etiquette in cases like this is simple: If you see something you weren't meant to see, act as if you didn't see it. However, if you notice a chill in the air, you might say something like this:

> *"I'm really sorry I barged in on you the other day. I was in such a rush to find a pencil that I forgot to knock. I had no idea you were, uh, sleeping. I promise I'll knock from now on."*

"Yesterday I walked in on my parents having sex."

"Sex?!? But they're in their forties!"

Dear Alex

"My parents say I have to be nice to their friends. Why? They're not my friends. I don't see why I have to greet them and stay around while they talk about boring things."

Which would you rather encounter when you go over to your friends' homes—parents who express interest in you as a person and are glad to see you, or parents who are grouchy and give you the cold shoulder? Everybody feels more comfortable in a courteous and respectful environment, whether it's somebody's home, a restaurant, or a store.

Kids shouldn't have to be present the entire time their parents are entertaining, nor would most parents want them to. It should be enough to greet your parents' guests, engage in some conversation, pass the hors d'oeuvres a few times, and then excuse yourself. If the conversation is dull, do something about it. Ask questions about current events or topics that you find interesting.

Tip: Your parents' friends can be good resources for jobs, references, career and college advice, travel tips, etc. Many of my parents' friends have become my friends—especially those with nice vacation homes.

Dear Alex

"My mother gave me this big lecture about not being rude to people who do work in our house. All I did was tell this guy who was cleaning the carpets to come back to my room later, since I was in the middle of something. What was so wrong with that?"

There's nothing wrong with making a polite request:

"Do you think it might be possible for you to clean my rug last? I'm just finishing up here, and I can be out of your way in 10 minutes."

But only employers—in this case, your mom—have the right to *tell* an employee what to do. And even then, politeness is required. You got hauled on the carpet because it wasn't your place to give instructions to someone your parents had hired.

Most households entertain a steady stream of service people: newspaper carriers, meter readers, caterers, landscapers, electricians, painters, house cleaners, Roto-Rooter routers, cockroach poisoners, cable guys. Just because these people are paid for their efforts doesn't mean you can dispense with good manners.

Think of yourself as a fringe benefit for those who work at your house. Be polite and helpful to everyone—even if you're unlikely to see the person again. And if some people come regularly, try to build warm, respectful relationships with them. (One can never be on *too* good terms with the cook.) Without being intrusive, show interest in their lives and skills. Offer them a beverage. Compliment their work. Everyone likes to have their efforts and expertise appreciated. You do this because:

1. these people are human beings who deserve your friendliness and respect

2. good help really is hard to find

Besides, imagine what might happen if parents had to choose between a rude child and a reliable plumber.

Dear Alex

"Do parents have the right to kiss their kids?"

Yes. But teenagers who wish to head off this behavior when peers are present can do so by politely asking their parents to please not kiss them in front of their friends. This request is most likely to be honored by parents whose kids spontaneously go up to them in private, say "I love you," and give them a hug.

Fighting Fair

No family is an island of perfect peace and harmony. All families argue at times. In general, there's nothing wrong with arguing—as long as it occurs in a context of love and mutual respect. Arguing is okay if people listen to what others say, and work toward a resolution that respects everyone's needs and feelings. This is called *fighting fair.* Unfair fighting is when people break or throw things, commit acts of violence, reveal confidences, issue threats, call names, and/or say things they know will hurt. This kind of fighting rarely leads to solving a conflict. It only escalates it.

All families (especially large ones, in which it's easy for individual voices to be lost) should have a family meeting once a week. This is a regularly scheduled time when everybody gathers to share news, set goals, air grievances, and solve problems. You can propose this to your family. Explain that people who share common interests and objectives—be they basketball players, management teams, faculty members, or parents and kids—need to get together regularly to discuss their plans and concerns.

Here's how to make family meetings work:

Establish a regular time to meet. If someone can't come because of an unavoidable conflict, try to reschedule. If one or more family members just decide not to show up, don't reschedule. It's their loss, and they have to abide by decisions made without their input.

Post an agenda in a conspicuous place. Encourage your parents and siblings to write down items they'd like to discuss. While late-breaking issues can always be brought up, the agenda lets people do some thinking ahead of time.

Appoint a "chair" for each meeting. This is the person who brings the agenda and runs the meeting. The position should be rotated among all family members so no one person dominates.

Don't meet for too long. When people get restless, tempers flare and thinking gets sloppy. Better to schedule another meeting than to run overtime.

Take notes. Appoint a scribe for each meeting. The scribe's job is to write down ideas, decisions, plans, etc. He or she can also remind people between meetings of actions they need to take.

Use the structured problem-solving method. Virtually any conflict can be resolved if you:

1. define it in terms that don't accuse people of wrongdoing
2. brainstorm solutions together
3. discuss the options available to you
4. pick the best one and make a plan of action
5. monitor and adjust the solution

Keep the mood positive. While family meetings are the place to bring problems and complaints, they shouldn't degenerate into gripe sessions. This can be avoided if you all agree to stick to the following rules:

- Listen when others speak.
- Think constructively. Focus on solving the problem rather than placing blame.
- Don't label people's ideas as lame, clueless, or silly.
- Don't accuse. Say how you feel.
- Make sure there's a fun item on every agenda (for example, taking a trip, getting a dog, deciding what to do for Grandma's birthday).
- End each meeting on an upbeat note. Watch a movie, make ice cream sundaes, play a game. Try not to end a meeting when people are angry or upset.

*SEE PAGES 136–138.

Dear Alex

"What do you do when your parents are rude, mean, and unfair? I've tried yelling, throwing things, threats, and giving them the silent treatment, but I just get in more trouble."

Rudeness in response to rudeness just causes more rudeness. You need to break the cycle—to set an example of politeness which, in time, your parents will probably adopt.

Talk to them. Don't try to win arguments; try to solve problems instead. Approach your parents at a calm moment and proceed as follows:

1. If needed, start with an apology:
   "I'm sorry about breaking the window. It was very careless of me."

2. Follow up by offering to make amends:
   "I'll pay for it."

3. Then define the issue of unfairness in a neutral way:
   "But I'd feel terrible if it means I can never use my boomerang again."

4. And propose a problem-solving session:
   "Do you think we could talk about this and try to come up with a way that I can have it back and you can feel safe?"

See if this helps. Most parents respond well to reasonableness, respect, and empathy . . . in other words, to good manners. Meanwhile, ask your parents if they would be willing to start having family meetings.

Dear Alex

"Whenever I do something my parents don't like, they dock my allowance or stop it totally. I think this is rude. If they make a mistake at work, they still get their salary."

But if they make *enough* mistakes, they could get fired. Because parents don't have the option of giving kids the pink slip, they use other methods—like withholding or stopping their allowance.

I don't agree with this approach to discipline. I believe that children should get an allowance with no strings attached. Simply because they're family members, they're entitled to a small share of the family income. They shouldn't have to beg their parents for money every time they want to buy a book or go out with friends.

Before you run to your parents and show them this letter, there's something else you should know: I also believe that children should do more around the house than collect an allowance. Because they're family members, they should act like it. This means doing chores and meeting certain standards of behavior. If you forget or refuse to do your chores, if you're rude and uncooperative, if you're a pain in the butt, you're not keeping your part of the bargain.

If you don't like having your allowance docked, here are two things you can do:

1. Consider stopping the behaviors your parents don't like.

2. Propose alternative consequences for your actions. For example, maybe you can't go out with your friends until you do your chores. Or, if you leave tools out in the rain, you either have to replace them or you can't borrow them anymore.

Docking or withholding your allowance won't change your behavior. What *will* are consequences that relate directly to that behavior.

Now you can run to your parents and show them this letter.

Dear Alex

"If I do something wrong at home, I say I'm sorry. But my parents keep harping on it over and over. Surely this isn't polite."

It *is* rude not to accept a *sincere* apology. Maybe your problem has to do with the *way* you apologize. Sometimes, when kids are embarrassed, angry, or defensive, they just mutter a quick "Sorry." Even if they are genuinely sorry, this doesn't get communicated. Instead, parents hear "Why are you making such a big deal about this?"

An even worse form of apology is "Well, I SAID I'm sorry!" This comes across as "Get off my back!" It implies that mere words of regret should be sufficient.

If you want your apologies to be accepted, show that you're sorry in word *and* deed. Saying you're sorry is only half an apology; doing something about it is the other half. The real test of a person's regret is whether they try to set things straight. The next time you get scolded for something you did wrong, try saying something like this:

"Oh, no, I can't believe I did such a thing. How could I have been such a mush mind? You must think I'm the worst child that ever lived. I wouldn't blame you if you grounded me for life. I promise I'll be much more careful in the future."

Then offer to make amends for your actions by repairing, replacing, rebuilding, or reflecting. Your parents may take you up on your offer, which is only fair. Or they may be so impressed by the sincerity of your words that they'll be satisfied.

Around the House

TV or not TV? That is the question—along with a thousand others that come up when families share the same living space:

"Who took my baseball glove?"

"Who used my razor?"

"Who left these crumbs here?"
"Why can't I go barefoot?"
"Meatloaf AGAIN?!"

If you want to witness manners mayhem, all you have to do is step into the family room, kitchen, or bathroom of the typical household. The way family members quibble, nibble, or dribble can be a recipe for disaster. Read on (especially page 129) to learn how to do your part to keep pleasant family rituals from turning into free-for-alls.

Dear Alex

"I'm a 15-year-old boy with two older brothers. My mother makes us wear shirts inside the house, even when it's 95 degrees out. It's not like this is a McDonald's. Shouldn't you be able to be comfortable in your own home?"

All people have quirky little habits and preferences that make no sense to anyone else. For a three-year-old, maybe Mr. Moose has to be next to Thomas the Tank Engine or she can't go to sleep. For your father, maybe all lights in a room must be turned off when you leave, even if you're coming back in 30 seconds. For your mom, maybe young men must wear shirts in the house.

Problems arise when quirks conflict. For example, you like to leave projects you're working on in the living room ("I'll be coming back to it tomorrow"), but your mother wants the living room kept tidy ("You never know when company will drop by"). When these conflicts involve public areas of the house, the "higher" standard of behavior (neatness, cleanliness, modesty, serenity) usually wins. But the "loser" retains the right to indulge himself in private.

Here's what this means for you and your brothers: Wear shirts in the public areas of the house—with the understanding that you can take them off in the privacy of your bedrooms. If your mother will agree to knock before entering, this will give you time to indulge her by throwing on a T-shirt.

Dear Alex

"Whenever I do something wrong at the table, my mother says 'Where were you brought up, in a barn?' It's so annoying! What can I say back?"

"Moo."

THE FIFTY DO'S AND DON'TS OF FAMILY ETIQUETTE

Do

- treat each other with kindness and respect
- say "Please" and "Thank you"
- be courteous when answering the phone and door
- use proper table manners
- think before you speak as you cannot take back what you have said
- ask without demanding
- listen attentively
- keep your room tidy
- be willing to compromise
- be appreciative
- share willingly
- do your part to keep the house neat
- help set and clear the table
- treat each other's property with care and respect
- turn down the volume when asked
- apologize sincerely when apologies are called for
- greet each other first thing in the day by saying good morning, and last thing at night by saying good night
- rejoice in each other's successes
- offer to help without being asked
- put your dirty clothes in the hamper
- express your thoughts and feelings in words and not facial expressions
- notify parents of your whereabouts when out with friends
- respond to requests from adults the first time
- take responsibility for your own actions and words
- smile

Don't

- lie
- hit
- snoop
- whine
- interrupt
- use crude language
- make a mess in the kitchen
- text during conversations/meals/social gatherings
- open a closed door without first knocking—and waiting to be invited in
- tell each other's secrets
- leave your backpack and sports equipment in the hall
- ignore each other's requests
- be afraid to speak up when you feel something is wrong
- "borrow" others' belongings without first asking
- expect to get everything you want
- throw your jackets, hats, and shoes all over the house
- spend all day or night on the computer
- get up from the table before being excused
- embarrass your parents or siblings in front of their friends
- schedule commitments for each other without clearing them in advance
- drop your clothes on the floor
- leave dirty dishes all over the house
- forget to do your chores
- yell across the house when you need someone or something
- bully anyone

TV Civility

The invention of the remote-controlled television brought about a new era in TV watching. No longer did viewers have to leave their chairs and walk across the room to change channels; no longer were they forced to sit passively through commercials. The remote also led to a new variety of vegetable: the couch potato. And it gave rise to a new subject for family fights and arguments: who controls the remote.

> *"Whenever we watch television as a family, my brother grabs the remote. Every time there's a commercial, he starts flipping through the channels. Then he'll see something that appeals to his intellectual level, like mud wrestling, and everyone has to start yelling 'Change back, change back,' and by the time he does, we've missed some of the program we were watching and everyone's in a bad mood."*

In every family, one person usually emerges as the Keeper of the Remote. Ideally, he or she won't be a dictator or a hog. Instead, that person will hold the remote in trust for the rest of the family, and honor the responsibilities of such guardianship. These include:

- adjusting the volume to an acceptable level

- changing (or not changing) channels, based on the wishes of the majority

- leaving the remote in a convenient location so the next person to watch TV won't have to spend three hours looking for it

Being the Keeper is like carrying the basket on a picnic. This is a position of honor, but it doesn't give the carrier the right to eat all the deviled eggs or decide who gets tuna and who gets liverwurst. Siblings who abuse their power should be sat on by the rest of the family until they surrender the remote or agree to operate it according to the wishes of the majority. Parents who turn into TV tyrants should be invited to a family meeting for the purpose of discussing this issue.

There are other protocols of polite TV watching. They include:

Choosing what to watch. This is done either by vote (all those in favor of *Wall Street Week* raise their hand), alternation ("I decide tonight, you decide tomorrow"), or fiat ("Because I'm the parent, that's why"). Multi-TV households can cut down on these conflicts, as can those with DVRs—simply record one show while you're watching another.

Talking. Unfortunately for those who wish to concentrate on the screen, talking during family TV viewing is allowed. Sparkling commentary followed by a chorus of "Shut ups!" is what makes the experience so warm and delightful.

The typical family includes many different personality types. They are easily identified by the remarks they make while watching:

- *The Disdainful One:* "The whole space station is nothing but a bunch of cheesy miniatures."

- *The Literalist:* "That's so lame. He just fired eight shots and that gun only holds six."

- *The Distracted One:* "Are we going to the lake again this summer?"

- *The Clueless One:* "Is that the same woman? Where are they now? Why did he let her go?"

- *The Critic:* "The filmmaker's homage to Godard and the French new wave falls flat, in my opinion."

- *The Beans-Spiller:* "I already saw this movie. The kindergarten teacher did it."

- *The Cheerleader:* "Yeah! Kill 'em! Blast 'em in the kneecaps!"

- *The Heckler:* "Where did she learn to act? Who wrote this terrible script? And why did we just see a microphone dangling over their heads?"

- *The Shusher:* "Sssshhhh!"

Dear Alex

"My parents don't let us watch TV at all. Doesn't this violate some rule of etiquette?"

I don't know why so many parents are so opposed to television. We should consider ourselves fortunate that a medium exists for the purpose of providing children with countless examples of people behaving badly. How else are kids supposed to learn what *not* to do?

As long as your parents are polite about laying down the law, their position lies outside the bounds of etiquette. Doubtless you've tried all the arguments about the educational value of watching PBS, the History Channel, and the Learning Channel. And you've probably thrown a few TV-related tantrums, only to be told "Someday you'll thank us for this." Meanwhile, you're limited to whatever watching you can do at your friends' houses.

It's tough when parents forbid television in the home. But the worst that can happen is you'll grow up to be a fascinating, creative, self-sufficient person with a million goals—and the intelligence and motivation to reach them.

Dear Alex

"Whenever we have company, my parents make us turn off the TV and socialize. It's always in the middle of a good show. What can I do?"

This policy is based on two assumptions: First, that people are more fascinating than television (this, of course, is not always the case). And second, that it's rude to give the guests the impression that they are less captivating than a TV show.

Try a compromise. When your parents' friends come to visit, go to greet them. Say hello, ask a few questions, submit to their inane remarks ("My, how you've grown!"), and then say "Please excuse me, I have a lot of homework tonight." You've fulfilled your social obligations, but you'll have to keep the volume low. (This assumes that the TV is in a different room from the one they're in.)

If the company can't be shaken that easily (such as relatives, or parents' friends with kids your age), you may be stuck. But you live in the digital age. So, program "Record," and you won't miss a thing.

Sometimes it's okay to watch TV with company—for example, when guests drop by unannounced ("We're all watching *Real Houseflies of Beverly Hills,* come on in and join us"), or when TV watching is the main event (as on Super Bowl Sunday).

In the Kitchen

Kitchens are a prime source of calories, cholesterol, and conflict, as in:

"Don't drink out of the milk carton."

"Don't stand there with the refrigerator door open."

"Wipe up your crumbs."

"Why is there a four-foot stack of dirty dishes in the sink?"

"Who do you think I am, the maid?"

Here are the basics of proper kitchen protocol:

Clean up after yourself. This means putting away food, sweeping up crumbs, wiping the counter, and rinsing out your dishes (or putting them in the dishwasher).

Be a good inventory clerk. If you eat the last piece of bread, drink the last gulp of milk, or scarf the last pineapple popsicle, tell someone—preferably the person who does the food shopping for your household. Many families keep a shopping list on the refrigerator door just for this purpose. (There's no rule against trying to sneak your favorite foods onto the list.)

Check before you chomp. If something looks rare, special, and appetizing, chances are it's not for you. It may be hors d'oeuvres for company, or a cake for a bake sale. Ask.

Pretend you're a waiter. Let's say your family is watching TV together. If you get up to go to the kitchen for a soda or to make a sandwich, ask if anyone else wants anything. Why? Because it's rude to help yourself to food without offering some to others.

It's possible that your courtesy will be abused. This occurs when family members come to rely on your treks to the kitchen and stop getting up themselves. It's not fair if every time you say "May I bring anyone anything from the kitchen?" the responses are:

Dad: *"I'd love a ginger ale."*

Mom: *"A cup of tea would be nice."*

Sister: *"Could you get me a grapefruit with the sections cut out?"*

Brother: *"Yeah, bring me a ham-and-Swiss on whole wheat toast with lettuce, tomatoes, and mustard, tortilla chips with medium salsa, lemonade, and three pickles. Don't let the pickle juice get on the bread."*

One hopes that with your good example, other members of your family will offer to make their fair share of service runs to the kitchen. If they don't, you can always suggest that a different person be "on duty" each evening.

In the Bathroom

Bathrooms rank way up there on the list of family squabble generators:

"Mom, Christine's hogging the bathroom!"

"Who used up all the hot water?"

"Someone stole my shampoo!"

"Whose slimy hairball is that in the drain?!"

"How many times do I have to tell you, DON'T LEAVE WET TOWELS ON THE FLOOR!"

Want to avoid these conflicts? All you have to do is install a 3,000-gallon water heater and provide each family member with a personal lavatory attendant.

Or you can establish a Fair Use Policy.

If six people all need to use the same bathroom within the space of 20 minutes, family members will stack up like planes at LaGuardia. When needs conflict, try not to fight. Instead, work to solve the problem. Sit down with your family at a calm moment. Identify the issues. Phrase them in nonaccusatory ways ("The water is always cold when I take my

THE 14 DO'S AND DON'TS OF TOILETIQUETTE

- -

Do

- hang your wet towel on the rack, not the floor
- raise or lower the toilet seat, as the case may be (either way, make sure the seat is down and the lid is closed when you leave the bathroom)
- willingly give way to those whose need is greater than yours
- rinse out the tub after using it
- remove your shed hairs from the soap and sink
- clean the mirror after brushing and flossing
- flush when you are done

Don't

- pee on the toilet seat
- finish a roll of toilet paper without replacing it
- use more than your fair share of hot water
- appropriate the towels or toilet articles of others without permission
- enter without knocking and being invited in
- comment on the sounds or scents generated by others
- hang your unmentionables where they will smite others in the face

- -

shower," not "Jeffrey uses up all the hot water"). Then brainstorm solutions. Maybe some people can shift to evening showers. Or get up earlier. Or use the laundry room sink for shaving. The solution may not be perfect, but it will be a lot better than starting every day with an argument.

Dear Alex

"Why do parents make such a big deal about how you squeeze the toothpaste tube? What difference does it make? You wouldn't believe the fights we get into over this."

The "proper way" to squeeze a toothpaste tube is usually defined by parents as "my way." While parents would be smart to ignore little issues (such as missqueezed toothpaste) and conserve their energy for big issues (like drinking from the milk carton), this is unlikely to happen. Therefore, you'll need to take some action. Here are three proposals for solving the problem:

1. Accommodate your parents' neurosis (er, preference). Train yourself to squeeze and roll from the bottom up.

2. Buy your own tube. Squeeze it anyway you like and keep it out of sight.

3. Have your family switch to toothpaste in a pump. No-squeeze is bound to pleeze.

Sharing a Room

In the adult world, one generally gets to choose one's roommates. And if things don't work out, one can unchoose. With kids, it's different. You're forced to share a room with your sister or brother—or maybe several sisters or brothers. If you're lucky, such cohabitation can lead to closeness and camaraderie. If you're unlucky, it can ruin your life.

Meanwhile, parents aren't very sympathetic. They tell you that "sharing a room is a learning experience." And that "you need to learn how to live with people you don't always get along with." You say "Isn't that what marriage is for?" But it doesn't do any good. You're stuck.

Siblings can be a joy to live with—IF you know the secrets of proper roommate etiquette. The key to getting along with roommates is to lock them in the closet until they behave. If that's not an option, try using *consideration* and *negotiation*.

- **Consideration** means anticipating the consequences of your actions on others.

It's not enough to just consider the effect *(Hmmm, if I throw a water balloon, he'll probably get wet)* and then go ahead and do it anyway. The idea is to refrain from those behaviors that infringe upon the rights, property, and serenity of others. If you're not sure, you can always ask:

"Is it okay if I throw this water balloon at you?"

"Do you mind if I get rid of this, or are you doing a science project on the regenerative properties of three-month-old bologna sandwiches?"

"Would it be all right with you if I rearranged the furniture and put your bed in the garage?"

- **Negotiation** enters the picture when roommates have conflicting wants, needs, tastes, and metabolisms.

For example, you need to throw a water balloon, and your roommate needs to remain dry. Or you prefer to see the floor, and your roommate prefers to hang her clothes on it. This doesn't mean that all siblings who share space are destined to fight. Yours may be as tolerant, considerate, generous, and cool as yourself. If that's the case, here's my advice for you:

As you can see, when things are going swimmingly, there's not much to say. It's when things *aren't* going well that you need help.

You can be sure that conflicts will arise. Conflict is natural, and sometimes it's even healthy. Conflict *per se* is not what harms relationships. Rather, *unresolved conflict* and *unfairly resolved conflict* do the damage. While kindness, empathy, and consideration go a long way toward minimizing conflict, don't expect to eliminate discord from your relationships. Rather, strive to recognize conflict early and address it in ways that respect people's needs and feelings.

People who share space are bound to come into conflict because they have different definitions of noise and neatness, different aesthetic tastes, different daily rhythms, different priorities and attitudes. To nip potential problems in the bud (and solve those that do sprout), try this simple five-step problem-solving strategy:

1. Identify the problem. Gather the parties involved with the conflict. Ideally, this should be done when you're not screaming at each other. State the problem in terms of your needs and feelings rather than your roommate's transgressions. Examples:

Right	**Wrong**
"I can't study with music on."	*"Your music is driving me crazy."*
"I went to play tennis, and my racquet was gone."	*"You're always taking my things without asking."*

This approach creates the type of nonaccusatory climate that leads to thoughtful discussion and creative problem solving.

2. Brainstorm solutions. Come up with as many ideas as you can for addressing the issue. The more the merrier; the sillier the better. Don't censor your thoughts or anyone else's. Sometimes it's the wild ideas that lead to the best solutions. No criticism or analysis is allowed at this stage.

3. Discuss the possibilities. This is where you evaluate the options generated by your brainstorming. Some will strike you as impractical or unrealistic. But don't label them "stupid" or "lame." State your reasons for rejecting a suggestion without dumping on anyone. Be wary of "solutions" that sound great but are, in fact, wishful thinking unlikely to work.

4. Choose the best solution. Decide which option seems to resolve the conflict most fairly and effectively. Identify the actions that must be taken to carry it out (such as buying a partition, seeking permission from a parent, or writing out a schedule). Then determine who will do what and when you will do it.

5. Monitor your progress. Check to see how things are going. Sometimes solutions get snagged and have to be retooled. If an unexpected glitch turns up, make any necessary midcourse corrections. If things are going well, acknowledge that fact. It will give you and your roommate pleasure to know that you can handle any problems that might come up.

This problem-solving method can be applied to virtually any conflict between roommates as long as *fairness* rather than *winning* is your goal. This assumes that the conflicting desires are equally legitimate—a question of *different* rather than right or wrong.

Sometimes it's very difficult to determine who's "right" and who's "wrong." In the meantime, the following "roomietisms" will help you figure out when the position of one roommate should be granted priority over that of another:

- Illegal behavior must yield to legal behavior.
- Rule-breaking behavior must yield to rule-following behavior. (Although, if both roommates agree to break the rules of etiquette, this is no longer an issue of manners and they may do so at their own risk.)

- Health comes first. (Allergies to animal hair outrank the desire to keep a pet llama in the room.)

- Virtuous behavior takes precedence over nonvirtuous behavior. Virtuous behavior is defined as that which is creative, productive, charitable, compassionate, beneficial to humankind, and/or morally and spiritually uplifting. Nonvirtuous behavior is defined as that which is selfish, disgusting, manipulative, destructive, distracting, dishonest, impositional, and/or likely to cause itching in others. But let's not get carried away. The minute virtuousness turns into self-righteousness, it goes to the end of the line.

What do you do when *both* roommates' positions are reasonable? Look for the most sensible and easy-to-implement solution. If your roommate wants to play music and you need to study, it's easier for your roommate (the noise aggressor) to use headphones than it is for you to screen out the sound or leave the room. Or, let's say you like to sleep with the window wide open during winter (room temperature a nippy 50 degrees), and your roommate likes to sleep with it closed (room temperature a toasty 90 degrees). You can't say that either preference is "better" than the other. Since it's easier to make yourself warm in a cool environment (load on the blankets and flannel p.j.'s) than it is to keep cool in a warm environment (sleep naked and remove several layers of skin?), the simplest solution would be to crack the window open a bit (room temperature 63 degrees) and lend your down sleeping bag to your roommate.

As a last resort, roommates can petition the authorities for a divorce. Maybe you can swap with someone else who's unhappy with his or her living situation. Or scour the house for a corner that might be turned into a space for yourself.*

*TO LEARN MORE ABOUT LIVING WITH ROOMMATES, SEE PAGES 247–249.

Dear Alex

"My brother taps. He uses pencils, fingernails, feet, knuckles—you name it, he's tapped with it. He's the one who's nervous, but I'm becoming a nervous wreck. What's a polite way to ask him to stop his %$#@! tapping?"

The issue here is unwanted noise. Unwanted noise comes in many varieties. The most common is music you don't like. Others are tapping, drumming, excessive volume, talking in one's sleep, and banging into objects that jump in front of you when you return late at night to a dark room and your roommate is sleeping (er, *was* sleeping).

In this case, a tap-free environment takes precedence over a tappy one. In other words, it's more reasonable to focus on cessation of tapping as the goal than to expect you to leave the room whenever your brother experiences a tap-attack. Decency, however, still requires you to take a sympathetic attitude toward your roommate's excess nervous energy.

Use the problem-solving method outlined on pages 136–138. Approach your brother when he's tapped out. Introduce the problem in a nonaccusatory way. Say:

"I'm sure you don't realize it, but sometimes you tap, old chap. And when I nap or work on my lap—top, my concentration goes snap. Let's not scrap or cause a flap, but have a rap. So put on your thinking cap."

If your roomie doesn't call the poetry police, you can then brainstorm possible solutions. Examples:

- Your brother agrees to get counseling.
- You buy him a nervous energy ball to squeeze whenever he gets the urge to tap.
- You work together to build an isolation chamber.
- You tie his hands and feet to the chair.
- You banish him to the Tappan Zee Bridge.
- You'll say "Tapping" whenever he starts. He'll try to stop.
- Your brother agrees to increase the frequency of activities known to dissipate excess energy.

When your list is done, weed out the wild suggestions. Then choose the one or ones that solve the problem most fairly. If things improve, congratulate yourselves. If they don't, go back to the drawing board.

Here are some other solutions that work for noise problems:

- Be quieter.
- Use earplugs.
- Use headphones.
- Schedule "quiet times" and "high decibel times."
- Build sound barriers with carpeting, blankets, foam, etc.

Dear Alex

"Is neatness automatically better than messiness?"

No. Messiness in the absence of an offended beholder is a victimless crime. This raises two questions: What grants a beholder the right to legitimacy as an interested party? And what constitutes an "offense"?

Generally speaking, the beholder must be affected by the mess in some tangible way. This raises another question: Is injury to one's aesthetic sense a tangible affront? YES—if the mess intrudes (visually or olfactorily) on the public areas of the house. NO—if the mess is contained within the child's domain. In fact, wise parents grant their underage roommates the right to keep their rooms anyway they like, as long as the following conditions are met:

- The door to the room remains shut.

- Children maintain parental standards in the rest of the house.

- Mutant life forms growing on leftover food and overripe clothing are not permitted.

- Housing and safety codes are not compromised.

- Possessions damaged by disarray are the inhabitant's responsibility to repair, replace, or do without.

Some parents will argue that the mere knowledge that a mess exists, even if it's hidden from view and doesn't stink, is more than their sensitive selves can handle. These parents should get a life. Parents should ensure that their children have adequate storage space, they should instruct their children on methods for ordering one's material world, and then they should butt out. For many children, neatness is an acquired skill. It comes with age as they decide they don't want to spend half their days looking for things, or half their allowances replacing things they step on. It comes when a friend visits and says "How can you live in this pigsty?"

But what if it's not a case of a child's own bedroom? What if two siblings share a room, one a neatnik and the other a messnik? Then you've got a conflictnik. So dust off the problem-solving strategy described on pages 136–138. Identify the issues. Brainstorm solutions. As in:

- Hang blankets or build a partition to divide the space. (This way, you won't have to look at the neatness.)

- Define acceptable and unacceptable messes. (Examples: Cluttered desk—okay; food on floor—not okay.) You might establish a kitty so that any roommate who forgets and violates the agreed-upon standards has to deposit a dollar. When enough money accumulates, the kitty treats you to a movie or snack.

- Schedule a time twice a week when you turn up the music loud and blitz the room with a thorough cleanup.

- Hire a sibling to clean for you.

- Get a trunk or a big box. Throw the things you used to throw on the floor in there instead.

"Permission to enter your side of the room?"

"Are you shedding?"

Dear Alex

"What's so important about making your bed? I think it's a total waste of time because you're only going to unmake it again."

I've spent many years trying to discover an unimpeachable argument for why one should make one's bed—some scientific finding that would settle the dispute once and for all, like: *Children who don't make their beds are 18 times more likely to have tapeworms than are those who do.* But the evidence just isn't there. The closest I can come to a justification for making your bed is this: If you ever turn up missing, a detective could come into your room, lay his hand on the mattress, and say "Hmmm, this bed hasn't been slept in."

So, where does this leave us? With bedmaking as an issue of *aesthetics* and *ritual*.

To many people, a made-up bed is more visually pleasing than an unmade bed. I belong to this camp. My interior life is so disordered that I need all the external help I can get, and a neat bed means one less thing cluttering up my mind. I'm not a fanatic about it—not anymore. When I was a lad, I had a thin blue bedspread with a busy plaid pattern on it. It took me so long to get the lines properly parallel and perpendicular that by the time I finished, I was ready to hop back into bed. Nowadays, I use a big, fluffy comforter. I can fling it over my bed in three seconds, and if the sheets are still bunched up at the foot of the bed, no one is the wiser. (**Tip:** If you get a thick comforter, you, too, can make your bed in three seconds.)

To other people, making one's bed is a ritual that signals the start of a new day. The phrase "make the bed" meant something entirely different during the Dark and Middle Ages. In those days, it was a luxury just to sleep indoors. Sometimes, people would take straw or leaves and stuff them into cloth sacks to "make a bed," which they would lay out on the floor or on a bench or table. There was just one problem: Because the stuffing was organic, it would attract rats, mice, bugs, and mold. (This is probably where the expression "Don't let the bedbugs bite" originated.) Thus, people would literally make and unmake their bed each day to dry out the stuffing, squash fleeing bugs, and hit rats and mice over the head with frying pans.*

Now that our history lesson is over, let's get straight to the bediquette:

- Parents should not harangue their children to make their beds. Bedmaking has taken on mythological proportions as one of those things children *should* do. But there's no reason a bed must be made other than to honor the parents' aesthetic sensibilities. And aesthetic tastes are subjective. Therefore, parents should lighten up and recognize that *it's not that big a deal.*

> *FASCINATING AS THIS TALE IS, YOU PROBABLY DON'T WANT TO SHARE IT WITH YOUR PARENTS. FOR IF YOU DO, THE NEXT TIME YOU HAVE A DISPUTE OVER MAKING YOUR BED, THEY'LL SAY "YOU SHOULD CONSIDER YOURSELF LUCKY THAT YOU HAVE A BED TO MAKE!"

- Because *it's not that big a deal,* children whose parents refuse to follow the above advice should make their beds. Why? Because *it's not that big a deal.* Take three seconds, throw a comforter over your bed, and preserve the peace. Save your energy for the really big issues (like curfews).

- Children who are overnight guests in somebody's home must always make their beds. If it turns out that nobody in the host family makes their bed, and you have violated household standards of sloppiness, you may never get invited back. But you will be a martyr to the cause of good manners.

The Blended, Shaken, Stirred, or Mixed Family

Families come in so many configurations these days that there's no longer a single definition of what "family" means. A mom, dad, two siblings, and a dog? Sometimes. A mom, dad, stepdad, stepmom, two siblings, four stepsiblings, a dog, and a stepdog? Two moms, three siblings, and an ocelot? A dad, a grandmother, six cousins, and a hundred hamsters? These are all possibilities, along with lots of others. You might be born into a particular type of family, then watch it change before your eyes. The most common type of change these days is divorce.

When parents get divorced, it's not only your home life that's affected. Friends and acquaintances at school ask questions like:

"Why are your parents splitting?"

"Who are you going to live with?"

"Whose fault was it?"

But it's none of their business, and you don't feel like talking about it. What's the polite way to respond?

It's easy. Just say:

"I appreciate your concern, but I'd rather not talk about it."

Some of the kids (and adults) who ask you these questions are simply insensitive boors who are sniffing for juicy gossip. Others, however, are well-intentioned. While their questions may be nosy and clumsy, what they're really saying is "I'm here if you'd like to talk about it."

You have every right to keep your personal life private. But I hope you'll talk about your feelings with someone you trust—a parent, teacher, close friend, counselor, or relative. This doesn't mean you have to spill the beans on private family matters. Teenagers whose parents are going through a breakup can feel scared, angry, ashamed, and guilty. They sometimes blame themselves for the divorce, or think their parents won't love them anymore, or take it upon themselves to try to get their parents back together. These feelings, if they're kept bottled up inside, can make it hard for kids to concentrate, enjoy life, trust people, and build new family relationships.

The following Codes of Etiquette give everybody a fair chance to get along and act like civilized, caring human beings during this difficult time. The "Code of Etiquette for Divorced or Divorcing Parents" on pages 144–145 may be copied and left lying about by children and teenagers. Similarly, the "Code of Etiquette for Children of Divorce" on page 146 may be copied and left lying about by parents.

CODE OF ETIQUETTE FOR DIVORCED OR DIVORCING PARENTS

- Answer fully your children's questions about your divorce, especially those that relate to how it will affect their lives.

- Don't share intimate details about your marriage or the reasons for your breakup.

- Encourage your children to continue the rewarding relationships they have with your ex's relatives, such as grandparents, cousins, aunts, and uncles.

- Don't ask your kids to carry messages to your ex unless the message is purely logistical.

Okay	Not Okay
"Tell your mother I'll pick you up at eight."	*"Tell your mother she'll get her money when they pry it from my cold, dead fingers."*
"Tell your dad that your sister loves anything having to do with Curious George."	*"Tell your dad that if he ever brings that hussy here again, I'll see him in court."*

- Never badmouth or blame the other parent in front of your children. If the divorce truly was somebody's fault, older children already know it and younger children aren't ready to.

- Never ask your children to take sides.

- Don't say "We did it for the children's sake." Kids hear this as "It's our fault."

- Be sure your children have all the necessary gear for shuttling between abodes.

- Don't use material objects to buy your children's love or assuage your guilt. Use love, interest, and time spent together.

➔

CODE OF ETIQUETTE FOR DIVORCED OR DIVORCING PARENTS (CONTINUED)

- Ascribe only the best motives to your children's other parent and or stepparent.

Okay	**Not Okay**
"I'm sure your mother didn't mean to ignore you. She must have been worried about something."	*"Well, what did you expect? Your mother's never been able to think of anybody except herself."*
"Felicia didn't mean to embarrass you. It's hard being a brand-new stepmother. I bet if you give her a chance, you'll like her."	*"Of course little Miss Pom-Pom flirted with your boyfriend. She's barely out of high school herself."*

- Be unfailingly polite to your ex in the presence of your children. What better way to show your children proper behavior for dealing with people who drive you bananas?

- Don't ask your children for the scoop on your ex. ("So, is your mom seeing anyone these days?")

- If you're an every-other-weekend parent, be a parent, not a party host. Share your life, interests, and routines with your child. This is more meaningful than 26 visits a year to the aquarium.

- Minimize the disruptive aspects of your children's shuttle between two dwellings. In fact, have you considered having the children stay put in one house while you and your ex make the switch? ("What! Live in two places?! Me? I'd never know where anything is! How would people reach me? I'd go crazy without a permanent home." My point exactly.)

- Don't conceal new romantic interests from your children. While your children should treat these guests with the courtesy they extend toward all guests, don't expect them to necessarily welcome such rivals for your affection into the bosom of your family.

- Take things slowly with stepchildren. Older kids, who are used to their independence, may resent the appearance of a new authority figure. If you focus on building a caring, respectful relationship, your authority will evolve. If a problem develops, work out a strategy for dealing with it with your partner.

CODE OF ETIQUETTE FOR CHILDREN OF DIVORCE

- Don't play one parent off against the other. ("Daddy doesn't mind if I stay out 'til two in the morning, so I don't know why you do.")

- Treat your parents' new romantic interests with the same courtesy you extend toward all guests.

- Don't assume that your parents' dates wish to steal your mom or dad's affections from you.

- Don't ask your parents for details of what they do on or with dates.

- Never brag about one parent's "new friend" to the other parent. ("He's so cool, Dad. He drives a Ferrari and he said he'd teach me to fly his helicopter!")

- Put yourself in your parents' shoes. They, too, may feel angry, confused, scared, lonely, and betrayed. Try to help each other rather than hurt each other.

- Give stepparents a break. It's as hard for them as it is for you.

- Don't get caught in the middle of your parents' arguments. As you leave the room, say "I love you both, and I'm not going to take sides."

Dear Alex

"My parents are divorced, but they both live nearby. Even though I live with my mom, I'm very close to my dad. The problem is, every time they get within 50 yards of each other, they start sending out these vibes, and the atmosphere gets spoiled even if they don't have an actual fight, which they sometimes do. Both my parents want to be active in my life, and I appreciate that, but do I have to invite both of them to things like plays or games or even graduation if it's going to spoil it for me?"

You have a tricky situation, but with some thought and advance planning, you can handle it. The answer to your question is yes . . . and no. Yes, you have to invite both your parents to certain once-in-a-lifetime events, such as graduation. No, you don't have to invite both of them to less significant or repeated events.

For example, if you're in a school play, you can ask your dad to opening night and your mom to closing night. They can alternate football games. If there's an open house at school, invite your mom for 7:00 PM and your dad for 8:00 PM. If it's your birthday, have the party at your mom's, and ask your dad if you could have a special birthday dinner for just the two of you (double celebrations are one of the benefits of divorce). The secret is to make each parent feel as if he or she is getting the best deal.

Should your parents suspect that you're purposely keeping them apart, all the better. It may cause them to reflect on their immature behavior. If, however, they confront you with their suspicions, don't say "It's because you and Dad fight so much." Instead, say "I just wanted to be able to spend time with you without worrying that Dad was feeling left out." If they believe you, great. If they don't believe you, maybe they'll get the message. Equally great.

Dear Alex

"I call my stepfather 'Larry.' What should my friends call him?"

Anything he asks them to. If he doesn't ask for anything specific, they should call him Mr. Whatever-His-Last-Name-Is.

Dear Alex

"I live with my dad, and he's divorced. He's 37 and goes out a lot with different women, and sometimes they stay over for days, weeks, or months. My problem isn't really with my dad, it's with those women. They act like they own the place. They're always telling ME what to do. I refuse, but this leads to some nasty scenes. I couldn't care less what they think, but I don't want to be a drag on my dad. How can I politely tell these women to get lost without upsetting my dad?"

That's a bit like asking "How can I politely throw a bucket of sludge at one Siamese twin without splattering the other?" It can't be done. When two adults are in a relationship, things that affect one affect the other. And your behavior is one of those things.

The situation you describe is a lapse of etiquette all around—his, hers, and yours. Let's start with your dad. Many people would disapprove of a parent bringing a string of overnight female guests into a house where impressionable minors live. Your disapproval won't necessarily change things, however, and might make them worse. In an ideal world, your dad (and ditto, Dad's dates) would be sensitive to the disruptive effect rotating "authority figures" can have on you. Thus, your father would invite each guest to enjoy your company and get to know you—but to leave the disciplining to him. He would make his expectations clear to them and to you. Each guest, recognizing that a "temp" has no claim to a parenting role, would happily agree. And you, absent provocation, would extend not rudeness but courtesy and social grace. Right? Right! But because he did and didn't, and she didn't and did, and you did and didn't, something's wrong.

The main problem here is that the situation is ambiguous. A guest, by convention, is allowed to be a total pain without suffering repercussions other than not being invited back again. (This appears to be what eventually happens with your father's lady friends.) Also by convention, a guest is not permitted to correct or chastise her host's children. At some point, however, if a "temp" stays long enough, she turns into a "long-hauler." When this occurs, she is no longer a guest, but a new adult member of the family. The change in job title vests her with the authority and responsibility to discipline, although even this may be limited by various factors (for example, if she's 22 and you're 17, this won't work).

How do you know when this change takes place? The easy answer is: when Dad marries her. The next easiest answer is: when Dad announces that she'll be living with you permanently as part of the family and he expects you to honor and obey and blah, blah, blah. Since Dad isn't announcing, the expectations for everyone's behavior are unclear.

Therefore, it's up to you to seek clarity. Go up to your dad at a calm moment when it's just the two of you. Say something like this:

"Pops, could we talk about what you expect of me when you have guests over? 'Cause I get upset when they act like a parent and tell me what to do. I know that's no excuse for my being rude, and I'm sorry for the times I've made a scene. But maybe if I try to be more polite, you could say something to them so that they won't try to be my mom, and that way everybody will get along better."

If you're reasonable and respectful in bringing up the subject, your dad should be responsive to your feelings. Have a problem-solving session (see pages 136–138). Brainstorm ways to improve the situation. Then put the best ideas into action. Since you can't control what other people do or say, there's always a chance the problem will continue. The best way to minimize the possibility of your father's friends disciplining you is to be as courteous and well-behaved as you can. If they still butt into your business, don't take the bait and get all riled up. Instead, respond as you would to any unauthorized comment from an insensitive adult.[*]

*FOR TIPS ON HOW TO DO THIS, SEE PAGES 368–371.

Dear Alex

"People always tell me how much I look like my mother. The thing is, she's not my biological mother. What should I say?"

Try "Thank you" or "Yes, we do look alike, don't we?" The people who say this are likely to be people you're never going to see again or with whom you have a superficial relationship. You're not required to correct them with a lengthy explanation:

"Oh, it's just a coincidence because, you see, even though she's raised me for the past 10 years, she's not actually my birth mother, who moved to Iowa with the owner of a stud farm when I was in first grade."

Keep in mind that introductions are simply a social shorthand. They are designed to paint relationships in broad brush strokes, to suggest people's roles and functions. There's no need to issue DNA samples or a genealogical chart every time an introduction is made. Nor is there any need to correct people who make an erroneous assumption—unless allowing the assumption to stand would cause harm or embarrassment.

For example, if the conductor of your school orchestra says "I really enjoyed meeting your parents at the concert," you can just say "Thank you." There's usually no purpose served in saying "Oh, that wasn't my father, that was my mother's steady boyfriend who lives with us." If, however, your father is coming to the next concert, you might want to say "Actually, that was a friend of my mother's. My father will be attending next week, and I hope you can meet him."

As long as everyone's comfortable, it's perfectly fine to refer to your half-brothers as "brothers," your stepmother as "Mom," and the parents of your father's second wife as "Grandma and Grandpa." And, if you're really stuck, you can just introduce someone as a "family friend," "one of my relatives," or simply by their name and leave it at that. That's a lot better than "I'd like you to meet the fiancée of my once-the-divorce-is-final ex-stepmother's soon-to-be husband's sister-in-law's son."

Dear Alex

"I never knew my father. About five years ago, my mother married this guy, Ed, who has two kids. I really love him and, as far as I'm concerned, he IS my father. But whenever he introduces the family, he always says 'These are my boys, Sean and Ed Junior, and this is Sharon's daughter, Lindy.' It really hurts my feelings, but I don't know what to do."

Of course it hurts your feelings. But it doesn't mean that Mister Ed feels any less love for you than he does for his biological children. Maybe he's just a methodical man who likes everything in its proper category. (He probably has one of those labelers so he can make signs to show where all of his tools go.)

When families reconfigure themselves, it's not always easy to come up with names that make everyone comfortable. Kids may not be sure whether to call Dad's third wife (with whom they are now living) "Kathy," "Mom," "Stepmother," "Mrs. Remington," or "Female Parental Unit Number Three." And she may not be sure whether to refer to you kids as "my kids," "my stepkids," or "Bill's kids."

The best thing to do in situations like these is get it out in the open. Tell Big Ed how you feel. Say "I love you as my real father, and I would like it if you would introduce me as your daughter." Chances are he'll be glad you told him, and he'll follow your wishes.

Dear Alex

"I'm 12 and an only child. I've been living with my father, and everything's been fine. But now he's getting remarried, and I just learned that he and my stepmother are going to have a new baby. I don't see why they need another kid. I'm thinking of running away."

It can be very upsetting when suddenly there's a big change in your life. You've been living happily with your father and BOOM, along comes the double whammy of a new stepmother and sibling. No wonder you're thinking about running away. But is that who you want to be? Someone who "runs away" from life? Nah. You can handle the rough spots.

One thing that can help is some "attitude work." It's natural to feel hurt that your father "needs" another kid when he already has you. Or to worry that he won't love you as much or have as much time to spend with you. Thoughts like these lead to the sort of anger and pain you're feeling. If you can question these assumptions and change your thoughts, you can change the way you feel.

For example, one of your assumptions seems to be that love is like a pie. The more pieces it gets divided into, the less there is for each person. Love doesn't work like that. Love is infinite. In fact, the more love someone gives, the better they get at it. A new child in the family may make your father love you all the more! He'll appreciate your maturity, your accomplishments, the help you are to the household; he'll remember with affection your infancy and early childhood; he'll thank his lucky stars that he doesn't have to change *your* diapers anymore.

Instead of thinking of the new baby as "taking something away," think of it as "giving something." Like what? Like the chance for you to be the best big brother any kid ever had. Or the chance to have someone who will adore and idolize you. Or the chance to learn exactly what babies are like and how they develop. Or the chance to feel good by helping out your father and stepmother.

In fact, this baby may come in quite handy. It could be a great tourist attraction for all your friends. Plus, a lot of people your age want more privacy and independence from their parents. If you stayed an only child, think of all the scrutiny you'd get. With a new baby, you can have a bit more breathing room. Yes, this kid-to-be sounds like good news. In fact, you may end up asking your dad and stepmom for six more.

Relatives

We can choose our friends, but not our families. And especially not our extended families. This is a shame, because relatives as a category seem to include a higher-than-average proportion of people who put one to sleep.

You might be tempted to avoid your relations. This would be a mistake. It's very important to go and see them. Why? Because this gives you the chance to stay in the good graces of rich aunts, to lord your successes over the less fortunate branches of the family tree, and to keep family feuds alive. Also, family is a precious thing. This is what people mean when they say "Blood is thicker than soy sauce." When push comes to shove, when you're down on your luck, your relatives will be there to offer love, support, and loans. So here's the kinetiquette you need to know.

Dear Alex

"Whenever relatives or friends of my parents come to visit, my mother tells embarrassing stories about me—like the one about the time I got splinters in my behind from sliding down a banister. And sometimes I'm right there in the room with them! Isn't this bad manners?"

Yes. But the road to rudeness is often paved with good intentions. These stories are probably nothing more than the by-product of your mother's boundless affection for you. Still, parents shouldn't talk about their children in front of them, as if they were statues. The only exception to this rule would be sharing news of your accomplishments:

> *"I know Shannon is too modest to tell you, but she just won a blue ribbon at the county fair for her woodworking project."*

The thing to do is to let your mother know how you feel when she does this. For best results, take the nonblaming approach.

Okay	**Not Okay**
"Mom, I get very embarrassed when you tell people stories about me, especially when I'm right there. I'd really appreciate it if you didn't do that."	"You ALWAYS talk about me in front of people and you have NO right to do that and I HATE it!"

Chances are good that your mother will respect your wishes, although you might have to repeat your request a few times to break her of the habit. If this doesn't work, the next time your mother embarrasses you, say to the audience "If you think that story was funny, wait 'til you hear the one about my mother going to the bathroom in the woods and—." At that point, your mother will remind you of something you have to go do RIGHT AWAY. But she probably won't tell any more questionable stories about you in your presence.

THE SURVEY SAYS . . .

When I asked parents "Have your children ever embarrassed you in front of your friends?" here's what they said:

YES 57%   NO 43%

"What was it they did?"

"Interrupted an adult conversation."

"Asked someone how much money she made."

"Took off his clothes in public."*

"Kicked in a school window in an emotional display."

"Talked back."

"Spoke disrespectfully to me and my friend."

"Used inappropriate language."

"Had a temper tantrum."

"Refused to do as I asked."

"Revealed family secrets."

"Didn't say thank you when given a gift."

*THE CHILD WHO DID THIS WAS ONLY THREE YEARS OLD, BUT LET IT SERVE AS A REMINDER TO ALL YOU TEENAGERS TO KEEP YOUR CLOTHES ON WHEN YOU ARE OUT WITH YOUR PARENTS.

When I asked parents "Have you ever embarrassed your children in front of their friends?" they said:

YES 75%   NO 25%

"What was it you did?"

"Things they tell me only kids should do."

"Reprimanded them in front of their friends."

"Told a story of an embarrassing moment from their childhood."

"Scolded their friends and sent them home."

"Dressed too formally."

"Said 'Why can't you be like so-and-so?'"

"Corrected their friends' poor use of grammar."

"Told them I loved them in front of their friends."

"Hung out with them too long."

Dear Alex

"My parents are always making me do things I don't want to do. Just this past week, I had to go to my cousin's for a barbecue, to church, and to this stupid art gallery opening of this artist friend of my parents. I don't see why I should have to do these things."

Much of childhood consists of doing things one doesn't want to do. But take heart. Once you grow up, much of adulthood consists of doing things one doesn't want to do. So, in many ways, you're getting excellent practice for later in life.

There are three reasons why you should do things your parents ask, even if you don't want to:

1. **It's only fair.** Your parents do many things for you that they would rather not do.

2. **It's satisfying.** The route to happiness is not found in giving to oneself, but in giving to others. When you fulfill your parents' requests, think of the pleasure it brings them rather than the pain it brings you. If you do this right, their happiness can become yours. (This is how parents endure doing things for their kids that *they* don't want to do.)

3. **It's in your own best interests.** Showing that you're willing to share in the boring, dreary, unfair, unpleasant tasks of life indicates to your parents that you're mature enough to share in the fun, exciting, adult privileges of life.

Dear Alex

"We have a very big family with lots of relatives. Practically every week we go to my aunts' or uncles' or grandparents' house for some boring meal or picnic. I don't even think my parents like doing it. But whenever I ask why I have to go, they just say 'Because.' That doesn't answer my question. Why do I have to go?"

Because.

This falls into the category of Doing Things One Doesn't Want to Do. For three reasons why one does these things, see the answer to the preceding question.

It's understandable that being smothered in the bosom of a tedious, nosy, gossipy relative isn't your first choice for a sunny Sunday afternoon. When duty calls, the thing to do is change your *attitude* so you can change your *experience*.

Instead of thinking of a visit to relatives as a dreary chore, think of it as an opportunity. Instead of being passive, be active. What about the visit bothers you the most? The food? Sitting around indoors talking? Doing the same thing every week? No other kids around? No matter what it is, you can do something about it. Volunteer to take charge of the cooking next time. Propose that people play a game, go for a hike, or visit a local attraction. Bring your bike and explore the neighborhood. If you see any kids, stop and talk to them. With your relatives' permission, ask a friend to come along. (You may have to promise that you'll accompany her to her relatives' at some future date.)

Another thing you can do is take charge of the conversation. Instead of being bored, think of things to talk about that interest you. This is a *great* opportunity to find out all about your parents. Go off with your aunts and uncles and grandparents and ask them for the scoop on your folks as kids.

What are your relatives into? Maybe one of them flies a plane or knows a lot about horses, computers, or photography. Use the visit as a chance to learn new skills and knowledge. Or incorporate one of *your* interests into the visit. Bring your guitar and play. Make a video. Offer to do some gardening. Whatever.

Dear Alex

"Whenever I go to my grandparents' house, they make a big point about dressing nice for dinner and using proper table manners. What should I do?"

Thank them.

Dear Alex

"I'm a 17-year-old girl. My grandparents live nearby, and I used to visit them a lot. But my grandfather always wants me to sit on his lap or give him a hug, and it just feels weird. I don't like it, and I've started making excuses about going there, but now my mother is mad at me and says my grandparents are very hurt that I don't see them anymore. I don't know what to do."

You've already done the best thing you could possibly do: You've removed yourself from a situation in which another person's physical contact makes you feel "weird." From this "safe" distance, let's look at your options.

In the most innocent scenario, it may be that your grandfather is an affectionate gentleman who has simply not recognized that his granddaughter has grown up. If that's the case, you could say to him:

"Grandpa, I really liked it when I was little and I sat on your lap, but now that I'm older I would prefer it if you treated me like a young lady."

Note that you haven't accused him of anything. You have "owned" the situation as a personal preference of yours, which is the essence of good manners.

A less innocent scenario would be that your grandfather is knowingly taking inappropriate liberties with you. The same request as above, delivered more pointedly, might work equally well in this case. By all means, tell your mother why you've stopped going to your grandparents'. In fact, she could be the one to say something if you would rather not:

"Dad, Rosa is a young lady now and feels uncomfortable when you cuddle with her as if she were a little girl. You're going to have to start treating her as a young woman and not a child."

These responses give your grandfather the benefit of the doubt. They assume that his behavior is unintentionally discomforting to you; hence, the polite tone of your reaction. It's important to note, however, that children don't always have to be polite or to respect their elders. Good manners may be suspended in the face of abuse. So, if your grandfather were to touch you in a private place under the dinner table, you have every right to jump up, interrupt the conversation, and shout "Grandpa, don't you ever touch me there again!"

If for some reason you can't talk to your mother, and if your grandfather (or any other relative) persists in behavior that feels "weird" to you, tell another adult you trust. This might be a teacher, counselor, pastor, rabbi, or friend. Don't give up. Keep looking until you find someone who will listen to you and help you.

Dear Alex

"I hate family reunions! All these relatives slobber all over me, and I end up with lipstick on every square inch of my face. What can I do to keep from getting kissed without being rude?"

Short of wearing a sign around your neck saying "Bubonic Plague Carrier," probably nothing. Overaffectionate relatives present a ticklish situation. It's hard to reject a kiss without insulting or hurting the person offering it. If you can, try to grin and bear it. Or grimace and bear it. Since your expression is hidden from the kisser, no one will be the wiser.

THE SURVEY SAYS . . .

And now, for some good news—just what you need after reading all about family life and strife.

When I asked parents "Which best describes how you feel about your children's manners and social behaviors?" here's what they said:

VERY DISAPPOINTED 0%

DISAPPOINTED 10%
SATISFIED 67%
VERY SATISFIED 22%

Just look at how satisfied most parents are. You know what this means? All of those rude kids belong to other parents!

What some parents said:

"My children are generally thoughtful and considerate of others."

"Their everyday behavior at home and in public is fine. We're proud of them."

"While there is room for improvement, I believe that my daughter genuinely cares that she not hurt people."

"My son is totally lacking in social awareness, but is inherently good-natured (except when he gets upset)."

"My children very seldom engage in behaviors that offend people in public. However, they have a lot to learn about good manners, such as expressing appreciation and praise."

"We have spent lots of energy teaching and role modeling, but they just don't get it. I sometimes question whether or not I expect too much when I see how other families deal with the same situations."

"I feel my children are respectful and considerate of others. I know they are well-liked, and I can rest easy knowing that when they are with others they will do the 'right' thing, such as pick up after themselves, offer to help with dishes or clean up, etc."

"Once in a while, they have to be reminded, but I guess we all do at times."

"Most of the time, my kids are great!"

You can also try sticking out your hand. This creates a barrier that would have to be breached if someone were to plant a juicy one on your face. Another strategy is to go for an air kiss by turning your cheek. You might also try saying "Better not kiss me. I've got a cold. I'd feel terrible if you came down with what I have." This, accompanied by a handshake and repeated every time you see the person, often gets the message across. Your final recourse is to be explicit about your feelings:

"Auntie Jane, how lovely to see you. No, no kisses, I'm getting too old for that. But let me give you a hug."

Chapter Quiz

1. *You walk in on your parents making love. Do you:*

a) laugh

b) say "You guys still do that?!"

c) leave quietly and immediately

2. *You and your brother are at each other's throats. The best way to settle your differences is to:*

a) run his underwear up the flagpole at school

b) run *him* up the flagpole at school

c) have a problem-solving session

3. *Your divorced dad just remarried, and you have a new stepmom. Since things may feel strange for a while, the best thing to do is:*

a) check into a hotel

b) treat her like dirt and hope she'll leave

c) be kind, respectful, and friendly

4. *Your parents have several of your aunts, uncles, and cousins over for the afternoon. You go to use the bathroom and discover that someone has really stunk it up. When you return to the company, do you:*

a) stick out your tongue, clutch your throat, and pretend to choke

b) ask "Who let off the butt bomb in the bathroom?"

c) say and do nothing

5

ARTFUL LODGERS

Taking the Guesswork out of Guestwork

If you gain just one piece of wisdom from reading *How Rude!*, let it be this:

**Get to know as many people as you can
who own beautiful vacation homes.**

Live according to these words, and you will find much happiness and free lodging. Success in this area depends on knowing how to be a considerate, responsive guest—the type whose departure will cause hosts to exclaim "Good guest!" and not "Good riddance!"

Good guests get invited back. *Great* guests get invited to stay when the hosts are away! This, of course, is your ultimate goal, for nothing can ruin a week at the beach more surely than hosts running around the house as if they owned the place. On the occasion of your first house-sitting assignment (this term is preferable to "mooching"), follow another guiding principle:

**When you stay in people's homes,
always leave them cleaner than you found them.**

This way, when your hosts next use their place, their jaws will drop at the sparkling kitchen, the freshly dusted furniture, the polished faucets, the vacuumed carpet, the shiny floors, and the scrubbed bathtubs. They will think *When can we ask him (or her) to house-sit again?* They may even experience a moment of embarrassment when they realize how dirty the place must have been upon your arrival. But this will quickly pass. They will whip out their calendar, flip through the months, and come up with all sorts of possible dates when they would love to have you clean, er, stay again.

Right now, you may be thinking *Won't all that cleaning cut into my sunbathing? Doesn't it take a lot of time?*

Of course it takes time. Which is why you need to invite a friend or two as *your* guests while you have the run of the place. (With your hosts' permission, of course.) Just be sure they're around at the end of your stay when the work has to be done.

This conscientious approach to guestwork has rewarded me with repeated stays in many beautiful homes over the years: a beach house in Delaware, a condo in Florida, a flat in London, townhouses in San Francisco and Washington, an estate in Connecticut, a ski chalet in Vermont, an apartment in Paris, a chateau in the Dordogne, a farm on Martha's Vineyard—to name but a few. My presence is so coveted by absent hosts that the demand far exceeds my supply. Thus, I sometimes find myself having to say "Hmmm, your villa in Tuscany for the month of May? I just don't know if I can squeeze you in this year. Does it come with a car?"

Your career as a guest began the first time you went to a friend's house to play. Now you get invited to dinners, parties, celebrations, and sleepovers. And one day, if you have shown yourself to be a guest above the rest, you, too, may be asked to house-sit.

Being a Guest with the Best
Responding to Invitations

Being a great guest starts with responding appropriately to invitations. Hosts find this helpful. It's rather difficult to prepare a reception for 100 people when you're not sure whether 9 or 99 are showing up. How you reply to an invitation is determined by how it's given.

Example #1: Informal Passing-in-the-Hall or Text Invitation

"Hey, fish face. How 'bout coming over after the game?"

This rather breezy invitation may be answered in kind:

"Okay. And don't call me fish face."

Example #2: Informal Telephone Invitation

"Oh, hi, Lei. Say, look, uh, my parents, see, like, um, they're letting me have a party this Saturday night, 'cept they don't know 'cause they'll be out of town, but anyway, it starts at eight, can you come?"

Since we're talking here about invitations rather than honesty, we'll overlook the subterfuge. This slightly more formal verbal invitation may also be responded to verbally:

"I think so. I'll have to check with my dad, but I think I can. I'll call you back tomorrow."

If Lei follows through on her promise to call, she will have done the right thing.

Example #3: Informal Written Invitation

Look what came in the mail!

To: Buffy

From: The Kissimees

It's a party!!!

What: Beach and Barbeque

When: 3:00–7:00 p.m., Saturday, August 11

Where: Jellyfish Beach State Park

Why: Why not!!!

Bring: Beach towel

RSVP: 626-555-6377 (by August 5)

This is an informal multipurpose invitation that probably has tacky little pictures (balloons, confetti, party hats) printed all over it. Nonetheless, it's very kind of them to invite you.

Note the "RSVP" at the bottom. This is French for *Répondez, s'il vous plaît,* which means *Veuillez me donner une réponse,* which means "Respond, if you please." But it doesn't *really* mean that. OF COURSE YOU HAVE TO RESPOND! Whether it pleases you to do so or not. The phrasing is just a social nicety not to be taken literally.*

Because the Kissimees included their phone number, you would call with your response. If they had given their address, you would send a short, friendly note:

Thanks so much for the invitation to your beach party. Count me in! I'll be there with bells on my toes and sunscreen on my nose!

*SIMILARLY, WHEN SOMEONE SAYS "WOULD YOU BE SO KIND AS TO PASS THE SUGAR?" YOU DON'T HAVE THE OPTION OF SAYING "NO."

Or:

Thanks for your kind invite! I regret that I must decline. I'm grounded until the year 2029!

You don't *owe* people an explanation for declining an invitation. In fact, it's rude for anyone to ask. This is because it either exposes the ugly truth ("You bore me to tears and I'd rather floss my teeth than waste an evening at your house"), or it forces you to concoct an excuse:

You: *"Because, uh, um, er, I have to babysit my little brother."*

The inviter: *"But you don't have a little brother."*

See what happens when people violate the etiquette of invitations?

Sometimes you'll want to give an explanation so the person will know that you really, truly wish you could have accepted. This is especially important if you hope the invitation will be reissued on another occasion.

Some hosts put "Regrets only" instead of RSVP on an invitation, the idea being that people should respond only if they *can't* attend. But what usually happens is something like this: You invite 200 friends, relatives, and acquaintances to your Bar Mitzvah Dinner Dance. Twelve call with their regrets. Does this mean you can safely assume that 188 will show up? Not on your yarmulke! It means that you can't distinguish those who haven't called because they have no regrets to extend from those who haven't called because they can't be bothered. So you're in the dark. And if you start phoning people you haven't heard from (so you can tell the caterer how many guests there'll be), those who are coming and didn't call because you said "Regrets only" will think you're daft for calling them.

So you're much better off using RSVP. You'll still have to check up on some people, but at least you'll know who. Give them a call and say "I hadn't heard whether you'll be able to come to my party, so I'm calling to make sure you got my invitation." They'll probably squirm and apologize (as well they should), but you'll get the information you need.

Example #4: Electronic Invitations

You have mail! Email, that is. And when you follow the link it's a cool invitation with music and animation—why, the card actually pops out of an envelope right before your very eyes. Your aunt is having a baby shower! Online invitations, whether via email, Facebook, or other social media, contain all the info you'll need to know—who, what, where, when, and what to bring. They even provide new ways to fail to RSVP.

Online invitations come with many advantages. Most are free; they're quick and easy to set up; you can choose from hundreds of designs; you can upload your own photos; you can create a link to directions; there's no licking or sticking; and they're paperless, so they don't cause the death of innocent trees in the forest. Plus, guests can RSVP with the click of a mouse. Disadvantages? They're not as personal as a written or verbal invitation so they might not be suitable for certain occasions; they could end up in someone's spam filter; you can't put 'em in a scrapbook.

If you do decide to send an online invitation, keep the following tips in mind:

- Make sure you include your name as the host; the type of party (e.g., dinner dance); the occasion (e.g., your graduation from driver's ed); the time and place; and how to RSVP.

- Consider carefully the options the site offers. Some may be pre-checked. For example, there's usually a feature that allows guests to see the entire guest list, and who's RSVP'd "yes," "no," "maybe," or "not on your life." Some hosts like this feature since it allows guests to see who's coming, contact each other for rides, chip in for group gifts, know who not to mention the party in front of (since they weren't invited), and decide not to go if a mortal enemy is attending. Other hosts don't like this feature and turn it off. They want to respect their guests' privacy and/or keep everyone in suspense.

- If the online invitation has a place for a personal message, be sure to include one. It makes the invitation more, er, personal.

- Proofread your invitation for typos and missing information before you hit "send." You don't want to email 200 invitations and then discover you've invited everyone to a Fool Party instead of a Pool Party.

Example #5: Formal Engraved, Calligraphed, or Handwritten Invitation

My, you're popular! Let's see what you're invited to:

> ꙮ
> *Mr. and Mrs. Ralphie Malone*
> *request the honor of your presence as their son,*
> *Bugsy Albert,*
> *performs his first tumbling routine on Friday,*
> *the thirteenth of March, at half after one o'clock*
> *Nadia Comaneci High School*
> *The Gymnasium*
> *Lakeville, New Jersey*
> *Luncheon following the cartwheels*
>
> *RSVP*
> *112 Lottery Lane*
> *Atlantic City, New Jersey 98765*

If the envelope contains nothing else, you must send a handwritten reply by mail to Mr. and Mrs. Malone at the given address. It's not enough to catch Bugsy at school and accept (or decline) verbally. He is not the host. Use good quality note-sized paper (frayed edges okay). Then get yourself centered (because that's what your reply to a formal invitation needs to be) and write:

> Miss Moll Flanders accepts with pleasure the kind
> invitation of Mr. and Mrs. Malone for Friday,
> the thirteenth of March, at half after one o'clock.

You may wonder why formal replies have to be centered and handwritten, and why, instead of just saying March 13 at 1:30 P.M., you have to spell everything out. BECAUSE IT TAKES MORE TIME, THAT'S WHY! It's assumed that people who issue and receive formal invitations either have a lot of leisure time or have other people who do their dirty work for them.

"But why do I have to tell the Malones when their stupid party is? If they don't know, who does?"

The Malones may be such social lions that they send out waves of invitations to all sorts of different events. This way, you let them know which particular party you plan to attend.

If the Malones are extra-smart, they'll make it extra-easy for you to RSVP. They'll include a response card and a stamped, self-addressed envelope along with the invitation. A response card is a bit like a miniature true-false exam.

Just fill in "iss," "s.," "rs.," or "r." after the multipurpose "M," followed by your name. Check the appropriate box. Stick the response card in the envelope and don't forget to mail it.

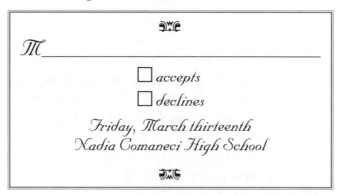

You *really* have to be lazy, inconsiderate, and/or disorganized to fail to reply to an invitation that includes a response card.

Guestly Behavior

Now that you've responded properly to the invitation, here are 12 protocols of proper behavior that will establish your reputation as a best guest.

1. Show up. You've made a commitment. People are counting on your scintillating presence and smiling visage. If it turns out that you are *not* able to attend after all, let your host know ASAP.

2. Be on time. Invitations to some events, such as open houses or skating parties, usually list hours of operation (for example, 4:00–7:00 PM). This typically means that guests are free to arrive and depart at any time within the stated range. Other events, such as sit-down dinners, graduations, and religious services, are time-sensitive and must occur on schedule. Don't be late. You'll either miss the main event or cause others to. What's worse, you might have to spend the rest of your life with some host's dried-out chicken on your conscience.

3. Don't arrive early. The air of relaxation hosts affect when they answer the door is an act. Five seconds earlier, they were running around in a state of total panic—cooking, polishing, setting, cleaning, counting, checking, supervising, and yelling at their kids. The last thing any host needs is some guest coming early and interrupting all this anxiety. So, if you've arrived ahead of schedule, sit in the car. Go for a walk. Feed the squirrels. Do anything—but don't ring that doorbell.

4. Never bring people who weren't invited. It's the host's job to make up the guest list. Guest lists reflect interpersonal likes, dislikes, obligations, and aspirations; the number of plates in the pie pantry; the number of Cornish game hens that can fit in the oven. Bringing one uninvited guest can poison the chemistry of an evening, disrupt the seating plan, and precipitate a shocking scandal. Despite these attractions, it's something you must never do.

"I hope you don't mind, but I brought a few friends."

For large events where an additional guest is unlikely to cause undue expense or problems for the host, you can ask for permission to bring someone. Another way to ask is to decline the invitation with an explanation:

"I'd love to come. But a friend from my old school will be staying with me that weekend."

This gives the issuer of the invitation the opportunity to say either:

"Oh, well, let's do it another time then."

Or:

"Bring your friend. I'd love to meet her."

5. Dress appropriately. Chances are you'll know just what to wear. When in doubt, ask your host or someone who's been to these types of affairs before. It's better to err on the side of being too dressy rather than not dressy enough; this shows respect for your host and the occasion. It's a lot easier to remove a jacket you brought than to put one on that you didn't.

6. Introduce yourself. The first thing a host wonders after all the guests have left is *Did they have a good time?* A good host creates a setting and supplies raw material for an enjoyable event. After that, it's up to the guests to liven things up with spirited conversation and positive energy. If there are people you don't know, introduce yourself. You may meet the person who will become your best friend for the next five years. If you see people just standing around, talk to them or ease them into your group. If you help make a party work, everybody will want you at theirs.

7. Don't hog the food. A fellow came (early!) to one of my parties and, while I scurried around with last-minute preparations, ate the entire beautiful oozy wedge of Brie cheese I had set out. Remember that the food is there for everybody's enjoyment.

8. Don't bring anything illegal. Underage drinking and the use of illegal drugs by guests puts hosts in legal and financial jeopardy. This is an abuse of their hospitality and is, therefore, rude, rude, rude.

9. Don't snoop. Even people with impeccable manners are tempted to know more about the private lives of friends and acquaintances than is wise or healthy. You must resist the temptation to peek into the closets, medicine chests, and bureaus of your friends, parents, and the people for whom you babysit. Once you discover those amazing photos in the bottom drawer, you'll never be able to think of those people in the same way again.

10. Do your best to be cheerful. True, it's a bad idea to bottle up your feelings. But it's an even worse idea to come to somebody's party and let your woes dominate the mood.

You've probably seen this happen. Everybody's looking forward to having a great time. The party starts . . . and then Aisha arrives. She looks tearful and washed out, and word quickly spreads that she was just dumped by Scott. Before you can say "What?!" the party has turned into a group therapy and crisis-management session. Six girls in the bathroom plan the demise of Scott; four guys in the basement talk about how Aisha had it coming; Ryan practices shuttle diplomacy between the basement and the bathroom; a group in the den tries to figure out where love went wrong; Sally gets on the phone to Scott; and the poor host wonders what happened to her party.

Of course, Aisha has every right to be upset. But she doesn't have the right to turn her misfortune into the theme of somebody else's long-planned event. She could have stayed home, or used the party to get her mind off of Scott, or talked privately to one or two close friends.

If one of your personal problems ever threatens to intrude on a public event, keep a stiff upper lip and remember that the show must go on. This will only add to the drama, for the next day people will say "Can you believe it?! Aisha didn't breathe one word about it last night!"

11. Don't linger. Watch for clues that the hosts wish to wrap things up. Such clues include yawning, turning off the music, turning up the lights, bringing things to the kitchen, and saying "I had no idea it was so late." Many hosts, however, are too polite to hint people out the door. So it's your responsibility to leave at a reasonable time. If an end time for the event was mentioned in the invitation, be prepared to honor it. Otherwise, look for signs that people are beginning to leave, and go with the flow. Sometimes a party will really click and continue waaaay past everyone's bedtimes. You'll know when this happens, because any efforts on your part to leave will be genuinely resisted ("Don't go. The party's just getting started!"). In such cases, it's perfectly fine to let your arm be twisted.

12. Thank the host. For informal teenagers' parties, it's usually enough to thank your host when you leave. It's nice to repeat your thanks the next day. If your host's parents helped sponsor the event, be sure to thank them profusely as well. For smaller or more formal events, a written thank you is never out of order and will identify you as an especially well-mannered individual.*

The Polite Overnighter

There are many advantages to spending the night at a friend's house:

- You get a vacation from your parents.

- Your parents get a vacation from you.

- You learn all sorts of things that Carlo's mother lets him do, which you can use as ammo at a later date.

- You learn all sorts of things that Carlo's parents *don't* let him do, which you can keep to yourself.

- Carlo's parents observe how polite and well-behaved you are and compliment your parents on it. Your parents wonder *Are we talking about the same kid?*

*FOR A REFRESHER ON WRITING THANK-YOU NOTES, SEE PAGES 43–45.

- You see how other families operate. You can go home to your parents and say "You know, you guys aren't that bad after all!"

Everyone benefits from swapping parents and kids on occasion. Here are the basics of the polite overnight:

Bring what you need. Arrive prepared. Bring your toothbrush, comb, pajamas, sleeping bag, lounging jacket, blankie, teddy bear, etc. If you wear orthodontic headgear or take medications, be sure to bring those, too. If you're in great demand as a guest, you may wish to keep a small overnight kit in your school locker or knapsack. That way, you can accept spontaneous invitations without having to make a pit stop at your house.

"Hi, Mrs. Canoli. It's real nice of you to let me stay over tonight."

Take home what you bring. The ideal sleepover guest leaves behind only two things: profuse thanks and fond memories. Everything else you bring should leave the premises when you do.

Do what your friend does. She'll give you valuable tips on family rules and routines. Follow them. For example, if she gets up to clear plates, you do, too. If she says "I have to be quiet after 10:00 PM," you do, too.

Don't do what your friend does. If your friend's behavior is at odds with that of being a good guest, don't go along. Instead, do what your friend's parents *wish* she would do. In this way, you become what's known as "A Good Influence." Good influences are welcome in any home. If you get caught in the middle and your friend asks "What are you being so perfect for?" you can say "Because I want to make sure your parents will let me stay over again."

Be nice to everybody. Your friend may ignore her parents or bully her brother. You, however, must exhibit courtesy to all living things in your host's household. This means being friendly to siblings, respectful to parents, and kind to animals.

Make the bed. Your friend may have an ongoing battle with her parents about neatness. You, however, should keep the immediate zone you occupy orderly and clean. Hang up the towels you use. Stow your gear someplace other than the middle of the living room floor. Take your dishes to the sink. Brush up your crumbs. And make the bed.

Ssshhh! Everybody knows that the whole point of a sleepover is *not* to sleep. (Whoever heard of a slumber party where people actually slumbered?) The successful nocturnal get-together requires:

- resisting parental suggestions of bedtime until the last possible moment, then

- taking ages to settle down, then

- having to rearrange where people are going to sleep, then

- getting up because you a) forgot to brush your teeth, b) have to go to the bathroom, and/or c) need a drink of water, then

- having a pillow fight, which brings Dad in for Warning #1, then

- talking about girls, boys, ghosts, and what's on the other side of the wall at the edge of the universe, then

- having an outbreak of giggling, which brings Dad in for Warning #2, then

- doing something not very nice to the first person who actually falls asleep, then

- drifting into slumberland one by one until everyone wakes up and denies that they fell asleep

However, if this fun-filled event is ever to be repeated, it's essential that you not interfere with the host family's sleep. The party mood can fade awfully fast after Warning #2 if things don't quiet down. Therefore, thoughtful sleepover guests will do their part to keep a lid on the after-hours noise.

Give advance warning. You may have allergies, phobias, and/or non-negotiable habits or eccentricities that require adjustments or extra effort on the part of your host. If so, advise your host ahead of time:

"I'd love to come, but I'm allergic to feathers and wool. Should I bring my own pillow and blanket?"

"It sounds terrific, but I'd have to sleep with my head facing west."

"I sleepwalk, so is it okay if we don't bed down in the hayloft?"

Don't overstay your welcome. You want to leave with your hosts wishing you could stay longer, rather than wishing you had left sooner. Don't hang around. Let people get on with their errands and other plans.

THE SURVEY SAYS . . .

Here, according to my survey of adults, are the 20 Rudest Things Their Children's Friends Do When They Visit:

1. Enter the house without saying "Hello" and/or leave without saying "Good-bye."

2. Not say "Please" or "Thank you."

3. Throw their shoes, jackets, and backpacks all over.

4. Are loud and disrespectful.

5. Question house rules.

6. Damage or break items without apologizing or offering to replace them.

7. Hint broadly for things they can't have, or ask for them outright.

8. Don't look parents in the eye.

9. Don't acknowledge adult's presence or engage in conversation.

10. Wander into every room of the house without asking permission.

11. Use bad language.

12. Text all the time.

13. Not pick up after themselves.

14. Whisper behind parents' backs.

15. Look in cabinets and drawers; touch things that are considered private (read mail on counter, flip through calendars, etc.).

16. Not thank parents for preparing snacks, picking them up, etc.

17. Wear hats at the table.

18. Take food or drink out of the refrigerator without asking.

19. Not call home for a ride, but wait for parents to suggest a departure time and/or to drive them home.

20. Eat like pigs. (Oink, oink.)

Five Ways to Be a Good Friend

As a guest in a friend's home—for a special event, an overnight, or longer—you have at least two hosts: your friend and your friend's parent(s). Your obligations toward each host differ. When you're alone with your friend, you can fight and make up, share secrets, insult each other, argue about what to do, and engage in all the other activities that make your relationship so special. When you and your friend are in her parents' presence, however, you must:

1. **Be discreet.** No spilling secrets!

2. **Be supportive.** ("Mrs. Huffy, did Kate tell you how she got the highest mark in Algebra?")

3. **Be courteous.** Your behavior is a reflection of your friend's judgment. If you're a jerk, she's the one who'll be in the hot seat after you leave.

4. **Be loyal.** Don't let your presence interfere with your friend's responsibilities toward her family. ("Come on, Kate. I'll help you with your chores and then we can go to the mall.")

5. **Like everything.** Particularly when you're staying longer than just one night, conscientious adult hosts will ask all sorts of questions.

Behind every question, though, they already have a decided preference, attitude, or agenda in mind. For example, the innocent question "Are you hungry?" may mean:

"I hope you're not, because I don't want to eat until much later."

"We're all starving and want to eat."

"I don't have the faintest idea when I feel like eating, and it would be great if I could use you to make the decision for me."

Without knowing which of these subtexts is at work, you risk stepping into a trap. You don't want to come across as demanding and spoiled, nor do you want to appear wishy-washy and indifferent. So what do you do? *Like everything.* Present yourself as an open-minded individual of limitless flexibility and curiosity. This doesn't mean you can't express preferences and guide your host toward the choices you favor. You just have to do it in ways that escape detection.

Let's say you're visiting a friend who lives in another city.

Your friend's parents ask: *"What would you like to see while you're here?"*

You say: *"I dunno."* (You sound lifeless, unimaginative, and bored. Not good.)

Or you say: *"I want to go waterskiing."* (You may be proposing something that's impossible to do or very undesirable to your hosts. Also not good.)

Or you say: *"I don't care."* (Ouch! Three strikes! Try again.)

They ask: *"What would you like to see while you're here?"*

You say: *"Oh, I've been so excited about the trip, I haven't even thought about it yet. I've always wanted to go to Disney World, but what are some of your favorite things?"* (You float an idea but pass the ball back to your hosts.)

If you couch your desires in accommodation, you'll usually get what you want while maintaining your status as an ideal guest. The following remarks can be infinitely reworked to respond to almost any question:

Desire	Flexibility	Parry
"I've heard wonderful things about the seafood . . .	. . . but it all sounds so delicious . . .	. . . what did you have in mind?"
"It's so quiet here I could sleep forever . . .	. . . but there's so much I want to do . . .	. . . when do you usually get up?"
"I've always wanted to try hang gliding . . .	. . . but I'll have many opportunities . . .	. . . what do you feel like doing?"

Dear Alex

"Is it bad manners to play tricks on people while they're sleeping?"

You mean, like moving their bed into the middle of the freeway? Strictly speaking, it's quite rude to take advantage of a human being at his or her most vulnerable state. How would you like to be tucked away in slumberland, drooling onto your pillow, a sweet smile on your face, while your friends see how creative they can be with bowls of warm water, shaving cream, scissors, magic markers—and you?

You could, as a group, agree to suspend the manners prohibition against such subversive deeds. This often occurs among friends who have regular sleepovers. They know that this sort of activity is likely to happen—indeed, they consider it one of the high points of the evening. As long as the humiliation is evenly rotated, nobody should object.

Being a Host with the Most

Let's look at things from the other side of the doorbell—when you're the host rather than the guest.

Hosting the After-School Guest

This is hosting at its most informal. Strays brought home from school may enter and exit so quickly that their presence goes unnoticed—except for the unwashed dishes on the kitchen counter. Sometimes after-school visitors travel in packs, roaming from house to house in search of the perfect snack.

In time, these frequent fliers may come in for so many landings at your home that their status changes from guest to quasi-family member. This confers special privileges and responsibilities. The privileges include increased access to your family's trust, affection, and refrigerator. Your parents will drop the host facade, and "adopted" offspring will get to hear genuine family squabbles and see your mother without makeup. But this comes at a cost. Honorary family members lose the untouchability of guests. Without this protection, they are prey to the same obligations and expectations as their "siblings." This means kitchen cleanup, trash duty, and "don't slam the door."

Your responsibilities as a host for after-school guests are simple:

Communicate with your parents. Is it okay to bring friends home from school without asking? What if your parents aren't there? Can you invite friends to stay for dinner? Avoid misunderstandings by negotiating and knowing your parents' expectations ahead of time.

Introduce your friends to your family. In general, parents like to know the names of those who are eating their food, watching their television, sprawling on their furniture, and leaving their smelly shoes by the door. You can keep introductions simple:

> *"Mom, this is Paulo. He's just moved here. And you already know Biff, Bill, Bob, Ben, Bart, Brett—and Sticky."*

Explain house rules. If you don't want to be embarrassed by cameo parental appearances, you'll need to assume the role of disciplinarian. This puts you in that delicate spot between the maxim that "guests can do no wrong" and the reality that "guests can be total pains in the butt." The way to resolve the conflict is with tact. Phrase your admonitions so they come across as concern for your guests' comfort and/or safety:

> *"It would be best if you didn't go into my sister's room. She's a terror when intruded upon, and I wouldn't be able to guarantee your safety."*

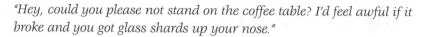

"Hey, could you please not stand on the coffee table? I'd feel awful if it broke and you got glass shards up your nose."

Alternately, you can state house rules as parental pronouncements that you're required to enforce. This is one of the handiest uses to which parents can be put. For example:

"I'm afraid my parents don't let us play croquet with the crystal."

"If you want to throw the football you'll have to go outside. My parents don't allow team sports in the house."

"My folks get very upset when people paint the dog."

Help with extra burdens. Your parents may truly enjoy your friends and welcome the fact that their house doubles as a community recreation center. Still, running a home for wayward teens involves extra work and expense. Do your part to lessen the load. After you've finished eating, put away the food (if there's any left). Stack plates, glasses, and silverware in the dishwasher (or help wash and dry the dishes if there's no dishwasher). Straighten the furniture. Your parents may not begrudge the extra 73 gallons of milk, 144 loaves of bread, and 35 quarts of peanut butter your friends consume each week if you do your part.

Assume the role of activity director. Few things annoy parents more than bored kids hanging around the house. If being bored is one of your favorite things, do it outside your parents' vision. Otherwise you're going to hear "If you guys have nothing to do, the garage needs cleaning." To avoid this scenario, be prepared. Suggest to your friends that you could shoot some hoops, watch a movie, play a game, redecorate your bedroom, etc. Bothering siblings doesn't count as a legitimate activity.

Don't use guests to get away with murder. Some teenagers use the presence of visitors to violate household regulations. They're banking that their parents aren't going to scold them in front of their guests. This doesn't accomplish much. For one thing, the scolding will just come later. For another, it takes unfair advantage of parents who respect their kids' feelings enough to refrain from public reprimands.

Hosting Groups

Your first responsibility is to issue a clear invitation. Maybe friends who have been to your house 17,892 times know that "Ya wanna come over Friday?" means "Do you want to take the bus home from school with me, stay for dinner, go to a movie, spend the night, and sleep until 1:00 PM the next day?" Individuals less well-acquainted with your routines and verbal shorthands might be confused by such an economical invitation.

Before your guests even arrive, they should know what it is they're arriving for. Otherwise they'll worry about what to wear, what to bring, how to pack, when to tell their parents to pick them up—and you will have made them uncomfortable before they even set foot on your premises. Therefore, every invitation, be it written or verbal, should contain the following information:

The Event: Is it a birthday party? A swim party? A Super Bowl party?

The Time: When does it begin and end?

The Place: Is it at your house? The skating rink? The park?

The Hosts: Who should one blame, er, thank for this delightful occasion?

The Attire: Snowsuits? Bathing costumes? Formal wear?

The Response: Just show up? Regrets only? RSVP?

In addition, the invitation should contain any special instructions or reminders essential to the event's success and the guests' comfort, such as:

Please bring rope, shaving cream, and sleeping bags. Sunblock and insect repellent recommended!

As the host of an event, your primary responsibility is to make your guests feel welcome and at ease. Your secondary responsibility is to see that this doesn't occur at the expense of the furniture. Accordingly:

- **Answer the door.** Guests feel dumb if they ring the bell and nobody comes to the door. They don't know whether to ring again and risk feeling dumber, or to walk in and risk being mistaken for a burglar.

- **Greet your guests.** Say "Hello. I'm glad you could come." Every arrivee should be made to feel that now the party can begin.

- **Take coats.** Visitors often arrive with coats, bags, and, one hopes, gifts. Relieve your guests of these burdens or point out where they can put them.

- **Say "Thank you" if you are handed a gift.** But don't dump your guest to go open it. You wouldn't want to give the impression that you're more interested in her presents than her presence.

- **Offer nourishment.** Take beverage orders or, if it's self-serve, point your guests toward the food and drink.

- **Make introductions.** Smooth your guests' entry. Introduce them to people they don't know. Provide conversation cues, as in "Beefy's been my trainer for the past year at Club Cholesterol."

- **Circulate.** Spend time with all your guests. Don't invite people just to ignore them for the evening.

- **See that everyone has a good time.** Make sure that no one is excluded from group activities. Similarly, make sure that no one feels pressured into group activities they wish to avoid.

- **Thank your guests for coming.** When the party or event is over, tell your guests how much you enjoyed having them. Walk them to the door. Their departure should not be something that goes unnoticed. Rather, portray it as a sad event that, with sufficient fortitude and time, you hope to get over.

Dear Alex

"I get invited to a lot of parties, and I want to have one of my own. But my parents won't let me. Aren't you supposed to invite people who have invited you?"

Certainly. This is known as *reciprocation*. It's how we thank people for their hospitality—and ensure that invitations continue to flow in our direction.

In my experience, parents who forbid their children to entertain usually have their reasons. These range from the practical to the fantastical, the sound to the silly. If you don't know the source of your parents' objections, find out. Approach your folks when they're in a good mood. Pose your question as intellectual curiosity rather than angry accusation ("Could you please tell me your reasons for not wanting me to have a party?" as opposed to "Why can't I have a party? That's no fair! Everybody else's parents let them!"). Once your parents have told you their reasons, thank them and drop the subject for now.

Meanwhile, come up with a plan that addresses their concerns. Too expensive? You'll share the cost. House too small? You'll have your party at the rink. Fear of crashers? You'll have your friends from the football team as bouncers. If it's still no go, maybe you could cohost a party at a friend's house.

You can also reciprocate with kind gestures. Buy or make a gift. Bake a pie. Your friends will know you appreciate their invitations, even if you're not able to respond in kind.

Dear Alex

"My parents said I can have a party, but there's no way they'll let me invite all the people I want to. How do I invite some without offending others?"

First, don't issue the invitations at school. Mail them or call people at home. Word will still get out that you're having a party, and people will still know they weren't invited. But at least the process will be a little less public. Since you're going to work so hard to make the party a success and show your parents how responsible you and your friends are, chances are you'll be able to have a second party. This means you can tell those friends you were unable to invite:

> *"I really wanted to invite you to my party, except my parents said I could only have a few people. But I'm going to have another party, and you have to promise me that you'll come."*

Dear Alex

"There's a girl I'm friends with. I've invited her to sleepovers and parties at my house, but she's never invited me to her house. Isn't this rude?"

One of the hardest lessons in life is that we can't control other people, no matter how much in need of our guidance they may be. Does your friend invite other friends over? If so, they may be students from her dance class, or people she doesn't think you'd mix with, or friends she wouldn't be able to see otherwise—guest list categories to which you don't belong.

If your friend doesn't invite anyone over, it may be that she has never been taught the principle of reciprocation. Or perhaps her parents don't allow her to have guests. Or it could be that she's ashamed of her house or some family secret. Since you don't know the reasons, you shouldn't take offense or be hurt.

Your friend has the right to invite whomever she wishes to her house. Even the best of friends have social engagements that don't include each other. Since it would be rude of you to ask "How come you never invite me over?" your choices are as follows:

1. **Maintain the status quo.** If you enjoy her company and she seems happy to have you as a friend, the issue of where you see each other shouldn't really matter. It's just part of the package deal.

2. **Stop inviting her to your house.** The lack of reciprocation may mean that she wants to cool the friendship. If this *isn't* the case, she may eventually say something like "Hey, when can I sleep over again?" You could reply "I don't know, how about doing it at your house sometime?" Since you're not exactly inviting yourself over, this would pass manners muster. Her response may give you a better idea as to why she's never invited you over.

Staying in Hotels

From time to time, you may be the guest of the Hiltons, Marriotts, or Super 8s. On these occasions, you're likely to be accompanied by your parents. Hotels are often the settings for parent-child rudeness. This is because the two generations have different and conflicting agendas. Parents want to unpack when they get to the room. Kids want to go to the pool. Parents think beds are for sleeping in. Kids think they're for roughhousing on.

So we can all get a good night's sleep, here are some guidelines for proper hotel behavior:

Walk, don't run. You know those long passages with all those doors? They're not tracks for running a 100-yard dash. They're corridors for getting to your room. Even if you've been cooped up in the car all day, even if you have so much energy you feel like you're going to explode, try not to run in the hallways, bang on the doors, jump on the bed, or play tennis against the wall. Instead, go for a walk. Find the pool. Use the health club.

Watch the volume. Keep conversation, roughhousing, and radio or television volumes at a level where they won't disturb your neighbors. During sleeping hours (no, that's not 3:00 AM to noon, that's 11:00 PM to 8:00 AM), be extra sure that you're not committing decibel mayhem.

Don't push all the buttons. If you're in a hotel with those neat glass elevators, just enjoy the ride. Go where others need to go. Don't make someone traveling from the 40th floor to the lobby stop at 39, 38, 37, 36, 35, 34, 33, 32, 31, 30, 29, 28, 27, 26, 25, 24, 23, 22, 21, 20, 19, 18, 17, 16, 15, 14, 13, 12, 11, 10, 9, 8, 7, 6, 5, 4, 3, and 2 before getting to 1.

Leave some ice for the other guests. If it's 98 degrees and you use the ice machine to fill your cooler chest, there may not be any ice left for anyone else. Ice machines are meant for beverages, not igloo construction. If you need a lot of ice, buy a bag at a nearby convenience store.

Resist temptation, Part One. Many hotel rooms come with small refrigerators called mini-bars. They are so named because the portions of candy, chips, cookies, and beverages are microscopic. The prices, however, are not. Don't take anything without your parents' permission. Otherwise you could end up with a $48 bill for M&M's and a soda.

Resist temptation, Part Two. In crummy hotels, about the only things you can take with you for free are fleas. In finer hostelries, the innkeepers provide an array of little items guests are welcome to take. These include soap, shampoo, conditioner, hand cream, shower caps, postcards, three-inch-long pencils with no erasers, travel literature, little chocolates on your pillow, and fruit. (Do not confuse food set in the room with food set in the maxi-price bar.) Hotel rooms also contain many other items you might wish to have as souvenirs. These include towels, bathrobes, remote controls, radios, blankets, pillows, pretty paintings, and air conditioning units. If you take any of these items, the management does not think of it as availing yourself of the establishment's hospitality. They think of it as stealing.

Don't be a total slob. If you're with your parents, they'll probably help you with this.* A lot of people have the same attitude toward hotel rooms that they do toward rental cars—namely, that they can trash 'em to pieces. Of course, there's the other extreme: Some people actually *clean up* their hotel room and *make the bed* because they're embarrassed to have the maid see a mess. Needless to say, this approach is a bit excessive. But there is a middle ground. When you leave, bed linens should be on the bed, not on the floor. Toilets should be flushed. Towels should be on racks or counters. Messy trash such as food and wrappers should be in the wastebaskets. The room should look as if somebody slept in it and used the bathing and toilet facilities, not as if the Mardi Gras passed through on its way to New Orleans.

Petiquette

You're sitting on a sofa as a guest in somebody's home. Their dog comes up to you and nuzzles at your crotch. Do you:

    a) pretend it isn't happening

    b) punch the dog and ask your host "What kind of a pervert animal is this?"

    c) firmly steer the dog's snout away, allowing the owner the opportunity to make apologies and say "Down, Casanova! Bad dog!"

Sooner or later, you're bound to be the target of an overly inquisitive animal sticking its nose where it doesn't belong. You have the right to "just say no" to unwanted advances from four-legged suitors.

*NOT WITH BEING A SLOB. WITH BEING NEAT.

TRUE STORIES

FROM THE MANNERS FRONTIER

Quelle Horreur!

I was dining at my favorite restaurant in Paris *(Paree)* when a large dog *(chien)* came in (no, it was not a French poodle) accompanied by its owner and her companions. While the owner affected indifference *(indifférence)*, the dog proceeded to wander all about the place, nuzzling customers and begging at tables.

Now, I, for one, do not appreciate having a dog sniffing at my sweetbreads while I'm eating. So I summoned the waiter and requested that the dog be restrained so I could eat in peace *(manger en paix)*.

The dog's owner, having nothing to tie it with, "borrowed" from the coat rack *(porte manteau)* a long, knit scarf that belonged to someone else and used it to tie up the dog.

Vraiment!

Of course, such overtures would never happen in the first place if pet owners exercised proper authority over the nonhuman members of their family. Call me unfriendly, but I have never developed a fondness for creatures that place muddy paw prints on my clothes or shake their wet, smelly, flea-infested hair in my face. The same parents who send their child to his room for the tiniest infraction are offended if you suggest that they send Romeo the Rottweiler to his kennel for assaulting the guests.

I am all for animal rights, so long as said animals keep their paws, snouts, and slobber to themselves. If they don't, it's the owner, not the animal, who is guilty of being rude.

So that you are never the agent of such a *faux pas,* here's all the petiquette you need to know to keep a well-mannered menagerie:

Control your pet. Guests should not be assaulted or smothered with affection by any member of your household unless you have established that said guests enjoy such attention.

Pick up after your dog. Doggie-doo is a *don't* if it's done in a public space or on someone else's property. I take my hat off to those dog walkers who bend down with an inside-out plastic bag to pick up the poop and carry it away. When I see this supreme act of conscience and public-mindedness my first thought is *Eeeeyooo!* My second thought is *Bravo!*

Keep Fido on a short leash. Nothing spoils one's day like tripping over a dog leash and getting a face full of concrete. If you're walking your dog where other people are present, keep the leash short.

Respect the allergies and/or phobias of your visitors. Some people are allergic to feathers and dog and cat hairs. Others are terrified of animals. If you discover this to be the case with any of your guests (often the ones covered in hives or cowering behind the credenza), take appropriate steps to rectify the situation. Let Rover romp in the backyard. Put Felix in the family room and Polly on the porch. Tell Boris the Boa to go stretch out in the sun and leave your visitor alone.

If you belong to the category of pet owners who refuse to restrict their animals' freedom, you must let guests know this in advance. You can say:

"I can't wait 'til Friday, when you're coming over after school. I just wanted to let you know that I have a very friendly ferret who is as dear to me as Mumsie and Popsie. I'm sure you'll all get on famously, but . . . ."

Most people will respond by telling you how much they're looking forward to meeting your family—bi-, quadri-, and octapeds alike. If, however, your friends are ferret-averse, you must be prepared to forgo them in favor of your animal's freedom.

Never bring a pet with you unless you have received permission. In this regard, pets are just like people. You would never bring an uninvited friend to a party without first asking the host. By the same token, you would never bring an uninvited animal. Ask first.

Assume responsibility for your pet's behavior. If your pet bites someone, soils her clothes, or damages her property, it's fair and proper for you to assume the costs of this misbehavior. Whether you take it out of your dog's allowance later is for you to decide. At the time of the incident, however, there's only one thing to do: Apologize profusely and make things right. Don't attempt to shift or minimize your responsibility.

Wrong	**Right**
"I'm sure it will brush right off when it dries."	"I absolutely insist on having it dry cleaned for you."
"It didn't even break the skin."	"We must get a doctor to look at that right away."
"Dogs will be dogs."	"I should have been watching. Fifi and I will come over tomorrow afternoon and plant some new ones."

"Don't worry. Rex just LOVES children."

If you've been effective in assuming your rightful responsibility, the victims of your pet's misconduct will often minimize the occurrence, as in:

"It's only a small slobber. No big deal."

"It's just a little bruise."

"I meant to transplant those tulips anyway."

You can then defer to their protests. But you will have fulfilled your duties as a polite pet owner.

If you're neither the pet nor the owner, you're the *pettee*—someone who comes into contact with other people's pets. Here are some protocols for being a polite pettee:

Be kind to animals. It's rude to cut worms in half or throw cats from a moving train. Treat animals you dislike as you would humans you dislike—with courtesy. Don't tease or torture them.

Ask the pet's owner for guidance. With some animals you meet, it will be love at first sight. An instantaneous bond will spring into force. This is called *animal magnetism*. You'll know without words that it's fine for the two of you to nuzzle and snuzzle all over the ground in an ecstasy of furry friendship. At other times, you, or the pet, may be unsure of the bounds of your relationship. In such cases, ask the owner if it's all right to pet the dog, feed the horse, stroke the bird, or tap the turtle.

Be firm but polite about your limits. Animals have an unerring instinct for identifying those who don't like them. Therefore, in a room of 12 people, the animal will invariably bestow its attentions on the one person who doesn't want them. If this person should be you, you're well within the rules of petiquette to say so. You may first address yourself to the offending animal. Remove its body or head from where you don't wish it to be. In a firm yet respectful voice, say "Down" or "No. Don't lick me there." Many animals are sensitive to the language of rejection and will go off in search of greener pastures. If, however, the animal doesn't take the hint, turn to its master and say:

"Reginald, could you please keep Reggie Jr. away from me? He's the cutest little koala I've ever seen, but I'm just not comfortable around animals."

If your host doesn't control the little beast, you might innocently remark:

"Have you noticed the price of dry cleaning these days?"

Or:

"I can't believe what they're charging at the emergency room lately to treat an animal bite."

Dear Alex

"My neighbor's dog goes to the bathroom in our backyard. This is a real pain because my friends and I like to play baseball there. What can I do?"

This certainly gives new meaning to the term "sliding into home." Your first recourse is to provide the dog's owner with the scoop on the poop. You do this in a polite tone of voice that suggests you're certain he's unaware of the problem (since otherwise it wouldn't be happening). Ask him if he could please mind his own dog's business—especially as it has been done in your backyard up to now.

If no positive results are forthcoming, then the caca is going to hit the fan (or, as the case may be, the rotary blade). At this point, you'd be doing your neighbor a kindness if you and your friends shoveled up the offending offal and placed it in a prominent location on his lawn, perhaps near the front door of his home. It's always polite to return things guests have left at your house. You might include a courteous note for your neighbor:

> Dear Mr. Smith,
>
> Your dog left this at our house. I just wanted to see that you got it back.
>
> Signed,
> A Friend

Chapter Quiz

1. *The reason you must strive to be a perfect guest is:*

    a) you get more food that way

    b) a happy host is more likely to pay for everything

    c) you never know when Santa is watching

2. *You're invited to a party you don't want to attend. The proper response is to:*

    a) picket the event

    b) tell the host you're coming but not show up

    c) toss a stink bomb through the window

3. *You're entertaining two friends from school for the afternoon. One of them is getting quite rowdy, and you're afraid he's going to break your mother's favorite lamp. You should immediately:*

    a) bean him with a frozen burrito

    b) break the lamp yourself so he won't get blamed

    c) say "Chill, dude! That lamp's lookin' mighty peeved and I'd feel terrible if it electrocuted you."

4. *It's fine to bring a pet with you to someone's house as long as:*

    a) it's not in heat

    b) it matches their decor

    c) your dog can beat their dog

5. *You're looking down from the 16th-floor balcony in one of those fancy atrium hotels. A kid comes up to you and asks if you want to have a spitting contest. The best response is to:*

    a) yell "Ptooey!"

    b) prepare a loogie

    c) say "Sure, but you have to aim for the bald guys."

6. *Every written invitation should include:*

    a) the entire guest list, showing who's going with whom

    b) a detailed breakdown of how much the party is costing

    c) chocolate mints

6

SCHOOL RULES

Civility in the Land of Tater Tots

Schools, by their very nature, are breeding grounds for rudeness. You've got stressed-out kids competing for grades, popularity, and college admissions.

You've got homework, dissections, tests, and report cards.

You've got wedgies, squeaky markers, dumped books, and metal detectors.

You've got prepositions, expositions, prohibitions, inquisitions
Computations, conjugations, confiscations, condemnations
Allegations, altercations, instigations, indignations
Derivations, deprivations, degradations, defamations
Preparations, palpitations, protestations, on-probations
ARRRRRGGGGGGHHHHHHH!!!!

People wonder why there isn't more politeness in schools. How much politeness can there be in a place where toilet stalls have no doors? Where, every 43 minutes, you get bowled over by a million stamping sneakers? It's hard to keep etiquette uppermost in mind when your entire future depends on knowing that in 1492, Marco Polo launched a line of men's sportswear.

It's a miracle there's as much politeness in schools as there is. But there needs to be *more*. Why? Because teenagers spend more of their waking day in school than anyplace else. And they deserve a school climate that's safe, respectful, and friendly.

The *climate* of a school is essentially what it feels like to be there. Research shows that the better a school's climate is, the more likely its students are to enjoy school, do well academically, behave morally, and stay out of trouble with the law. Schools with outstanding social climates share a number of characteristics including:

- a prideful sense of community
- explicitly stated values
- high expectations for student behavior and achievement
- respect for the needs and feelings of others
- close student-teacher relationships
- creamed corn for lunch every Tuesday

Translated into English, this means that in the best schools—schools that students enjoy attending and do well in—people are polite to one another. To come up with a code of school etiquette, we need to know more about what makes a school climate polite or rude. If only we could find out what students and teachers think about the climate in their school. Guess what—we can! Why? Because in my survey, I asked students and teachers all about . . .

Rudeness in the Learning Environment

The first thing I did was get a general idea of whether rudeness is a problem. Hold on to your baseball caps, because when I asked teachers "Do you think students today are more polite, less polite, or the same as when you were growing up?" 73 percent said "less polite."

And when I asked those same teachers how they felt about the manners and social behaviors of the students they teach, 57 percent said "very disappointed" or "disappointed," vs. 43 percent who said "satisfied" or "very satisfied."

Before you conclude that these teachers were just dumping on kids, you should know that roughly the same proportion of teachers (71 percent) also said that *adults* are less polite today than they were a generation ago. In fact, they blamed parents, media, and society for the sorry state of kids' manners. As one teacher put it:

"I don't think ANY of us spend enough time teaching manners and politeness."

Another teacher said:

"Schools and students today are but a reflection of society's tolerance for lower standards of behavior."

Before you say "You see, it's not our fault," keep in mind that soon *you'll* be the adults. So it's up to *you* to raise the standards. To do this, you'll need to identify what those standards should be. So let's look at rudeness in schools from the teachers' perspective. Then let's look at it from the students' perspective. Then let's break for lunch. When we return, let's come up with a code of etiquette that will make the school climate warm, enriching, supportive, respectful, and joyful.*

*WOULD YOU SETTLE FOR BEARABLE?

THE SURVEY SAYS . . .

When I asked *teachers* to describe the Rude Things Students Do to Teachers—things that cause them to go home at night, tear out their hair, and sob "Why do I do this?! I can't go on. I'm going to find a nice, stress-free job clearing minefields!"—I came up with this Top 15 list:

1. Talk while the teacher is trying to teach.

2. Not raise their hand.

3. Not say "Please," "Thank you," and "Excuse me."

4. Talk back.

5. Text, check email, surf Internet during class.

6. Make no attempt to hide their boredom, irritation, or anger.

7. Not pay attention.

8. Not take responsibility for their actions.

9. Not make eye contact.

10. Lie.

11. Swear.

12. Say "whatever."

13. Continue a behavior after being asked to stop.

14. Use disrespectful body language (rolling their eyes, slouching, etc.).

15. Not prepare assignments.

THE SURVEY SAYS . . .

When I asked *teenagers* to describe the Rude Things Students Do to Teachers, here's what they said:

"Disobey them." • "Humiliate them." • "Mimic them." • "Swear at them."
"Ignore them." • "Threaten them." • "Contradict them." • "Interrupt them."

"Talk back." • "Talk during class." • "Text during class."
"Make weird noises." • "Make stupid jokes."

"Keep doing something after they tell you to stop."

"Tell them you hate their class."

"Gossip or spread rumors about the teacher."

"Pack up before class is over."

"Insult their looks and/or sexual orientation."

"Make obscene gestures behind their back."

"Skip class." • "Come late." • "Come unprepared."
"Get up and leave." • "Fall asleep." • "Not pay attention."

"Copy." • "Take advantage of a sub."
"Cheat." • "Complain about the work."
"Mess up books." • "Not show up for appointments."
"Pass notes." • "Not raise their hands."

"Hit them." • "Make fun of them." • "Lie to them."
"Burp in their face." • "Call them names." • "Be a total nuisance."

"Not do the work. Teachers go to great lengths and really do their best to teach. Students who don't do schoolwork make their teachers' lives meaningless. Making a life meaningless is rude."

THE SURVEY SAYS . . .

When I asked *teachers* to describe the Rude Things Students Do to Other Students—things that cause teachers to go home at night, tear out their hair, and sob "I can't stand it when students are so mean to each other!"—here are the Top 15:

1. Say cruel things to each other.

2. Call each other names.

3. Put each other down.

4. Hit, push, shove, and cut in front of each other.

5. Single out a scapegoat.

6. Gossip or spread rumors about someone behind his or her back.

7. Trip each other in the hallways.

8. Dump books.

9. Take personal belongings without asking.

10. Exclude each other.

11. Fail to apologize to each other.

12. Invade each other's space.

13. Interfere with each other's education.

14. Tease about sexual orientation and call each other "gay" or "fag."

15. Bully.

THE SURVEY SAYS . . .

When I asked *teenagers* to describe the Rude Things Students Do to Other Students, here's what they said:*

The Top 10

1. Call you names.

2. Taunt you for no reason.

3. Deliberately pass gas near you.

4. Bully you.

5. Talk about you behind your back.

6. Exclude you.

7. Spread rumors about you.

8. Put you down if you're different.

9. Play with your feelings.

10. Embarrass you to make themselves look good.

*WARNING! THE LISTS YOU'RE ABOUT TO READ MAKE THE TEACHERS' LIST SOUND LIKE IT'S DESCRIBING THE BEHAVIOR OF CHOIR BOYS HAVING AN AUDIENCE WITH THE POPE.

More Rude Things Students Do to Each Other

"Ignore you." • "Tell inside jokes in front of you." • "Tell someone's secrets."
"Have an attitude with everyone who isn't their friend."
"Borrow things without returning them."

"Run into you without saying 'Excuse me.'" • "Step on your shoes or sneakers."
"Sexually harass you." • "Beat you up." • "Flip you the middle finger."
"Trip you in the hallway."

"Curse." • "Gossip." • "Brag." • "Shove." • "Lie." • "Spit." • "Tattle." • "Kick."

"Make prank calls." • "Burp the ABCs in your face."
"Text and talk at the same time." • "Steal your boyfriend or girlfriend."

"Trick you into doing things." • "Call each other gay."
"Close your locker on purpose when you just opened it."
"Talk trash about you on Facebook or Twitter."

"Dis your family." • "Send you fake letters or breath savers."
"Ditch you intentionally." • "Call you degrading ethnic names."
"Not give you a chance." • "Insult your body size and looks."

You're probably sitting there with plumes of smoke rising from your ears, thinking: *Hmmm . . . rude things students do to teachers; rude things students do to each other. Isn't something missing? Like all the rude things TEACHERS do?*

You're absolutely right. School climate is just as much a function of how teachers behave as it is of how students behave. So let's turn the spotlight on *les professeurs*.*

*WARNING: TEACHERS READING THIS ARE ADVISED TO SIT DOWN AND TAKE A DEEP BREATH. YOU'LL BE SHOCKED TO LEARN HOW RUDE OTHER TEACHERS CAN BE!

THE SURVEY SAYS . . .

When I asked *teenagers* to describe the Rude Things Teachers Do to Students, here's what they said:

The Top 10

1. Make fun of us in front of the whole class.

2. Deliberately ignore us.

3. Give us too much work.

4. Punish the whole class for something one person did.

5. Call on us when they know we don't have the answer.

6. Say sarcastic things.

7. Talk down to us.

8. Accuse us of doing things based on suspicion, not facts.

9. Not listen to our side of the story.

10. Play favorites.

More Rude Things Teachers Do

"Yell at us."

"Snap at us."

"Call us names."

"Make us feel stupid."

"Say that we're good for nothing."

"Underestimate our intelligence."

"Overestimate our intelligence."

"Call on certain people more than others."

"Not call on us when we raise our hand."

"Act impatient."

"Act like they know everything."

"Assume that all teenagers act the same."

"Assign too much homework."

"Accuse us of cheating."

"Lose our work and blame it on us."

"Grade according to their frame of mind."

"Let the rest of the class know a student's grade."

"Not return our papers or tests."

"Fail us because they don't like us."

"Take their crabbiness out on us."

"Breathe on us with their bad breath."

"Act like their class is the only class in a student's schedule."

"Treat us like we're still in grade school."

"Say that we can't use the bathroom."

"Judge us by our clothes or speech."

"Take points off for talking in class."

"Act nosy about our personal lives."

"Think of us as 'teenagers,' not as human beings."

"Make boring lesson plans."

"Assign busywork."

"Not take the time to explain things."

"Act like they don't want to help us."

"Break up good discussions."

"Refuse to negotiate."

"Assume the worst without letting us explain."

"Put down our ideas."

"Condescend. Condescend. Condescend."

"Most teachers are mature and smart enough to not be rude to students."

There you have it. Enough rudeness at school to last a lifetime. The point of reporting these rude behaviors is not to start an argument. Students and teachers can have different opinions about what's boring, or how much work is too much, or whether a given remark is disrespectful. The point is to make everyone aware of the types of attitudes and actions that injure feelings and interfere with every student's right to learn—and every teacher's right to teach—in a safe, respectful school climate.

Dear Alex
"Is not doing your homework rude?"

It depends on whether this is a pattern or a singular event. If something makes it impossible for you to finish an assignment, that's not rude at all. These things happen. Even teachers aren't always able to grade papers or prepare lessons on time because something unexpected comes up. The best thing to do is to offer an honest explanation:

> "I'm sorry, Mrs. Rousseau, but I wasn't able to do my assignment last night. There was a gas leak in our neighborhood and we had to evacuate our house. But I'll bring my paper in tomorrow."

If you're usually responsible about doing your homework, your teacher should accept your explanation and appreciate your forthrightness.

But what if you've really fallen behind? This, too, is not necessarily rude—if you have a legitimate reason. For example, you may be feeling depressed, or your parents may have just split up, or other students may be bullying you. Being sad, upset, or scared doesn't mean you can ignore your schoolwork. But sometimes circuits get overloaded, and no matter how hard you try, you just can't cope. Most teachers are very understanding and supportive of students who show initiative and take responsibility for their actions and education. You don't have to tell a teacher personal details about your life if this makes you uncomfortable. You could say something like this:

> "I'm sorry I've gotten so far behind in my work. I'm having some problems at home, and I haven't been able to concentrate lately. I want you to know that I really like your class, and I'm trying to get caught up again."

When *is* it rude not to do your homework? When you're just goofing off. This behavior affects others. When some students don't live up to their part of the teacher-student bargain, the pace of learning slows for everyone. Class discussion is hindered when students are unprepared. Teachers often feel hurt, frustrated, and dispirited. But the person who suffers most when you don't do your homework is *you*. Why? Because you restrict your options for the future. You miss out on the pleasures and benefits of learning. You create a reputation that is unlikely to garner much respect. Why be so rude to yourself?

Dear Alex

"What's so bad about getting good grades? In my school, kids act as if it's cool to flunk everything. They tease me all the time and treat me like a traitor because I do well."

You have my sympathies. But you'll also have the last laugh.

Why do some students badmouth others who get good grades? Because they're jealous, resentful, and hurting; because their own insecurity makes them think you look down on them; because your grades remind them of how poorly they're doing; because they know, deep down, that you're going to be able to do things and go places in life that they, most likely, will not. Dissing you is a defense mechanism.

What can you do? First, be sure you're not flaunting your grades or projecting a sense of superiority. Then approach the people who tease you. Ask about their interests and activities; congratulate them on their accomplishments. They may stop bothering you once they see that you're a regular person who doesn't put on airs.

Finally, hold your head high. Don't feel you have to apologize to anyone for your intelligence, motivation, or success. If people ask you how you did on a test, say "I did fine." If they press you, say "I've decided to keep my grades private from now on." Your astute friends will figure out why.

Dear Alex

"There's this teacher who really likes me, and people keep calling me his 'pet.' I don't think this is very polite of them. It's not my fault."

Ideally, teachers shouldn't let their personal likes and dislikes influence the way they relate to students. Good teachers make an effort to treat all students fairly. But it's only natural that they will like some students more than others, just as you like some teachers (and friends) more than others.

In most cases, students who are labeled "teachers' pets" are simply those who are interested in the subject and treat the teacher with respect. (Most teachers are turned off by students who butter them up.) If people bug you about being a teacher's pet, you might say:

> *"It's not my fault if Mr. Lime finds my winning personality, alert mind, and cheery demeanor so appealing. I'm no different in his class than I am in Miss Lemon's, and you know she can't stand me."*

If, however, you're being phony with the baloney, your classmates have a genuine beef and the right to rib you. So, if you don't want to get lamb-basted for being a bratwurst, hold your tongue and go cold turkey with the sucking up. After all, your reputation is at steak.

Dear Alex

"My school does random drug testing. It's already happened to me. I don't use drugs, and I don't think I should have to take the tests. Isn't there some etiquette rule against this?"

There certainly is. Good manners are based on extending the benefit of the doubt. They reflect the assumption that one's fellow citizens are trustworthy people of goodwill who, if treated with respect and fairness, will respond in kind. Random drug testing violates these principles. It says to children "We don't trust you. You must, on demand, prove that you're not behaving improperly—even if, from all outward appearances, you're a model student."

You've probably heard the standard argument for drug testing: "If you're not using drugs, you have nothing to fear." But would politicians and school board members submit to random hidden cameras in their homes to prove that they're not doing anything illegal?

People in favor of drug testing in schools insist that the tests are no different in principle than sobriety roadblocks, metal detectors, or screenings given to employees such as nuclear plant operators. But they are. Driving, flying, and working in certain fields are voluntary privileges that, if practiced irresponsibly, may put the lives of others at risk. If people object to the "test," they don't have to drive, fly, or apply. Schoolchildren, however, are required by law to attend school. They can't avoid being tested by choosing to stay home.

Students aren't yet driving school buses or piloting jumbo jets. Until they are, politeness demands that school administrators show more interest in the process of education and less in the process of elimination.

Classroom Decorum

This doesn't refer to the color of the drapes in Room 201. Rather, it refers to those behaviors that have proven over time to be most conducive to teaching and learning, such as shooting spitballs, texting—oops, wrong list. I meant behaviors such as paying attention, coming prepared, and respecting the rights and opinions of others.

Why is etiquette important in school? Because etiquette is the first line of defense against unpleasant and illegal behavior. When people refuse to control themselves voluntarily, all sorts of disagreeable things happen. In school, students find themselves harassed, bullied, suspended, afraid, and unable to learn. In the "real world," the collapse of etiquette leads to anarchy, lawsuits, and violence. Wouldn't you rather say "Oh, excuse me, I'm terribly sorry" than be slapped with a summons?

Everyone benefits (except lawyers) when people behave civilly to one another. If you don't want etiquette to play hooky from your school, look at the codes of conduct on pages 198 and 199. They're guaranteed to create a warm, productive climate for students and teachers alike.

Dear Alex

"Teachers in my school act like they don't want to help you. Isn't that their job?"

It certainly is. The fact that something is somebody's job, however, doesn't relieve others from the duty of requesting services politely and acknowledging them gratefully. This may be a problem in your school. A teacher's willingness to help is not encouraged by students who whine "I don't get this stupid stuff. Why do we have to learn it anyway?" Nor do teachers feel warmly toward students who slack off all term and then appear the day before the final demanding private instruction.

You may be suffering the fallout from a school climate where these attitudes and actions prevail. If you need help, approach your teacher politely and respectfully. You might say:

> *"Excuse me, Miss Pinchley, I'm having trouble understanding why Attila the Hunk nailed Lex Luthor to a door with 97 species during the Spanish Imposition. Is there some time when you could please help me?"*

With this well-mannered query, you'll awaken all the reasons Miss Pinchley went into teaching in the first place. You'll be a ray of sunshine and a breath of fresh air in the otherwise dank swamp of her classroom. (**Tip:** If your teacher has turned into a human storm cloud, unmoved by the courteous supplications of an eager young mind, you'll need to turn elsewhere for help—to a classmate, another teacher, or, if the problem persists, to your parents, guidance counselor, or principal.)

Dear Alex

"Sometimes I don't understand what's going on in class. But I'm afraid I'll look stupid if I ask a question."

Don't worry about appearing stupid. In fact, asking questions is a sign of intelligence. It means that you're listening and you care about learning. Teachers know that when one student doesn't understand something, chances are neither do others. Therefore, a good teacher appreciates questions. And you'll be a hero to your classmates for having the guts to ask the very question that was going through their minds.

Dear Alex

"What do you do when you're so confused you don't even know what question to ask?"

Raise your hand and politely say:

> *"Excuse me, Mr. Plato, I'm so confused I'm not even sure what question to ask. Could you please explain that again?"*

Mr. Plato will probably ask the class if others are confused, too. When all hands go up, he'll take another stab at the lesson.

Dear Alex

"Some kids in my school suck up to all the teachers. They're such brownnosers that nobody likes them. Is it okay to be rude to them?"

Rudeness can never be justified by the color of anybody's nose. We had brownnosers in my day, too. (Let's take the high road and call them "apple-polishers.") Those were the kids who, if the teacher said "You don't have to take notes on this," would write that down in their color-coded notebooks.

Someone who does well in school, turns in her homework, acts responsibly, raises her hand, participates in class, and treats her teachers and classmates with courtesy and respect is not an apple-polisher. She is a lovely human being whose friendship you should seek.

So what, then, *is* an apple-polisher? It's someone who does all of the above—while giving off fumes of superiority. In other words, it's someone whose considerate behavior is transparently self-serving. Why don't we like these people? Because they give etiquette a bad name! They appropriate its tools for their own advancement. The benefits of good manners should be a by-product of such behavior, not its cause. Etiquette becomes apple-polishing when insincerity ceases to be invisible.

THE 30 DO'S AND DON'TS OF CLASSROOM ETIQUETTE FOR TEACHERS

Do

- treat all students with patience and respect
- listen to your students
- avoid sarcasm
- encourage students to ask questions when they don't understand
- take the time to explain things
- keep your personal likes and dislikes from affecting student-teacher relationships
- empathize with the pains and pressures of adolescence
- treat students as individuals
- expect the best, not the worst, from students
- model tolerance and compassion
- allow students to go to the bathroom
- reward responsibility with extra privileges
- treat boys and girls equally
- make corny jokes at your own risk
- use breath mints

Don't

- ignore students
- talk down to students
- accuse students based only on suspicions
- punish the whole class because of one person
- call on students just to embarrass them
- make fun of students in front of the whole class
- prejudice other teachers' opinions of a student
- invade a student's privacy
- play favorites
- keep students after class just to inconvenience them
- take your own personal problems out on students
- assume the worst without letting a student offer an explanation
- judge students before getting to know them
- assume that all students who pass gas are doing it on purpose
- condescend

THE 30 DO'S AND DON'TS OF CLASSROOM ETIQUETTE FOR STUDENTS

Do

- listen to your teacher
- think before speaking
- clean up after yourself
- come to class prepared
- raise your hand to be called upon
- make eye contact when speaking and listening to others
- compliment each other
- remove your hat in class
- address your classmates and teachers with kindness and respect
- keep your hands and feet to yourself
- say "Please," "Thank you," "Excuse me," and "I'm sorry"
- find another response for displeasure besides anger
- work diligently in class, even if you must pretend to be interested in a subject or assignment
- talk directly to the person with whom you have a conflict, rather than to everyone else
- remember that teachers have feelings, too

Don't

- bully others
- be physically or verbally aggressive
- sexually harass others
- ignore a reasonable request
- talk when a teacher or classmate is talking
- take another's property without permission
- backbite or spread rumors
- put people down to look cool
- interfere with each other's learning
- act bored or fall asleep in class
- make hurtful comments about another person's looks, abilities, background, family, ethnic heritage, or sexual orientation
- pressure others into doing things that are mean, harmful, or illegal
- belch or pass gas on purpose
- text, game, Facebook, etc., during class
- cause the markers to squeak

To Cheat or Not to Cheat?

Over the years, many students have wondered *Is cheating bad manners?* Although that question ignores the more important issues involved in cheating, politeness demands a response.

What's *right* and what's *polite* are not always the same. A well-dressed gentleman could walk into a bank, remove his hat, allow a woman with two small children to go ahead of him in line, and then, when he reaches the teller, say "Excuse me, I'm terribly sorry, but this is a robbery. Could you be so kind as to hand over the money?" His manners are flawless, but his morals leave something to be desired.

Cheating is similar. If you use a crib sheet *and* no one notices *and* the teacher doesn't grade on a curve, cheating is not bad manners because it doesn't affect anyone but you. That does not, however, make it right. And if your cheating causes your classmates any discomfort, or places them in disciplinary jeopardy, or alters their class standing, then it definitely *is* bad manners and wrong besides.

The main defense you hear for cheating is that "everybody does it." Everybody dies, too, but that doesn't mean we should all rush out and croak. Cheating deprives you of self-respect and self-confidence. If you cheat, chances are your friends and teachers will know and think less of you for it. How can you feel good about a grade you don't deserve? How can you believe in your abilities if you don't put them to a fair test? How can you be mellow if you live in constant fear of being caught?

If you're honest, hardworking, and passionate about something, there are a lot of routes to success besides good grades. Do the best you can *without* cheating. Your sense of pride and self-worth will carry you a lot further than fake A's.

Dear Alex

"There's a kid in my class who always tries to copy off my paper during tests. I don't like it, but I don't know what to do."

There's a range of responses available to you:

Change your seat. This may not be possible in classes with assigned or ritualized seating (seating by cliques).

Rat on the cheater. Most schools have such a strong student code against ratting and tattling that *you'd* end up in the doghouse. So you may want to rule this out.

Semi-rat on the cheater. You could inform your teacher in general terms that "some people" aren't doing their own work on tests. This

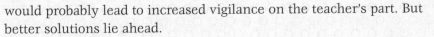

would probably lead to increased vigilance on the teacher's part. But better solutions lie ahead.

Cover your paper. This is probably the best initial action to take. Shielding your answers sends a strong message to the cheater that you're not willing to let her copy from you. It also sends a message to the observant teacher.

Speak to the cheater. Some students cheat because they're lazy or not interested in doing their schoolwork. Other students cheat because they're under great pressure to achieve. These students often feel confused, anxious, guilty, and ashamed. If you confront someone copying your answers, etiquette requires nothing more than polite limit setting:

"I'm sorry, but I don't let people copy my papers."

It's not your job to lecture anyone on her morals. You could, however, reach out to the person by adding:

"But I would be happy to help you or explain how to do the problems later, if you're having trouble."

She may tell you to take a flying leap off a quadratic equation. Or she may be touched and heartened by your kind offer. What do you have to lose?

Dear Alex

"All my teachers make their big assignments due at the same time. It's impossible to get everything done. So a few times I used websites that let you buy term papers. They even custom write them if your assignment doesn't fit a paper they already have. I go over each paper to make it better before turning it in. My friend says this is cheating. I say it's just using the Internet for research."

Of course it's cheating. There's a big difference between writing your own paper—using the Internet to locate primary and secondary source material, which you credit, to help you generate your own ideas—and buying a paper somebody else wrote.

I know teachers can really pile it on. And it's tempting to use the vast resources of the Internet to make life easier. But when you hand in an assignment as your own that came from Papers "R" Us, you're not being truthful about its authorship. Passing off someone else's work as your own is plagiarism.

Apart from the dishonesty of cheating, which in and of itself should be enough to make you stop buying papers, you're likely to get caught sooner or later. There's software out there for detecting plagiarism, and more and more teachers are using it. Imagine the shame and broken trust if you were caught. School is where you're supposed to learn how to manage time and write papers. If you cheat to get by, you're shortchanging yourself. Why not talk with some of your classmates. See if they feel overwhelmed in the same way. If so, you could form a small group and approach a few of your teachers to see if you can negotiate alternate due dates. Nobody wins if unrealistic pressure causes students to stress out so much that they can't produce their best work.

The Internet is a fabulous resource for information—some of which is gold and some of which is garbage—but it's not a personal research assistant that will write your papers for you. Don't expect strangers to do your homework. While it's fine to go to blogs or networking sites to research your topic, questions like *"Hey, I gotta write a paper on Lewis and Clark. Anybody know anything about them?"* are not appreciated. Specific questions like *"Does anybody know if Lewis and Clark ever stayed at a Motel 6?"* are always welcome.

Dear Alex

"My friend and I are very good at math. We like doing problems, but our teacher loads on so many it's ridiculous. If 10 will show that you know how to do them, she assigns 100. So what my friend and I do is this: She comes over to my house, I do half, she does half, and we swap answers. We almost always get them all right. Would you call that cheating?"

I would call that efficiency.

Getting Along with Teachers

If you follow "The 30 Do's and Don'ts of Classroom Etiquette for Students" on page 199, and if your teachers are sane and reasonable people, then getting along with them should be a breeze. However, you may encounter difficult teachers or special circumstances as you wend your way through school. Because it pays to be prepared, here's some advice to keep in mind for those challenging times.

Dear Alex

"I have one of those names that people always mispronounce. What should I do when a teacher says it wrong?"

Sensitive teachers make a point on the first day of school of asking any student whose name is not Pat, Chris, Bob, Luke, Grace, or Kate, if they are pronouncing it right. If your teacher doesn't do this, your best bet is to go up to him after class. This is because people bristle at being corrected in public. Don't say "You pronounced my name wrong," as this implies that your teacher made a mistake. Instead, say "Excuse me, Mr. Baggypants," and then tell Mr. B. how you like to pronounce your name. Be good-humored about it. There's no way a teacher will know that your parents, in their infinite wisdom, decided to name you "Karen" but pronounce it "Cahr-in." Or that you're French and therefore your name, Guy, rhymes with "key" and not with "sky."

Your teacher will be impressed with your good manners, and you'll be off to a great start for the year.

Dealing with the Problem Teacher

The global pool of teachers, like any group of people, includes many kinds. There are the saints, the nurturers, the lovable eccentrics, the quirky comedians, the inspiring orators, the dedicated mentors. But, by the law of averages, there are also bullies, crabapples, weirdos, and pontificators with superiority complexes and delusions of grandeur. And they will, on occasion, do things that are hurtful or unfair.

Outside of school, you can usually ignore or stay away from people you don't like. This isn't possible in the classroom. So what do you do? You follow the Five Golden Rules for Protesting the Bad Behavior of People in Authority:

1. Choose your moment well. Let timing work to your advantage. If you can possibly avoid it, don't approach a teacher who's in a rush or a foul mood. Wait until she has more time, patience, and warmth in her heart. Then say:

> *"Mrs. Moonshine, I wondered if I could please talk to you about something. Is this a good time?"*

2. Talk in private. Nobody likes to be challenged publicly. Audiences cause people to care more about scoring points and saving face than solving problems. If the injustice must be dealt with immediately and publicly, it's all the more important that you adhere to rules 3–5.

3. Empathize. Teachers are human, too. A few words of understanding from a student can go a long way toward laying the groundwork for a fruitful discussion. Try these for openers:

"It must be really frustrating when nobody pays attention."

"I bet it's hard to teach when no one's done the homework."

4. Explain, don't complain. Accusations—"That's not fair!" "You never listen to anything anybody says!"—put teachers on the defensive. If you're upset at something a teacher did, explain the situation from your point of view. Try not to mention the teacher's actions at all. For example, instead of saying "You had no right to make me take the test," say:

"I know I should have studied while I was out sick, but my headaches were so bad I couldn't read. My grade in this class is very important to me, because the only way I can go to college is if I get a scholarship."

5. Offer alternatives. When teachers are unjust, it's often because they're angry, hurt, frustrated, or at their wits' end. Help them. Maybe the class could hold a problem-solving brainstorming session for what to do about stealing or bullying. Tender your own suggestions for dealing with a situation:

"Now that my headaches have gone away, I wondered if I could write an extra-credit paper on the material the test covered and try to bring up my grade."

Most teachers admire initiative. If you're not just trying to evade responsibility or get out of work, you'll be surprised by how many teachers are willing to give you a fair shake.

Dear Alex

"There's a teacher who keeps the whole class after if one person does something wrong. I don't think this is fair. What can I do?"

First, let's acknowledge that you're learning a valuable lesson from her: Life isn't fair. Sometimes you can do something about it, sometimes not. But it's worth a try.

Go up to her at a calm, private moment. Without accusations, empathize, explain, and offer an alternative:

"I'm really sorry that someone broke your plaster bust of Beethoven. I know it meant a lot to you. But keeping the whole class after doesn't solve the problem, and it punishes a lot of innocent people. I missed half of history and got a detention. One of my uncles runs an antique shop. If you want, I can ask him to keep an eye out for Beethoven busts."

This approach focuses on solving the problem rather than blaming the teacher. She just may go along with it.

"And we're going to STAY here until the person who did it confesses."

50 YEARS LATER . . .

Dear Alex

"Every time I get called to the board, I get nervous and embarrassed and make these stupid mistakes, and then the teacher makes fun of me in front of the whole class. I hate it!"

Go up to your teacher in private. Explain that you get nervous at the board. Tell him how you feel when he makes fun of you. Suggest alternatives. Perhaps, instead of making you do the problem yourself, he'd be willing to let you lead the class in doing it. Or maybe you could complete a couple of extra problems for homework. If he insists that you continue to work at the board, he may at least be more sensitive to your feelings.

TRUE STORIES

FROM THE MANNERS FRONTIER

School Can Be Cruel

Few situations in life afford greater opportunity to show how much you don't know than being called to the blackboard (the ancient precursor to whiteboards).

I still remember my 10th-grade math class. I tried to cultivate an aura of invisibility so I wouldn't get called on, but it didn't always work. One day I was assigned a problem at the board. I struggled through it and stood there like a flagpole. Dead silence. Then a fusillade of chalk ricocheted around the room. (Throwing chalk was this teacher's trademark.) The teacher launched into a tirade against stupidity—mine for the mistake I had made, and the class's for not detecting it.

Making fun of a student is inexcusably rude. Teachers who shame kids for their mistakes should be ashamed themselves. Some students may contribute to the problem by being class clowns or troublemakers, but that doesn't excuse the teacher. For, as we all know, Two Wrongs Don't Make Polite.

The good news is: Even though you may feel humiliated and upset for days after the event, your classmates will forget about it the moment you return to your seat. They're much too worried about being called on next to focus on your errors.

If the problem persists, talk to your guidance counselor or parents.

Dear Alex

"A teacher accused me of stealing in front of the whole class. I didn't take anything. Later, they found out who did it, and I didn't even get an apology. I'm so mad!"

You have every right to be. It was rude of your teacher to accuse you. Since the accusation was public, the apology should be public. If your teacher doesn't offer one voluntarily, go up to him in private and say:

> *"Mr. Meaney, a lot of people in the class still think I stole Tracy's money and don't believe me when I say I didn't. I'd appreciate it if you could tell the class that it was someone else and I had nothing to do with it."*

Giving Teachers Gifts

The only "present" allowed in the classroom should be that which follows the calling of one's name during roll. The giving of gifts to teachers places burdens on the parents (who have to pay for them), the students (who have to choose them), and the teachers (who have to pretend they're thrilled to get them).

I speak from experience, having spent many glorious years inspiring young minds in the school environment. I witnessed the giving and receiving of truckloads worth of perfume, scarves, and calorie-laden candy. It's true that teachers deserve a bounty of appreciation. But gratitude should reflect heartfelt thoughtfulness rather than robotic ritual. If you *really* want to give a teacher a present, here are the best that money can't buy:

- *Your attention and enthusiasm throughout the year.* This is the greatest gift of all. Trust me.

- *A warm letter of appreciation.* Tell the teacher how much her teaching, example, and support have meant to you. Follow-up notes may initiate a lifelong friendship.

- *Support for better schools and teaching conditions.* Many schools are falling apart for want of money. Windows are broken, walls are peeling, and there aren't enough books to go around. While teachers make pennies, people who dribble make millions. If you want to give something back to your teachers, be an activist for higher salaries and increased funding for education. You can circulate petitions, speak at school board meetings, and encourage people to vote.

- *Something you make.* Take a photograph of the class and get everyone to sign it. Write a poem. Record a song you wrote. Create a work of art or craft. These are the gifts a teacher will want to keep forever.

In lieu of the above, a store-bought gift is fine—*if* it shows you made the effort to observe your teacher's interests. During the year, you can learn a lot about a teacher from what he shares with you, the way he dresses, and the physical environment of the classroom. If you discover that your teacher loves begonias, wild ties, and Tuscany, a floral print cravat from Italy may be just the ticket.

Coping with Crushes on Teachers

It's wonderful to have a teacher you really like. In fact, most kids have crushes on one or more teachers before they finish school. These crushes can be based on feelings of attraction and romance, or feelings of respect and admiration. Either is normal and natural.

It's fine to "worship" someone or to have fantasies about the person—as long as this doesn't get in the way of your schoolwork or social life. If all you can do is dream about a particular teacher, if your grades are dropping, if you're cutting yourself off from your friends, then it's not a healthy situation. Perhaps you feel the need to be close to an adult and are projecting this onto your teacher. Are you having problems that you yearn to tell someone about? Are you and your parents having conflicts? Your desires to be loved and listened to may fuel a crush when what you really need is someone to confide in. Talk to a school counselor, a relative, your parents, or an older sibling about your feelings. This may take some of the pressure off.

What if it seems obvious that your teacher likes you, too? He (or she) probably does . . . but not in *that* way. Your attentiveness, enthusiasm, and friendliness are pleasurable and rewarding to him as a teacher. But it would be a mistake to interpret his fondness as romantic interest. Because he's a teacher and you're a much, much younger student, he can't have a relationship with you—no matter how much you (or he) might wish it. This would be unprofessional and illegal.

Don't tell the teacher how you feel about him. This would force him to "reject" you—which would be painful and awkward for both of you. At the end of the year, write him a thank-you note. Tell him how much you enjoyed his class and appreciated his help and interest. But don't tell him about those daydreams of you and him alone on a tropical island.

Dear Alex

"There's a teacher I can't stop thinking about. I think he likes me, too. Is it okay to give him a Valentine's Day card?"

If students in your school have traditionally given cards to teachers, then yes, it's okay. If not, it's not.

If you do give a card to a favorite teacher, make sure it's not mushy or romantic. Better yet, if you give a card to *one* teacher, give cards to *all* of your teachers.

Suffering Substitutes

What is it about the presence of a substitute teacher that brings out the very worst in students? Why does a normally well-behaved class turn into a pack of spitball-lobbing rowdies when the "real teacher" is away? For what reason do otherwise polite students delight in tormenting temps?

Let's not bother with rationales. Our focus here is on etiquette. And it's bad manners to make subs squirm (or, as has happened on more than one occasion, burst into tears and flee the room).

"But our regular teacher lets us do this."

Substitute teachers enter the classroom at a disadvantage. They come on short notice, don't know the students, are unfamiliar with the teacher's rituals, and may never see the class again. They lack the teaching tools and clout that come from having historical knowledge of, personal relationships with, and future report cards for the students. To take advantage of this is the height of rudeness. It is like (and I mean no disrespect to the legions of wonderful substitute teachers) torturing a turtle on its back.

While it may be common practice in your school to give subs a hard time, that hardly makes it proper. The presence of a substitute presents you with a rare opportunity to reap the rewards of good manners. This is because the behavior of the class reflects upon the absent teacher. Being helpful and polite not only makes the sub feel welcome and respected, but also makes her think highly of your teacher. So when the sub leaves her report (which all subs do), it will be full of accolades for those students who made her stay so pleasant.

Bullying, Bigotry, and Bad Behavior

A parent of my acquaintance told me the following story. During a visit to her son's school, she was walking down the hall toward his classroom when two students emerged from the media center. One bumped into the other, and the following verbal exchange occurred:

"Watch it, @#$%&!"

"YOU watch it, @#$%&!"

"Make me, @#$%&!"

"I'll make you, @#$%&! Get over here and I'll kick your @#$%&!"

"Yeah, I'll kick your mother's @#$%&!"

"@#$%& you!"

"@#$%& you, you @#$%&!"

Did this happen at a high school? Or even a junior high? Had my friend overheard two teenagers showing off? No. She was visiting an elementary school, and the offenders were first graders. They were bullies-in-training. They were bigots-to-be (as evidenced by the racial slurs in among the @#$%&s). They were models of bad behavior. And you probably know students just like them in your school. Read on to learn what to do.

Bully for You

You've seen students at your school getting picked on, and you're sick of it. Bullying sullies your school climate. Not only is it rude, it's harmful and potentially lethal. Some targets of bullying have dropped out of school; some have committed suicide; some have killed their tormentors (and others wish they could).

Bullying comes in many varieties. There's verbal bullying: taunting, name-calling, teasing, threatening, insulting, making comments about someone's real or perceived sexuality. There's social bullying: spreading malicious rumors or lies, giving someone the "silent" treatment; excluding someone; embarrassing someone in public. There's cyberbullying*: the use of mobile, wireless, or Internet technologies to hurt, insult, humiliate, or endanger others. And, of course, there's physical bullying: hitting,

*FOR A DISCUSSION OF CYBERBULLYING, SEE PAGES 418–421.

kicking, tripping, shoving, punching, tickling, spitting, breaking, dumping, stealing, extorting, etc. No matter what form bullying comes in, it is rude, crude, and cruel behavior.

Bullying thrives on having an audience. But why do people let it happen? Many reasons. Bystanders may look up to kids who bully, who are often powerful and popular. They may find the bullying funny or entertaining. They may be afraid that the kid doing the bullying will turn on them if they say anything. And they may think that speaking up won't make any difference. Bullying can make bystanders feel guilty, helpless, and scared. The truth, though, is that saying something makes a big difference. In fact, research shows that much of the time, bullying stops if bystanders speak up! If you witness an act of bullying, don't just stand there. Don't give bullies that pleasure and silent support. Be brave. Try one or more of these suggestions.

If You Witness Bullying . . .

Confront the person publicly. This takes a lot of courage. But, since kids who bully other kids count on the silent complicity of others to get away with their bullying, if you see someone being hassled in the hall or bullied on the bus, and you feel safe doing so, say:

> *"Cut it out. Nobody finds what you're doing amusing."*
>
> *"Leave him alone. How'd you like to be treated that way?"*

Confront the person privately. Take him aside and voice your concern:

> *"Look, Fowler, you may not realize it, but people are upset about how you treat Chumpley. It's not funny and you're just getting a reputation for being a bully, which I'm sure you don't want. I know you're not that kind of person so I thought I'd say something since I figured you'd want to know how it's coming across."*

Of course, this is a total crock. And that's what makes using good manners so much fun—the total perversity of it all. Fowler may be so stunned by your appeal to his better nature that he'll actually lighten up on poor Chumpley.

Help the person being bullied get away. Walk with him to a safe place. Go someplace where adults are present. Interrupt the bullying and offer an escape route by saying to the kid being bullied, *"We need to talk about the biology test,"* or *"Mr. Zamboni wants to speak to you."*

Support and counsel the target. Say:

> *"Don't let what Fowler says get to you. Everybody knows he's a jerk."*
>
> *"He's just doing it because you get so angry. Stay calm, hang out with us for a while, and try not to show that it bothers you."*

Enlist the support of bystanders. In the face of an act of bullying, turn to those present and say:

"Does anyone else here find it objectionable when Fowler picks on people?"

Chances are good that others feel the same way you do and will lend their voices in protest. Make sure they know that watching, laughing, or egging on someone who's bullying makes them complicit in the bullying.

Show kindness to the person being bullied. Often, kids who are bullied don't have many or any friends. Be a friend. Talk to her. Walk with her. Eat lunch together. Sit with her on the bus. Call her at home. Send her a text message. The few minutes it takes could make a profound difference in her life—it could *save* her life.

Nip rumors in the bud. If you hear a rumor that you know isn't true, tell the person it's false gossip and not to spread it.

Steer the target toward an adult. It's important that someone being bullied has the support of an adult she trusts. Offer to go with her to talk to the principal or a teacher, counselor, or parent. If she won't go, volunteer to talk to someone on her behalf.

Increase awareness. Schools that consciously create an anti-bullying culture reduce bullying. Find out how you can help. Write about bullying on a blog; write a letter-to-the-editor or an article for your school newspaper; tweet about it. Push for an anti-bullying program. These work. Talk to your principal or a teacher or counselor. Ask them to bring together a group of students and teachers who will work to reduce bullying at your school.

Appeal to higher authorities. In the "good old days," the worst thing a kid might do would be to shake you down for your sasparilla soda under the threat of a bloody nose. Today, kids who bully may be packing AK-47s. This is no joke. "Normal" school-yard hazing has escalated to extortion, emotional terrorizing, physical torture, and cyberbullying. If these bullying behaviors happen in your school, it may be dangerous for you to confront them directly. Instead, talk to your parents, guidance counselor, school administrators, or the police. Make sure somebody in authority knows what is happening. They can increase vigilance, discipline kids who bully, talk to parents, and introduce anti-bullying programs into the school. You shouldn't have to attend a war zone to get an education.

Bullying is an awful breach of etiquette. The sad reality is that you'll encounter bullies your whole life. Some will go by other names: parents, professors, judges, police officers, bosses, bureaucrats. Etiquette depends on everyone agreeing to play by the same rules. If someone who bullies adheres even minimally to the standards of society, you can use your good manners to address and rectify the situation. If, however, the person refuses to acknowledge the conventions of society, you'll have to pull out an arsenal of other approaches.

If You're Being Bullied . . .

Ignore the person who's bullying you. Initially, if you can, pretend you didn't hear him. Don't look at him. Walk quickly to a place of safety. It's possible this was a one-time-only event that will never happen again.

Don't show you're upset. Most kids who bully are looking to get a reaction out of you. If you don't cry or get angry, they may get bored or go off in search of other targets. It's difficult to hold in your feelings. But people who bully want to control your emotions. The less you show, the less likely they are to continue to bully you. When you're safely away from the situation, you can work out your feelings in other ways. Keep a journal. Go for a run. Talk to a friend.

Tell the person who's bullying you to stop. Say, *"Cut it out." "Stop bothering me."* If you have a good sense of humor, make a joke of it. Laugh it off.

Don't fight back. This can just make things worse or get you physically injured or in trouble yourself.

Walk away. Run if you have to. Go someplace where adults are present.

Talk to an adult you trust. Don't keep your feelings bottled up. Tell your parents. If you don't feel you can talk to them, find someone else who will give you support: a teacher, coach, principal, or counselor; an older brother or sister or other relative; a priest or rabbi. If you don't get the response you need, find another adult to talk to. It may be easier to talk about the bullying if you go with a friend. It's especially helpful if it's someone who has witnessed the bullying.

Act confident. Yes, it may be an act. But stand up straight. Hold your head high. Look people in the eye. You'll be less likely to attract the attention of kids looking to bully someone.

Avoid being alone in places where bullying takes place. Don't go by yourself to locker rooms, bathrooms, or other unsupervised areas of the school. Roam in packs. Walk home with other kids. Go to recess or the cafeteria with friends.

Stay close to adults. Sit near the bus driver. Walk near teachers in the hallway. Most bullying takes place in locations where adults aren't present.

Label your belongings. They're less likely to be taken if your name is on them.

Know that it's not your fault. Kids who bully want to make you feel worthless. They want you to think you deserve to be bullied. That's nonsense. You're a great person who merits being treated with respect and kindness.

Build your confidence. Find things to do that make you feel good about yourself. Exercise. (This is one of the most effective things you can do to perk yourself up and keep from getting depressed.) Learn a martial art. Take classes in meditation or yoga. Pursue your interests in music, art, dance, bike riding, sports, designing apps. You'll feel good and meet people who care about the same things you do and who may become your good friends.

Take stronger action. Tell a teacher, a counselor, or an administrator what's going on. They are obligated, legally and morally, to take action if incidents of bullying are brought to their attention. If the bullying doesn't stop, if it gets worse, if adults at school can't or won't stop it, your parents may need to contact the police or consider legal action against the kid doing the bullying and his parents.

If You're Someone Who Bullies . . .

Bullying is at the extreme end of bad manners. What could be worse than behaving in such a way as to make other kids feel hurt, scared, lonely, persecuted, and depressed? If you bully other kids, ask yourself the following questions:

- Do you like having power over other people?
- Do you like to get attention?
- Do you want to be popular and have people think you're tough and strong?
- Are you in trouble a lot?
- Are you unhappy or depressed?
- Are you lonely?
- Are there problems at home?
- Is shouting and name-calling a way of life in your home?
- Do your parents hit you?
- Do you spend a lot of time watching violent movies or playing violent video games?
- Do role models in your life use anger or violence to get their way?
- Do you feel insecure, stressed, or enraged?
- Are you being bullied yourself?

If you answered yes to any of these questions, it may have something to do with why you bully people.

Or . . .

- Are you popular?
- Do you play sports?
- Do you get good grades?
- Do you have lots of friends and interests?
- Do people respect you and want to be your friend?

If the answers to these questions are yes, it may seem like you "have it all." But you don't. Something's missing. That something may be feelings of self-confidence or security. It may be that there are no loving, supportive adults in your life. Yup, something's missing because happy, healthy kids don't go around making other kids' lives miserable. They don't get pleasure out of making other kids feel humiliated, sad, and afraid. If you're doing this, deep down inside you are hurting. And if you don't do something about it, you can end up harming your life and future.

You need to find out why you're behaving in a way that is so destructive to other people and, ultimately, yourself. Talk to someone you trust. Tell them about your actions. Find ways to deal with your problems without hurting others. And if you are popular and powerful, find ways to use those gifts in positive ways that will bring you satisfaction and respect. Wouldn't you rather be thought of as a cool and kind leader instead of a mean and abusive bully?

Stopping Sexual Harassment

Sexual harassment is R-U-D-E. It's also illegal. Sexual harassment is neither loving nor complimentary. At its least offensive, it's an act of insensitivity or miscommunication: a misguided attempt to tease, be funny, show one's feelings, or "get back at someone." At its most offensive, it's an act of hostility, domination, or violence.

Like bullying, sexual harassment is common in schools. One study[*] found that nearly half (48 percent) of the 7th–12th graders surveyed reported being sexually harassed in school during the academic year that was the focus of the study. While most targets of sexual harassment are girls, it happens to boys as well (56 percent girls versus 40 percent boys in this study). And boys are far more likely than girls to sexually harass someone. Here are some examples of sexually harassing behaviors that have taken place in middle and high schools:

[*]"CROSSING THE LINE: SEXUAL HARASSMENT AT SCHOOL" BY CATHERINE HILL, PH.D., AND HOLLY KEARL, M.A. (AAUW, 2011).

- unwanted touching, hugging, kissing, stroking
- sexual assault or attempted sexual assault
- rape
- giving snuggies or wedgies (lifting someone up by their underwear)
- pulling down someone's pants or skirt
- physically intimidating someone (cornering, blocking, leaning over, or standing too close)
- pressuring someone for sexual activity
- making kissing, sucking, or smacking sounds that someone doesn't want to hear
- making suggestive facial expressions (licking, tonguing, kissing, winking)
- leering or staring in a sexual manner
- looking someone up and down
- catcalling, whistling
- asking intrusive questions about a person's sexual fantasies, preferences, experiences
- making unwanted verbal comments about clothing, looks, parts of the body, what type of sex the person would like or be "good at"
- calling someone gay or lesbian in a negative or taunting way
- name-calling ("fag," "babe," "honey," "bitch," "slut," etc.)
- telling lies or spreading rumors about a person's sexual behavior
- telling unwanted sexual or dirty jokes
- repeatedly asking someone to go out when she or he isn't interested
- making sexual gestures or movements with one's hands or body
- touching or exhibiting oneself sexually in front of others
- sending unwanted texts, IMs, photos, or emails of a sexual nature
- showing pornography or sexually oriented cartoons, graffiti, or pictures to someone who doesn't want to see them
- making books, lists, or websites with derogatory sexual comments about students
- publicly "rating" an individual's looks or body (e.g., on a scale from 1–10)
- posting private photos of a sexual nature on Facebook or other social media sites to embarrass, humiliate, or "get revenge" on someone

You might be feeling skeptical about some of the items on this list. In fact, you might be asking yourself, *What's wrong with a friendly touch, comment, or whistle? Is flirting a crime?* And even, *Can't a person have fun anymore?*

Of course you can have fun—just not at the expense of others. Maybe you don't intend to harass a lass (or lad) with your interest and/or affections. But sexual harassment is defined by the person on the *receiving* end, not the *giving* end. If your actions or words are unwelcome; if they cause someone to feel embarrassed, humiliated, fearful, powerless, invaded, or degraded, it's sexual harassment, not flirting. If the object of your attentions asks or signals you to stop and you don't, it's sexual harassment, not flirting.

Flirting makes people feel valued, flattered, attractive, and respected. Sexual harassment makes them feel confused, angry, intimidated, and demeaned. Flirting boosts self-esteem. Harassment undermines it. Flirting is reciprocal. Harassment is one-sided. Flirting is wanted. Harassment is unwanted.

Here's where things get tricky. During adolescence, you experience a lot of new sexual feelings and start to want deeper relationships with people. As you explore these new relationships, you may feel awkward or confused. You may not be sure if someone likes you or how they like you. You may wonder *Is it okay to put my arm around her? Is it okay to give him a good-night kiss? Is it okay to compliment an outfit she's wearing? Is it okay to tell him he turns me on?*

The answers to these questions aren't always clear. Human love and sexual desire are among the most powerful, mysterious, and profound feelings we experience. There's no way to regulate flirting or dating to guarantee that no one will get hurt or be misunderstood. And it would be a tragedy if schools, in their efforts to eliminate harassment, also eliminated warmth, trust, and affection between students.

You need not worry about overstepping the bounds of flirting as long as you practice courtesy in your relationships. This means being alert to verbal and physical cues. Taking things slowly. Asking permission. Saying "May I?" "Do you mind if . . . ?" "Is this all right with you?"

Another way to monitor your behavior and remarks is to ask yourself these questions:

Would I mind if somebody else did or said this to my sister, mother, or girlfriend (or brother, father, or boyfriend)?

Would I mind if a video recording of my behavior were shown to my parents, friends, teachers, and/or classmates?

Obviously, you might be doing something perfectly acceptable and mutually desired which, for reasons of privacy, you'd rather not see at your neighborhood multiplex. What we're talking about here is stuff that you'd be ashamed of—stuff that would reflect poorly on your character or reputation.

If you make a genuine effort to show sensitivity to the needs and feelings of others, you won't be considered a sexual harasser. But you might be considered very sexy.

If you witness or are a target of sexual harassment, many of the suggestions for responding to bullying can be used to confront these behaviors (see pages 209–213): Increase awareness. Work with student leaders and adults in your school to create a harassment-free climate. Know your legal rights and school policies. Get support. Find trusted people to talk to. Report the incident. Shoot down lies and rumors. And most important, speak up when you see or are a target of sexual harassment. Challenge the behavior by naming it and telling the person to stop: *"Putting someone down by calling them gay is really offensive. Quit it!" "What you tweeted about Oriana was rude, insulting, untrue, AND very childish. Delete it! Now!"*

Besting Bigots

You've heard the comments, the sneers, and the slurs, and you've decided that enough is enough. Time for action! The key to besting bigots lies in refusing to tolerate their offensive remarks.

Precisely how you respond will depend on the circumstances. Start by considering the motive behind the insult. Some bigoted or inappropriate comments result not from prejudice but from a lack of awareness. While this doesn't lessen their ugliness, the speaker's lack of harmful intent allows you to assume the role of an educator.

For example: Your five-year-old brother calls someone a "fag." Since little kids often repeat words they hear, ask your brother if he knows what the word means. If he doesn't, tell him. Because he's so young, you'll have to gear your words to his level of understanding.

Or: An exchange student struggling to learn English makes a comment about some "colored" students in your school. Explain to her that the word "colored" is offensive to many people because of its historical associations. Suggest that she use "black" or "African American" instead.

Or: Your grandfather, who lives with you, addresses your female classmates as "honey" when they come to visit. Since he means to be gracious rather than sexist, your job is to fill him in on the social changes of the past decades. Inform him that young ladies of today don't appreciate being called "honey," no matter how sweet their disposition. Suggest that he refer to your friends by their given names.

Unfortunately, most bigoted comments can't be chalked up to innocence or cluelessness. They are the result of fear, ignorance, and/or prejudice. Silence in the face of such bigotry suggests approval, and silence doesn't stop hatred. As the 18th-century English statesman Edmund Burke is reputed to have said, "All that is necessary for the triumph of evil is that good men do nothing."

It's easy to "do nothing" in school or work environments. There's a lot of pressure to fit in that can make it difficult to challenge injustice, racism, and homophobia. Deep down, you know it's wrong, but no one else is doing anything, so why should *you* be the one to stick your neck out?

Because if you're not part of the solution, you're part of the problem. If you take a stand, the bigots may respond "You say we should be tolerant. Well, where's *your* tolerance for *our* beliefs?" Don't be taken in by this devious "defense." Tolerate intolerance the same way you do toxic waste: Accept that it exists, recognize it as bad, and do everything in your power to eliminate it.

If you speak out against bigotry, the worst that can happen is you'll be disliked, scorned, or ostracized by people whose behavior is cruel, ignorant, offensive, hateful, and/or illegal. Like, big loss. The best that can happen is you'll discover that most of your classmates feel the same way you do. Once you break the ice, they'll cheer your courage and support your cause. You'll be a leader in creating a friendly, respectful, and inclusive climate for your school.

Following are five ways to respond to bigoted jokes and comments. Remember that bigotry is not an excuse for being rude back. In fact, politeness is the most powerful sword you can wield.

1. Walk out. You may attend a lecture or performance in which the speaker (or comedian, or musician) makes bigoted remarks. It may be impolite or impractical to speak out at the time. There may not be a forum for questions or discussion in which you'd have a chance to challenge the remarks. Therefore, get up and leave. Do it quietly. Don't disturb others. Your statement will be seen and "heard." It may cause others to follow your example. You will have taken a stand. Quite literally.

2. Stare. We all know that it's impolite to stare. So let's call this an "intense visual focus." Laser looks aimed at the perpetrator of an offensive remark can be an effective way of signaling disapproval. This is especially so if everyone present follows your lead. The target of 12 pairs of humorless eyes is likely to squirm, sweat, and wonder if he said something wrong. If however, your stare is lost in a general hubbub, you'll need to take more noticeable action.

3. Question the speaker. Many bigots assume that everyone present shares their view. Therefore, it can be quite unsettling to them if you draw attention to their remark by inquiring about it. Let's say a racist comment is made. With a pleasant expression and tone, you could say:

"Excuse me?"

"I beg your pardon?"

"I'm sorry, I must have misheard you."

If the person repeats the offensive remark, you can repeat yours:

"I'm sorry, I still think I've misheard you."

This is a bit like the parent who says "I can't hear you" over and over until a child says "Please."

4. Ask for an explanation. In the face of a racist or homophobic comment or joke, say:

"I'm sorry, I don't get it. Could you please explain the joke to me?"

A perfectly civilized question—but the spotlight it shines on the speaker and the remark is stunning. You could also ask:

"Do you consider that funny?"

5. Reveal a connection. Another way to respond to bigotry is by informing the speaker of your personal stake in the matter:

"You may not realize that my mother is Polish."

"I'm sure you're unaware that my father is gay."

The speaker may fall all over herself with an apology and say that she didn't mean anything disrespectful and some of her best friends are gay or Polish or both. Or she may escalate her abuse or accuse you of not being able to "take a joke."

You challenge discrimination, intolerance, and hatred because it's the right thing to do. Don't expect to change a bigot's mind. If that happens, great. If it doesn't, you may succeed in at least getting the person to keep his ideas to himself. But no matter what happens, you'll feel proud of yourself. Plus your actions will have a powerful effect on those who witness them and may lead to their speaking out in the future.

Dear Alex

"What's so bad about ethnic jokes? They're funny."

Which are the funny ones? Those about your ethnicity or someone else's?

Ethnic jokes are comparable to getting your pants pulled down in school. If it happens to someone else, it's humorous. If it happens to you, it's hurtful. It all depends who's the butt (so to speak) of the joke.

Don't get me wrong; some ethnic jokes are very funny. And we all need to lighten up before political correctness turns humor into an endangered species. Poking fun at a culture, an ethnicity, a religion, or a group of people doesn't automatically imply disrespect. Many jokes that do this are good-natured; they tease, but without maliciousness. Other jokes, however, are rooted in prejudice. They are mean-spirited and reinforce the stereotypes that feed bigotry.

In order to tell ethnic jokes (and "fat" jokes and "lawyer" jokes and "dumb blonde" jokes) and stay within the bounds of proper etiquette, you need to consider their *content* and *context*.

- **Content** means "What is the basis for, and character of, the humor?"

For example, a "Jewish" joke that makes fun of rabbis, yarmulkes, or gefilte fish is probably pretty safe to tell in the proper context. A "Jewish" joke about the Holocaust is likely to offend listeners no matter what the context may be.

- **Context** means "Where, when, and to whom are you telling the joke?"

Death jokes would be out of place at a funeral. Jokes about contortionists and Crisco would be out of place at your grandmother's dinner table (unless you have a very unusual granny). It's generally okay to tell a joke that skewers a group, a nationality, or a category of people if it falls into one of the following contexts:

1. The joke is at the expense of the person telling it. (A lawyer tells a joke about lawyers.)

2. Everyone present belongs to the target group. (The speaker at a convention of lawyers tells a joke about lawyers.)

Once you tell a joke, you can't control where it travels. For example, let's say you tell sexist dirty jokes in the locker room. Just because your teammates are all guys doesn't mean some of them won't be offended. They might tell their girlfriends. Word could get out that you have some pretty sick attitudes toward women. Maybe you do, maybe you don't. But people will make judgments based on the things you say.

I'm not suggesting that you stick to knock-knock jokes for the rest of your life. But before you tell a joke, consider its content and context. Ask yourself *Would I be comfortable if people associated this joke with me?*

Dear Alex

"There's a teacher in my school who's gay. He's the best teacher I've ever had, and I really like him. But now people are starting to say

that I'm gay (I'm not) and he's after me (he isn't). I don't want to stop being friendly, but I don't like what people are saying."

It would be a shame if you gave up a wonderful relationship just because of the rude gossip of bigoted people. Taking a stand always involves consequences. Sometimes fitting in and not making waves is the best course of action. But this is rarely the case when confronted with prejudice. As Martin Luther King Jr. once said, "Noncooperation with evil is as much a moral obligation as is cooperation with good."

Homophobia is a form of prejudice that breeds not only discrimination, bullying, violence, and hate, but also the depression and isolation that leads a disproportionate number of gay and lesbian teens to drug abuse and suicide. The people you risk alienating when you refuse to tolerate intolerance are probably not people you'd want to associate with anyway. This doesn't make it any easier, but it helps you to know you're doing the right thing.

Adolescence is a time of experimentation and discovery. Many teenagers are preoccupied with the feelings and fears that surround their emerging sexuality. They're trying to figure out what it means to "be a man" or "be a woman." People who question your sexuality are revealing concerns about their own. It's their insecurity that's showing. And because they're insecure, they need to put others—namely gays—down.

Your sexuality isn't anyone's business. If people call you gay, don't respond "I am not!" Defensiveness plays into their hands. It also suggests that there's something wrong with being gay. There isn't. Instead, ignore them or calmly say:

"Calling me gay as if it's an insult is rude and juvenile. If I were you I would want to stop doing something that reflects so poorly on yourself."

or

"You seem very interested in other people's sexuality. Did you have some questions or concerns about your own that you'd like to share with me?"

More and more schools today are establishing support groups for gay, lesbian, bisexual, transgender, and questioning (GLBTQ) teens. Many straight kids join as a way of expressing their solidarity. No school should tolerate taunting or gaybashing, and you may want to approach school authorities about establishing such a group or having someone speak to the school about these issues.

While cultural attitudes toward people who are gay are becoming increasingly equitable, respectful, and welcoming in the United States and certain other countries, it's still important for schools to counter the homophobic messages kids may receive from peers, politicians, and popular culture. Some teens have gay parents, relatives, or family friends already serving as positive role models. Other teens are prey to misinformation spread by intolerant and ill-informed groups. Since prejudice is based on ignorance, it's important to debunk some of the myths that fuel harassment of, and discrimination against, GLBTQ individuals.

Myths	Facts
AIDS is spread by gay people.	AIDS is spread by the exchange of bodily fluids, not by sexual orientation. New cases of AIDS are occurring at a far greater rate among heterosexual people than gay people.
Gay people are only interested in sex.	Gay people are just as desirous of finding and giving love and entering into a committed relationship as are heterosexual people.
People choose to be gay.	Sexual orientation isn't something people choose, it's something they discover about themselves.
Most child molesters are gay.	The vast majority of child molesters are heterosexual.
Homosexuality is an illness or perversion.	Neither the medical nor psychiatric professions view homosexuality as an illness or perversion.
You can tell if people are gay or not by the way they act.	There's no way to determine a person's sexual orientation from the way he or she looks or behaves.
Having a crush on, fantasy about, or sexual experience with someone of the same sex means you're gay.	Most heterosexual adults have had one or all of these experiences while growing up.
Gay parents and teachers recruit kids into being gay.	No one can be "recruited" to be gay or straight. Children with gay parents or teachers are no more likely to be gay than are children of straight parents or teachers.
Gay and lesbian people are unfit to be parents.	Gay and lesbian parents are just as capable of raising healthy, happy, emotionally sound children as are heterosexual parents.

Civility at School Sporting Events

Spectator Etiquette

Proper spectator behavior at interscholastic games differs markedly from that at other school events. For example, at a concert by the school orchestra, it is considered bad form to yell "Kill the bassoonist!" Audience members at school plays may not chant "We want an actor, not a weed whacker!"

"Go trombones!"

The standards are more relaxed at school sporting events. Tradition says it's acceptable to hurl mild insults at (and cast spells upon) game officials and opposing team members. To be considered appropriate, however, these aspersions must have a direct bearing on the target's athletic role, performance, and/or relevant body parts. Thus, the eyes of an umpire, the arms of a pitcher, and the I.Q. of a coach are all fair game. The umpire's mother, the pitcher's religion, and the coach's race are not.

That tradition allows invective from the stands isn't the same as saying that it's a good thing. After all, we allow brussels sprouts. Don't get me wrong; I'm very sympathetic to those who pepper the playing field with such creative taunts as "Swing!" How else can they survive the tedium of interminable timeouts? But if the idea is to get one's mind off how boring the game is, couldn't this goal be achieved equally well by vigorously supporting one's own team, rather than casting asparagus on the character and performance of the opposing team?

In an era when fewer and fewer people practice even the basics of politeness, do we really need to institutionalize rudeness? This only encourages those who would spit on umpires or throw iceballs from the stands. Look at World Cup soccer. It has been overrun by hooliganistic yobs out to hit someone over the head with a bottle of beer. And the fans are even worse!

It's time to reassess spectator behavior at sporting events. A bit more of "Well played, sir!" and a bit less of "Throw the bum out!" can do no harm. After all, teams should be uplifted by their athletic supporters.

Dear Alex

"I play baseball for my school team. I used to really like it, but I'm thinking of quitting because it's no fun anymore. Parents are always yelling rude things at the players from the stands. Two fathers got into a real ugly fight at our last game. I want to win, too, but it's just a game. Is there any way to stop parents from being so rude?"

Parents who do this should have to sit in the corner and then go to bed without supper. There's no excuse for such behavior. If they want to spend their afternoons being loud-mouthed and making ignorant remarks, they should run for Congress.

It's likely that many of your teammates feel the same way you do. Why not get together with them and talk to your coach? He can speak to particular parents or send a letter home to all parents reminding them of the importance of good sportsmanship. During a game, he can also approach offending parents and tell them that he won't tolerate any mean-spirited remarks addressed to his players.

Unfortunately, parental misbehavior is a common problem. Coaches as a group need to band together so that all teams, at the beginning of the season, inform parents that they must abide by certain rules of conduct if they plan to attend any games.

Player Etiquette

Sports etiquette is the ultimate test of good manners. This is because good sportsmanship sometimes requires you to act in opposition to your feelings.

For example, when you've had your face wiped in the mud all afternoon only to lose by one fluky goal in the last two seconds of play and be knocked out of the finals, it's difficult to extend your hand to the winners and say "Great game!" What you really feel like saying is "You lucky shmucks!"

The reason you must put your feelings aside is because "it's not whether you win or lose, it's how you play the game." Yeah, right. If you believe that, I've got another one for you: "Sticks and stones may break your bones, but names will never hurt you." OF COURSE IT MATTERS WHETHER YOU WIN OR LOSE! Self-confidence, scholarships, career paths, and endorsements can all be affected by your win-lose stats. But it's your behavior before, during, and after every match that determines whether, as a human being, you're a winner or a loser. You can be a winning athlete but a loser in life. And you can be a losing athlete but a winning person.

Here's how to be a winner no matter how the game turns out:

Have fun. What's the point of being out there if you're not enjoying yourself? Good vibes are contagious. Your teammates will catch your enthusiasm and the game will be that much more enjoyable for all.

Avoid temper tantrums. Nobody, with the exception of tabloid reporters and paparazzi, wants to witness an immature outburst. Resist the impulse to throw your tennis racquet, curse at umpires, or storm off the field. Only professional players making millions of dollars are allowed to do these things.

Don't make excuses. If you mess up, say you're sorry and let it go. You only draw more attention to yourself if you blame the sun, the wind, the ref, the racquet, or the gopher hole. If it truly wasn't your fault, that will be obvious to everyone.

Don't blame others. If your team members mess up, give them encouragement, not criticism. Saying "Good try" or "Don't worry about it" will do a lot more to help than "Smooth move, Ex-Lax."

Congratulate the winners. This is how character is built. Extend your hand and tell the victors they played a great game.

Compliment the losers. But be sincere. Don't tell them they played well when it's obvious they didn't. Instead, you might say:

"Thanks for the game."

"Thanks for playing us."

"You guys had an off day today, but you were great against Lincoln last week."

Choose up sides with tact. It feels terrible, time after time, to be the last person chosen for a team. You stand there, staring at your sneakers, hoping that the next pick will put you out of your misery. Finally, everyone's

TRUE STORIES

FROM THE MANNERS FRONTIER

Yer Out!

Once, when I was in fifth grade, I struck out in a softball game. One of my teammates called me a boner. So, naturally, I picked up a banana peel I saw on the ground and threw it at him. He charged me, and we began to roll around in the dirt. The gym teacher intervened and made us both run around the backstops 10 times.

The moral of this story is: *Don't go to a school where the backstops are far apart.*

been chosen except you and somebody says "Ha, ha. You get Wiley." This is the stuff of which lifetime traumas are made.

Many gym teachers, realizing this, now assemble teams randomly by counting off by twos or fours (or two-by-fours). If you're one of the captains choosing up sides, strike a blow for kindness. Tell the other captain (discreetly) to pick people in reverse order. Start with the worst players. Of course, everyone will know what you're doing. But I guarantee you that the people usually picked last will worship you for life. And the star athletes will get a useful lesson in humility as they experience what it feels like to stand in the dwindling line as everyone else high-fives their way onto the team.

Well, that just about covers etiquette on the playing field. A few final suggestions:

- If you mistakenly kick the goalie's head instead of the ball, say "Excuse me" or "Sorry!"

- If you tackle someone, upon removing your cleats from his groin and your fingers from his eyeballs, it's a nice gesture to help him up.

- In basketball, don't pull down anyone's shorts as he or she goes up for a jump shot.

Dear Alex

"My school forces students to take showers after gym class. I HATE it. People say rude things and make comparisons about people's . . . you know."

It's very impolite to make disparaging remarks about the sports equipment of others.

Let's begin with a basic fact: Teenage boys and girls are often sensitive about their body's development, or perceived lack thereof. This sensitivity is heightened when you're naked in front of 90 classmates. Perfectly normal teenagers can feel too fat or too thin, too short or too tall, too big or too small. It's important to remember that the development of secondary sex characteristics in kids typically starts anywhere between the ages of 9 and 15. This causes great curiosity as to who's matured how far. Such interest is natural but must be pursued discreetly so as not to cause offense. After all, it's rude to stare.

The operative rule for locker room etiquette is *Look, but don't touch.* The corollary to this is *Don't get caught looking.* Therefore, these are the Top 10 rules that should be posted in every locker room:

1. Don't hang people up by their underwear.

2. Don't snap your towel at anyone.

3. Don't run unless you enjoy slipping and hitting your head on a bench.

4. Don't lock anyone in his or her locker.

5. Don't drip on anyone.

6. Don't hide anyone's clothes or towel.

7. Don't point, laugh, gape, or giggle at unclad classmates.

8. Don't make comments about anyone's body or body parts.

9. Don't bend over without saying "Excuse me, do you mind my butt in your face?"

10. Don't bring a tape measure or magnifying glass into the showers.

And don't you dare pull out a cell phone or tablet to take pictures!

If you're self-conscious about changing in the locker room, you can wear your gym clothes under your regular clothes. You can also protect yourself from mean-spirited classmates by sticking close to your friends. Grab lockers that are next to each other. Go as a group into the showers. And remember, the students who make the comments are usually those who are most insecure about themselves. If someone offers a disparaging remark about your anatomy, you can ignore it or respond by smiling and saying "I wouldn't talk if I were you."

Cafeteria Courtesies

Throwing food. Spitting. Screeching. Chewing with their mouths open. Are we in the monkey cage? No, we're in the typical school cafeteria.

It's no wonder that students at lunchtime act like they're in a zoo. After all, they've been kept in cages all morning. Pent-up energy and chipped beef on toast are a dangerous combination. While good table manners are always preferable, there are factors in the school environment that mitigate against them. For instance, if you only have 11 seconds to eat lunch and get caught up on the latest news, the pressures to combine chewing with talking are enormous. Best behavior is not encouraged by the sight of boiled hot dogs and barfaroni. Gelatin that's still alive invites remarks of dubious taste, particularly if the droopy whipped cream has the consistency of skim milk.

Nonetheless, you can rise to the challenge and resist these downward forces. Here are some etiquette tips for feeding time:

- Always be kind to food servers and other lunch counter personnel.

- Don't dump anyone's tray.

- Don't trip or tickle anyone carrying a tray.

- Don't laugh, clap, or cheer if somebody drops a tray or glass.

- Ask permission before you grab food off of anyone's plate. On second thought, don't grab. Allow it to be passed to you.

- Schedule jokes and disgusting remarks so they don't occur when your luncheon companions are drinking. This will minimize those occasions upon which milk comes snorting out of someone's nostrils.

- Throw out your trash. Don't, however, fling objects halfway across the room so their trajectory passes over others. Nobody wants your "miss" in their lap.

- Be inclusive. It's natural to want to eat with your friends. The tradition of "reserved" seats and designated tables exists in many schools. If someone who's not part of your circle sits down at your table, be friendly. Staring, holding your nose, making snide remarks, or telling the person to get lost is rude, crude, and bad attitude.

- As you leave the cafeteria, give thanks that you don't have to wash the dishes.

Applying to Colleges

One day before too long, many of you will start applying to colleges. You will have prepared for this over the years by ensuring that your social media presence contains nothing that would give college admissions officers pause when they go to check you out online. Most colleges require applicants to write an essay describing their interests, goals, and/or reasons for wanting to go there. Some ask prospective students to relate an experience from which they learned something. If you find yourself facing the latter type of essay question, you may wonder how truthful to be. Is this a case where honesty isn't necessarily the best policy?

In fact, there are times when the truth, the whole truth, and nothing but the truth could lead to that Great Rejection Pile in the Sky rather than the Land of Fat Acceptance Envelopes. Telling a college that your major interests are sex and getting away from home is not the way to win the heart and mind of an admissions officer.

The key to applying to college is the key to life: *Balance.* You want to say what they want to hear without sounding phony. You want your application to stand out without drawing attention to the fact. You want to elucidate your achievements without appearing boastful. You want to show that you have the motivation to make a success of yourself (i.e., you'll be able to contribute to Alumni Giving Campaigns) without coming across as money-grubbing. In short, you want to present yourself as:

- creative but not flaky
- cooperative but not spineless
- independent but not rebellious
- confident but not cocky
- principled but not intolerant
- enthusiastic but not ditsy
- well-rounded but not unfocused
- socially aware but not self-righteous

Thus, the act of applying to a school is the culmination of everything you've learned (and are learning) about good manners: Present yourself as a sincere, tolerant, observant, secure individual who, while marching to your own drumbeat, is ever mindful of the rights and sensibilities of others. Toward that end, here are six tips for school applications and interviews:

Remember that the purpose of filling out an application is to get into that school. It is not to commence an autobiography entitled *Confessions of a Young Miscreant.* Anything you include that reflects negatively on yourself must be portrayed as a profound learning experience from which you have grown.

Dress appropriately for interviews. College admissions officials have no interest in seeing the top six inches of your underwear or the bottom six inches of your cleavage. Wear something casual enough to help you feel comfortable and natural, yet formal enough to show that you respect the occasion and have made an effort to look nice.

Be on your best behavior. This is the time to pull out all the manners stops. Rise when the interviewer comes to greet you. Offer a firm handshake. Look 'em in the eye. Use "Sir" and "Ma'am." Sit up straight. Try not to fidget. When the interview concludes, thank the admissions official and say that you enjoyed talking with him or her.

Show enthusiasm. It's not a good sign if your interviewer falls asleep in the middle of your interview. Don't be a lifeless lump. Speak up. Put a sparkle in your eyes. Don't mumble. Convey the kind of energy you will apply to your studies. No, on second thought, better not.

Demonstrate knowledge of the institution. Show that you've read the catalog. It would be embarrassing to reveal a passion for architecture and then learn that the college to which you're applying because your father went there doesn't have a design school.

Come with questions. It never hurts to have a few intelligent queries ready in case the interviewer asks if you have any questions. You can inquire about the curriculum, cultural life, volunteer programs, academic policies, sports requirements, social opportunities, etc. Try not to ask anything that would be obvious to anyone who'd done her homework (as in "How many years does it take to get a degree?").

There are several fictions to the application process that both sides agree not to examine too closely. For example, applicants pretend that all of their extracurricular activities were motivated by altruism and love of learning, rather than by the craving to get into college. They also pretend that the college they are currently considering is their first choice. Meanwhile, colleges pretend that the decisions they make are objective. They aren't. Most students are amply qualified to attend the schools to which they apply. The choice of whether to accept the straight-A student who loves history, captains lacrosse, plays flute, and works with the homeless or the straight-A student who loves math, captains tennis, plays guitar, and works with inner city youth is arbitrary. The ultimate decision is not going to be made on the basis of you, but on the basis of how the tennis and lacrosse teams have been doing. Therefore, while an acceptance should make you feel proud, deserving, and successful, a rejection should never be taken personally.

In sum, applying to college is like going on a first date. You want to be honest about who you are. At the same time, you don't want to reveal anything less than salutary about yourself until the relationship has reached a point where your deficiencies will be seen in the light of your many fine qualities.

Chapter Quiz

Keep your eyes on your own paper. You may begin.

1. *Your school springs a random drug test on you. What's the proper response?*

    a) don't take it sitting down

    b) stand up for your rights

    c) grin and bare it

2. *You're taking a final exam. The student in the seat next to yours is trying his hardest to copy your paper. Do you:*

a) hand it to him so he doesn't strain his eyes

b) yell "Brian's cheating, Brian's cheating!"

c) use your arm to shield your paper

3. *A teacher wrongly accuses you of cheating. Do you:*

a) slap him with a wet noodle

b) slap him with a sexual harassment suit

c) go up to him after class and calmly make your case

4. *Your teacher is out sick and you have a new sub for the day. Classroom etiquette requires you to:*

a) switch seats so she won't know who sits where

b) hang a jock strap from the fluorescent lights

c) make a special effort to be cooperative

5. *It's especially crowded in the cafeteria one day. An unpopular student has to sit at the table usually reserved for you and your friends. The polite response would be to:*

a) throw coleslaw at her

b) pinch your nose and say "What's that rotten smell?"

c) engage her in friendly conversation

7

FRIENDS, ROMANCE, COUNTRYMEN

Lend Me Your Peers

Adolescence is a time of many firsts—and lasts. Adults, having repressed their own painful memories, often describe the teenage years as the "best years of your life." But teenagers know firsthand the worry, cruelty, and competition; the pressures and responsibilities; the fears and confusions; the humiliations and torments; the jealousies and rivalries. They know how deep their feelings go; that it's *not* just a crush, they *won't* get over it, it *was* real love.

The greatest pleasures of adolescence are usually linked to one's social life—and so are the greatest pains. A lot of the aches and embarrassments could be eliminated if teenagers behaved politely toward one another. The very idea of being polite to one's peers may generate hoots of derision in some circles. This is because many teens seem to feel that the best way to avoid getting hurt is to get the first punch in. They don't want to be teased, taunted, badmouthed, and ostracized, so they tease, taunt, badmouth, and ostracize others.

Teenagers who practice good manners with their peers can dodge much of the suffering and anxiety that runs rampant in school corridors.

And they will enjoy closer and more rewarding relationships with their friends and romantic interests. Let's look at some of the ways you can put politeness to work with your peers.

The Etiquette of Friendship
Making New Friends

Is there a proper way to make new friends? Yes: *Act as if you already have as many as you need.*

This may seem like strange advice. But, for some reason, teens are turned off by people who seem desperate to have friends. Maybe they figure that if you want to be friends with *them*, there must be something wrong with *you*. (That's what low self-esteem does for people.)

So do your best to exude confidence. Be relaxed, yet respectful. Cool, but without an attitude. Eager, but not fawning. Mysterious, but not aloof. Smile enough to show you're at peace, but not so much as to suggest you're coming unglued. Once your aura is properly adjusted, you can commence operations.

1. Observe. Get a sense of who's who. Check out the pecking orders and group affiliations (jocks, preps, Goths, geeks, nerds, punks, slackers, skaters, stoners, loners, posers, gangstas, artists, emos, rockers, cheerleaders, metalheads, wannabees, etc.). This will give you a better idea of people you'll want to steer clear of and people you'll want to approach.

2. Inquire. In a low-key way, ask questions. These can be procedural ("How do you think the teacher wants us to do these papers?") or personal ("What's it like being on the debate team?"). Since most teenagers find themselves interesting, they appreciate anyone who asks them questions.

3. Compliment. If someone says something noteworthy in class, wears a nice outfit, or makes a good play, tell him or her so. We all like to be around those who recognize our fine qualities.

4. Join. Go out for the team, audition for the band, sign up for the school paper, get involved with the service club. Being with people who share your enthusiasms is one of the best ways to find kindred spirits and new friends.

5. Resist. You may be approached by teens who are looking for new partners in crime. These are the kids who'll be your friends if you'll be mean to their preselected targets, or if you'll use drugs or cut school with them. These are the sorts of friends you can do without.

6. Nurture. Friendships require time to develop and maintenance to thrive. Once you make a new friend, give her your support, encouragement, loyalty, and empathy. These are things we all wish to receive. And when we do, we keep coming back to the well that provides them.

Dear Alex

"I try to be polite and to think about how my actions affect other people. But I get teased a lot for having good manners, even by my friends. Why is it considered bad to be polite?"

There are still a few bugs to work out in teenage human software. One is the tendency to put people down for being smart, well-behaved, industrious, and moral. The idea is, if you devalue those traits in others, you don't have to feel bad about not possessing them yourself.

Don't ever apologize for being polite, principled, responsible, or virtuous. Those very friends who tease you now will discover later on—when it may be too late—how valuable those characteristics are. While they desperately play catch-up to try to acquire them, you'll already be reaping the benefits.

Dear Alex

"Is teasing always rude?"

It's sometimes okay to tease people about their positive attributes—looks, accomplishments, popularity, etc. This form of teasing, if done with a light, affectionate touch, is usually intended and taken as a backhanded compliment.

It's never okay to tease people about aspects of their appearance, background, or behavior that they can't help and/or feel self-conscious about—an accent or stutter, poor grades, a parent in prison, etc.

How do you know whether someone is pleased or embarrassed to have attention drawn to, for example, good grades or a British accent? You just know! A teenager's most highly developed radar is the one that detects the sensitive spots of others.

Coping with Cliques

You may think (and you may be right) that cliques are the height of rudeness. It's fine if people want to be with their friends. There's nothing wrong with that. But do they really have to treat everyone else like dirt?

Of course they don't—and they shouldn't. But knowing that won't make them stop. So what are your alternatives when you're faced with (or shut out by) a clique?

- You can start by understanding why some people form cliques. Many teenagers are unsure of themselves socially. They lack self-confidence and certain social skills. Cliques and gangs (which are really just cliques carried to an extreme) furnish love, approval, protection, and support. The more a clique's members put down other people, the cooler they think they are.

- You can decide whether belonging to a particular clique is really that important to you. What, if anything, do they have that you want? When you closely examine a particular clique, you may find that they're not as special or elite as they'd like you to believe.

- If you're convinced that your life will be meaningless and empty if you're not part of a certain clique, then do what you can to join. You can try making friends with one member. (**Tip:** Approach the person when he or she isn't surrounded by other members. Your chances of being scorned and rejected will be somewhat reduced.) Maybe you have interests in common. Once you've established that friendship, you may find that you're automatically part of the clique. (And once you're in, you can try to influence the clique to stop being so nasty to outsiders.)

Of course, you have another alternative: You can ignore the clique. Follow the steps in "Making New Friends" on pages 233–234. Find other people who are warm, interesting, inviting, and open-minded. The chances are excellent that they'll welcome you and return your friendship.

Handling Friendship Problems Politely

Peer Pressure

What if you learn that the people you hang out with do things that are questionable or against the law? How can you avoid getting involved without seeming holier-than-thou when pressured to do something you don't want to do?

Simply respond with one of these phrases:

"No, thank you."
"I'd prefer not to."
"Count me out."
"No can do."

Beyond that, you don't owe anyone an explanation. With certain people, in certain situations, you may wish to provide one. For example, you might want to explain to someone with whom you've been seriously involved why you don't want to have sex. Otherwise, he or she might take your refusal in a way you don't intend. Or you might try to dissuade friends from spray painting racist or anti-Semitic graffiti on the walls of the school by explaining why you won't do it.

Whatever the circumstances, stand firm. Nobody can make you do anything you don't want to do. And you may discover that the minute one brave soul (namely you) says no, others will follow.

Dear Alex

"I've decided that I don't want to use drugs. But some of my friends keep pressuring me to get high with them. What's the polite thing to say in these circumstances?"

You can take some comfort in the fact that at least your friends have been taught to share. But when they offer you something you wish to decline—whether it's a joint or a jelly sandwich—simply say "No, thank you." If the person who's inviting you to get high has good manners, the matter will go no further. But what do you do if the person persists? Watch:

"Wanna get high?"
"No, thank you."

"Why not?"
"I'd prefer not to, thank you."

"Whatsa matter, ya scared?"
"I'd prefer not to, thank you."

"Oh, come on."
"I'd prefer not to, thank you."

"It's not gonna kill ya."
"I'd prefer not to, thank you."

"Just try it."
"I'd prefer not to, thank you."
"Oh, forget it!"

You see the power of good manners. Just remember that you don't owe anybody an explanation for your decision. In fact, it's rude of the person to ask. Responding to such pressure just prolongs the discussion and puts you on the defensive. See what happens if you try to answer the questions:

"Wanna get high?"
"No, thank you."

"Why not?"
"Because I don't want to."

"Whatsa matter, ya scared?"
"No, I'm not scared."

"Then what?"
"I just don't want to."

"Have you ever tried?"
"No."

"Then how do you know?"
"I've never jumped off a cliff, but I know I don't want to."

"That's different. Jumping off a cliff could kill you."
"So could drugs."

"How do you know? You think you know everything?"
"I didn't say that."

And so on.

If you stand firm and show no room for debate, you'll wear down your interrogator. This strategy can be used to decline participation in any event:

"I'm sorry, but I'd prefer not to shoplift, thank you."

"Count me out. I'm just not able to smash mailboxes."

As a matter of etiquette, it's not your responsibility to make judgments or point out dangers associated with those behaviors in which you're asked to participate. As a matter of friendship, it may be.

"Hmmm, rob the First National Bank this afternoon? Thank you for asking, but I have other plans."

Drinking and Driving

You and your friend go together to a party. He drives. Alcohol is available, and your friend partakes. As the party comes to an end, he grabs his coat, fumbles for his keys, and says "Lesh go, hokay?"

He's so far out of his gourd that he doesn't know which end is up, he's about to turn 4,000 pounds of steel into a lethal weapon, and he expects *you* to sit in the passenger seat. You haven't been drinking, so you're still mindful of your obligation to exercise good manners. You say:

"No way. I'll talk to the host. I'm sure you can just spend the night here."

"You really don't look well. Come. I'll show you where you can lie down."

"Hand me your keys, please. I'll call a cab."

"I know you think I'm overreacting, but I could never forgive myself if I let you drive and something happened. You're simply going to have to indulge me."

"Amy said she'll take you home. We'll arrange for you to get your car tomorrow. I'll get a ride with Micah."

Or, if you're a licensed driver:

"I'll drive you home, drop you off, and return your car in the morning."

If these approaches don't work, gather several of your largest friends. Then sit on the person and pry the keys out of his fingers. This is not impolite. Etiquette grants considerable leeway to those engaged in the saving of lives. For example, shoving a total stranger would, in normal circumstances, be bad manners. Doing so to move him out of the path of an oncoming bus would be a heroic act.

Don't worry about being seen as rude. It's likely the person won't even remember what was said or done. And if, the next day, he should give you a hard time, simply put on a resolute, I'll-have-none-of-that air and say:

"Your friendship and safety are so important to me that I'm happy to put up with your anger. And I'll do it again if it will keep you from killing yourself or someone else."

Backbiting

You've just heard that Andy, one of your friends, has been saying mean things about you behind your back. Understandably, you're hurt and upset. Should you say something or drop him as a friend? That depends.

You have only the word of the person who told you—who spoke behind the back of the friend who allegedly spoke behind *your* back. But where did Person B (the tattler) get the news about Person A (your friend)? Did she hear it directly from your friend (A)? Or from someone else (C) who heard it from someone else (D) who heard it from someone else (E) who heard it from your friend (A)? In other words, how many people were involved in passing this information along to you?

It's best to receive this sort of communication with skepticism. You have no idea what Andy actually said. To put this another way, imagine that he bakes a big plate of brownies as a gift for you. He hands the plate to a friend and says "Please give these to Gina." The friend figures no one will miss one brownie, so she takes one and hands the plate to another friend with instructions to "Give this to Gina." The plate goes through 12 more people, and each takes a brownie, rearranges the remainder, and passes it on. By the time it gets to you, there's just a bunch of crumbs. And you think *What kind of a lousy cheap present is this?*

Now watch what happens when words instead of brownies get passed along:

Andy: *"I'm worried about Gina. Her parents are getting a divorce, and she seems pretty upset. I wish there was something I could do to help."*

Sandy: *"Andy's really upset that Gina's parents are divorcing. He wishes he could do something to help her."*

Mandy: *"Andy said that Gina's parents are really upset about getting divorced. Apparently Gina's been getting some kind of help."*

Randy: *"According to Andy, Gina's parents are getting divorced because Gina is in some kind of trouble and needs a lot of help."*

And this is what finally reaches you:

Candy: *"Andy's been telling people that it's all your fault that your parents are getting divorced and that you're going to have to go to this special school that helps kids who are in trouble."*

The only way to check out the backbiting rumor is to talk to Andy. He probably said *something*. But there may have been a context, or additional remarks, that didn't get passed along. Give him the benefit of the doubt. Tell him what you heard and how it made you feel:

"I can't believe that you'd say something like that, so I wanted to ask you about it."

You may discover that the whole thing was just a misunderstanding. Or you may find that your friend is guilty as charged. In that case, you'll have to decide whether and/or how things can be patched up.

Shunning

One day, for no apparent reason, your friends start acting like jerks. They don't return your calls or texts, and when you see them in school, they don't stop to talk. You know they're getting together without you. What's up . . . and what can you do?

It can feel very lonely and disorienting when people you like and trust suddenly give you the cold shoulder. If *one* friend does this, maybe she *is* a jerk and you should just write her off. But if you're having problems with *all* of your friends, it may be because of something you did (or they mistakenly think you did).

Take a close look at yourself. Has your behavior changed? Have you been upset, negative, or cranky? Have you said or done anything that might have hurt someone or caused offense? Even if your friends are behaving badly toward you—even if they're being selfish, snooty, or petty—make the effort to consider your own words and actions. Keep in mind that you can't control your friends; you can only control *yourself*.

The way to get other people to change their behavior is to change your own. This works with friends, parents, teachers, bosses—anybody.

If you can't identify any reasons for the way your friends are treating you, seek out the one friend you trust the most. Approach her when she isn't with the rest of the group and doesn't have to put up a front. Tell her that you value her friendship, but you've noticed that she and the others don't seem to want you around lately. Explain that this has upset you, and you wonder if you've done something to alienate them. She may give you some feedback that will point the way to changes you can make, or reveal a misunderstanding that you can set straight.

It's also possible that you're simply out of favor. Sad but true, relationships among teenagers can be fickle, painful, and short-lived. Friends drop friends for reasons both good and bad. If this particular group has decided to reject you, you can't force them to take you back. But you can hold your head high and make new friends. If your old group should later decide that they want to include you again, you can choose to resume those friendships or not. But whatever you do, don't drop your new friends. You know how much that can hurt.

Dear Alex

"I did something terrible to one of my friends. We've been avoiding each other ever since. I'd apologize, but I don't think it will help. What should I do?"

The only thing you *can* do is apologize. You can do this in person (if she's willing to talk to you) or by writing a note. Don't hedge your apology. Don't make excuses, or minimize what happened, or place any blame on your friend for "being too sensitive" or "not being able to take a joke." Take full responsibility for the terrible thing you did, and make it clear that you're profusely and abjectly sorry. Say that the last thing you'd ever want to do would be to hurt or embarrass a friend; that you don't know how you could have been so careless, unthinking, and inconsiderate; that you can understand if she never wants to see you again; that you'd give anything to turn back the clock and erase the event; and that you know you don't deserve it, but you hope she'll be able to forgive you.

If your friendship is strong, your friend *will* forgive you. After hearing how miserable and guilty you've been feeling over the incident, she may even console you.

Taking Sides

If you have more than one friend (and let's hope you do), chances are that at some point two of them won't get along. And each will want you to take sides against the other.

Adults face this same situation when couples they have been friends with divorce, and each spouse tries to convince his or her friends that it was the other person's fault. It's best to stay out of the crossfire. Friendship doesn't obligate you to enlist every time one of your friends goes to war.

When your friends begin to badmouth each other, simply hold up a hand and say:

> "Stop! I'm very sorry that you and Meg are angry with each other, and I know how upsetting that must be. But I like you both too much to get caught in the middle or choose sides. I'm sure that if you and Meg sit down and talk about the problem, you can resolve it."

This doesn't mean that you can't use information you glean from one or the other to try to effect a rapprochement. For instance, if one of your friends said "You know, if she'd just apologize, I'd be willing to forget the whole thing," you could mention to the other friend "You know, I'm sure if you'd just apologize, Meg would be willing to forget the whole thing."

Telling Secrets

Have you ever had a friend (note the past tense) who couldn't keep a secret? This is one of the most serious—and most common—of all friendship problems. Keeping secrets is difficult, and the temptation to share them is great, because information is power. When someone blabs a secret, they're saying "I know something you don't know. I'm 'in the loop' and you're not."

Not all secret spillers are intentionally malicious. In their mind, they're not really breaking a confidence, because they're only telling a friend they know they can trust. Of course, that friend tells *her* best friend, who tells *her* best friend, and before you know it, your secret makes the rounds of the entire school.

There's only one surefire way to keep someone from spilling one of your secrets: Don't tell it in the first place. But if you must tell someone, make sure it's a person who's told *you* a lot of secrets. This is known as *mutual deterrence*. It's what two countries do when they point nuclear weapons at each other. Since either has the power to destroy the other, neither makes the first move.

Dear Alex

"This so-called friend of mine read my diary and told everyone what I'd written about them. I'm so embarrassed I could die. But first I want to kill him. Why are people so mean?"

All thoughtful, moral people ask this question at some point in their lives. The answer has to do with evolution, human nature, psychology, genes, temperament, self-image, the environment in which one lives, and how one was brought up. Add in the fact that not all meanness is equal, and the issue gets even more complicated. Dumping someone's books is mean, but it's nowhere near as mean as taunting someone because of his ethnic background, which is nowhere near as mean as executing all of the people in a village because of their religious beliefs.

Meanness is usually the result of:

Thoughtlessness. People may be "sloppy" about the way they go through life. They don't take the time to think before they speak or act.

Lack of empathy. People may be self-centered and fail to consider how things look from someone else's perspective.

Intolerance. Children learn intolerance from their parents, political and religious leaders, societal messages, prior generations, etc. Prejudiced people, because they're self-righteous, wouldn't call their behavior "mean." But of course it is—and worse.

Entitlement. People who feel that life has treated them unfairly may believe that they're entitled to take what they want and abuse others. They see this as "righting the scales," not as being mean.

Poor self-image. People who hurt others are often in great pain themselves. Putting down others is a power trip that masks their own insecurities.

None of these "causes" of meanness is an excuse for being mean. But each helps us understand it—and ourselves—a little better.

Meanness is an extreme form of rudeness. In the case of your "friend's" betrayal, you have three choices:

1. You can make a conscious decision to drop him.

2. You can wait and see what happens. The friendship may dry up and die on its own; it may return to normal with time; your own feelings may change; or your friend may apologize.

3. You can try talking to your friend. Tell him how you feel about what he did. Don't accuse or attack. Focus on your own shock,

embarrassment, and hurt. He may be feeling terribly remorseful, and your overture may give him the opportunity to apologize.

Dodging a Debt

You're a kind and generous person, so you occasionally agree to loan money to a friend. But what should you do when the friend doesn't pay you back? Since dodging a debt is rude, you can treat this as a "responding to rudeness" situation.* You might say:

> *"You know that 20 dollars I loaned you last week? I'm sure it's just slipped your mind, but I need it back."*

By giving your friend the benefit of the doubt, you offer her a face-saving way out. If she says she doesn't have the money right now, try to set up a payment plan in which, for example, she gives you five dollars a week. You'll quickly learn whether she intends to repay you or string you along with a bunch of excuses. If she's a bad debt, you may have to absorb your loss.

When loaning money to friends whose creditworthiness hasn't yet been established, it's a good idea to see whether they repay their *first* loan before you agree to a second (or a third). This way, you cut your losses early. For larger loans (for example, the $100 a friend needs toward a new pair of track shoes), it's a good idea to draft a letter stating the amount and outlining a payment schedule. This prevents misunderstandings and impresses upon both parties the business-like nature of the transaction.

Many friends loan money back and forth to tide each other over during lean periods. This is fine, as long as things stay relatively even. If, however, you keep coming up on the short end of the deal, you may need to cut off the cash flow.

"You're my best friend. Of course I'll lend you the money. Introductory interest rate of 5.9% for the first three months, 18.9% for the next three months, monthly P&I payments amortized over 15 years, $10 late fee, balloon for the balance in six months. Sign here."

*FOR A REFRESHER ON THE BEST WAYS TO RESPOND TO RUDENESS, SEE PAGES 19–21.

FRIENDS,
ROMANCE,
COUNTRYMEN

Dear Alex

"I have this friend I really like, but she stays at my house forever—even when I hint that it's time for her to go. How can I get her to leave without being rude? She also keeps me on the phone forever when we talk."

You'll have to be a bit more assertive—and forearmed. When you issue an invitation, include an end time. Say:

> *"Do you want to come over this afternoon? I have to start my homework at 6:00. But you could stay until then."*

For those never-ending phone calls, have an arsenal of excuses handy:
> *"I have to eat dinner now."*
> *"I need to make another call before it gets too late."*
> *"My dad's calling. I gotta take it."*
> *"My mom wants me to help her with something."*

When you offer an excuse, preface it politely. As in:
> *"I wish you could stay longer, but . . . ."*
> *"I'd love to talk more, but . . . ."*

Another good phrase to have handy for those interminable phone calls is "I'm going to let you go," as in "I know how busy you are so I'm going to let you go." It works because it sounds as if you're doing the person a big favor by releasing her from the captivity of the phone call.

Jealousy

Sometimes it may seem as if your friends are better than you. Maybe they're winning more prizes or getting better grades or wearing cooler clothes. Perhaps they're more popular or more attractive or smarter. In any case, you wake up one day feeling like a total loser—and jealous besides.

It's difficult when other people seem to have all the luck and success, especially when they're your friends. It's natural to feel jealous. But you're overlooking one thing: They have chosen *you* for their friend. Do you think they'd hang out with a total loser? No way. This means there must be something wonderful in you that they see and you don't.

People are successful in all sorts of different ways. Maybe you're a terrific "people person"—considerate, well-mannered, responsible, trustworthy, helpful, empathetic, caring, loyal, supportive, and fun to be with. Those are *real* talents. They're just not as easy to quantify as grades or votes or numbers of goals scored. You may tell yourself that those things don't count. But they do. In fact, you'll go a lot further in life, and find a lot more fulfillment, than will people who are great students or athletes but lack those skills.

Being a friend means showing pleasure in your friends' prizes, trophies, and honors—even when you're hurting inside. But that hurt will go away if you take the friendship of these high achievers for the compliment it is. Focus on the strengths and talents you have, rather than the ones you may not have.

True Confessions

Do your friends bring their problems to you? This can be a compliment—and a burden. Sometimes you might not know what to say, or you might be afraid of saying the wrong thing.

Chances are you're already saying the right things, or you wouldn't have so many friends confiding in you. For everyday problems and normal teenage mood swings, here are some good ways to respond:

Be a shoulder. Most people, when they have problems, just want somebody to listen. They're feeling isolated, abnormal, confused, or afraid. If you lend an attentive and empathetic ear, you might give your friend 90 percent of what she needs. If you've dealt with a similar problem in your own life, share your experience. If you see a possible solution, suggest it.

Ask questions. This is a good way to help people get their troubles in perspective. Essentially, what you're doing is leading a problem-solving session.* First, help your friend define the problem. (Often we just feel overwhelmed. Once we get a handle on the problem, it becomes less scary or upsetting.) Then let your friend brainstorm attitudinal and/or practical ways to deal with it. Encourage her to pick the best ideas and to make a plan of action. You can then help her follow through.

Be sure not to minimize the problem. In an effort to make your friends feel better, you may say things to comfort them that end up belittling their feelings or situation:

> *"You'll get over it."*
> *"It's not that big a deal."*
> *"You'll get another chance."*
> *"That happens to lots of people."*
> *"It'll be all right."*

Of course, these things may all be true. But people who are upset don't want logic or platitudes. They want sympathy, love, understanding, and acceptance. They want you to know that they're hurting. To be a real friend, show that you know and give them what they need.

*FOR A REFRESHER ON HOW TO DO THIS, SEE PAGES 136–138.

For example, if a friend says that her father has to have an operation for cancer, don't say "Oh, I'm sure it will be fine." Even though you're saying it to cheer her up, you don't know how the operation will turn out. Neither does she, and that's why she's scared to death. Say "That must be really frightening" or "I'd be so worried if my father had to have an operation."

Offer assistance. When friends come to you with problems, ask them if there's anything you can do to help. They'll probably respond "No." When they do, say "Okay, but promise you'll tell me if there is. I really want to help." When you make your caring explicit, it lets your friends know that they're not alone.

Show that you're not afraid to talk about difficult things. Sometimes, after sharing a problem, teenagers will feel embarrassed or wish they could take back what they said. The next time you talk to your friend, tell her how glad you were that she told you about her troubles. Then ask her how she's feeling and how it's going. If it's obvious that she doesn't want to talk about it anymore, let it pass.

Be alert to the possibility that there's more to the story than you're being told. Friends with serious problems will sometimes only tell you the tip of the iceberg. They may be in denial; they may be ashamed; they may be hesitant to spill a family secret.

For example, someone says that his parents aren't getting along, but what's really happening on the home front are knock-down-drag-out fights. Or someone says he's been "experimenting" with drugs when in fact he's been using them daily for six months.

If you suspect that you're not getting the whole story, you'll need to encourage your friend to say more. Asking "Do you want to talk about it?" makes it easy for him to say "No." Instead, try saying "Sounds like things are pretty rough. Tell me what's going on." In your friend's mind, this turns talking from a self-indulgence into a kindness he can do for you.

Know when you need to turn to others. The approaches described previously should work for most everyday problems. But what about a friend who says she's going to kill herself? What about a friend you suspect is being abused at home? What about a friend who's shooting heroin? These are terribly difficult situations, and you shouldn't expect or attempt to solve them by yourself.

Your friend may be confiding in you in the hope (conscious or not) that you'll "force" her to get help. Even if she resists, try to get her to see a counselor, talk to a trusted adult, or contact a hotline. Explain that you're very concerned about her and will do everything you can to help. If your friend refuses or makes you swear not to tell, don't back off or let it go.

Talk to your parents or another trusted adult. Tell them what you know about your friend and ask for their help.

It's worth risking the friendship if your friend's life or health are in danger. She may be angry at first. But if she gets the help she needs, she'll eventually think of you as the best friend she ever had. And if she drops you or comes to greater harm, at least you'll know you did everything you could to help.

Dear Alex

"What are you supposed to say if a friend tells you he's gay?"

It depends on how and why it's said. If it's just mentioned in passing—as in "I'd love to come to your party, but my boyfriend and I will be attending the Gay Pride rally that day"—treat it as you would any other piece of information. Say "We'll miss you" or "Have a good time!" or "You'll have to tell me how it went."

If it's said to set things straight (so to speak), say "Thanks for telling me."

If it's said as a proud disclosure of identity, offer the person your best wishes for a life full of much love and happiness.

If it's said in confidence by a friend who's troubled by his sexuality, respond with warmth, support, and empathy. Encourage him to talk. Ask questions and use active listening.* If specific things are upsetting him (for example, how to tell his parents or harassment at school), help him explore options for dealing with these issues. If your school is "gay-friendly," he may find a gay-straight alliance and/or empathetic counselors. He could also look online or in local bookstores for some of the excellent books written for GLBTQ teens. Tons of blogs, support groups, and other resources for gay and lesbian teens can be found online or by calling a hotline.

There's no need for a gay or lesbian teenager to deal with these issues alone. The best thing you can do for your friend is see that he doesn't have to.

*TO LEARN HOW TO USE ACTIVE LISTENING, SEE PAGES 357–359.

Getting Along with Roommates

You're thrown into a cabin at Camp Meneemoskeetoes with seven kids you can't stand. Or you go away to school and get stuck with the dork from New York. If you're lucky, these loathsome creatures will become your best friends. If you're not, they'll make your life a living hell.

When it's time for you to have a roommate, ideally you'll be matched with people with whom you have something in common. Realistically, you might find yourself sharing close quarters with beings who, like you, are airbreathing bipeds—and that's where the similarity ends.

Roommates can be soul mates—simpatico companions you end up loving as much as (or more than) your siblings.* Or they can be schmucks who charge you for a stamp, leave crumbs on your bed, take your things without asking, and tell you to get lost so they can make out with their boyfriend or girlfriend.

Improve your chances of getting along by doing your part. Start by respecting your roommate's privacy. It's very important for roommates to respect each other's privacy because there isn't any. Since *physical* privacy is usually impossible to achieve, you have to create *psychological* privacy. Here's how:

- Never read your roommate's letters, email, journals, or papers.
- Stay out of your roommate's desk and bureau drawers.
- Keep your hands off of your roommate's computer and smartphone.
- Always ask permission before borrowing your roommate's possessions.
- Don't reveal personal things you learn from living with your room-mate. ("Hey, did you guys know that Damani drools in his sleep?")
- Never rat on your roommate unless his transgressions harm you personally, or place him or others in physical, legal, emotional, or reputational danger.

Non-Rattable Offenses	**Rattable Offenses**
Your roommate sneaks out during every full moon to sing Verdi under the stars.	Your roommate sneaks out during every full moon to get drunk and play chicken with freight trains.
Your roommate uses cheat sheets for French quizzes.	Your roommate deals drugs from your room.

Of course, it's best for your relationship if you first try to deal directly with your roommate about even the rattable issues.

If you're scrupulous about honoring these principles, your roommate is likely to follow suit. Setting a good example is better than saying "Mess with my things and I'll pull your tongue out." Since people have different attitudes toward sharing, it's also perfectly fine to establish limits: "You're welcome to borrow my racket, but I'd appreciate it if you'd check with me before using my toothbrush." You can also negotiate such things as who

*FOR A REFRESHER ON ROOMING WITH SIBLINGS, SEE PAGES 134—138.

gets the upper bunk, whether you sleep with the window open, and what to do when your roomie's clothes take up the whole closet.

Another way to create the illusion of privacy is to make your presence invisible when circumstances require. Let's say your roommate is in the middle of a private and painful conversation with a friend. You'd leave the room except you're waaaay behind schedule on a paper and you have to keep working at your desk. Your roommate would leave except it hasn't occurred to him. Therefore, create the illusion of privacy by intensifying your concentration. This will reduce the self-consciousness your roommate would feel if you made faces in response to the conversation, or even entered into it. When the friend leaves, your roomie will probably want to talk about what transpired. Even though *he* knows *you* know that something went down, let him tell you what happened. It reinforces the illusion of privacy.

A final aspect of roommate privacy involves respecting routines. Let's say you go to soccer practice every afternoon between 3:00 and 4:00. One day your coach is sick and practice is canceled. You head back to your dorm barely five minutes after having left it. Your roommate, however, may be counting on having an hour of private time. If you barge in unexpectedly, you might catch him doing something that he'd be very embarrassed to have you discover—like, say, studying. Therefore, when you get near your door, bang against it. Fumble with your keys. Drop your books. Yell "Hi!" to a friend. Take a lonnnnnnnnng time to open the door. Your roommate will appreciate this act of courtesy.

Dear Alex

"What do you do when your roommate is a jerk? I mean, this guy is hopeless."

Whoa. Let's back up for a minute. First, we need to confirm that your roommate really *is* a jerk, because sometimes the label is unfairly applied. For example, these characteristics might be misinterpreted as jerkdom when really they're a matter of perspective and preference:

- lines pencils up by height
- wears funny glasses
- has a weird haircut
- studies too hard or doesn't study hard enough
- writes letters to his or her parents
- uses a knife and fork to eat an apple
- likes Wiener schnitzel

In contrast, these characteristics indicate that you're dealing with a genuine jerk:

- spreads malicious rumors about people
- bullies new kids
- takes your sweater without asking
- refuses to do his or her fair share of cleaning
- spits on someone's tuna sandwich as a joke
- refuses to turn off music so you can sleep
- blabs your secrets to everyone
- likes Wiener schnitzel

You can see that the first list reflects the intolerance of the beholder rather than the jerkiness of the beheld. These surface behaviors have nothing to do with the substance of a person. Judging people in this manner is *character bigotry*. It says "If you don't do things my way, you're a jerk." Isn't that the very attitude teenagers hate so much in adults?

The second list portrays a bona fide, Class A jerk. These behaviors are not harmless superficial traits. They are acts of aggression. People get hurt. This person is self-centered and inconsiderate.

The first thing you need to do is diagnose your roommate's jerkiness. Is he just different, or is he a certifiable jerk? If it's the former, suspend your judgment long enough to get to know him. You may discover a terrific person beneath those uncool (to you) surface characteristics.

If, however, the person is truly a jerkmeister, you have three choices:

1. **Set him straight.** If you're willing to invest some time and energy, you can use your insight and people skills to try to help your roommate. Maybe he doesn't know how to make friends. Maybe he feels awkward and stupid. Maybe nobody's ever told him how his actions affect others. Maybe he's hurting from something in his background or home life. Be his friend. It could work wonders.

2. **Maintain your distance.** Be polite. Stay cool. Establish limits as to what you will and won't tolerate in your roommate's behavior. And count the days until you and he part ways.

3. **Change roommates.** Most school and camp officials would probably say that learning to get along with people you don't like is a valuable life lesson. That's all well and good, but they don't have to live with them. If you've really tried to handle the situation, if your roommate is really making life miserable for you and others, there's no reason to put up with it. Talk to your advisor or counselor.

It may be possible to engineer a roommate swap or move one of you to a different room.

The Etiquette of Romance

During elementary school, most kids' energy goes into the three Rs. But once junior high rolls around, a fourth R is added: *Romance*. Hormones start percolating, and suddenly the world looks very different. Obnoxious boys turn into *cute* obnoxious boys; giggly girls turn into *cute* giggly girls. The fear of cooties is set aside and the hunt is on.

Romance doesn't just happen. It takes careful strategizing and armies of friends to pull it off. This is because junior high etiquette doesn't permit the couple-to-be to negotiate on their own behalf. The reason: the fifth R—*Rejection*—which must be avoided at all costs.

Here's how the ritual works: A guy texts a girl. He pretends that he has questions about homework or carpool. Then, with all the offhandedness he can muster, he types *btw do u like tim?*

The girl is absolutely bonkers wild in love with Tim. So she writes back *he's ok*. And the conversation continues:

> *do u like him?*
> *y, does he like me?*

Since this could go on all evening, the guy tries a different tack:

> *if he asked u to go w/ him—and i'm not saying he wld—*
> *but if he did, wld u?*
> *i might*
> *well wld u?*
> *prolly*
> *prolly yes?*
> *yeah, i guess*
> *so u wld, right?*
> *yes*
> *hey guess who just walked in, it's tim. he wants to type smth*

At this point, Tim takes the phone whose screen he was watching the whole time and, now that he knows he won't be rejected, asks Beth to go with him. By 8:20 the next morning, the news is all over school. Tim and Beth are seen holding hands. Their friends are free to spread rumors and participate in all the major and minor crises of the relationship.

Which probably won't last very long, because nobody wants to be dumped. And the only way to avoid getting dumped is to dump the other person before he or she dumps you. So, at the first signs of strain, boredom, or wandering eyes in the relationship, one of the parties will enlist a friend to tell the other "You're dumped." The dumpee can then either deny having been dumped or use being dumped as a way to get sympathy and attention. Friends will rally 'round, be extra nice, and say nasty things about the dumper. The school will have a new source of drama, and cell phones will beep and buzz all night.

From an etiquette standpoint, this system leaves a lot to be desired. In an effort to spare one person from hurt, it inflicts hurt on others. It opens up personal matters to widespread scrutiny and gossip. But in junior high (and sometimes into high school), it's the way things tend to happen.

The first steps toward a new skill—be it reading, riding, or romancing—are often awkward and scary. As you start down the rocky road to love, you can expect to undergo a period during which your relationships are orchestrated by emissaries. You might compare this to training wheels. When you first learned to ride a bicycle, they kept you up and running with maximal speed and minimal injury. But if you use them longer than you need them, they can foster a dependence that ultimately slows your future progress. Therefore, training wheels—and emissaries—should be discarded at the first opportunity.

Dear Alex

"Girls are always falling in love with me. How do I let them know I'm not interested without hurting their feelings?"

Assuming that the infatuated ones are asking you out, the simplest way to deflect their affections is by being "too busy." (There's no need to issue preemptive rejections to anyone rumored to be swooning over you.) Simply say:

"I'm sorry, but I have plans for that night."

If they ask again, respond with the same statement. If they call, say:

"I'm sorry, but I'm busy and can't talk."

It should soon become clear that you're too engaged to squeeze them into your life. If they press you further ("Is there *any* time in the next five years when you don't have plans?"), say:

"I'm afraid I'm just too busy to have much of a social life."

Of course, they'll eventually realize that you find time to go out with *other* girls. So a feeling of rejection is unavoidable. But etiquette doesn't erase hurt from the face of the earth; it merely tries to minimize it. And those who refuse to take face-saving hints only open themselves up to greater hurt.

Dear Alex

"There's a boy I really love, but he doesn't even know I exist. How can I get him to like me?"

If there's anything worse than being in love with someone who doesn't know you exist, it's being in love with someone who knows and doesn't care. Romance would be easier and less heartbreaking if we could *will* people to like us.

It might also be less fun.

You can't "get" him to like you. But you *can* try to attract his attention—and eventually, maybe, win his affection—by being your best self. Don't show off. Don't force yourself on him. And follow the strategies outlined in the answer to the next question.

Dear Alex

"How do you show a girl that you like her?"*

If you're seven years old, pull her pigtails and put a spider in her lunch box. If you're older, try these strategies instead:

Pay attention to her. Smile. Say "Hello!" Ask questions about her classes, interests, opinions, experiences, teachers, friends, parents, and siblings. Showing interest in another person says *I like you.*

Spend time with her. Do things together. Walk with her between classes. Call her on the phone. Send her a text message. Wanting to be with someone says *I like you.*

Treat her with respect. Say "Please" and "Thank you." Show pleasure in her accomplishments. Comfort her when she's disappointed. Never say anything behind her back you wouldn't say to her face. Being supportive and trustworthy says *I like you.*

Be thoughtful. Bring her a flower. Write a note. Listen carefully to everything she says. Give her a small gift that follows up on an off-handed remark she makes. Being sensitive and attentive says *I like you.*

Get the word out. Have *your* friends make it known to *her* friends that you like her. This is the sort of thing that makes school so interesting.

Tell her! The direct approach works wonders. Say "I really like you." If that seems too forward, say "I really like being with you" or "I really like it when we do things together."

*****THESE IDEAS ALSO WORK FOR SHOWING A BOY THAT YOU LIKE HIM.**

Asking Someone Out

Before you plant, you must prepare the soil. Similar groundwork must be undertaken before asking someone for a date. Here are nine tips that will increase your chances of success:

1. Get to know the person first. Invitations out of the blue are usually rejected because most of us are taught never to go anywhere with strangers. So take the time and make the effort to learn about the other person—and give him or her a chance to learn something about you. Talk in class (but not during class). Sit together at lunch. Hang out in the same group(s). See if you have things in common and if you enjoy each other's company. If all systems are go . . .

2. Ask early. Give the person advance notice—three to four days for informal dates such as dinner, a movie, or paintball. This allows plenty of time to check with parents, earn some extra money, reschedule an appointment, decide what to wear, and, of course, look forward to being with *you.*

Last-minute invitations are likely to be rejected. Either the person has other plans, or the person doesn't have other plans and wants to hide the fact, or the person assumes (rightly or wrongly) that you couldn't get anyone else to go.

There is an exception to the ask-early rule: an occasion that couldn't have been anticipated. As in:

> *"I just found out that my uncle is sailing his boat up tomorrow. Do you want to go out on the bay with us?"*

3. Don't ask *too* early. Being overeager isn't attractive. Also, it makes both parties involved feel silly:

> *"Would you like to go to the senior prom with me?"*
>
> *"Gee, I don't know. I'm really flattered that you asked. Let's see how we're feeling about each other in two years."*

4. Choose the right moment. You know how important timing is when asking your parents for permission to do something. The same holds true for asking someone out on a date. You don't want to pop the question if your intended is upset, distracted, surrounded by other people, or rushing madly to class. Wait for a calm, private moment.

5. Do the asking yourself. Throughout history, certain individuals have willingly done the dirty work of others. In the adult world, these people are called *lawyers.* In the teenage world, they're called *friends.*

Obviously, rejection is easier to take if it comes secondhand. If you don't do the actual inviting, you have what's known as *plausible deniability.*

When the rumors of your rejection start to fly, you can say "What do you mean? I never asked him out." Despite this advantage, using friends as proxies can backfire for three reasons:

- *Secondhand invitations make you look like a wuss*—someone who's scared or lacking in confidence. Of course, you may actually be scared and lacking in confidence on certain occasions. That's perfectly natural. But courage means taking action in spite of your fears. It's an attractive, admirable quality—one we like to see in people whose dates we accept.

- *Secondhand invitations promote miscommunication.* Are you positive your friend said just what you told her to say? Did she get the day and time right? Did she ask at a good moment? And if your invitation was rejected, was it with an "I-never-want-to-go-out-with-him" no or an "I-might-go-out-with-him-but-not-to-that" no or an "I'd-love-to-go-out-with-him-but-can't-that-night" no?*

- *Secondhand invitations encourage gossip and rumors.* If you ask someone out and get turned down, only two people know. It's a private matter. There's a good chance that the respect you've shown in asking the person yourself will be reciprocated by her not blabbing all over creation. If, however, you get a friend to do the asking, it becomes a public matter. Your friend may tell a friend, your prospective date may tell a friend, and before you know it, the gory details are all over school.

So resist the temptation to use friends as social secretaries. Issue your invitations face-to-face, phone-to-phone, text-to-text, or in writing.

6. Go s-l-o-w-l-y. Some people (there are three in North America) have no trouble asking for a date. Full of confidence and charm, they pick up the phone, propose a wonderful evening, wait for the yes, and carry out their plans with aplomb.

Most people are a bit less sure of themselves. You know what that can be like. You agonize for weeks or months: *Does she like me? What if I don't have anything to say? What if the answer's no? What if I make a fool of myself? Where would we go?* Finally, you muster the courage to pop the question. With pounding heart and flip-flopping stomach, you pick up the phone and start to dial. And immediately hit end. After eleven tries, you let it ring. She answers. And in a firm, confident voice, you say "Gulp."

When you ask someone out for the first time, take it easy. Think date with a small *d*. Don't plan a six-hour evening where you'll be all alone in new or stressful circumstances. Do something low-key and informal. Go

*FOR MORE ON THE VARIATIONS OF THE DECEPTIVELY SIMPLE WORD "NO," SEE PAGES 258–259.

FRIENDS,
ROMANCE,
COUNTRYMEN

to a basketball game with a group of friends. Play tennis. Go skating. See a movie. Do some shopping. Your comfort and friendship will grow, and you'll know when the time is right to ask for a date with a capital *D*.

You may be thinking *But I'm cool. I can handle anything.* That may be true, but your date might not feel the same way. Take things slowly for his or her sake.

7. Be specific. If you issue a vague invitation, you're asking for it. Not a date—a major hurt. As in:

"You wanna go out sometime?"

"No."

Even if the person replies "Sure," she may be thinking *In a hundred million years.* And you have no way of knowing.

Here's the difference between being vague and being specific:

Vague—No!	Specific—Yes!
"What're ya doin' Friday night?"	"Are you free Friday night to go trick or treating?"
"Ya wanna go out with me?"	"Would you like to go to the Halloween Dance with me?"
"How 'bout doin' somethin' sometime?"	"I'm wondering if you'd like to see that new documentary on bighorn elks at the Rialto. Maybe this Saturday? It's only showing for a week."

Once you've issued the invitation, you can provide further details on time, place, mode of transportation, curfews, special clothing or equipment required, etc.

8. Be positive. Negative invitations plant the idea of rejection in the mind of the person you're asking. And they make it easy to say no in response.

"You wouldn't want to go to the movies with me, would you?" (No, I wouldn't.)

"I don't suppose you're free next Thursday?" (No, I'm not.)

Negative invitations soften the blow of rejection ("I got turned down, but at least I guessed right!"). They also tend to be self-fulfilling prophecies. Because they reveal your lack of confidence, they require the person to contradict you in order to accept, and that's too confusing and too much work.

"You wouldn't want to go to the movies with me, would you?" (Well, yes, I would, but if you think I wouldn't, then maybe I shouldn't.)

"I don't suppose you're free next Thursday?" (Actually, I am, but if you think I'm not, then I probably shouldn't be, because what does that say about my social schedule? So I'd better find something else to do.)

Remember that an invitation from you is a compliment. It says *I and my wonderful self desire your company.* Let that be your message. If you still get turned down, at least you gave it your best shot.

9. Be up-front about money. Let's say you want to invite someone out but you don't have enough moola. Should you forget about asking? Or you've been invited to a concert but the tickets cost $85—too much for you. Do you say no? Either way, don't let money keep you from extending or accepting invitations. It's normal for teenagers to be flush one week and broke the next.

If you're doing the inviting, you can signal your intentions with certain words and phrases. For example, if you plan on paying, you can say:

> *"My treat."*
>
> *"Would you be my guest for . . . ?"*
>
> *"I just got my birthday money, and I'd love to take you to . . . ."*

If you don't have the bucks, you can mention that you'll have to "go Dutch," which means each person pays his or her way.* Or you might say "I can cover the tickets if you can spring for the food."

If you're on the receiving end of the invitation, don't be embarrassed about raising the question of who pays. If money isn't an issue, you can just bring some to cover your expenses should the need arise. If it is an issue, say "I'd love to go, but I'm short on funds right now." That will get things out into the open.

Being Asked Out

Someone you know has just asked you out. It's Decision Time! What you say and how you say it will depend on whether you like the person, whether you like the person enough to go out with him or her, whether you're free to date, and about a zillion other factors. But basically your answer will be "Yes," "Maybe," or "No." Let's look at the protocols of each.

If your answer is "Yes" . . .
Shout it from the rooftops of your heart. Say:

> *"I'd love to!"*
>
> *"That sounds great!"*
>
> *"I've always wanted to do that!"*
>
> *"I was hoping you'd ask me!"*

Convey enthusiasm, appreciation, anticipation, eagerness, and anything else you can think of along those lines. The person who asked you probably sweated bullets for three weeks before popping the question. He or she deserves more than:

*FOR MORE ON "GOING DUTCH," SEE PAGE 306.

"Okay."

"Sure."

"I guess."

"Why not?"

Never accept an invitation and back out later unless there's an emergency or you become ill. It's not fair to leave your date high and dry. He or she might have already made arrangements, spent money, or told other people. Your reversal might be inconvenient and/or embarrassing. And it would give you a reputation for being hurtful and unreliable.

If your answer is "Maybe" . . .

Sometimes you'll need to check with your parents or reschedule a conflict before you can accept an invitation. If this is the case, convey your enthusiasm, just as you would if you answered "Yes." Then, in a verbal footnote, explain the catch. Let the person know when you'll have a definite answer. Don't invent a phony excuse to keep someone on hold for days while you wait to see if a better offer comes along.

"Hi, Ben. Would you like to go to the Turnabout Dance with me?"

"I dunno. Maybe. When is it?"

"Oh, man, if only she'd ask me to the Turnabout Dance this Saturday, my life would be perfect. I'd be the happiest guy on the planet. Please, oh please, let her ask me."

If your answer is "No" . . .

There are three types of no:

1. The "I'm-hoping-someone-else-will-ask-me" no. Let's say you've been invited to a school dance by someone you feel lukewarm about. You're hoping someone else will ask you. You can't say "I'm holding out for someone better" or "I'll go with you if no one else asks" because that would hurt the asker's feelings. And you can't say "Sorry, but I'm going to be away that weekend" because then, if you turn up at the dance, you'll be caught in your lie. So there's only one thing you *can* say, and that is:

"I'm sorry, but I already have plans for Saturday. Thank you for asking."

If you show up at the dance with someone else, it'll be apparent what those other plans were.

It would be rude for anyone to ask what your plans are. Should this happen, you're under no obligation to respond. Just be a parrot and repeat what you said about already having other plans. Eventually the person will give up.

2. The "I'd-love-to-but-I-can't" no. The key here is to make sure the person knows that you really *want* to be asked again. When you refuse the invitation, make sure you convey your regret, dismay, disappointment, and heartbreak:

"Oh, Nigel, I'm soooo sorry, but that's the night I have my acupuncture sessions and I just can't get out of them. But please ask me again. I'd love to do it some other time."

3. The "I-wouldn't-go-out-with-you-for-a-billion-dollars" no. The first time someone in this category extends an invitation, you can use the "I already have plans" response or "Thank you, but I'm not free that evening." Be polite. There's no need to carve the person's feelings into mincemeat with a reply such as "Are you kidding? What makes you think *I* would ever go out with *you?*"

The second time this person extends an invitation (which may occur then and there—"Well, how about *next* Saturday?"), you can respond in the same way. If after several refusals he or she still doesn't get the hint, you'll need to be more direct, but in a gentle, considerate manner:

"I'm very flattered that you keep asking me, but I just don't see us going out together."

If the person presses you for a reason, take it upon yourself:

"I'm just not the person for you."

"I'm interested in someone else."

"I'm not dating anyone these days."

This type of response accomplishes two good things. First, it respects the other person's feelings. And second, it closes the door to rebuttals. Only someone who's completely clueless will fail to take the hint.

Finally, don't blab. If you asked someone out and got turned down, you'd feel hurt or disappointed. Imagine how much worse you'd feel if the person went around telling everybody. There's not much you can do to stop others from indulging in such rudeness. But you can make sure that *you* never do it yourself.

Dear Alex

"Is it okay to go out with someone if your friend likes him, too?"

If your friend is currently going out with him, no. If neither of you is seeing him, talk to your friend before taking any action. It's difficult to maintain a friendship when you're both competing for the same guy.

You might try to find out how he feels about you and your friend. If he doesn't like either of you, or he just likes one of you, knowing that might save you some needless conflict. Once you've got the lay of the land, you can negotiate with your friend about the best way to proceed. For example, you might decide that the person who's liked him longest gets first dibs.

Sometimes sensitive teens voluntarily refrain from going out with their friends' ex-boyfriends or crush objects. But one should never ask somebody to do this. It's hard enough to manage one's own social life without trying to run the social lives of others.

Dear Alex

"When my boyfriend picks me up to go out, he just sits in his car and honks. My parents get mad at me because he won't come into the house. He gets mad at me because I tell him he should come in. And I get mad at everyone. What does etiquette say about this?"

Etiquette says "Young man, get out of that car this instant!" A gentleman *always* comes to the door the first time he picks up a young lady at her home. He does this for three reasons:

1. so the girl's parents can meet him

2. as a sign of respect for his date

3. so he can wear a T-shirt that says "I Met My Girlfriend's Parents and Survived"

You're beyond the first date stage, but it's not too late to amend the situation. Tell your boyfriend that the next time he picks you up, he *will* and *must* get out of his car and come into your house.

You can ensure that the occasion will go smoothly by doing a little prep work. Tell your parents a few things about your boyfriend:

"Henry is on the chess team. He spent last summer on an archaeological dig in Levittown."

This way, they'll have some leads for conversation. Coach your boyfriend in the same manner:

"My dad helped design the Mars Rover. My mom is a crime reporter for The Journal. *They just built a new addition on our house. Tell them you like it."*

Greet your boyfriend personally when he arrives. None of this up-in-your-room-still-getting-dressed business. Instead, make introductions and let the conversation flow. If your parents are the sort who really push their luck, they may invite you to sit in the living room for a few minutes. Once you've done this, you're free to depart.

On subsequent dates, you can watch for your boyfriend from a window and go out to meet him when he drives up. It's not necessary for him to come to the door. But a wise young gentleman will do so anyway. And this goes for young ladies who take gentlemen on dates, too.

Dear Alex

"If somebody sets you up on a blind date and you meet the person and don't like her, is it okay not to go through with the date?"

No. That would be rude and hurtful. You can, however, take certain steps to minimize the awkwardness:

- Only go out on blind dates in a group. This doesn't mean that you audition four hopefuls at once. Instead, it means that you go out with several other couples or friends. This allows you to dilute the contact with your date, if need be.

- Pick an activity that doesn't force you to talk or stare into each other's eyes all night. A movie, ice-skating, shopping, or a football game all fit the bill.

A blind date can be fun and interesting if you go with the right attitude. At best, it can result in a wonderful new friend. At worst, it's a great chance to practice your patience, tolerance, and charm.

Dear Alex

"Sometimes my boyfriend comes over to my house, and I'll cook a snack or a meal. He never helps. He won't even do the dishes. He says it's the woman's job. Another thing I don't like is when I'm with him and we run into people he knows, he never introduces me. Other than those two things, I love him."

If your boyfriend has an allergy to kitchen work, you might overlook it as long as he does the laundry. But it sounds as though he has an allergy to respecting women. He wants you to serve him in private and stand in his shadow in public. If you probe your relationship, you may find other examples of this attitude.

Your boyfriend is living in a time warp. He'd probably love the following advice, taken from a 1950s home economics textbook:

How to Be a Good Wife

Have dinner ready. Most men are hungry when they come home, and the prospect of a good meal is part of the warm welcome needed.

Minimize the noise. At the time of his arrival, eliminate all the noise of the washer, dryer, dishwasher, or vacuum. Try to encourage the children to be quiet. Greet him with a warm smile and be glad to see him.

Some don'ts: Don't greet him with problems and complaints. Don't complain if he is late for dinner. Count this as minor compared to what he might have gone through that day. Make him comfortable. Have him lean back in a comfortable chair or suggest that he lie down in the bedroom. Have a cool drink ready for him. Arrange his pillow and offer to take off his shoes. Speak in a low, soft, soothing and pleasant voice.

Make the evening his. Never complain if he does not take you out to dinner or to other pleasant entertainment. Instead try to understand his world of strain and pressure, his need to unwind and relax. ✿

You're excused if you need to go puke or laugh yourself silly. This sort of sexist garbage was actually taught in home ec classes all across America. But that was then, and this is now, and there's no excuse for such Neanderthal behavior.

There's nothing wrong with being sensitive and considerate to someone you love. This is the bedrock of good manners and successful relationships. But it has nothing to do with gender—and it works both ways. Since you say you love your boyfriend, it's probably worth making the investment to try to bring him out of the Stone Age. Don't attack him. Simply tell him how you feel. Say what you need in order for things to work out between you:

"I need to feel that you respect me as an equal."

"I need us to share responsibilities without regard to gender."

He may not have a clue what you mean. In that case, you'll have to be more explicit. If he begins to come around, be supportive and encouraging. If he doesn't, drop him. But don't get discouraged yet. He's young, and he may still be teachable.

Dance Decorum

You're at a school dance. The band is playing a song you like. The mirror ball suspended from the ceiling is casting sparkly confetti through the air. You're tired of hanging around the food table. How do you ask someone to dance?

You say "May I have this dance?" You don't say "Wanna dance?" unless you're willing to hear "Sure, with that gorgeous guy over there!"

How do you refuse if someone asks *you* to dance? Believe it or not, this is trickier than doing the asking. First, you never *refuse*. You *decline*, which is more polite. You do this by invoking one of the following:

1. A physical incapacity. As in:

"I'm sorry, but . . .

> *. . . I'm feeling a bit tired right now."*
> *. . . I'm just too overheated."*
> *. . . I think I slipped a disc on that last dance."*

Honor demands that your subsequent behavior be that of one who is too tired, overheated, or out of alignment to dance. After a reasonable period of recuperation (for example, 10–15 minutes), you can consider yourself back to speed and return to the dance floor.

2. An urgent mission elsewhere. As in:

"I'm sorry, but . . .

> *. . . I simply must get some air."*
> *. . . I have to make a phone call."*
> *. . . I'd like to freshen up a bit."*

Here, too, you need to disappear for a few moments to uphold your integrity.

3. A prior obligation. As in:

"I'm sorry, but . . .

> *. . . I promised this dance to someone else."*
> *. . . I told Mrs. Lilliliver I'd help with the punch."*
> *. . . I said I'd show Kalaya how to do the tango."*

You're probably wondering why, if someone asks you to dance, you can't just say "No, thank you." Picture this:

You say: *"May I have this dance?"*

The other person says: *"No, thank you."*

You think: *What th' . . . ?*

And you stand there for a minute or two—perplexed, hurt, not knowing what to say. Then you slink away wondering *Why not? Is there something wrong with me? Am I too sweaty? Is it my dancing? Was it just this dance they didn't want? Should I ask again?*

In other words, a polite excuse—*even if it's not really true*—allows both parties to maintain their dignity and self-respect. And that's the essence of good manners.

Dear Alex

"I've been taught that if someone asks you to dance and isn't a total loser, it's polite to accept. But the problem is how to get rid of them afterward. I'm willing to be polite, but I'm not willing to go steady based on one dance, if you know what I mean."

Use the same strategies you would to decline a dance in the first place. The only difference is that you excuse yourself from the field rather than the sidelines. Thank your partner for the dance, then declare a physical incapacity, urgent mission elsewhere, or prior commitment. You might also smile warmly, say "Thank you for the dance. Excuse me," and then make your exit.

Dear Alex

"I'm taking my girlfriend to a fancy school dance. Do I have to buy her those flowers you pin on?"

No, you don't "have to." You're perfectly free to bring your date unadorned. Let her look like a patch of crabgrass while the other girls burst forth in the blossoms of spring.

If, however, you wish your relationship to flower, a *corsage* is just what the gardener ordered. Before the dance, ask your date the color of her dress so you can order one that matches (no, not a *dress* that matches, a *corsage* that matches). For example, if she's wearing a plaid dress, you won't want to bring a polka-dot corsage.

"But," you say, "won't knowing about the corsage ahead of time spoil the surprise?"

No. Tradition demands that the young lady act surprised when she receives it.

Now comes the hard part—pinning it on. Start by asking your date where she would like it. Corsages can be pinned up near the shoulder (make sure her dress actually goes up that far before pinning) or at the waist (try not to crush it when dancing). Or she may prefer that her corsage be pinned on the fancy little evening bag she's carrying.

Once you've determined the proper location, follow these simple steps:

1. Hold the corsage so the flowers are at the *top*.

2. Take the pin (the long, nasty-looking one that should have come with the corsage) and push it *horizontally* into the dress and back out through the fabric at one side of the stem of the corsage.

3. Slide the pin *over* the stem, then back *into and out of* the fabric. This not only holds the corsage securely, but creates four holes in the dress. (**TIP:** Some corsages come with two pins, supposedly so you can crisscross them and hold the flowers more securely. But the real reason is so you can make *eight* holes in your date's dress.)

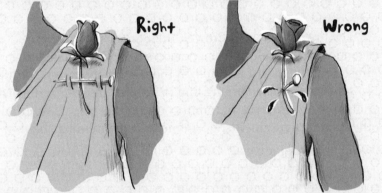

Some girls—perhaps those who don't like mutilating their dresses—prefer to receive a *wristlet* (a corsage worn around the wrist like a bracelet) or a *nosegay* (a little bouquet of flowers meant to be carried). If you want to know which your date prefers, ask.

Your date may present you with a *boutonniere*—a small flower to be pinned on your jacket lapel where the buttonhole is (or would be if your jacket had one). It's pinned on in the same manner as a corsage, except the pin goes *through* the flower stem rather than over it.

The reason a young lady gives her date a boutonniere is not, as you might think, to be kind. It's to get even for all those holes you've just poked in her dress.

- -

Breaking Up

You've been going with the same person for a month (or a week, or a year). For whatever reason—boredom, a new love on the horizon, changing interests, incompatibility, unhappiness—you think it's time to break up. But you're a thoughtful, sensitive individual, and you'd rather not trash the other person in the process. What's the best way to behave?

It's kind of you to ask. This means that you're willing to take the appropriate steps to minimize pain and suffering. Whether you wish to break off all contact or redefine the relationship as "just friends," the technique is the same:

1. **Do it face-to-face.** This will be difficult, but presumably you did other things face-to-face. Don't send an emissary or text message. Don't write a letter or simply post something online. Find a private moment when you can speak without an audience present.

2. **Don't accuse or lay blame.** Doing either will only increase the hurt and the likelihood of an argument. Saying "You never pay any attention to me" or "I'm fed up with your being late and forgetful all the time" gives the other person the chance to say "You're misjudging me" or "I'll change!"

   The one situation where you might choose to make an exception to this rule is if the person's behavior is dangerous to himself or others. For example, if the person-about-to-be-dumped is a substance abuser, telling him that his drinking is the reason you're breaking up is a mini-intervention that might, along with other people's comments, push him to do something about it.

3. **Avoid "making a case."** Unless you think it's important to express a specific reason, you want the breakup to seem fated, not the result of anyone's behavior. Simply say "I want to go out with other people" or "I guess I just don't feel the way I used to." Make it clear that your feelings have changed and you're responsible for them. It's not the other person's fault.

There's no magic formula for breaking up. Ending a relationship can be messy and painful. But if you do it quickly, directly, and resolutely, you'll lessen the suffering and may even stay friends.

Dear Alex

"I just learned that my girlfriend dumped me. She sent her best friend to tell me that she doesn't want to go out with me anymore. What's the best way to get even?"

It's unfortunate that your girlfriend chose to convey the news in such a rude manner. You have every right to be hurt and angry. The best way to get even is to . . .

. . . respond with perfect graciousness. Show that your poise and confidence exist apart from any relationship. Since your friends and classmates will know you were dumped, they'll be watching to see how you react. If you fly into a rage or badmouth your girlfriend, you'll be playing into her hands. She might even say "That's why I didn't tell him myself. I knew he'd turn ugly." Other girls may hesitate to go out with you if they see you as vengeful and out of control.

Be calm, philosophical, and understanding. If friends press you for a response, you can say:

"People change. Life goes on."

"I'll always cherish the memories of our time together."

"I wish her all the best in her future relationships."

Your impeccable politeness will indirectly highlight your girlfriend's bad manners. When she learns how "well" you're taking it, she'll probably feel low, cowardly, and guilty, proving once again that politeness is the best revenge.

P.S. When you get home, by all means, rant, rave, and beat up your pillow. Cry yourself to sleep. Talk with a best friend. But then get back on the horse. Stay active and involved. Don't let yourself get isolated. Spend time with your friends. Do something nice for yourself. Your friends will admire you for the stoic, upbeat way you carry on with a broken heart. Keep it up and you may find yourself in a new relationship sooner than you think.

Beyond Rude: Abusive Relationships

You know when someone treats you right: You feel valued and respected and cared for. But it's not so easy to know when someone treats you wrong. Teenagers are often confused about what's normal or acceptable in a relationship. Those who grow up in a home with two adults who love and respect each other have a model for what a healthy relationship looks like; those who grow up in a home with parents who fight a lot may think *that's* normal.

If you're wondering about your relationship and you want to understand it better, here are some questions you can ask yourself. They apply to any relationship and can be asked by boys or girls.

Does your boyfriend or girlfriend . . .

    . . . put you down in front of other people?
    . . . publicly tease or embarrass you?
    . . . demean your ideas?
    . . . disregard your feelings?
    . . . badmouth people or things you care about?
    . . . use alcohol or other drugs as an excuse for his/her behavior?

. . . try to cut you off from your friends?

. . . stalk you with text messages?

. . . take things out on you?

. . . get angry at you when you don't know why?

. . . treat you poorly, apologize, promise to never do it again—and do it again?

. . . blame you for things he/she has done?

. . . deny that he/she has hurt you?

. . . make it clear that he/she calls the shots?

. . . threaten or intimidate you to get his/her way?

. . . use physical force or violence against you?

. . . make you engage in sexual activity you don't enjoy or aren't ready for?

If you answered yes to one or more of these questions, it means that you're almost certainly in an abusive relationship. Of course, an otherwise wonderful, loving person might have the *one* annoying habit of telling embarrassing stories about you in public or the *one* flaw of an authoritarian streak that he or she needs to work on. A caring boyfriend or girlfriend, if told that his or her behavior upsets you, will make a genuine effort to respect your needs and feelings. So you'll have to use your judgment in assessing how these issues apply to your situation.

In general, though, answering yes to these questions suggests that you're in trouble. Abuse can be emotional or psychological as well as physical. If you think you might be in an abusive relationship, get help. Talk to your parents, a teacher, or a school counselor, or contact a teenage or domestic violence hotline. Another person's bad behavior is never your fault. And you don't have to take it anymore.

Sex-Ediquette

Most etiquette books steer clear of sex. That's generally because the behavior of consenting adults in the privacy of their bedrooms is their own business. But this is a book for teenagers, which allows a certain license (as opposed to licentiousness).

Whether teenagers should or shouldn't be sexually active isn't our topic here. What you decide for yourself is up to you and your partner. Your decision will depend on your values, maturity, religious beliefs, self-image, aspirations, and personal morals. It will depend on what your parents have taught you, what you've learned on your own, and ultimately what you feel is right for you. It should *not* depend on what your friends think, what your boyfriend or girlfriend wants, or what the advertising media tell you in the myriad mixed messages they send.

Now that we've made these disclaimers, let's focus on what *is* our topic here: the etiquette related to sex.

If you plan to be (or are) sexually active, it's beyond rude to:

- give someone HIV
- give someone a sexually transmitted infection
- get someone pregnant
- trick someone into getting you pregnant
- bring a child into the world before you're financially, emotionally, or logistically able to care for it
- expect society or your parents to assume the responsibility for such a child
- pressure someone to have sex
- force someone to do sexual things that make him or her uncomfortable
- use alcohol or other drugs to weaken someone's resistance or awareness
- ignore the word "No"
- use, abuse, and lose someone
- say things you know aren't true just to get someone into bed
- spill intimate secrets or spread sexual rumors
- have sex with your best friend's partner
- sexually harass someone[*]
- make disparaging comments about someone's body or sexual performance

If you plan to be (or are) sexually active, it's essential that you:

- treat your partner with respect and kindness
- make every effort to be honest in your relationship
- show sensitivity to the wishes and signals of your partner
- go no further or faster than your partner wishes
- always use condoms and other forms of protection to lessen the chance of disease and/or pregnancy
- refrain from blabbing intimate details about your relationship

*FOR MORE ON SEXUAL HARASSMENT, SEE PAGES 214–217.

Dear Alex

"One of my friends has just been diagnosed HIV-positive. My parents told me I can't see him anymore. I don't believe this. We've been friends since kindergarten. There's no way I'm not going to see him. What can I do to get my parents to listen?"

You're right to want to be there for your friend. It would be rude, as well as uncaring, to drop him because he has the virus associated with AIDS. Your parents are probably frightened because they know there isn't a cure for AIDS yet. This fear, coupled with their love for you, has led to their prohibition.

If you haven't done so already, explain the medical facts to your parents. Tell them that the only way HIV can be transmitted is by the exchange of bodily fluids. These include semen, blood, vaginal secretions, and saliva (although the possibility of acquiring the virus from saliva is considered very remote). This means that it can only be passed from one person to another through sexual intercourse, tainted blood transfusion, the commingling of blood (as in "blood brother" rituals), or sharing needles. As long as you don't take drugs intravenously, have sex, or exchange blood, you're protected against AIDS. You can't get AIDS from toilet seats or swimming pools. You can't get AIDS by dancing or holding hands. You can't get AIDS by hugging, sleeping next to, or being breathed upon by a person with AIDS.

Once the shock of the news wears off, your parents may relax their prohibition. It wouldn't hurt to leave some medical pamphlets around for them to read. In the meantime, you have a difficult decision to make. Should you ignore your parents' wishes and keep seeing your friend, even if it involves subterfuge on your part? This is an issue for your conscience and morals to decide. As far as etiquette is concerned, it would be terribly rude and hurtful to shun a good friend just because he has a virus.

Dear Alex

"My boyfriend wants me to have sex with him. He says there's no way he could have AIDS, so he doesn't want to use a condom. Could this be true? Can you know for sure that you don't have AIDS?"

Assuming they weren't born with AIDS, someone who has *never* had sex, shared needles, received a blood transfusion, or otherwise exchanged bodily fluids with anybody can be sure he or she doesn't have AIDS. If your boyfriend has engaged in any of those activities, he could be carrying HIV. He could even be carrying it if he just had a test saying he was HIV-negative! (This is because it can take some time before the virus is detectable.)

Most people who are HIV-positive don't know it. People who say they couldn't possibly have AIDS may be speaking the truth, or they may be deluded, in denial, or ignorant of the facts. If your boyfriend had sex just once with just one person, he could have acquired the virus. If, five years ago, he and a friend cut their palms with a pocketknife and shook hands to signify everlasting friendship, he could have acquired the virus.

Even if your boyfriend doesn't have AIDS, condoms offer additional protection against pregnancy and sexually transmitted infections. It's a mark of good manners to do whatever one can to make a sexual partner feel comfortable and safe. Therefore, your boyfriend should use a condom if for no other reason than you asked him to. If it turns out you didn't "need" to, no harm has been done. If, however, you needed to and didn't, a lot of harm may have been done.

Trust is critical to any healthy relationship. And you probably wouldn't want to have a sexual relationship with a boy you didn't feel you could trust. But remember, more lies have been told to get someone into bed than for any other reason.

Dear Alex

"Who's supposed to bring the condom, the boy or the girl?"

An excellent question, because no teenager today who chooses to be sexually active should have intercourse or oral sex without protection.

Traditionally, the man brought the condom. This goes back to the days when men were considered the initiators of sex. It would have been scandalous for a woman to acknowledge having a sex life, let alone buy condoms. In today's world of changing attitudes and sex roles, this tradition no longer makes sense. Unless you have an explicit division of responsibilities—for example, you bring the condoms and your partner brings the breath mints—it's the responsibility of *both* partners to ensure that they take every precaution, every time, to protect themselves and each other against pregnancy and/or disease.

A BRIEF HISTORY OF THE CONDOM

Since you were wondering, it was a 16th-century Italian physician named Gabriel Fallopius (of Fallopian tube fame) who is generally credited with designing the first male prophylactic. Its purpose was not to prevent pregnancy, but to combat the epidemic of venereal disease ravaging Europe. Dr. Fallopius's invention quickly led to the manufacture of medicated linen sheaths a uniform eight inches long. They were secured to the base of the penis with a pink ribbon (cute). In the mid-1600s, King Charles II of England supposedly asked his personal physician to devise a method of protection against syphilis. Legend has it that the doctor created a sheath out of oiled sheep intestine. His name? Dr. Condom.

Making Out in Public

You're waiting at a bus stop with your boyfriend, and the bus isn't due for another 10 minutes. You kiss him, he kisses you back, and nine minutes later you come up for air—and dirty looks from the other people at the bus stop.

You might ask *Why is it rude to make out in public? With all the violence in the world, what's wrong with showing a little love?* Good questions. But the fact remains that what you call "showing love," others call "rude behavior."

While affection in general is to be applauded, affection in public is to be avoided. Why? Because nobody likes a show-off. It's rude to rub people's noses in the fact that you have something they don't.

This isn't about holding hands, kissing good-bye, hugging at the airport, or strolling arm-in-arm with the one you love. It's about physical contact that's basically sexual in nature. The kind that makes your heart beat faster and your blood pressure rise. (And that's just for the people who are watching.) Things like petting. Tongue wrestling. Rounding the bases between first and home.

Making out is a wonderful thing to do with someone you care about. But it should be done in private. When you do it in public, you force people to witness behavior that may be distracting or discomforting. And that, as you know, violates the basic principles of etiquette.

P.S. The prohibition against public displays of affection is lifted under certain situations. For example, as long as it's raining, couples are permitted to kiss passionately along the Seine River in Paris during the entire month of April. Similar license is granted to those watching the sunset by the ocean in Key West. You may apply to me if you wish to propose additional exceptions for consideration.

TRUE STORIES

FROM THE MANNERS FRONTIER

PDA

I was downtown when I saw this young couple, hands plunged in each other's rear pockets, locked in an embrace. At first I thought they were trying to dry-clean each other's blue jeans. But then, after watching for 45 minutes, I became convinced that they were doing something entirely different. I found the entire episode highly distracting, and it made me late for where I was going.

Dear Alex

"My boyfriend is a terrible kisser.* Is there a polite way to tell him this?"

No. How would you feel if he told *you* something similar? If you enjoy his company in other ways, if you're a good match in terms of your

*OR WHATEVER.

personalities and interests, then you can probably assume that he *wants* to please you. Use his desire as a teaching tool. Don't say "Ewwww!" or "You kiss like a fish." Instead, say "I love it when . . ." or "Do you think you could . . . ?" On the other hand, if he has no desire to please you, you might want to send him out to pasture.

Being Discreet

If you've dated, you've had this experience: You go out with someone, and the next day all of your friends ask nosy questions. Like "How far did you get?" and "Did you _____?"

It's not surprising that your friends would feel they have the right to know such intimate details. After all, look at all the things people post about themselves online. Look at the bad example set by politicians who feel they have the right to legislate people's love lives. Nevertheless, you have the right to privacy. So when your friends pry into your personal affairs, smile and reply:

"A gentleman [or a lady] never tells."

"I prefer not to discuss things of that nature."

"I can't imagine why you would be interested in things of such a personal nature."

The more secretive you sound, the more—or less—they'll assume you did. But you can't be held responsible for other people's assumptions.

Dear Alex

"My boyfriend and I are in love, and we had sex. Now he's told everybody about it and he's ignoring me."

Nothing ruins a good relationship like sex. Some boys (not all) view sex as a conquest. It's a notch they put on their belt once it's back around their waist. In laying the groundwork for sex, they may even convince themselves (and you) that they're in love. After the sex, however, they discover that it wasn't love but horniness, and they're no longer interested in the relationship. So they move on to another conquest.

Of course this is terribly hurtful. If your boyfriend's behavior was unintentional, it's a sign of immaturity and insensitivity. Immature, insensitive people shouldn't be having sex. If your boyfriend's behavior was deliberate and manipulative, it's a sign of unforgivable rudeness and disrespect. Either way, you're better off without him.

Chapter Quiz

1. *You've just started attending a new school, and you're eager to make new friends. Do you:*

a) hand out $20 bills

b) offer to do everyone's homework

c) project a confident air, ask questions, and join clubs and groups

2. *You have a friend who always overstays her welcome. The polite way to get her to leave is:*

a) drop a mouse on her lap

b) toss a tear gas canister at her feet

c) say "I wish you could stay, but I have to do something with my mother."

3. *Your best friend informs you that he's gay. Do you:*

a) tell him it's just a stage he's going through

b) say "I'm feeling a bit giddy myself."

c) reassure him of your friendship and thank him for telling you

4. *Your roommate takes things from your desk without permission. The best way to get him to stop is to:*

a) throw out your desk

b) put a tarantula in the top drawer

c) request that he ask permission before going through your things

5. *Half of the boys in school want to go out with you. Do you:*

a) tell them to take a number

b) print up little rejection cards and pass them out in study hall

c) use "having plans" and "being busy" as polite excuses when turning down requests for dates

6. *You're in love with a girl who doesn't know you exist. The best way to get her attention is to:*

a) push her down the stairs

b) do a striptease in the cafeteria

c) maneuver into her vicinity and start a conversation

7. *When a boy pins a corsage on a girl, it's essential to:*

a) check it for bugs

b) offer the young lady an antihistamine

c) confirm that the place you're about to stick the pin is a shoulder strap and not a tan line

8. *Public displays of affection aren't bad manners as long as:*

a) you keep three feet on the ground

b) one of you remains fully clothed

c) you're both on the honor roll

8

EAT, DRINK, AND BE WARY

Tabled Manners and Food for Thought

Ever since the first caveman threw a few dino-chops in the microwave and invited the neighbors over for dinner, eating has been the central social event in people's lives. Whether a romantic dinner, a wedding banquet, a power lunch, or a Thanksgiving feast; whether a sacrificial slaughter, a Passover seder, a funeral wake, or a two-straw shake at the mall, food and drink play a part in virtually every human activity. No wonder so many rules and rituals have evolved around the what, when, where, and how of eating.

It's important to learn the food-related rituals and practices of any culture you live in or visit. Bad table manners can get you chewed out by your mom, embarrassed in front of your friends, or dumped by your date. First impressions are often formed around a dinner table. And if the impression you give makes people sick, you won't be invited back. So here are the ABCs of minding your peas and cukes.

Place Settings: Cracking the Code

You've been invited to a formal dinner party at your boyfriend's house. He's told you that his parents are going all out, and you're already nervous. You arrive on time, and after a brief period of chitchat in the living room, dinner is announced.

The moment you catch sight of the table, you know you're in trouble. Deep trouble. You've never seen so many dishes, plates, glasses, bowls, knives, forks, and spoons in your life—and that's just *your* place setting. Your whole body breaks out in a sweat. There's nowhere to run, nowhere to hide. Within 30 seconds, you'll be revealed as an ignoramus.

Wake up! It's only a bad dream. Cracking the code of the formal place setting isn't as hard as it looks. Read on to learn everything you need to know to be suave, sophisticated, and self-assured at even the most daunting dinner table.

Setting the Well-Mannered Table

To avoid awkward moments in other people's homes, start by practicing in your own. Take out your family's best dishes (ask first) and announce that you've decided to learn how to set a proper table. Once your parents recover from their initial shock, they may even offer to help you (or learn along with you).

It's easy to set a table correctly. In fact, the basic rules are so simple that even an adult can understand them:

- Set out only what you need for that meal.
- Place the silverware* and glassware so people work their way *from the outside in* as the meal progresses.

Like this:

1. Forks go to the *left* of the plate (except for that tiny seafood fork, which goes to the *right* of the spoons).

2. Knives go to the *right* of the plate, with their sharp edges facing in.

3. Spoons go to the *right* of the knives. Dessert spoons are set *above* the plate, or they can make a grand entrance later with the dessert.

4. Salad plates go to the *left* of the forks (unless the salad is served as a separate course).

5. Bread-and-butter plates go *above* the forks.

6. Glasses go *above* the knives.

> *SILVERWARE NOT ACTUALLY MADE OF SILVER SHOULD, STRICTLY SPEAKING, BE CALLED FLATWARE.*

If you're a dinner guest in somebody's home, you'll start with the silverware farthest from your plate for the first course. Once that's cleared away, you'll use the silverware that's *now* farthest from your plate for the second course, and so on. Of course, if your hosts have taken liberties with the arrangement, all bets are off. You'll have to watch them for cues as to which utensils to use, or you might end up trying to cut your steak with a spoon.

A Formal Dinner, Course-by-Course

Since learning about proper place settings and how to use them can be a lot to digest, let's imagine you're back at your boyfriend's house, only now you know what you're doing. (NOTE: A less formal family dinner would be similar to the one described here, except some of the courses and place setting pieces would be eliminated.)

The Initial Service

Dinner begins with raw oysters. Of course you're not going to have any, but you should still know about that tiny fork to the right of your plate. That's what you'd use if you weren't so busy thinking *Ewwww, I'm gonna puke if I have to keep looking at these slimy things.* Fortunately, your neighbor says "If you're not going to eat those, can I?" and quickly swaps plates with you. This, at a formal dinner party, is a lapse of both manners and grammar. But who's picky in an emergency like this? Finally, the oyster plates are cleared away. (**Tip:** Throughout any meal, dishes are cleared from the *right* and served from the *left.*)

Soup's On

Next up is a soup. Since you don't eat soup with a fork, you look to the far right, *et voilà*, there's your soup spoon.

By now you might be wondering *Isn't there usually a teaspoon on the far right?* And the answer, bouillon brain, is: Yes, there is. And it's not supposed to be there! That teaspoon has no business on the table unless tea is the first course. So ignore it. If you're the one who's setting the table, leave it in the drawer.

As for your soup: Don't slurp.

The Salad Course

Still hungry? Of course you are! Never fear; it's salad time. A small fork on the far left is rarin' to go, as well as a salad knife on the right for those who need it. Lettuce proceed.

Something's Fishy

After the salad comes a fish course. With the salad fork retired to the great dishwasher in the sky, next up on the far left is the fish fork. On the far right you'll find the fish knife.

Let's take a breather as you dab your mouth with a napkin and join the chorus of compliments offered to the host and hostess.

Once the fish plates and utensils are cleared away, clean plates are set in front of you. It's time for . .

The Meaty Course

A platter of thick, sizzling venison is brought to the table. (Oh, deer, it's Bambi's great, great, great, great grandson.) The proper knife and fork for the meat course have now reached the head of the utensil line. *Bon appétit.*

NOTE: During dinner, your hosts will serve those beverages that best accompany each course, keeping in mind the ages and preferences of their guests. Depending on how old you are and/or whether the hosts are serving alcohol, these beverages might include water, milk, juice, or soda. If it's a very fancy dinner the hosts might serve sherry with the soup, white wine with the fish, red wine with the meat, and champagne with the dessert. And, since the table was correctly set, you'll find just the right glass each time you move along the lineup of glassware from the outside in.

What if you're not old enough or you prefer not to drink alcohol? No problem. If there's a wine glass at your place setting and someone comes to serve you simply decline by saying "No, thank you." Don't place your hand over the glass or turn it upside down on the table.

Just Desserts

Since everybody knows that the purpose of dinner is to whet one's appetite for dessert, you're probably in a panic because you've used up all your silverware and the *pièce de résistance* has yet to arrive. Fear not. See that spoon and fork lying facedown above the space where your plate used to be? That's your dessert service.* Notice that the spoon is not a teaspoon. (Teaspoons are used for tea!) Dessert spoons are larger.

A 22-layer pecan torte with a dollop of white chocolate ice cream soon arrives. It's history in no time. You turn to the neighbor who saved you from oyster hell and say "Excuse me, if you're not going to eat that, may I?" It's still a lapse of manners, but at least your grammar's good. No one's looking—quick—you swap plates.

*IF IT'S NOT THERE, BE PATIENT. IT WILL BE COMING WITH THE FINGER BOWL. (SEE PAGE 289 FOR FINGER BOWL FACTS.)

Dear Alex

"What should you do if you use the wrong fork?"

Just keep using it. If you're feeling particularly daring and you're in a private home, wait until no one is looking, then lick it clean and put it back where you found it.

Dear Alex

"I'm not a very religious person. What should I do if I'm at someone's house for dinner and they say grace? I know I shouldn't start eating, but do I have to bow my head, say 'Amen,' or hold hands with the people on either side of me?"

Etiquette insists that you follow the "when in Rome . . ." principle and do as your host family does. But all that's required of you is the *appearance* of respect for their tradition; you don't have to convert to their religion. So bow your head, join the circle of hands, and mutter "Amen." If, in the process, you figure out some batting averages, no one will be the wiser. In the future, try to sit next to those persons whose hands you would most like to hold.

Dear Alex

"I'm going out with this girl, and my parents want me to invite her over for dinner. I keep putting them off because she has the world's worst table manners and my parents would fall out of their chairs if they saw them. Even I, who's been known to put an elbow or two on the table, am pretty disgusted. How can I tell my girlfriend that her table manners are terrible?"

Pointing out flaws in a person's manners, behavior, and/or character is always risky and often rude. Most people can handle the news that they have gravy on their chin. It's a bit harder to swallow the notion that one isn't fit to be taken out in public.

Try this: Tell your girlfriend that she's the most wonderful creature on the face of the planet, that you love her more than words can say, and that you soooo want your parents to like her. Then, in an embarrassed tone of voice, confide that they have this weird thing for table manners. Mention a few of the behaviors your girlfriend exhibits that would drive your parents up the wall: using fingers as utensils, sucking entire strands of spaghetti into one's mouth, talking while chewing, etc. Ask your girlfriend if, as a special favor to you, she'd make a point of being extra careful when she comes over for dinner.

And in case you need to polish your own table manners, read on for a refresher course.

Basic Table Manners

You've just learned how to navigate your way through a formal table setting. But there's more to table manners than using the correct fork or saying "Excuse me" if you bump into a sideboard.

Following are some rules and guidelines that will give you food for thought. Abide by them at other people's homes, in restaurants, and, if you want to amaze your parents, at your own dinner table.

Playing with Food

It's never proper to catapult pudding across the dinner table (something I learned as a child when I responded to my grandfather's teasing in such a manner), nor shall peas and other tiny vegetables be used as artillery against one's siblings. As for all those other imaginative things you can do with your food while eating, now that you've thought about them, forget about them. Playing with food is not allowed.

Pushing Food Around on Your Plate

If you're having fun, this counts as playing with food and isn't allowed—no matter how artistic your arrangement may be. This means no making mashed potato dams or clearing paths with sausage plows.

There's one exception to this rule:

Food You Don't Like

When you're a guest in somebody's home, you may be served food you don't like. It's rude to leave your plate untouched. If your dislike is mild, try to eat as much as you can. If you absolutely can't bear to consume a single morsel, move your food around on your plate so it appears to have seen some action. Tuck a little slice of liver under the lettuce. Cut a few more bites and slip them in with the green beans. Try to reduce the overall surface area of the food. Meanwhile, engage in animated conversation so people will look at your brow, not your chow.

You don't want anyone to notice that you're not eating; this defeats the purpose of surreptitious food relocation strategies. And if someone is so rude as to ask "Don't you like the liver?" or "Aren't you eating?" just smile and say "It's delicious."

Dear Alex

"I'm a vegetarian, and when my friends invite me to dinner, they usually serve meat. What's the polite thing to do?"

Take the opportunity of the invitation itself to explain your food preferences. Tell your friend that you don't eat meat, then hasten to explain that you'll be perfectly satisfied with the salad, vegetables, rice, and/or other nonmeat items people normally serve along with the meat course. In other words, they don't have to change their menu just for you. Then simply pass the meat plate when it comes your way.

In time, most of your friends (and their parents) will remember that you're a vegetarian, and they might even prepare vegetarian meals when you're their guest. Especially if your manners are so impeccable and your conversation so engaging that they can't wait for you to grace their table again.

Dear Alex

"My parents force me to eat things I don't like. Isn't that rude?"

Children shouldn't be forced to eat things that make them gag, vomit, and keel over at the table. And parents shouldn't have to cook five different entrées to satisfy the finicky eating habits of family members. What's needed is a middle ground—somewhere between the parent who insists that a child eat eggplant and the child who claims that she'll never eat anything but fish sticks for the rest of her life.

Here are Seven Reasonable Rules for Happy Home Dining:

1. Children must try a bite of a new food before they can proclaim that they don't like it.

2. Parents must respect the right of underage taste buds to declare certain foods off-limits.

3. Children who reject certain foods must not expect parents to prepare alternate meals for them.

4. Parents must make good faith efforts to prepare meals that all family members like.

5. Children must recognize that microwaved burritos are not nature's only food group and try to eat a well-balanced diet.

6. Parents must recognize that children can go quite a few days without vegetables or fruit before they begin to waste away.

7. Children and parents together shall determine household food policies to address the following questions:

- Can a child who doesn't like something make something else?
- Can a child who doesn't finish her dinner have dessert?
- Who determines the portions of food served?
- Can a child who doesn't eat her dinner cook something later?
- Can a child snack between meals?

Self-Service

A platter of food from which you're supposed to serve yourself normally arrives from your *left*. If it sits on the table (rather than being held for you), make sure it sits *on* the table. Otherwise the Escalope de Veau on Rice may end up as Escalope de Veau on Floor.

Use the serving utensils provided (never your own silverware) to take a portion. Often there are two utensils that look like a spoon and fork on steroids. Use the spoon to (duh) spoon out a portion. Use the fork to steady it from the top or side. Place the utensils securely back on the platter. If someone has been holding the dish for you, say "Thank you."

Some items will come to you in ready-made portions dictated by the recipe (Eggs Benedict, Salmon in Pastry Puffs, etc.). Don't cut yourself a half-portion or scoop off the toppings and leave the foundation behind. Take a whole portion of what's being served, even if you know you won't eat it all.

For all other dishes, take only as much as you can finish. In fact, when a platter of food arrives, do a quick mathematical calculation. Place yourself in the numerator. You're #1. (Don't let it go to your head.) In the denominator, enter the number of people dining minus the number of people who have already taken portions. If there are eight people dining and you're the first to be served, you would enter an 8 (8 – 0 = 8). If three people have already been served, you would enter a 5 (8 – 3 = 5). The resulting fraction (in this case, 1/5) represents the maximum amount of food you're allowed to take from the platter. This ensures that the last guests to be served won't find the platter bare when it finally reaches them. (Although it sure would be fun to see what a guest would do if you offered him some chicken while holding an empty platter.)

And you thought math was useless.

Dear Alex

"What should you do if you drop food on the floor?"

If the family dog is nearby, do nothing. He'll gladly take care of it for you. If the dog is absent and the food is of the nonmessy variety (such as a string bean or an apple slice), you can bend down, pick it up, and place it discreetly on the edge of your plate. (The same thing applies if you drop things on the table, although you can eliminate the bending down part.)

Messier droppings (such as chili or creamed corn) may require excusing yourself, saying "How could I be so clumsy?" and zipping into the kitchen for a spoon, sponge, or paper towel (unless you're advised to leave it until after dinner).

If you're at home and you drop a utensil, pick it up, excuse yourself, and get a clean one from the kitchen. In a restaurant, it's okay to leave it on the floor (unless you think someone might slip on it) and ask the waiter for a new one. You can also leave food you drop on the floor.

WHO'S ON FIRST?

If you're like most people, you've bolted upright from a sound sleep wondering about the correct order for serving people at a family dinner. Here it is:

- adults before children*
- females before males
- unrelated (guests) before related (family members)
- older before younger

If you're not sure of someone's age or gender, don't ask. Guess.

*CHILDREN TOO YOUNG TO BE ABLE TO WAIT SHOULD BE SERVED FIRST.

Thus, the oldest adult female who's not related to your family would be served first, followed by the next oldest. Once you run out of unrelated females, you turn to related ones such as grandmothers, aunts, etc. Once you run out of those, you serve females in your immediate family, such as mothers and sisters one would no longer consider children. (The point at which a child ceases to be a child is often a matter of dispute. The sensitive host knows that he can win an admirer for life by conferring adult status on older adolescents.) When you've finished with the women, you turn to the men and start over again.

Once all the adults are salivating at the food they're not yet allowed to eat, it's time to serve the children: girls first, guests first, oldest first, and then the boys. The person preparing each plate serves himself or herself last.

Sometimes people are determined to confound etiquette, and the person for whom the plate is intended insists on passing it to someone else, who in turn sends it on. If you're not careful, the same plate can circle the table four or five times. An experienced server often announces the destination of each plate by saying "This is Aunt Mary's."

Children shouldn't feel slighted by this system. Rather, they should feel privileged that their status allows them to exercise such generosity toward their elders.

Please Pass the . . .

Usually the things you want or need during dinner are stacked up in front of somebody at the far end of the table. If you want something, don't reach. Ask:

"Could you please pass the Mushrooms à la Grecque?"

Sometimes a dish being passed 'round the table comes to a complete halt in front of one oblivious soul. In such a case, it's perfectly fine to say:

*"Excuse me, Natasha, are you finished with the Mushrooms
à la Grecque?"**

Natasha will turn red in the face and pass the dish. She's allowed to take some before passing it because you phrased your request as a question.

It's improper to intercept an item being passed to someone who requested it. For example, if the gravy is traveling from person A to person F, persons C and E can't halt its journey. When F has finished, C and E can put in their own bids and wait their turns.

Items with handles (pitchers, serving utensils, gravy boats) should be passed so the handle is presented to the recipient.

***TRANSLATION: "NATASHA, GET WITH THE PROGRAM
AND STOP HOGGING THE MUSHROOMS."**

Dear Alex

"Are there rules about passing food?"

Platters of food should make their rounds from left to right counterclockwise around the table. Most people are right-handed, and it's easier to serve yourself by reaching across your plate to a dish positioned to your left. Attendees at a Convention of Left-Handers would be correct in passing food in the opposite direction.

When you're somebody's dinner guest, the food-passing route isn't up to you. If a platter blows in from the east instead of the west, don't reverse its direction—unless the dinner party is boring and you want to liven things up a little.

Dear Alex

"Why are you supposed to pass BOTH the salt and pepper if somebody just asks for one of them?"

Because condiments have feelings, too. They get lonely without each other. And if they stay together, you'll never have to send a search party across the tabletop to find the one that's missing.

Asking for Seconds

Don't ask for seconds if you're a guest in somebody's home. Your hosts may not have any, or they may be in a rush to finish up, or they may be counting on leftovers for tomorrow's supper.

If you're *offered* seconds as a guest at an informal dinner, it's usually all right to accept. Especially if you know that others will be doing the same. At a formal dinner, you're better off declining. This way, you avoid the risk of being the only person having a second helping while 11 other guests have to wait for the next course until you finish.

Offering Drinks

When you're hosting guests, don't say "What do you want to drink?" This can lead to awkward exchanges:

You: *"What do you want to drink?"*

Guest: *"How about some tomato juice?"*

You: *"We don't have any tomato. Would you like some cranberry juice?"*

Guest: *"Oh, I'll just have a Diet Coke, then."*

You: *"I don't think we have any diet sodas. Is Pepsi all right?"*

Guest: *"Do you have some tonic water?"*

You: *"No, but we have club soda. Only I think it's flat."*

It's much better to say:

"What would you like to drink? We have orange juice, apple cider, ginger ale, and I can make a mean chocolate milk."

Dear Alex

"Why do you have to hold your pinkie in the air when you drink tea?"

You don't. The reason people used to do this centuries ago was because cups didn't have handles. Since a cup of boiling water was HOT, the more fingers you kept away from it, the fewer got burned. Once handles were invented, there was no longer any reason to fly superfluous fingers in the wind. The custom, however, has been slow to die out. Therefore, many people, if served a dainty cup of tea, still hold their pinkies in the air.

Elbows off the Table

This is a much misunderstood point of etiquette. When parents say "Elbows off the table!" what they really mean is:

- Don't lean on the table.
- Don't rest your head in your hands.
- Don't eat with your elbows glued to the tablecloth.

These are all reasonable expectations.

You may, however, set the undersides of your forearms gently on the table while resting between courses or conversing since, technically speaking, these aren't your elbows.

As long as we're on the topic of elbows, keep yours *down and at your sides* while cutting and eating food. No flapping or jabbing your neighbors allowed.

Getting Food onto the Fork

Forks were designed to capture food without any help from bread, knives, or fingers. The combination of those handy little spears for stabbing, that long edge for pursuing, and that flat surface for shoveling provide all the tools you'll ever need to transfer food from plate to mouth.

Occasionally you'll encounter some defiant holdouts who refuse to board. Usually these are peas or beans, the very things your parents admonish you to finish if you want your dessert. If this should happen, tell your parents that you've done the best you can without committing an etiquette violation.

Eating with Your Fingers

At informal family dinners or picnics, it's okay to eat the following foods with your fingers: chicken (unless it's in a thick, gooey sauce); crisp bacon; fish sticks; shrimp cocktails; pizza; spareribs; chop bones (after you've eaten the meat with a knife and fork); artichoke leaves; crisp asparagus; corn on the cob; french fries; pickles; crudités (cold vegetables); fruit (apples, oranges, watermelon, bananas, etc.); and, of course, things set out without any silverware in sight, such as chips, nuts, olives, cheese and crackers, hors d'oeuvres, tiny sandwiches, and so on.

If you're a guest at an informal dinner at somebody's house, watch what your host family does and follow suit. If you're at a formal dinner, you're unlikely to be served any of these foods. But if, for example, a little gourmet pizza is presented as an appetizer, use a knife and fork.

- -

Dear Alex

"Is it okay to eat fried chicken with your fingers?"

Yes. But I prefer to eat my fingers plain, with just a touch of lemon.

- -

Dear Alex

"Is it okay to blow on your food?"

Only if it spontaneously combusts. If it's merely too hot, allow it to cool. Soup may be gently aerated by stirring.

Sopping Up Sauce

It's not proper to take a piece of bread and hydroplane across a lake of gravy. Still, it's a basic human drive to want to soak up that last bit of sauce. So, if you must, here's a compromise:

1. Break off a small piece of bread.

2. Place it on your dinner plate.

3. Delicately spear it with your fork.

4. Make like a sponge and mop. Gently.

Meanwhile, don't stare at your handiwork. Make it seem as if the bread has a mind of its own, like a Ouija Board pointer. And don't worry about capturing every speck of sauce. Your plate will still end up in the dishwasher, even if it sparkles by the time you're through with it.

Dunking

Almost everyone dunks at one time or another. It's a natural and satisfying human urge, and the pleasures it yields should not cause anyone to feel guilty. However, the joys of dunking are best reserved for private moments at home. It's simply not considered proper for anyone over the age of four to plunge donuts, cakes, or other soakables into milk or coffee in the company of others.

Ejecting Inedibles

Sometimes what goes in must come out again. Inedible food debris leaves the mouth by the same method it enters. In other words, a bite of steak delivered by fork, upon being recognized as a piece of gristle, exits the mouth by fork.

FINGER BOWL FACTS

Chances are you'll get through life without ever encountering a finger bowl. But if you should meet one in a dark alley some evening, here's what you need to know: A finger bowl is a small bowl, usually glass, in which you place finger bones.

Ha, ha. Let's start again.

It's a small bowl, half filled with water and set on a doily, that arrives with the dessert setting. It may have little things floating in it. These are not insects. They are flower petals.

If you want your dessert, you now have to work for it. Remove the finger bowl and doily and set it to the left of your dessert plate. Remove the dessert fork and spoon which came along for the ride, and place them, respectively, to the left and right of your plate.

Don't drink from the finger bowl or try to drown the flowers. Just barely dip your fingers into it, one hand at a time, and then dry them on your napkin.

Finger bowls are really quite silly. They're never around when you need 'em, like after a picnic of fried chicken and barbecued spareribs. Instead, they only show up at formal dinners, where fingers aren't likely to be messy in the first place. Go figure!

This is best done at a moment when all eyes aren't on you. Discreetly place the half-chewed glob back on your plate. If you can tuck it under some mashed potatoes, so much the better.

An olive popped in by hand returns its pit to the world by hand. Exceptions:

- *Fish bones.* Fish flesh enters by fork, but the bones leave by hand. This is because the skinny little vertebrae tend to stick to lips and forks if you try to remove them by utensil. They don't stand a chance against fingers.

- *Watermelon seeds.* Although they sneak into the mouth via hand-delivery, watermelon seeds may, by unanimous consent of all present, leave by oral projectile. This approach is known as a spitting contest. It's restricted to outdoor locations and must never be tried inside. And, of course, never spit seeds in the direction of anybody.

Eating Out of Containers

I confess: I eat ice cream out of the carton. But I only do it when I'm by myself. As far as good manners go, this transgression doesn't exist. Similarly, if nobody sees you having an open-refrigerator-door buffet, sampling from this container and that, polite society won't be offended. If your mother sees you, that's a different story.

Concerning containers on the table, the High Etiquette rule is simple: Don't. Never bring a milk carton, a pickle jar, or a cardboard silo of parmesan cheese to the table when serving company. Transfer the milk to a pitcher, the pickles to a small platter, and the cheese to a serving dish with a spoon.

But High Etiquette often goes on hiatus when the family sits down to dinner. This is because serving foods in the containers they come in cuts down on preparation time, cleanup time, and dishwashing time. Your family will have to seek its own comfort level regarding such things as pizza and cereal boxes, carryout Chinese food, jam jars, and ketchup bottles.

Buffet Behavior

The world is divided into two types of people: those who pig out at buffets and those who don't. Whichever category you fall into, there are three rules to follow when you're dining the buffet way:

1. Don't sneeze on it.

2. Don't bring your dirty plate back to it for refills. Get a clean one each time you go up.

3. Don't get more than one course ahead of the other people you're with. Wait until everyone is finished before you go up for dessert.

THE BREAKFAST CLUB

Breakfast differs from other family meals in that many rules of conduct are relaxed. This is because people clawing their way to consciousness are in a fragile emotional state. Children and parents about to head off, respectively, to school and bullies, work and bosses, need to indulge in certain ritualized eccentricities if they are to face the day. These include:

- arriving and departing at different times
- reading at the table
- sitting in dazed silence
- consuming the identical menu day after day

This need not be the same menu as anyone else's, since definitions of breakfast in most families range from light (toast and coffee) to hearty (pancakes, scrambled eggs, bacon, juice, cereal, and French toast).

While conversation isn't necessary (or, in some families, advisable), good mornings and good-byes are. Under no circumstances shall critical comments be made that would undermine any family member's belief that he or she is a lovable and capable human being. This will happen soon enough after leaving the house.

Leaving the Table

One leaves the table when everyone is through with the final course. A host might signal this moment by saying "Why don't we move into the living room?" and a parent by "Whose turn is it to do the dishes?"

If you're a guest and you must leave the table for any reason, simply say "Excuse me" and depart. At home, it's proper to ask "May I please be excused?" (Children who say "may I" as opposed to "can I" receive bonus points.)

Dear Alex

"If you're eating over at a friend's house, should you help clear the table?"

Follow your friend's lead. If he gets up to clear, you get up to help. If a chorus of protests tells you to stay seated, that's what you should do. After dinner, offer to help your friend with any dishwashing or drying chores he may have been assigned.

THE EIGHT DINNERTIME DUTIES OF CHILDREN AND TEENS

1. To come when called. (Astute parents will issue five-minute, three-minute, and "You'd-better-get-down-here-right-now-or-else" warnings.)

2. To present yourself at the table clean and clothed, hands washed.

3. To wait until your parents sit down before starting to eat, unless they insist otherwise. For extra credit, hold your mom's chair and push it in for her when she sits down at the table.

4. To use good table manners.

5. To contribute to the conversation with:

   - topics of general interest (for example, a supply-side economics analysis of how the unified European currency will affect bond rates in the Tokyo stock exchange).

   - narratives of personal experience (for example, how you saved your best friend's life on the way to school this morning).

6. To listen (or give the appearance of listening) to the conversation of others.

7. To remain at the table until permission is granted to leave.

8. To participate cheerfully in post-dinner cleanup chores as requested.

You may be thinking *Ha, ha, ho, ho. I don't really have to do all that.*

Yes, you do. If it's your parents' responsibility to bring home the bacon, it's your responsibility not to be a pig while eating it.

Dear Alex

"My parents nag me about not talking with my mouth full, but every time I take a bite of something they ask me a question. How can I answer without talking with my mouth full?"

If you're caught *in flagrante mouthful,* try to park the chew in your cheek long enough for a brief response. Some people consider this cheating, but if you can do it without spraying food particles, nobody will object and it's a handy skill to master.

If all that's required is a yes or no, nod or shake your head.

More detailed responses require a different approach: signaling to the questioner that a reply is forthcoming as soon as you swallow. You do this by raising your hand, index finger extended, as if testing for wind. Such a gesture, when accompanied by gleefully raised eyebrows, says *I can't wait to answer your question—but you're going to have to—since you wouldn't want me to talk with my mouth full, would you?*

Or you can take smaller bites. This way, your mouth is more conversation ready at any given moment.

Dear Alex

"I hate eating dinner with my parents. Every two seconds it's 'Hold your fork right,' 'Sit up straight,' 'Don't talk with your mouth full.' What should I do?"

Hold your fork right. Sit up straight. And don't talk with your mouth full.

Dear Alex

"My parents are always making snide comments about how much me and my friends eat. It's not our fault we're hungry. Don't you think this is rude?"

Look on the bright side. Your parents could be making snide comments about your grammar.

The truth of the matter is that the feeding habits of the adolescent are astonishing to behold. Like sharks, teenagers just open their jaws and consume whatever is in their way: cold pizza, chocolate fudge peanut butter ice cream, leftover Chinese food, 30 gallons of milk. And that's just for breakfast! These creatures usually forage in packs, drawn to the kitchen by familiar scents (brownies baking, sauces simmering) and sounds (the slam of the silverware drawer, the sizzle of bacon frying).

If dinner is still 20 minutes away, this means there's time for a snack: pretzels, bagels, microwaveable pizza, microwaveable soup, microwaveable ravioli, microwaveable waffles. In the old days, a teenager could starve to death between the onset of hunger and the end of sandwich-making. Nowadays, a 12-course dinner can be zapped in less time than it takes to say "Medium high."

Of course, the remarkable feeding habits of adolescents don't justify rudeness on the part of those who track them. Your parents should pick their jaws up off the floor, stop gaping, and say nothing to your guests other than "Another piece of pie, boys?"

Napkin Niceties

Here's everything you always wanted to know about napkins but were afraid to ask:

- Place your napkin on your lap as soon as you sit down. It's not a waiter's job to do this. He has no business in your lap. Some restaurants fold their napkins into cone shapes; resist the temptation to put these on your head.

- Huge napkins may be left folded in half. Small napkins should be fully unfolded.

- Don't hold your napkin out to the side and unfurl it with a chivalrous flourish as if you were Henry VIII's barber.

- Never tuck your napkin under your chin. Bibs were invented for this purpose, and they are meant only for children under three and persons eating lobster who don't mind feeling foolish if it will spare their upper garments from attack.

- Use your napkin to dab at your mouth, not scrub the skin off of your face.

- Don't use your napkin to blot lipstick, clean eyeglasses, or wipe off silverware between courses.

- If you get up during dinner, leave your napkin on your chair until you return. If dinner is over, leave your napkin loosely folded on the table to the left of your plate (or where your plate used to be).

- Never use napkin rings with company. It's a common mistake to assume that these little devices were originally intended as a decorative way to present napkins and impress guests with how much silver one owned. Actually, they were designed as a way to tell family members' napkins apart in the days before paper napkins and washing machines. It was impractical for most families to wash cloth napkins after every use; thus, each person had a napkin ring engraved with his or her own initials or symbol. This permitted bonding between increasingly soiled napkins and their respective owners until the relationship was ripped asunder on wash day.

- Finally, never use your napkin as a handkerchief. If you blow your nose into your napkin, everyone else at the table will spend the rest of the evening picturing your slimy snot slowly solidifying and will experience the same reaction you're having now.

Utensil Essentials

There are three ways to hold and use silverware while cutting and eating your food: the American Way, the Continental Way, and the Wrong Way. Lefthanders may reverse the following instructions for left and right. They should not, however, reverse the actual place setting.

The American Way	The Continental Way	The Wrong Way
1. Hold the fork in your left hand, tines down. Use your index finger to steady it and apply pressure. Cup the handle in your palm.	**1–3.** Hold and use the fork and knife as you would in the American Way, but think Continental thoughts.	**1.** Hold the fork in your left fist.
2. Hold the knife in your right hand, sharp edge down.		**2.** Hold the knife in your right fist. (Picture yourself gripping a pair of toothbrushes.)
3. Slice gently. Don't saw. Keep the knife close to the fork or you risk flinging your filet across the table.		**3.** Saw away. Flap your elbows and slop food over the edges of your plate.

The American Way	The Continental Way	The Wrong Way
4. Set the knife at the top of your plate so the blade faces inward.	**4.** Continue to hold the knife or set it down, depending on how soon you'll need it again.	**4.** Using both your knife and your fork, shovel food into your mouth.
5. Transfer the fork to your right hand, tines facing up. Lift or spear a bite of food.	**5.** With the fork still in your left hand, tines down, spear a bite of food.	**5.** Talk with your mouth full.
6. Raise fork to mouth. Eat. (The food, not the fork.)	**6.** Raise fork to mouth. Eat.	**6.** Ask your dinner partners why they are leaving the table before the meal is through.

Silverware Signals

Silverware has its own body language. Here's what various positions mean:

"I'm still eating."

"I'm about to pass my plate for seconds."

"I'm done."

"I'm a slob."

Using Chopsticks

If the chopsticks are stuck together, separate them. You'll notice that they taper at one end. Use the smaller, narrower ends for picking up food; usually they're round, while the top ends are square. You'll hold the chopsticks about half to two-thirds of the way up, keeping the ends even.

Hold the upper chopstick—the one that moves—as if it were a pencil (almost). Support it between your second and third fingers, but extend them a bit straighter than if you were writing.

Don't rest the upper chopstick in the hollow between your thumb and index finger, as you would a pencil. That's where you'll rest the upper half of the bottom chopstick. Support the lower half with the tip of your ring finger. The bottom chopstick stays fixed, while the upper chopstick pincers up and down when you move your second and third fingers.

On second thought, never mind. It's impossible to explain how to use chopsticks. Get a friend to show you—or ask the waiter for a fork.

How to Eat

1. Open mouth.

2. Insert food.

3. Chew and swallow.

Beyond these rudiments, you may have questions about the proper way to eat certain types of foods. From Artichokes through Tea, the chart on pages 297–302 tells you everything you want and need to know.

THE DO'S AND DON'TS OF DELIGHTFUL TABLE MANNERS

Do

- wait to sit until everybody is present and all ladies have been seated
- wait to eat until everybody is served—unless your host tells you to please start
- take small portions when food is passed
- offer to pay the dry cleaning bill of anyone upon whom you spill food
- learn to talk with a little food in your mouth and your lips closed (this skill will serve you well at business lunches)
- finish swallowing one mouthful before taking another (or a sip of your beverage)
- take small bites and chew with your mouth closed
- pace your eating so you don't get ahead of or behind the others in your group
- sit up straight and lean slightly over the table when putting fork to mouth
- keep your humming to a minimum

Don't

- redip the bitten ends of veggies or chips into the communal bowl of dip (you may redip the other ends)
- pick your teeth at the table
- reach across another person to get something (ask for it to be passed instead)
- smack your lips (although an ecstatic "mmmm" may be exhaled in the direction of the host)
- use common serving utensils (sugar spoons, butter servers) to stir your own tea or butter your own bread
- tilt your chair
- mop the table with your napkin if you spill water (just right the glass—and don't mop your dinner partner if you spill water on her)
- hold your silverware in a fist
- gesture with a knife or fork in your hand
- play footsie unless you're very sure whose feet belong to whom

Food	Do's	Don'ts	Fine Points
Apple or pear	Hold. Bite. Chew. Swallow.	Don't eat an apple or pear by hand in a formal setting. Stab it with your fork. Then cut it in quarters and eat bite-sized pieces by fork.	If you swallow a seed, it takes approximately 60 years for an orchard to grow in your stomach.
Artichoke	Pull off a leaf. Dip the pulpy end into the sauce. Slowly draw the leaf through your teeth. Repeat until you finish or get fed up with so much effort for so little return. When all leaves are gone, you come upon a tender heart surrounded by tough bristles. Use your knife and fork to cut off the fuzzy "choke." Eat your heart out.	Don't stick the whole artichoke in your mouth.	Leaves that you have scraped clean or rejected may be stacked on the plate.
Asparagus	Use your knife and fork to cut and capture bite-sized morsels.	Don't stick the spears in your ears.	According to etiquette, crisp asparagus may be eaten with the fingers. Few people know this, so you may not want to try it in a fancy restaurant.
Baked beans	Consume with a fork, but only when you anticipate being by yourself for the next 24 hours.	Beans should never be eaten with the fingers.	Ask yourself: Why are beans primarily cooked on camping trips, where you'll be sleeping in a closed tent with 12 other bean-digesting campers?
Banana	Hold by the bottom. Strip the peel a little bit at a time. Eat the fruit.	Don't lick a banana as if it were a lollipop.	At a formal dinner, peel the banana all at once and eat it with a knife and fork.

Food	Do's	Don'ts	Fine Points
Berries and cherries	Use the fingers to grasp the stem. Insert the berry/cherry into mouth. Clamp lips. Pull on stem with hand. Berry/cherry should pop off. Place stem on plate, in trash, or gently upon Mother Earth. Remove pits, if any, from mouth by hand.	Never spit pits at your dinner partner.	Formal settings require the use of a spoon. Use the tongue to redeposit pits on the spoon.
Bread and butter	Break off a small piece of bread by hand. Butter it. Eat it. Repeat. (Exception: Toast may be buttered all at once.) If you don't have a bread plate, place the bread (or roll) on the edge of your dinner plate.	Never stuff an entire buttered slice or roll into your mouth. Never hold the bread in the palm of your hand while slathering gobs of butter on it.	When taking a pat of butter from the butter dish, use the butter knife traveling with it. Place the butter on your butter plate (or dinner plate, if a butter plate is not provided). Then use your own knife to butter your bread.
Cake	Eat with a fork. True aficionados always begin at the point of the triangle.	Don't eat cake with your fingers, unless you're sneaking a piece in the kitchen.	Cake left sitting on the counter quickly disappears, despite the fact that nobody's had any. This is because everyone who takes some thinks his or her slice is too thin to be detected.
Candy	All teenagers are genetically programmed to know how to eat candy.	Don't leave telltale chocolate smears on your face.	With boxed candy, you must "take the one you touch," and *only* one, unless your host insists that you take several. (This would be the mark of a *very good* host.) The little paper tray comes along for the ride and may be placed in a nearby ashtray or candy-wrapper-discard-dish.

Food	Do's	Don'ts	Fine Points
Cherry tomatoes	Small cherry tomatoes should travel by fork to the mouth and be eaten in one bite, thus producing a squirt of tomato seeds inside your cheek. Larger cherry tomatoes should be cut in half.	Never bite into a cherry tomato unless your mouth is fully closed.	*Cherry* tomatoes should be eaten with a big grin and a happy disposition.
Club sandwich (and other food too tall to fit in your mouth)	Discreetly compress the sandwich. Eat over the table so falling food will land on your plate and not in your lap. Use your fork to pick up the droppings.	Never stand on a club sandwich to flatten it.	The toothpicks with shrubbery on top are not meant to be eaten.
Corn on the cob	Ears are eaten from left to right. You may nibble horizontally (the "typewriter" method) or vertically (the "rotary" method).	Making typewriter sounds is forbidden.	These methods are designed to maximize the number of corn bits that get stuck in your teeth.
Fish	Use the fish fork, tines down, to anchor the fish. Holding the fish knife as you would a pencil, cut through the skin from left to right. Lift up the top flap of skin and eat from left to right. Then lift the bottom flap and repeat. Break off the fish meat carefully so you don't pry up any bones. The backbone will now be exposed. Gently remove it and place it on the edge of your plate. The fish's other flank is now available for eating.	Never use a toy guillotine to decapitate the fish. If you can't stand the sight of a fish head, cover it with your lemon.	While fish may come to the table with their heads on, it's considered rude for them to wear hats.

Food	Do's	Don'ts	Fine Points
Grapefruit	There's no way to eat a grapefruit properly unless you're furnished with a serrated grapefruit spoon, or the sections have been previously loosened in the kitchen.	Try not to squirt people in the eye while eating grapefruit.	Someday when you're bored, try to figure out how grapes and grapefruit are related.
Grapes	Use your fingers to place grapes in your mouth one by one. Remove any seeds by hand.	Don't pick single grapes off of a communal bunch. This leaves an unappetizing grave yard of stems for others.	If a bowl of grapes is passed, use your fingers or the scissors (if provided) to break off a small bunch.
Ice	Consume with an iced tea spoon. Or hold the glass to your lips *after* the liquid has been consumed, tilt, and pop cube into mouth.	Don't chew the ice. You'll sound like a trash compactor.	Ice is a refreshing, no-calorie, highly underrated treat.
Ice cream in a bowl	Eat with a spoon and a rapturous look on your face.	Don't mush it into ice cream soup. If you really can't eat it any other way, wait patiently while it starts to melt. Then allow your spoon to travel in genteel circles around the bowl until the ice cream reaches the desired consistency.	Greedy children who gulp down their ice cream are punished with headaches.
Ice cream in a cone	Immediately attack the overhanging lip to prevent drips. Push the scoop into the cone with downward tongue pressure to prevent tearful "scoop-on-the-sidewalk" scenes. Be gentle to avoid agonizing "my cone broke" scenes.	Don't work your way up from the bottom.	Dripless and dropless techniques must be practiced and mastered in order to maximize carryout cone-in-the-car opportunities.

Food	Do's	Don'ts	Fine Points
Ice cream soda	The only way to eat an ice cream soda is with two straws, two spoons, and somebody you really like.	It's acceptable to slurp up the last remains of soda and melted ice cream—but the sound must not be audible to those in the next booth.	Always offer your date the cherry on top.
Lemon	When squeezing a lemon wedge, use your other hand as a shield to prevent lemon spritzes from flying into people's eyes.	Don't bite into a lemon wedge in company. This will make everyone pucker up.	When life gives you lemons, make lemon chiffon pie.
Orange	Either cut in quarters and burrow your face in the fruit, or peel by hand and separate into sections.	Never tell "Knock, knock." "Who's there?" "Orange." "Orange who?" "Orange you glad . . ." jokes at formal dinners.	In a fancy restaurant, eat the fruit with a fork.
Peas	Consume with a fork. The last few peas may be cornered against a wall of mashed potatoes. If the peas are the only food remaining on the plate, the holdouts are generally impossible to catch and must be sacrificed.	Never use bread, fingers, or a knife to push peas onto your fork.	Parental commands to "Finish your peas!" are unreasonable unless permission is granted to snare the stragglers using improper methods.
Pizza	For informal occasions, pizza may be lowered into the mouth from above for that first delicious bite of the triangle. The remaining wedge may be kept flat or folded by breaking the spine of the crust with your forefinger.	Don't pull long strings of cheese with your teeth.	For formal occasions, use a knife and fork. If you must pick off the olives, do it with your fork.

Food	Do's	Don'ts	Fine Points
Salad	Use a salad fork and knife if provided. Otherwise use your main course utensils. Large pieces of lettuce may be cut with your knife.	Refrain from cutting your lettuce so fine that it looks like it went through a shredder.	In Europe, salads are typically served *after* the main dish; in America, before.
Soup	Hold the soup spoon so its length runs parallel to the table edge. Fill by submerging the far side first and moving the spoon toward the back of the bowl. Sip from the *near side* of the spoon, not the tip. Pour the liquid into your mouth. Tilt the soup plate *away* from you to get the last drops.	Don't put the spoon in your mouth unless it has chunky goodies on it. Don't suction the contents of your spoon as if you're cleaning out a septic tank. Don't crumble crackers into the bowl. Don't use a knife to cut things in your soup. Don't drink from the bowl unless it has handles or the soup arrives in a mug.	When pausing or finishing, leave your spoon in the bowl if the bowl is large, or on the saucer underneath if the bowl is small.
Shish kebab	Eat from the skewer if the kebab is served as an appetizer.	If the kebab is served as a main dish, hold the skewer with one hand while using your fork to slide the pieces off.	Do not use the skewer to have sword fights with others at the table. Place it on the edge of your plate.
Spaghetti etiquetti	Capture a few strands in the tines of your fork and twirl. (Not you. The spaghetti.)	Don't slurp or lower linguini into your mouth as if it's feeding time at Sea World. Don't sever strands with your teeth so they fall onto your plate.	It's not considered proper to twirl spaghetti on a spoon. It doesn't matter if everybody does it.
Tea	Let it steep. Allow the teabag to drip into the cup before removing it.	Don't bounce the teabag up and down in your cup or squeeze it by wrapping the string around it.	Place the used teabag on your saucer.

Dining Out

You'd like to take your girlfriend to a fancy restaurant for dinner. You've never done this before, and you're not quite sure how to go about it. Here's precisely what to do to ensure that a good time is had by all.

When you pop the question, give your girlfriend clues for how to dress. If you want to surprise her with your choice, you can say:

"Are you free for dinner Saturday night? I'd like to take you to this fancy little place I know."

Or you can be more direct and ask:

"Would you like to go to Le Snob on Saturday night?"

Next, make a reservation. It's not necessary to speak French. Call the restaurant. Tell them you'd like a table for two on Saturday night at 8:00. If you have any special requests (for example, a table near the window, or a birthday cake) make them known at this time.*

When you arrive, you'll be greeted by the maitre d'. State your name and say that you have a reservation. He'll check to make sure that you do, then lead the two of you to your table. Your girlfriend should go first—after the maitre d'. So you don't get lost, you should follow her. If there's any problem with the table (too close to the kitchen, in a draft, next to noisy neighbors, etc.), politely request a different one. You have every right to do this.

> *IF THE RESTAURANT IS ESPECIALLY POPULAR OR VERY SMALL, MAKE THE RESERVATION *BEFORE* ASKING YOUR GIRLFRIEND. YOU CAN ALWAYS CANCEL YOUR FIRST RESERVATION AND MAKE ANOTHER ONE IF SHE'S ALREADY BUSY THAT NIGHT. BUT DO CALL TO CANCEL YOUR FIRST RESERVATION. NO-SHOWS ARE RUDE.

The maitre d' will either pull out the woman's chair for her to sit down, or, if your table is a banquette (a bench against the wall instead of chairs), slide out the table so she can gracefully scoot in. Once your girlfriend is seated, you may sit down.

Menus come next. If you want to communicate subliminally to your girlfriend that she'd better not order the most expensive item on the menu, you can mention dishes that look interesting to you. She will then check them out, note their prices, and order accordingly.

As long as you don't eat with your fingers or use the tablecloth as a handkerchief, there's no need to feel uncomfortable in a fancy restaurant. Snootiness isn't the same as elegance; disdain isn't the same as good service. If a restaurant indulges in either, it's the restaurant, not the patrons, who are rude. Demonstrate your opinion of their behavior by never returning.

Dear Alex

"What are you supposed to do with those pretty little things that come with your plate of food?"

I assume you're referring to the garnishes. It's perfectly fine to eat the various sprigs and ferns that doll up a dish. Do, however, keep a sharp lookout for miniature Oriental parasols, plastic palm trees, and toothpicks with greenery on top. While nonfattening, these are not readily digestible.

Dear Alex

"What do you do if you find a bug in your food?"

First, resist the urge to scream and throw your dish against the wall. In a restaurant, discreetly tell the waiter. He will remove the dish and bring you a bug-free replacement. At a friend's house, you must walk a fine line between not embarrassing your hosts and wanting to eat your food. If you've eaten most of your food when the discovery is made, simply stop eating as if you're full and say no more. If you discover the crunchy critter right away, quietly mention it to your friend or host. They will bring you a fresh dish. What you don't want to do is make it the center of attention of the entire dinner party. If you encounter the little Bugsy at home, excuse yourself and go into the kitchen to take a new dish and portion of food. Of course, if you'd rather have a bit of fun, it's perfectly fine to say, "Eeeeeek, there's a bug in my couscous!"

Dear Alex

"How do you decide who gets the best seat when you go out to dinner?"

This is usually determined by clever planning and quick footwork, since possession is nine-tenths of the law. Traditionally, the woman was given the "best" seat—the one against the wall, from which you can look out and see everything. This left the man better positioned to pay the bill, taste the wine, and beckon the waiter. Since women today perform many of these tasks, there's no longer any gender-based reason for who sits where. People who go out together frequently can alternate "best" seats.

Deciding What to Order

When someone takes you to dinner, what should you order? Why, the most expensive thing.

Just kidding.

It's best to order something in the mid-price range. If you order the cheapest item, your host will think you think he's cheap. If you order the most expensive, he may wish you thought he was cheap.

Listen for clues. If your host says "This place is famous for the lobster" or "I think I'll have the chicken, but I hope you'll try the steak," he's giving you permission to order whatever you want.

If he puts you on the spot with "What do you think you're going to have?" you can say "Everything looks good. What are *you* thinking of having?" Similarly, if a friend's parents take you out, ask if there's anything in particular they'd recommend. Even if they've never been to the restaurant before, they'll mention some items that sound good, and you'll get the menu guidance you need.

Dear Alex

"I was invited to dinner at a country club. My menu didn't have any prices on it. I was afraid of ordering the most expensive thing by mistake. What's the polite thing to do when this happens?"

The idea behind the "priceless" menu is that it's gauche for hosts to let on exactly how much their generosity is costing them. (We remove price tags from gifts for the same reason.) This makes sense in a country club, where it's assumed that the members will pay for their guests. In public restaurants, however, there's no way (short of mind reading) for waiters to know who the lucky check picker-upper will be. It's the height of sexism to give menus with prices to men and menus without prices to women.

If you're handed a menu without prices, use the strategies discussed above to solicit clues and suggestions. Generally speaking, things like lobster, seafood, shellfish, and fine cuts of meat are more expensive than chicken, pasta, salads, and sandwiches.

TRUE STORIES

FROM THE
MANNERS FRONTIER

Beaucoup de Bucks

I was once taken out to dinner at a three-star Michelin restaurant in Paris. It was the kind of place where you could spend more on lunch than most countries spend on defense.

Our party consisted of three men and a lady. As the men stared at the menu prices in stunned silence, the lady exclaimed "Doesn't this look fabulous! We must try the lobster-stuffed raviolis, and the crab timbale, and the salmon, and—" on and on through half the items on the menu. We were a bit surprised at her extravagance, until we discovered that her menu had no prices.

It was at this moment that the brothers Slobola walked in. No, not really; it was at this moment that the waiter arrived. We ordered everything we wanted. And then we economized by eating dry cereal for the next eight days.

Going Dutch

Going Dutch doesn't mean dining in Amsterdam. It means that each person pays his or her own share of the bill. The tricky thing is, if you're invited out, how do you know if it's Dutch or not?

If you're lucky, the person will make it clear by saying "Let's have dinner together Saturday, my treat" or "I have some good news and some bad news. The good news is I'm inviting you to go out to dinner with me. The bad news is I'm flat broke, and we'll have to go Dutch."

If you're not sure who's paying, you can:

- wait and see, being sure to have enough money with you in case you need to cover your share

- say "I'd love to go, but I'm broke until next Friday." This will generate either "Oh, that doesn't matter, I'm paying" or "Why don't we wait 'til then, okay?"

If you do go Dutch, split the bill evenly by the number of people. This saves endless hassles over who had coffee and whose appetizer cost 35 cents more. If, however, you know that your share came to much more than anyone else's, you should insist on putting in more money. If your share of the bill was much smaller—for example, you had a bowl of soup while everyone else had four-course dinners—you may, unfortunately and unfairly, end up having to contribute more than you owe to avoid an awkward math brawl at the table. One trick you can try if your share was much smaller is this: As soon as the check arrives, put in what you owe (tax and tip included) and say, "This should cover my share."

Dear Alex

"What can you do if you order something in a restaurant and you don't like it?"

If the item is well-prepared, you're probably stuck. You could see if anyone at your table wants to swap with you, or you could order a different dish. A truly classy restaurant might not charge you for the order you didn't eat, but don't count on it.

If you order something and it's unsatisfactory, discreetly bring it to your waiter's attention. Say:

"Excuse me, I ordered my steak rare. This one is well-done."

"The soup is delicious, but I wonder if you could have it warmed up."

As long as you're polite, the restaurant should agree to make things right. If you don't get satisfaction from the waiter, ask to speak to the headwaiter or manager.

It's also perfectly proper to ask the waiter to replace dirty forks, dishes, or glassware.

Dear Alex

"Why are waiters so rude to teenagers?"

Because *some* teenagers are very rude and rowdy in restaurants. They yell, swear, make out, blow bubbles in their drinks, snort through their noses, play with their food, throw things, create salt mountains on the tablecloth, treat servers with contempt, leave little or no tip, and even bolt from the restaurant without paying. Unfortunately, their behavior puts *all* teenagers under suspicion. Therefore, some waiters groan inside when a group of teenagers sits down at one of their tables. This doesn't excuse rude service, but it may help explain it.

Naturally, when *you* dine out, your behavior should be exemplary. Use your best table manners, treat the staff with respect, tip well,* and leave the restaurant intact when you depart. The next time you visit that establishment, the waiters will fight for the right to serve you. Look at the following chart for a summary of acceptable vs. unacceptable acts.

It's okay to:	It's not okay to:
request a particular table	rearrange the room
ask for descriptions of menu items	ask the waiter to repeat them more than once
ask the prices of specials	blurt "What a rip-off!"
send back an improperly prepared dish	stomp into the kitchen and throw your plate against the wall
address a request to any staff person who serves your table or passes within its vicinity	yell across the room "What do I have to do to get some service around here?"
ask for a doggie bag	ask for a barf bag
glance at the check to make sure there are no errors	bring along your accountant
discreetly apply a little lipstick at the table (as long as you're with friends or relatives)	comb your hair, apply full makeup, or squeeze zits at the table

*FOR TIPPING TIPS, SEE PAGES 308–312.

"Is it proper to hand plates to a waiter?"

Only if you're tucked away in an awkward corner and the waiter would have to reach over other diners to take your plate. Otherwise it might be seen as an affront to his professionalism. On a similar topic: Never stack the dishes at your table. Let the staff do it when they clear them away.

Sharing Food

You're at a restaurant with a friend, your orders arrive, and you notice that her onion rings look spectacular. Meanwhile, your french fries are especially crisp and golden. You wonder if it's all right to share.

If she agrees, it is. But ask first. Or, better yet, wait until she offers. Don't just reach across the table. (If she's slow to offer, you might casually remark *"Boy, those rings look good. How are they? By the way, want some of my fries?"*)

Although it's rude to pass mashed potatoes from one person's mouth to another in public, it's perfectly fine to share some types of food at restaurants. For example, grub that's brought in communal serving dishes— Szechuan spicy chicken, pizza, big bowls of pasta—is meant to be enjoyed by all. In fancy restaurants, where one oohs and ahhhs and thinks *six dollars* every time you take a bite, you may put a taste of food on your fork and pass it to a close friend or loved one. For people you know less well, samples should be delivered on their forks or onto their bread plate.

If you plan to go halvesies on two entrées or split one, tell the waiter when ordering. Many restaurants will make the division in the kitchen. This might upset the chef's carefully laid out squiggles and sprinkles, but every artist needs to be challenged once in a while.

Tipping Tips

In a perfect world, there would be no tipping. Workers would be paid a fair wage to do their jobs. Instead, they get caught between cheap employers ("Yeah, but you'll make a fortune in tips") and cheap customers ("Tip? They earn a good salary"). The fact is that people in service jobs earn very low base salaries—often below minimum wage. They depend on tips for their income. If a waitress serves a party of 12 businessmen who hog three tables all night, run up a bill of $2,500, and leave a $10 tip, that waitress has been stiffed for her work. Imagine if you babysat for an entire evening and got paid a quarter.

The first rule of tipping in the United States is that it's *not* optional. If the hairdresser cuts off your ear, or the cabby runs over your foot, you can leave a small tip—or none at all. But you should make it known why you aren't leaving a standard tip. In Europe, a service charge is added to the bill in most restaurants, and it's perfectly acceptable to leave without tipping anyone. In the United States, the convention is different. Tipping is an "honor system" in which customers are trusted to ante up most of the worker's wage.

Some teenagers tend to leave low tips. Often it's because their own funds are limited or because they don't know how much to give. But it's not fair to penalize workers who are trying to make a living. So here are the rules for being a tip-top tipster wherever you go:

Restaurants. Tip a minimum of 15 percent of the total bill—20 percent or more if the service is exceptional, the restaurant fancy, or you want to become known as a "preferred" customer. Never leave less than 50 cents, even if all you had was a cup of coffee and it means you're leaving a 25 percent tip.

A debate rages over whether you should tip on the total bill including tax, or just on the food and beverage costs. Let me settle it for you. Tip on the tax. Why? Because you're not a CHEAPSKATE! If your food bill is $20 and your state has an 8 percent tax, the amount you'll save by not tipping 20 percent on the tax is 32 cents. On a $100 food bill you'd save $1.60. Is it really worth complicating the math and shorting the waiter a few cents to make the point that nobody "served" you the tax and therefore that amount should be excluded when calculating the tip? Sheesh!

If the food was bad, don't take it out on the waitress. She didn't prepare it. As long as she or the manager was responsive to your complaints, you should still leave a tip. Just don't go back to that restaurant again.

If you're part of a large group, check to make sure that the restaurant didn't already add the tip (sometimes referred to as a "service charge" or "gratuity") to your check. Otherwise you'll end up tipping twice.

Sorry, but you still need to leave a full tip in buffet-style restaurants where you serve yourself.

It's not necessary to tip the maitre d' or headwaiter if all he does is show you to a table, pull out your chair, and hand you a menu. If, however, he provides a special service (rearranging tables, securing a birthday cake, squeezing you in without a reservation), a tip of $10 to $20 is customary. This should be discreetly slipped into his hand as you leave.

The *sommelier* (wine steward) need not be tipped if all he does is serve the bottle ordered. If, however, he helped with the selection, a tip of 15 percent of the wine bill is appropriate.

Restroom attendants. These are people whose job is to listen to you pee. You are forgiven if the idea of a bathroom attendant creeps you out. If the attendant does nothing for you, no tip is required. If he or she hands you a towel, you can tip 50 cents to $1. If other services are performed (although I can't imagine what they would be), or if you partake of the display of mints, hand lotion, candy, or hair gel they sometimes maintain, tip $2–$3.

Checkroom attendants. You can usually tell if tipping is expected by the presence of a little tray full of money on the counter. Don't be fooled by any large bills you see. They represent what the person would like to get, not what you're obliged to give. The going rate for checking a coat or parcel is $1 per item.

On a personal note, I'm happy to tip checkroom attendants in restaurants, museums, galleries, and concert halls. I refuse to tip in stores that presume me to be a thief upon entering and require me to leave my parcels or bags.

Airport skycaps. $2 for the first bag, then $1 per bag is standard for curbside check-in. If the skycap ferries your bags to the check-in counter, you can tip $2 per bag. Some airlines charge a curbside check-in fee. Keep in mind that this does not go to the skycap.

Hotels. If you stay in a fancy hotel, you should arm yourself with a roll of dollar bills. These can be handed out to bellhops ($1 a bag; minimum $2) and doormen ($1–$2 for strenuous cab hailing). Now you know why motels were invented.

For hotel maids, leave $1–$5 per day in the room (depending on the cost of your room), when checking out. Few people observe this custom. Be one of them.

The *concierge* (which is French for Person Who Knows Everything) may perform a special service for you, such as obtaining tickets for a sold-out show or finding a psychiatrist for your homesick dog. A gratuity of $5 to $10 is standard; for really hard-to-get tickets or reservations, tip $15 or 15–20 percent of the ticket price.

Many hotels add a 15 percent service charge to the bill for room service (plus a delivery charge). Check your bill, and if this has been done, no further tip is required when your breakfast or midnight snack is delivered to your door. It's fine, when you place your order, to ask whether the service charge includes a gratuity (tip) for the person who delivers your food. If not, then you'll want to tip the server $2.

The pizza delivery guy or gal. Usually $2 per pizza with a $2 minimum. For larger orders, tip 15 percent of the bill (10 percent for lackluster service). Be a bit more generous if you live in a sixth floor walk-up or the delivery person had to trudge through snowdrifts to find you.

"Keep the change."

Taxi drivers. The minimum tip is $1. For fares over $7, tip 15 percent. Tip another buck or two for help with bags. No tip is necessary if the driver runs out of gas and you miss your flight.

Shoe shiners. If you ever have time on your hands and want to get those Nikes shined up, tip $1–$2 for shoes and $2–$3 for boots, depending on the level of service.

Hairdressers and manicurists. Tip 15 to 20 percent of the bill. Give the shampooist two bucks.

Wandering musicians. I have often been tempted to offer them a dollar if they will stop playing. No tip is required if a strolling musician just stops by your table, plays, and moves on. If you make a request, tip a dollar. More requests, more dollars. Pay when he or she leaves your table.

Valet parking. Tip $3 in great metropolises, $2 in lesser ones—when they bring your car. No tip is necessary if your car is returned with 200 more miles on the odometer than when you left it.

Owners. Don't tip the owners of establishments when they provide services for you (for example, Jean-Louis himself cuts your hair, or Mel of Mel's Deli personally brings you your Reuben). Instead of money, give profuse thanks and many referrals.

Tour guides. Museum docents and sightseeing tour guides are sometimes tipped. Watch what others do. For a short tour, $2 is adequate. If someone has been your tour bus guide for three weeks through Siberia, a much larger tip would be proper.

And finally:

Never tip a **police officer.** For some reason, this is interpreted as a bribe. Others who should never be tipped include flight attendants, bus drivers, train conductors, pilots, elevator operators (if there are still any left), government officials, teachers, and owners of bed-and-breakfast establishments. This doesn't mean, though, that you can't give a nonmonetary *gift* to someone you see frequently and have gotten to know such as a school bus driver, a doorman, or the lifeguard at a pool.

Chapter Quiz

1. *You're at a dinner party. You ingest a mouthful of soup and discover that it's burning hot. Do you:*

a) spit it out

b) sue your hostess for $4,000,000

c) quietly breathe air into your mouth to cool it

2. *You're having dinner at the home of some friends of your parents. When the main dish is brought from the kitchen, you realize that it's something you don't like. Do you:*

a) knock it out of your hostess's hands and hope she'll serve something else

b) say "Yiccch. I hate that!"

c) take a small portion and eat as much as you can

3. *A vegetarian comes to your house for dinner. She loads up on the salad and pasta but doesn't touch the meat. The proper thing to say is:*

a) "If humans were meant to be vegetarians, animals would be made out of rice."

b) "Have you ever had scurvy?"

c) nothing

4. *You're having lunch in the school cafeteria. While munching on a morsel of Salisbury steak, you encounter a huge piece of gristle. Do you:*

a) throw it at the gym teacher

b) go "ARRRGH, ARRRGH, ARRRGH" and try to swallow it

c) deposit it on your fork when no one is looking and transfer it to your plate

5. *Etiquette permits family members to read at the table so long as they:*

a) don't move their lips

b) provide plot summaries for one another

c) are eating breakfast

6. *You're dining out at a fancy restaurant. The waiter brings your entrée, and it's not what you ordered. The best response is to:*

a) dump it on the floor

b) try to jerk the tablecloth out from under the dishes

c) say "Excuse me, but I ordered the duckling."

EAT,
DRINK,
AND BE
WARY

ON YOUR BEST BEHAVIOR

Etiquette for the Milestones and Celebrations of Life

Life is full of special events: weddings, funerals, bar mitzvahs, graduations. Some of these are happy occasions; others are sad. But they all have one thing in common: uncomfortable seats. So you don't trip the groom, tickle the bride, or fill your canteen from the baptismal font, here are some tips for minding your manners at the milestones of life.

Dear Alex

"What are you supposed to do at a funeral?"

Just lie still.

Funerals

The thought of attending a funeral or memorial service may make you uncomfortable. You may think *I won't know what to say. I won't know anybody there. What if I cry? What if I laugh?*

Our culture is squeamish about death. People don't like to talk about it, and most people grow up without knowing how to deal with grief—whether their own or somebody else's. While it's natural to feel ambivalent about going to a funeral, it's important that you do attend. It's a way of supporting the bereaved, consoling yourself, and honoring the dearly departed. You never get a second chance to go to someone's funeral. Here's what to do and why:

Dress conservatively. You don't have to wear black, but loud, attention-getting outfits are out of place. This isn't the time for fashion statements other than one of respect for the solemnity of the occasion and/or the traditions of the family.

Sign the registry. There should be a book at the church or funeral home for guests to sign. Presumably its purpose is to allow the family of the deceased to appreciate those who attended rather than depreciate those who didn't ("And after everything Harry did for him!"). There may also be an online guest book you can sign. Say what you would say in person: express what is in your heart; offer sympathy and support; leave an anecdote or special memory involving the person who died.

Respect the rites. The death of a person can involve many separate events: a viewing of the body, a religious service, a procession, a burial, a wake, a messy lawsuit over the will. Depending on the family's cultural and religious traditions, there may be wailing and keening—or stiff upper lips; there may be wild, life-affirming parties—or subdued reminiscing. You aren't required to participate in behaviors that are foreign or objectionable to your culture, language, religion, or relationship to the deceased. For example, nobody would expect you to make the sign of the cross, to kiss the corpse, to recite a prayer in a language you don't know, or to become hysterical. What you can always do, however, is be observant and respectful. Stand and sit when others do. Try to blend in with the tone and traditions of the occasion.

Feel free to decline. You may be asked to throw dirt on the coffin. You may be asked to say a few words. (Tributes and recollections from people who knew the departed are included in some services.) You may be offered an opportunity to view the body. If you're comfortable doing any of these, your participation will be appreciated. But such rituals are never obligatory, and you won't cause offense by declining. A simple "No, thank you" should suffice. If asked to speak, you could say "Oh, I'd love to, but there's no way I could get through it."

If you're asked to be a pallbearer*, however, it's *not* considered proper to decline—unless you recently dislocated your shoulder.

*A PERSON WHO HELPS CARRY THE COFFIN AT A FUNERAL

Don't be too jolly. Let's say the father of one of your friends has just died. You feel for your friend, but you didn't know his father. At the funeral are many of your classmates. Since you're not grieving yourself, it might seem natural to greet them jubilantly and engage in animated conversation. Don't. Behavior that's too upbeat might be misinterpreted as a lack of respect for the somber nature of the occasion. While you don't have to put on fake grief, you do have to maintain a subdued decorum to show your empathy.

Express your sympathy. Right after the service, guests usually form a line to extend their condolences to the family. This is the moment most people have in mind when they worry about what to say.

Stop worrying. *All you have to say to each person as you pass through the line is "I'm so sorry." Or, "Please accept my sympathy." Or, if you know the person, "I'm here for you if you need anything."* If this taxes your tongue too much, you don't have to say anything. If the person is someone you know well, you can simply hug him or her. If it's someone you don't know at all, you can engage in a mournful handshake. Instead of a vigorous up-and-down squeeze, embrace the person's hand between your own two hands, as if you were holding a bug. Either a hug or a handshake can be accompanied by a sad look that says "I feel for your pain."

Probably more important than knowing what to say is knowing what *not* to say. Avoid any and all of the following:

"I know just how you feel."

"You must be heartbroken."

"It's much better this way."

"At least he's out of his pain."

"Now you can get on with your life."

"You never liked her much anyway."

"I suppose you'll get the house?"

"Your parents can always have another kid."

"I'm sure he wouldn't want us to be sad."

These sentiments are inappropriate because:

- They presume to tell others what their emotions or grieving process should be.

- They put words and thoughts into the mouths of those who can no longer speak for themselves.

- They frame the death in terms of its impact on you.

- They suggest that people who die can be replaced as easily as lightbulbs.

Send flowers. It's traditional to send flowers to the church where the funeral will be held, or to the family of the deceased. Of course, if 300 people do this, there'll be so many flower arrangements that it will look like . . . a funeral. No one will be able to get in the door.

This is why many families ask that, in lieu of flowers, contributions be made to the deceased's favorite charity. Giving the money to a good cause is not only a lovely, lasting tribute to the one who was called away, but also a kindness to hay fever sufferers.

Write a letter of condolence. This, like a thank-you note, is nonnegotiable. Write it by hand, in ink, on good quality personal note paper. Do *not* send one of those tacky store-bought sympathy cards with canned messages:

Roses are red,

Violets are blue,

Sorry he's dead,

Boo-hoo, boo-hoo.

Instead, send a short, warm note. Acknowledge the death. Include a fond recollection. Close with an expression of sympathy. Avoid euphemisms such as "passed away" or "left us." These suggest that the deceased just overtook a slow-moving car or stepped out of the room for a moment. The use of email, texting, or IM'ing is inappropriate for sending condolences.

Dear Mr. and Mrs. Bereaved,

I was so sorry to hear the sad news of Billy's death. His friendship was very special to me. When I came to Buford in the middle of my freshman year, he went out of his way to make me feel welcome. I don't know what I would have done without his friendship (and his answers in math!). Please accept my deepest sympathy.

Sincerely yours,

Arthur Graves

Let it out. Somebody's death, even if you didn't know the person, can set off all sorts of feelings. Don't keep them bottled up inside. Write them down in a journal. Talk to people about how you feel, about the person who died. If you don't find the comfort or support you need from your family or friends, talk to a teacher, counselor, or member of the clergy.

Dear Alex

"Is it true that when a person is cremated, people at the funeral have to spread the ashes?"

If the person who died was cremated, there may be a ceremony in which her ashes are scattered. This doesn't usually take place at the time of the funeral, since ashes flung around the church would just end up in a vacuum cleaner. Most people who are cremated make it known (*before* they die) where they would like their ashes scattered. It's usually a place that holds special meaning for them (for example, the Rocky Mountains, the Tiber River, or the Walmart parking lot). If you participate in one of these ceremonies, you don't have to dish out the dust. But if you choose to do so, stand upwind.

Dear Alex

"I have this friend whose mother died about six months ago. I'm feeling guilty because I haven't seen much of my friend since then. She isn't much fun to be around anymore, plus I don't know what to say. How much longer do you think she'll be like this?"

There's no way of saying, because there's no "correct" way to mourn a death. Some people cry; others don't. Some people become depressed for a long time; others snap out of it quickly. Some people go through periods of anger and guilt for having done (or not done) something to or for the deceased. Some people may even be angry at the person who died—for dying. What you see on the surface may bear little resemblance to what a person feels inside.

Your friend had the rug pulled out from under her life. Her mother's untimely death will be a part of her identity forever—long after her acute feelings of grief and sadness have subsided. Six months ago, her friends and relatives probably rallied to offer their love and support. They came to the funeral, brought food, sent flowers—and then disappeared. The bereaved are often abandoned, emotionally if not physically. Other people expect them to "get on with their life," or they assume that those who have suffered a loss want to be left alone, or they are simply uncomfortable being around someone in so much pain.

The best thing you can do for your friend—and yourself—is to *be* her friend. Call her, spend time with her, and include her in social gatherings. If she hesitates or declines, apply a little pressure. Tell her you miss doing things together. Don't make her feel she has to put on a happy face. Let her know you want her company just the way she is.

When you're together, ask her how she is, how things are at home, and how her family is doing. Get her talking. People who suffer loss often feel isolated from those around them—because they have experienced something others haven't, and because people tend to avoid the subject. It's okay to talk about your friend's mother. Share some memories you have of her. Bringing them up won't make your friend feel worse by "reminding" her. She's already thinking about her mother all of the time.

If your friend starts to share her feelings, just be a good listener.* Don't try to cheer her up or talk her out of her feelings. If she speaks of problems at home, or if she seems terribly troubled or inconsolable, encourage her to talk to a counselor or another trusted adult.

*FOR TIPS ON LISTENING, SEE PAGES 357–359.

Religious Services

Presumably you know how to behave at your own house of worship, provided you attend one. In the event you're invited to attend a religious service outside your faith—perhaps for a special occasion—follow these guidelines to avoid offending the Higher Powers-That-Be:

- Respond promptly to the invitation.**

- Arrive on time.

- Don't skip the ceremony and just go to the party.

- Don't talk during the service unless audience participation is an integral part. (Whispered requests for a prayer book or page number are fine.)

- If you have to go to the bathroom, there's no need to raise your hand until the priest or rabbi calls on you. Simply exit quietly—preferably during a boisterous moment in the ceremony.

- Don't tell jokes. No environment is more conducive to uncontrollable fits of giggling than a house of worship. Should you suffer an attack, bite the insides of your cheeks. Whatever you do, don't look at your friend while he's reading from the Torah. If he breaks up, all is lost.

- Dress appropriately. Your friend and/or other classmates who belong to the same church or synagogue can advise you.

- Participate in the rituals. You don't have to take communion, kneel while praying, or immerse yourself in the baptismal font if these

**FOR TIPS ON RESPONDING TO INVITATIONS, SEE PAGES 160–164.

ON YOUR
BEST
BEHAVIOR

rituals are foreign to your faith. But you should stand when others stand, sing when others sing, and honor the traditions of worship practiced by that congregation.

- Don't take the money. At some services, a plate full of money will be passed. This is not an hors d'oeuvres tray of free samples; it's a collection plate to raise money for the church. If you feel so inclined, you may make a donation.

- Send a gift.* Honoring your friend and the occasion with a gift is a thoughtful thing to do. It's best if you don't bring your present to the church or synagogue. Send it to your friend's home ahead of time, or take it with you to the party later in the day. Checks and cash may be passed discreetly immediately following the service.

Bar and Bat Mitzvahs

A bar mitzvah (bat mitzvah for girls) is a religious ceremony that occurs shortly after a Jewish child's 13th birthday. It marks the child's initiation as a full-fledged adult into the Jewish faith.** The service, which takes place at a synagogue, is open to the congregation as well as to the invited guests of the bar (bat) mitzvah and his (her) family. (The name applies both to the ceremony and the person being initiated into religious adulthood.) After the service, there's usually a reception at the synagogue, during which people offer their congratulations and consume large amounts of herring.

Later in the day, there's often a more elaborate by-invitation-only party. This is for relatives, family friends, and classmates. I attended numerous such events myself between ages 12 and 14, as I was blessed with many Jewish friends. My respect for religion grew by leaps and bounds as I realized that sacred traditions could be celebrated by bowling, swimming, skating, dining, dancing, and sneaking onto the golf course to discuss theology with a member of the opposite sex.

If you're a bar (bat) mitzvah, fulfilling the following responsibilities will reinforce your newly minted adult status:

Prior to the event . . .

- Show your maturity by recognizing your family's financial limitations. Bar (bat) mitzvah parties are not a competitive sport. Just because some other kid's parents hired a Grammy-winning rock band to perform live is no excuse for saying "If you loved me, you'd take out a second mortgage."

*FOR THE NITTY-GRITTY ON GIFT-GIVING, SEE PAGES 38—39.
**IN THE CHRISTIAN FAITH, A CONFIRMATION CEREMONY ADMITS A YOUNG PERSON TO MEMBERSHIP IN THE ADULT CONGREGATION. IF YOU'RE INVITED TO ATTEND A CONFIRMATION, OR IF YOU'RE BEING CONFIRMED, MANY OF THE SUGGESTIONS IN THIS SECTION WILL APPLY TO YOU, TOO.

- When your parents and siblings propose inviting certain of their friends as guests, try not to say "Ewwww, do they HAVE to come?" Instead, encourage them. This ensures not only more gifts, but that family members will be occupied while you spend time with your friends.

- Reciprocate by inviting classmates who asked you to their bar (bat) mitzvahs. If you're limited in the number of guests you can invite to the party, at least issue invitations to the service itself.

On the day of the event . . .

- Enjoy being the center of attention, but do so with grace, charm, and modesty. Recognize that even though it's your day, you must still honor your social obligations.

- Great all guests with warmth and joy, even the ones your parents made you invite. Say "It's so nice to see you. Thank you for coming."

- Try not to grimace when kissed by relatives you don't know or like.

- Don't interrupt the festivities to announce that you've passed the $1,000 mark in gifts received.

- Be patient with adults who say "My, how you've grown" and "How does it feel to be an adult?"

- Introduce your friends to your relatives, to your parents' friends, and to each other.

- Write your thank-you notes pronto.* The longer you delay, the harder it gets. Begin each note with an expression of delight at having seen (or regret at not having seen) the person you're writing to. Never begin with "Thank you for the . . . ."

- Thank your parents for everything they did to make the day so special. Thank the rabbi, thank the cantor, thank Moses—make it an all-inclusive list.

- Leave some strudel for others.

Dear Alex

"I've been invited to a friend's bar mitzvah. I'm not Jewish. Do I have to wear one of those beanies?"

If you're referring to a beanie with a propeller on top, certainly not. If you're referring to the small cap worn by men and boys of the Jewish faith, then you mean a *yarmulke,* not a beanie.

Do you have to wear one upon penalty of being shot? No. Is it okay to wear one if you're not Jewish? Yes. It's a mark of respect, much like rising when others rise during a church service.

The Debut

First, *debut* is pronounced "day-byoo," not "duh-but." Knowing this ahead of time will save you from awkward moments like:

You: *"Dearest Amelia! I can't wait to see your duh-but."*

Amelia: *"My butt? Why would you want to see my butt?"*

A debut is the occasion upon which a young lady (the *debutante*), having attained the age of 18, is presented to society at a formal dance (the *debutante ball*). This ritual was much more prevalent in days of yore (that period when strenuous efforts were made to keep a woman's ankles from being viewed by the opposite sex). Because young ladies were kept sheltered from society, it made sense to have an event at which they were unveiled (the young ladies that is, not their ankles). This is why debuts were often referred to as "coming out" parties. Today, the custom has become so outmoded that most people, if invited to a "coming out party," would expect something quite different.

*FOR TIPS ON WRITING THANK-YOU NOTES, SEE PAGES 43—45.

The declining popularity of the debutante ball is related to the declining popularity of courtship. It used to be that a gentleman wouldn't dream of speaking to a young lady before they were properly introduced. Courtship was the period during which, and the process by which, he then showed his interest and affection for her, with the intention (if all went well) of eventually marrying her. The debutante ball was the perfect setting for making introductions and getting the word out that a young lady's hand (and presumably the rest of her) was available for marriage. The debutante's parents would invite their friends, particularly those with handsome, honorable, and well-endowed (financially, that is) sons. Since the parents knew the families of the young men in attendance, they could rest assured that all contenders would pass inspection.

Things today are quite different. The strictures against people getting together without being properly introduced have disappeared. This means that a young gentleman can approach a young lady in a laundromat, say "Yo, borrow your Clorox?" and three days later they're in Las Vegas being married by an Elvis impersonator. Potential partners can meet at the gym ("Spot me while I work on my pecs?"), at bars ("Are you going to eat that olive?"), and through online dating sites ("Fun-loving professional, age 28, looks 27 . . .").

It's not surprising that fewer parents are going to the trouble and expense of presenting their daughters to society (and that fewer daughters wish to be so presented). Where the custom does persist, it's usually stage-managed by a *cotillion committee*. These self-appointed social arbiters screen and select each season's candidates and orchestrate the event. With several dozen young ladies all making their bows at the same time, the tradition has been updated to resemble the modern assembly line—and enjoys similar cost and production benefits.

At least two or three male escorts are required for each debutante. This is so the young ladies will feel in great demand, and also so there will be enough young men to dance with their sisters, mothers, and great aunts. If the debutante has been properly protected up to her 18th birthday, she won't know three eligible escorts. Therefore, the cotillion committee must find them for her. This is accomplished by a careful computer search that cross-checks the senior class of St. Smithereens School for Boys against social register, country club, and Forbes 400 membership lists. Those boys whose families show up on all lists are invited. If this fails to produce enough eligible young men, a "Free Punch" sign is placed outside the ballroom.

If you're a young woman whose parents are planning to debut you, here are your responsibilities (please note that they are remarkably similar to those of the bat mitzvah):

- Be mindful of your family's financial limitations. It just may not be possible to charter a Virgin Airways jet to take your friends to the Bahamas for a postball beach brunch.

- Remember that the true purpose of a coming out party is to present you to your parents' society. This means they have every right to invite their friends (and even have them outnumber your friends) without your saying "Why do THEY have to come?"

- Welcome and chat with all guests, be they young or chronologically challenged. Tell them how pleased you are that they could come.

- If you aren't an innocent young child who's being cast, eyelashes a-fluttering, into the adult world, pretend that you are.

- Dress properly. Typically this means wearing a white gown, not cutoffs.

- Introduce your friends to your family, to your parents' guests, and to each other.

- Pay attention to all of your escorts. Dance with fathers, grandfathers, cousins, and family friends in such proportion as to pay equal homage to duty and pleasure.

- Smile and be patient with adults who say "Whatever happened to the little girl I used to know?"

- Acknowledge all presents promptly.

- Thank your parents.

If you're a young man who's been recruited from St. Smithereens or elsewhere to tour the debutante circuit, here are your responsibilities:

- RSVP promptly.*

- Dress appropriately. (Proper dress is usually indicated on the invitation.)

- Anoint your deb with a floral arrangement.**

- As there shall be no wallflowers, do your part to see that all ladies who wish to dance have the opportunity.

- Engage in charming conversation with the hosts and their invited guests.

- Flirt with grandmothers.

- Maintain sobriety.

- Send a thank-you note to your hosts.

*FOR A REFRESHER ON RSVP-ING, SEE PAGES 160–164.
**A.K.A. A CORSAGE. SEE PAGES 264–265.

Graduation

Twelve long years of school—worrying, struggling, hassling, dreading, hating, hoping, helping, longing, pleading, praying—and that's just what your parents have been through! No wonder they're so excited about their, er, your high school graduation. This is the moment they've been waiting for. Free at last! No more tests. No more homework. No more meetings with the vice principal. Now they can sit back, relax, and look forward to . . . *four more years?!*

Graduation may be your triumph, but it's payback time for your parents. They'll be so giddy with pride and joy that they'll forget about the backpacks left on buses, lost gym shorts, stolen sneakers, broken eyeglasses, misplaced notebooks, and report cards that never made their way home. In this euphoric, all-is-forgiven state, they may also do silly things. Like ask to be introduced to your friends. Or want to see your locker. Or insist that you stand on the steps of the school for the longest minute on record as they aim the camera, forget to turn on the camera, re-aim the camera, brush a fly from their forehead, re-aim the camera, focus, re-aim the camera, tell everyone to smile, wait for your little brother to look, and then, with all 380 of your classmates watching, take a picture.

Yes, graduation is a day you'll always remember. To be sure it's a day you'll *want* to remember, here are some pointers for proper commencement behavior:

Send out invitations. Typically, these are provided by the school. They look something like this:

> ꙮ
> *The Headmaster, Faculty, and Graduating Class*
> *of*
> *Bedlam School*
> *request the pleasure of your company*
> *at*
> *Commencement Exercises*
> *Saturday, the 20th of May*
> *at one o'clock*
> *on the Academy Lawn*

If you just stick this in an envelope, the recipient will have no idea who the lucky graduate is. Therefore, include your card along with the invitation. What? No card? Then buy some blank ones. In your most calligraphic scrawl, handwrite your name. If you and a number of friends all wish to invite the same person (for example, your soccer league coach), you may send one invitation. Just enclose all of your cards. That way, his mailbox won't get overstuffed.

Because seating is usually limited at commencement exercises, you may not be able to invite as many people as you wish. In this case, you'll have to prioritize. Start with anyone likely to give you a car. Then invite your immediate family and closest relatives. If you still have some seats left, you can broaden the net to include mentors, friends, and distant relatives.

Send out announcements. These you send to friends and relatives who would be thrilled to hear of your accomplishments. This list might include tutors, coaches, piano teachers, scout leaders, and treasured babysitters from your childhood. If you had hoped to invite them to the graduation but were unable to do so because of limited seating, include a note to that effect. Let them know how much their support and/or friendship have meant to you over the years.

Don't fish for presents. It's tacky to blanket the populace with news of your graduation. Don't send invitations or announcements to the diaper service driver or the doctor who removed your tonsils—unless they went on to become your close friends.

Be tolerant of parents and relatives. Your folks will be bursting with pride. This means that they'll stalk you with a camcorder, reveal your family nickname, leave lipstick on your cheek, and talk about you to anyone who will listen. Don't be embarrassed by your parents' behavior. Your friends have parents, too.

Shake, don't stir. When you go up to receive your diploma, restrict physical contact with the principal to a handshake. No hugs, playful slugs on the shoulder, or European air kisses allowed. Of course, if your principal initiates such activities, you are free to join in the festivities.

Thank your parents.

Dear Alex

"Does it matter what you wear under your gown at graduation?"

The safest bet is to follow your school's dress code for the occasion. You might wonder *But if you can't see it, what difference does it make?* In theory, it makes no difference. People attending a graduation ceremony should pay attention to the speeches, not speculate on what their classmates have on beneath

their robes. In other words, as long as what you're wearing (or not wearing) under your gown doesn't distinguish you from classmates who are properly attired, you're within the bounds of etiquette.

Dear Alex

"Is it rude to protest at graduation exercises?"

Some adults get teary-eyed at the sight of a class of graduating seniors standing with their backs turned to a distinguished speaker. For them, it evokes that Golden Age of protest known as "The Sixties." (You can read more about that time period in a textbook on Ancient History. Or ask your grandparents.) Nevertheless, such behavior is unacceptable. Commencement exercises aren't designed as forums for individual expression, whether artistic or political. Unless you go to the High School for the Artsy-Craftsy, where it's traditional for graduates to decorate their caps and gowns to look like postmodern cooking appliances, nix on the buttons, stickers, posters, placards, and pins.

Small ribbons, worn by group consent in loving memory of the 12 graduating seniors who were eaten by alligators on a field trip, would be an appropriate exception to this rule.

Dear Alex

"My school has invited a commencement speaker who's very controversial. Many students, myself included, are thinking of walking out. Would this be a breach of etiquette?"

Statements of personal belief—be they moral, political, or religious— by anyone other than a graduation speaker are inappropriate at a commencement. (The wise speaker knows to tread carefully in these domains.) Walking out, booing, hissing, or wearing incendiary slogans on your cap would all constitute breaches of etiquette. Since talking while someone else is talking is also rude, heckling and chanting belong on the list of unacceptable behaviors.

Virtually any speaker, with the possible exception of Kermit the Frog, is going to say *something* with which some audience members will disagree. Imagine the chaos that would result if students shouted, stomped, strolled in and out, and bobbed up and down every time they heard something they didn't like. (Imagine the fun!)

To be brutally frank, the individual student and what he or she thinks don't count for beans at a graduation. This is a ceremony of, by, and for the community. It's for the families and the faculty; for tradition and knowledge; for the graduating class as a whole. You have a lifetime in which to proclaim your individuality, express your opinions, and fight for the causes of your choice. But until the ceremonies are over, you must squash, squelch, and grind under your feet any such noble tendencies—even if the speaker expresses controversial beliefs that run counter to your own. Now, this doesn't mean that you can't picket and organize a social media campaign prior to the event to protest the *selection* of a particularly odious graduation speaker. There have been many times when the collective outrage of a school community succeeded in getting the person disinvited (or motivated to disinvite himself).

There's one exception to this no-protesting-at-the-event rule: hate speech. If a commencement speaker engages in verbal violence or sullies the dignity of the occasion by attacking members of the community, the community doesn't have to take it lying down (or slouching in their chairs). A calm, strong response to verbal abuse isn't rudeness, it's limit setting. The more dignified your response is, the more power it will have.

A quiet turning of backs or a solemn procession out of the auditorium would be a proper and restrained reaction to such provocation. A student who stood up and said "Sir, these attacks are hateful, and they dishonor this institution and occasion. I must ask you to stop them" would forever be a hero in my book.

Dear Alex

"Do you have any tips for giving a valedictory address without offending anyone?"

Keep it short. Don't swear. Hurt no one. Tell a few inside jokes. Radiate idealism. Thank all parents and teachers. Don't trip when you leave the stage.

Weddings

You've been invited to a wedding. And you've been asked to be a bridesmaid or an usher. Here's what you need to know:

Being a Bridesmaid

Despite their title, bridesmaids don't scrub floors and iron blouses for the bride. Rather, their duties are to look pretty and support the dress industry.

All you have to do to be a wonderful bridesmaid is show up and follow directions. For a wedding with all the trimmings, you'll need to attend a fitting for your gown (which you'll be expected to pay for), bridal showers (bring an umbrella), prenuptial parties, photography sessions, wedding rehearsals, and postnuptial receptions and parties. (Don't forget to go to the wedding.) You'll be told by the bride and/or maid of honor (chief bridesmaid), everything you need to know about where to be when and what to do where.

In general, your responsibilities as a bridesmaid might include any of the following:

- Help the bride plan the wedding
- Assist with pre-wedding tasks (shopping, sending invitations, decorating)
- Help plan, cohost, and share the cost of the bridal shower
- Provide emotional and moral support before and on the wedding day
- Run errands and assist with hair and makeup on the wedding day
- Help arrange table decorations or wedding favors
- Pose for photographs as part of the wedding party
- Walk behind the bride as part of the procession
- Dance with groomsmen and other guests
- Purchase a wedding present (sometimes done with other bridesmaids)
- Pick up confetti

Being an Usher

If you're asked to be an usher, it's an honor, and you must accept unless there's a good reason why you can't. (A football game that's on TV at the same time as the wedding doesn't count.) Your main responsibilities as an usher are to look handsome, act charming, and escort guests to their seats as they arrive.

You'll probably need to rent formal wear for the occasion. The best man and/or head usher will tell you the various times and places where your presence is required. These include dinners and parties before and after the wedding, the fitting for your penguin suit, photography sessions, the wedding rehearsal, and the wedding itself.

You'll need to show up at the church an hour before the ceremony, doff your coat and hat, don your gloves, pick up your boutonniere, and station yourself to the left of the entry door inside the church. The head usher will give you instructions on how people are to be seated (usually on their butts).

The bride's family and friends sit on the *left* side of the church; the groom's family and friends sit on the *right*.

- If a lady arrives by herself, offer her your right arm. (She must give it back, though.)

- If a group of ladies arrives, offer your arm to the eldest. (You may guess their ages but never ask them.)

- If a lady arrives with a male escort, the escort should follow meekly in your wake.

- If a male guest arrives, there's no need to offer him your arm unless he needs assistance.

- If a family arrives, escort the mother. Hubby and kids will follow.

Engage the being whose hand is stuck through your arm in gracious conversation. Even though the line of guests waiting to be seated is stacking up at the entry, don't rush. Act as if you have all the time in the world.

If the bridegroom has no friends and his section is empty, the head usher will ask you to start seating the bride's guests on the other side of the aisle. This is so the church doesn't tilt to the left.

If there are enough ushers to seat guests in a timely fashion, you may escort young ladies in the 10- to 15-year-old age range. This will be a thrill they'll never forget.

When everyone is seated, there will be a processional of ushers and bridesmaids (and other minor figures like the bride and groom) up the aisle. After the ceremony, there will be a recessional. These traditions follow the same basic principle of digestion: What comes in must go out. The head usher will tell you your responsibilities for crowd management during and after the recessional.

Dear Alex

"What are you supposed to say when you go through the receiving line at a wedding?"

"I'm so sorry." Oops, wrong occasion.

You congratulate the groom. To do this, say "Congratulations." You never congratulate the bride. Instead, you extend your best wishes for her happiness, as in "I wish you all the happiness in the world."

To those who had a minor role in bringing the occasion about as the result of certain exertions 25 or so years ago, you give your name and say "How do you do," "It's a pleasure to meet you," or "The ceremony was beautiful, just beautiful" as if you're still entranced by the breathtakingly magical occasion.

Visiting the Sick

Sooner or later, the body of someone you know will suffer some sort of mechanical breakdown. Let's hope it's not serious and they get better quickly. You'll want to visit them (or won't want to, but will feel you should). Good manners are indispensable to a healthy home or hospital visit. Here's what they are:

Ask first. Sometimes people don't want visitors. This may be because they're too ill, too embarrassed, or too intent on enjoying the first peace and quiet they have had in years. Respect their wishes. Call the patient or the patient's family to ask permission to come before putting in an appearance.

Leave the room at appropriate times. Honor the dignity of the person you're visiting. Leave the room when nurses or hospital staff come in, unless they're just dropping off a pill or a meal. Sponge baths, bedpans, and the rears of people in hospital gowns were never designed for public viewing.

Bring a gift. Or don't. In other words, it's optional—nice, but not required. How many balloons, flowers, or boxes of candy does somebody really need? If you do deliver flora, make sure it's ready to view and easy to carry. No cut flowers unless you also provide the vase.

Be sensitive in your gift selection. A box of cigars to a patient with lung cancer is a no-no. Books and magazines are usually appreciated, particularly if they're the trashy, gossipy type one would never buy but reaches for first in the doctor's waiting room. Homemade cards and artwork are always big hits, especially if they were made by the patient's friends.

Be imaginative. If the hospital will allow it, arrange for a band of school friends to play a concert for the wing. Bring in a DVD player, and rent a different movie for your friend to watch each day.

Ask the patient what she would like. An imported pepperoni pizza may be the thing she wants most in life at that moment. Of course, you'll need to clear it with the medical staff as patients are often under dietary restrictions.

Be upbeat. You're there to offer support, sympathy, and good cheer. Don't talk about how hard your life has been, or your aches and pains, or how serious or trivial the patient's problems are. If it's not a total lie, tell the patient she's looking well. This will cheer her up if she thinks she looks terrible. Follow the patient's lead as to whether it's okay to discuss her condition. Some patients want to talk about nothing but; others want to talk about everything but. Pay attention so you'll know whether the patient views her situation as humorous or tragic. Respond in kind.

Don't overstay. Patients may be medicated, tired, or in pain. They may have work to do or other visitors coming. Don't stay more than 20 minutes. If your imminent departure is greeted with a desperate plea of "Nooooo, don't go, please, please, please stay, I'm going crazy I'm so bored," you can allow your arm to be twisted. But not so much that it breaks.

There are many other ways besides visiting to support someone who is ill or in the hospital. With the patient and/or family's permission, offer to act as "Information Central" and provide the patient's friends, relatives, and acquaintances with updates on her condition. This way the family doesn't have to respond individually to 40 inquiries a day wanting to know how things are going. They can inform one person—you—of the patient's progress and you can pass that information along by sending group texts, tweets, or emails. Create a page for your friend on Facebook or one of those health event websites where people can go to learn how she's doing and leave messages of friendship and encouragement.

When someone is laid up there are often lots of practical things you can do to help like bringing over books or assignments. The person may have ongoing obligations like babysitting, cooking dinner for her family, or driving her little brother to practice three days a week that are now going unfulfilled. If you wanted to help out, there are websites where you can create a calendar and list these practical needs, and people can sign up to take care of them. It will be clear who has volunteered to do what when, and who will deserve thanks after the patient is better.

Chapter Quiz

1. *The reason you sign the registry at a funeral is to:*

a) get in the running for the door prize

b) practice your signature

c) show your respect and extend your condolences

2. *You've been invited to a friend's bar mitzvah. Unfortunately, it conflicts with your recital that same Saturday morning. The best way to handle this is to:*

a) ask your friend to change his bar mitzvah to Sunday

b) wear a yarmulke to your recital

c) send profuse regrets and a lovely gift to your friend

3. *You'll be serving as an escort at a debutante ball. Your duties include:*

a) spiking the punch

b) setting out whoopee cushions

c) being a charming dancer and conversationalist

4. *The commencement speaker at your graduation is a politician whose views you strenuously disagree with. The proper response is to:*

a) moon him

b) bombard him with tomatoes

c) listen politely but withhold your applause

5. *You're attending a wedding. You like the groom, but you don't approve of the bride. Should you:*

a) step on her dress

b) push her into the cake

c) be friendly and courteous despite your opinion

6. *One of your schoolmates had a bike accident and is lying with his arms and legs in traction in the hospital. When you go to visit, the polite thing to do is:*

a) tickle him in the ribs

b) place a spider on his nose

c) ask if there's anything he'd like you to bring on your next visit

10

TALKING HEADIQUETTE

The Art of Conversation

Rudeness comes in many forms. It can be physical (someone on a skateboard slams into you on the sidewalk); symbolic (wearing a National Rifle Association T-shirt to the funeral of a gunshot victim); behavioral (tailgating on the freeway); or omissional (not offering your seat to a person on crutches). And it can be verbal. All some people have to do is open their mouths and out pops a rude, insensitive remark:

"Can't you see I'm busy?"
"I wish I'd never had you."
"Who cares what you think?"
"Maybe Raoul would like to tell the class what he finds so amusing."

Insults. Put-downs. Slurs. Sarcasm. People who cut you off, interrupt, ask nosy questions, say mean things. People who accuse, criticize, whine, and compare. People who never say "Please," "Thank you," or "Excuse me."

Virtually every human, every day, interacts with other people—whether in person, over the phone, or by IMs, texting, email, or Facebook. The nature of these communications goes a long way toward determining the quality of our day and our relationships. If our interactions are pleasant and polite, we're likely to feel good about ourselves and the world we live in. If our interactions are disagreeable and rude, we're likely to feel angry and mistrustful.

What this means is that everyone needs to know the basics of courteous communication. Here they are.

Telephone Etiquette

Whether you're the caller or the callee, it pays to be well-mannered on the phone. So put down those potato chips, park your gum, set your cell phone to vibrate, and pay attention, please.

Now that almost everyone has a cell phone, shared household phones are becoming an endangered species. But many homes still possess this ancient device known as a landline telephone. So here's what you need to know so you won't be called out for poor telephone manners.

Making a Call

Ask politely for your party. If the person you wish to speak to doesn't answer the phone, you'll need to ask for her. Say:

"May I please speak to Muffy?"

Don't say:
"Is Muffy there?"

I learned this the hard way when I telephoned a friend and his four-year-old son answered the phone. "Is your daddy there?" I asked. "Yes," the boy said. After five minutes went by with no sign of Daddy, insight dawned. "Could you please get him?" I said. "Okay," the boy replied.

It's not necessary to tell the person who answers the phone who you are. In fact, it's a breach of etiquette for her to ask (unless she's been instructed to do so by a higher power, such as a parent or boss). If you know the person, it's a friendly gesture to say:

"Hi, Mrs. Beeswax, this is Mortimer Snerdhopper. May I please speak to Jack?"

Your friends' parents will adore you for this courteous acknowledgment of their existence.

Identify yourself when you reach your party. This has probably happened to you: Someone telephones, starts talking, and you don't have the faintest idea who it is. Unless you're calling a soul mate who would recognize your voice in a hurricane at 500 yards, say who you are. It could save you both from embarrassment.

Don't call at inconvenient times. Since households eat and go to bed at all sorts of different hours, find out from your friends when

TRUE STORIES

FROM THE
MANNERS FRONTIER

Sorry, Wrong Number
The other day my phone rang. I picked it up and said "Hello." A voice said "Who's this?" *How rude,* I thought. "To whoooom do you wish to speak?" I asked. This firm yet polite response made the caller realize his phone *faux pas.* It also taught him a thing or two about grammar.

CONTINUED »»

If you make a call and a strange voice answers the phone, never hang up or say "Who's this?" Instead, ask for the person you're trying to call. If it turns out that you reached a wrong number, apologize. You may want to verify the number with the person who answered. That way, you'll know whether the number itself is wrong or you just misdialed.

And now, if you're ready for today's truth-is-stranger-than-fiction bulletin, my phone just rang, affording us an invaluable opportunity for seeing these principles at work as I reproduce the entire conversation for your enlightenment:

< Ring. Ring. >
Alex: *"Hello."*
Caller: *"Meat Department."*
Alex: *"Hello?"*
Caller: *"What store is this?"*
Alex: *"I think you have the wrong number."*
Caller: *"I apologize."*
Alex: *"That's all right."*
< Click. >

All in all, it was a lovely exchange that reaffirmed my faith in etiquette.

it's okay and not okay to call. Many families don't appreciate interruptions during dinner or at two in the morning. It never hurts to ask "Is this a good time to talk?" or "How late is it okay to call?"

Ask permission to use the phone. If you're a guest in someone's home and need to use their phone, say "May I please use your phone?" before making any calls. Keep your calls short. Many phone service plans now include unlimited long distance calls. If you're dialing long-distance and aren't sure whether the call is free, ask your host.

Taking a Call

Say "Hello." A cheerful "Hello" is all you need when answering a residential phone. It's not necessary to say "Pedigree residence, Bartholomew speaking" or "Murray's Mortuary, you stab 'em, we slab 'em."

Your parents may want you to answer the phone in a particular way. If so, do as they ask.

Don't screen other people's calls. If you answer the phone and it's for someone else, it's none of your business who's calling, no matter how curious you are. Don't inquire about the caller's identity unless your parents or siblings specifically ask you to. In that case, say to the caller "May I tell them who's calling?"

Don't yell. It bugs parents to no end when their kids answer the phone and scream "MA! TELEPHONE! IT'S THAT LADY!" While yelling is one way to get a message from point A to point B, moving your body is another. If you need to alert someone to a phone call, relocate yourself more proximitously to the party whose attention you're trying to catch. Then say "Ma, telephone. It's that lady."

Never give out personal information. For safety's sake, don't reveal to strangers whether your parents are home or not. Don't give out your address or credit card numbers. And whatever you do, don't say that your dad is in the bathroom. People are never "in the bathroom" to callers. They are "unable to come to the phone."

Give the caller your full attention. It's rude to talk to someone while eating, watching TV, carrying on other conversations, or playing games on your tablet. If you can't focus on the phone call, tell the person that you're in the middle of something and will have to call back later.

Dear Alex

"My parents are always picking up the phone while I'm talking to someone. Isn't this rude?"

No, it's inevitable—especially if you're on the phone a lot. It's unrealistic for people to do a reconnaissance of all the extensions in the house before making a call. So this is bound to happen from time to time.

If you're the picker-upper, simply hang up right away. If you're the picker-upped-upon, say "I'm on the line." At this point, the picker-upper has the option of saying "Sorry" or "Excuse me" before hanging up. Except in an emergency, the picker-upper may not interrupt the conversation with questions ("How long are you going to be on?") or statements ("I have to use the phone. Would you please get off!"). These must be delivered in person, by note, or whispered so as not to embarrass those already on the line.

Voicemail

Prior to the invention of telephones, people would go "calling." They would show up at each other's houses unannounced. It was understood that these visits wouldn't always lead to an audience with the person one wished to see; he or she might be out, sleeping, entertaining, eating, practicing the lute, or painting his or her toenails. The housekeeper or butler would inform the visitor that "Madam is not at home." This had nothing to do with Madam's whereabouts; it was simply the convention for letting people know that Madam was not available. The visitor would leave a card, and Madam would know who had called on her. This is the origin of the term "calling card."

Today, of course, we have voicemail and caller ID. Think of these as an electronic butler. Surely you have the right to interruption-free moments in the privacy of your own home. Surely you have the right to know who's there before opening the telephonic door. Thus, there's nothing rude about using voicemail and caller ID to screen calls, as long as you follow these guidelines:

Keep your recorded greeting short. Unless your caller has been living on Pluto for the past century, he knows what to do when encountering voicemail. It's not necessary to issue such detailed instructions as:

"Hello, you've reached the voicemail of Steve, Mary, Grandpa, Fido, Billy, Willy, and Tilly McCarthy at nine-six-six two-three-five-one. We're sorry, but we're unable to come to the phone or we're away from our desks or we're in the middle of dinner, but your call is really important to us so please leave a message including your name, time of call, phone number, shoe size, person you're calling, reason for calling, and the best time to reach you and we'll try to get back to you as soon as possible. Remember to wait for the beep, which will come in approximately three point two seconds if this is working or in eleven seconds after five beeps and a screeching eight-second noise if it isn't. Have a great day and thanks for calling!"

Neither is it necessary to record Mahler's Symphony No. 2 or Lincoln's Gettysburg Address as your greeting. People, especially those calling long distance or who have limited cell phone minutes, don't appreciate having to twiddle their thumbs while some voicemail greeting gets its musical, political, or comedic jollies off. A simple "You've reached 401-9999" or "This is Alexander Graham Bell. Please leave a message after the tone" is more than adequate.

Keep your message short. Occasionally, you may need to leave a lengthy, complicated message. Whenever possible, however, try to keep your messages brief. And remember that with voicemail or answering machines, people other than the intended recipient may hear them. It's also a good idea to leave your phone number unless you're positive the person knows it by heart or has it in his or her contact list. This is because people often call in for messages when they're away from their home or office. Speak slowly and clearly. Otherwise, someone may have to play back your message 37 times to decipher the number.

Dear Alex

"People in my house always forget to give me my phone messages. Sometimes I'll be talking about a friend and my mother will say 'Oh, by the way, she called you yesterday.' This is so annoying. What should I do?"

You'll need a combination of high- and low-tech strategies to solve this problem. Start by getting a voicemail system with separate "mailboxes" for each family member. Your friends can leave messages directly in your box, and other family members can listen to their messages without touching yours.

But what if a live human being answers your phone? Since most messages get lost because people don't write them down, this calls for a low-tech solution. Place by every phone a pad of paper and a pen or pencil that can't be removed. Only a total dolt would stand by the phone, listen to a request to "Please tell her that Fran called," and not write down *Phran cald.*

Visual checks of message pads, combined with the occasional "Did I get any calls?" should take care of the problem, provided the dolt factor in your household isn't too high.

Obscene Phone Calls

It's never rude to hang up on an obscene phone caller. In fact, that's the best thing to do. Don't talk or stay on the line, no matter how bizarre the noises you hear. If the calls persist, contact the phone company. They have ways of tracking down those people.

Telemarketers

In case you're unfamiliar with the term, *telemarketers* are total strangers who have been trained to act as if they're your best friend in order to sell you something of dubious value. They're instructed to call at the precise moment you sit down to dinner:

> *"Hello Alex how are you tonight that's great because this is your lucky night you have definitely won one of the following great prizes that's right you have won either a brand-new Rolls Royce or a Gulfstream Jet or 10 million dollars or a genuine artificial tin-plated fake diamond pendant and all you have to do to claim your prize is purchase a vacation package for 600 dollars so if you'll just give me the credit card number to which you want to charge your vacation I'll tell you which of these four fabulous prizes you've won."*

Telemarketing is rude. But that doesn't mean it's okay to be rude back. Therefore, the proper response to these unwanted invasions of privacy is a polite "Thank you, but I'm not interested." Since telemarketers are trained to keep you on the line, they will respond, not by respecting your courteous attempt to end the conversation, but by escalating their pitch:

> *"Are you telling me you don't want to win 10 million dollars?"*

At this point you may issue a firm "Good-bye" and hang up.

Call Waiting

When someone with call waiting puts me on hold, I count to 20. That's ample time for the person to tell the second caller "I'm sorry, but I'm on the other line. I'll call you back in a few minutes." What usually happens, though, is that caller #2 goes to the head of the queue, while caller #1 (yours truly) continues to wait. At the end of 20 seconds, I hang up the phone.

This isn't rude since I'm not hanging up on anyone. I'm hanging up on *no one,* which is the whole point. Before I learned this technique, I would often be put on hold two, three, even four times during the course of a 15-minute conversation, eating up valuable cell phone minutes!

People with whom you use this strategy will call you back and say "I guess we got cut off." To which you may reply "Yes, it appears we did." In time, the coincidence of how often you get cut off will encourage these people to ignore call waiting when talking to you.

Call waiting is r-u-d-e. One expects to be put on hold when telephoning a business. One understands that the person one needs to speak to may already have another customer on the line. No such justification exists for putting personal callers on hold. It won't kill anyone to leave a message on voicemail.

You're doubtless aware of all the justifications for call waiting:

- so someone can reach you in case of an emergency
- so you can use the phone while expecting an important call
- so parents, children, or business acquaintances can get through when the line is tied up

Too bad. Rudeness often comes with its own rationalization(s). Putting people on hold is a way of saying "My time is more important than your time." In a genuine emergency, an operator can cut into a call.

If you're on the phone and it's equipped with call waiting, you can still behave politely in response to those obnoxious little clicks indicating someone else is trying to reach you. Here are your options:

Option A: Ignore the Second Call
This is the best and most polite option. Let's say a call comes in while you're already on the phone. Whether it's a number you recognize or not, you decide you don't want or need to interrupt the call you're on to take it. (Good for you!) You can then finish your first call and return the second call when convenient. The second caller also has the option of leaving a message or trying you again later.

Option B: Briefly Answer the Second Call
This time you recognize the second caller's number but feel you need to check out why he's calling (for example, let's say it's your dad and it's unusual for him to call you). So, to be polite, tell the person you're talking to that your dad is calling and you need to see why. Ask her if it's okay

to put her on hold for a sec. See what your dad wants. If it's not urgent, tell him you're on the phone with someone else and will call him back as soon as you get off. You can then return to caller #1 and continue your call. If you do need to take your dad's call, you'll have to quickly return to caller #1, apologize, and tell her you'll get back to her as soon as you can.

Option C: Take an Important Call You're Expecting

The only excuse for dumping someone you're talking to is if it's an emergency or an important call you've been expecting and must take. In this situation, you can be polite by letting caller #1 know up front that you're expecting an important call and will have to take it. If call waiting alerts you to the call you were expecting, tell caller #1 "I'm so sorry, but this is the call I need to take. May I call you back?" At this point you can conclude your call with caller #1 and connect to caller #2.

When rudeness is anticipated and apologized for in advance, it sometimes mutates into something we call *consideration*.

Tip: The only time it's *not* rude to use call waiting is with telemarketers. It's perfectly proper to put them on hold if another call comes in. Or even if it doesn't. You'd be amazed by how impatient telemarketers are. Most of the time, they're gone by the time you get back to them!

Cell Phones

The day they offer surgical telephone implants, half of America will sign up. It's a mystery why so many people are so eager to expand the ways in which bill collectors can reach them.

The ubiquity of cell phones, smartphones, walkie-talkies, and beepers affects us all. Even if you don't indulge, you're still exposed to second-hand sound. You can't go anywhere anymore without hearing so many chirping phones you'd think you were at a cricket convention. You're with somebody at a restaurant, and instead of talking to you he talks on the phone. Or there you are on an airplane, and the guy next to you is yelling in your ear:

"A MILLION TELEDEX, SHORT 'EM AT 29, AND TELL BEVERLY TO GET THE POOL CLEANED. OF COURSE I'M CALLING FROM THE PLANE. OF COURSE I'M SHOUTING. HOW ELSE WILL EVERYONE KNOW WHAT AN IMPORTANT PERSON I AM?"

All public spaces should be required to have phoning and nonphoning sections. Until that day comes, here are some basic rules of cell phone etiquette:

1. Turn off all beepers and ringers when you're at an event or place where quiet and/or respect are required: places of worship, libraries, concerts, plays, movies, lectures, funerals, restaurants,

private dinners at someone's home, etc. Silent ringers—the kinds that vibrate to give your thigh a thrill and let you know you have a call—are allowed as long as they're not audible when vibrating. But you're still not permitted to take the call. Instead, excuse yourself or slip out discreetly and call the person back.

2. Recognize that people talking to themselves—and that's how you appear to others, despite the piece of plastic growing out of your ear—are a distraction. Therefore, unless the call is of interest or relevance to everyone present (for example, a business negotiation or a loved one in common), take it to a private spot where your conversation won't intrude on those of others.

3. Public restrooms are a place where people go to conduct their business. But not their cell phone business. Why not? Because it's just too CREEPY, that's why! So please stay off your phone in public bathrooms. Everyone will be relieved.

4. The sound of a ringing cell phone is annoying to others by definition. It is often intrusive and unwelcome. SO WHY DO PEOPLE CHOOSE THE LOUDEST, MOST OBNOXIOUS RINGTONES? (AND YES, I AM SHOUTING!) Choose a ringtone that isn't going to rattle teeth or send shivers up one's spine. And turn the volume down to the lowest setting that still allows you to hear it.

5. If you're eating with others or attending a meeting, don't place your mobile devices on the table. Glancing lovingly at your tablet or smartphone gives people the impression that it is more important than they are. And we all know that's not true. Right? Right?

6. If you're out with people and expecting an important call, let them know upfront that you're going to have to take it and apologize in advance. When the call comes, excuse yourself and head to a private place.

7. No shouting please. People can hear you just fine if you talk in a regular voice.

"Phoning or nonphoning?"

THE 24 DO'S AND DON'TS OF CELL PHONE ETIQUETTE

- -

From the Minds of Genuine Teenagers

Do

- call your friends every once in a while instead of just texting
- be nice, polite, honest, and respectful
- call your parents if you think they'll be worried
- say "pardon" instead of "WHAT?" if you can't hear the person
- take the call outside or move away from the group
- put your phone on vibrate or turn off the ringer during dinner
- get off the phone when your parents say to
- talk quietly in public (no one cares to hear your conversation)
- refrain from eating while talking on the phone
- silence your phone in class and at the library and other places where people are trying to concentrate
- let people know if you're going to have to take an important call
- turn off your phone anyplace where quiet or respect is required (e.g., church, theaters, concerts)

Don't

- use loud, obnoxious ringtones
- talk in a public place and go "WHAT? WHAT? I CAN'T HEAR YOU! OH! SHE SAID THAT? REALLY?" etc.
- ignore the people who are with you to talk on your cell phone
- hang up without saying good-bye
- put a person on speaker without their knowing
- interrupt someone talking on the phone unless it's an emergency
- make prank calls or leave mean voicemails
- send embarrassing pictures to anyone
- talk or text in dangerous or inappropriate situations, e.g., while driving, crossing a street, riding in an elevator, ordering from a cashier
- carry on conversations with people in the room while talking on the phone
- put your phone on the table in restaurants
- use your phone in public restrooms

- -

Dear Alex

"I'm perfectly capable of checking out of a store and talking on the phone at the same time. Why is that impolite?"

First of all, the captive audience in line with you doesn't want to hear your conversation, no matter how fascinating you are. The cashier or person at the counter is probably stressed out from having been treated like dirt all day by rude customers. As a human being ringing up your sale, she deserves your full attention. To give any less treats her like a thing and not a person. So, stay off your phone, give her a big smile and a friendly hello, and you'll perk up her day and yours.

Interactive Voice Response Systems (A.K.A. Talking Computers)

It seems as if every time you make a call these days, you're presented with a menu of prerecorded voice prompts from a lovely and helpful computer lady ("Press 1 for . . . Press 2 for . . . Press 3 for . . ." *ad infinitum*). As soon as you make your first selection, you're presented with 500 more options, and then 500 more, and then 500 more. Eventually you reach a place deep inside the menu tree where you are put on hold for 23 minutes until at long last, finally—you get cut off and have to start all over again.

The good news is: Interactive computerized voice response systems aren't inherently rude. In fact, most prerecorded prompts and messages are quite polite ("We're sorry, but all our representatives are assisting other customers"). They even say "Please" and "Thank you," and "We

"All service representatives are currently helping other customers. Please stay on the line and your call will be answered shortly."

appreciate your call." They're a lot more considerate than humans who snap "Can you hold" and then, without even waiting for a response, disappear from your life.

But that doesn't mean you have to *like* spending half a morning pressing numbers on your telephone or speaking to an electronic brain. Especially when you also have to listen to horrible music that keeps you from concentrating on whatever you could be working on while holding if you weren't listening to horrible music.

It's unlikely that interactive voice response systems are going to disappear. If anything, soon we'll have talking robots serving tables, selling T-shirts, and cleaning teeth. But, the nice thing about talking with computers is that you can make faces and rude hand gestures and nobody will ever know.

Letter Etiquette

Letter writing is becoming an increasingly scarce art form. In days of yore, letters were the only means of getting a message from, say, Alexander the Great to Alexander Hamilton. And if one of them didn't like the message, he might kill the messenger. This was the origin of the expression "Hey, don't kill *me*, I'm just the messenger."

Today, of course, we have many additional methods of communication: email, telegrams, telephones, faxes, texting, IMs, Twitter, Facebook. These instant forms of communication are certainly handy. If you want to contact your neighbor across the valley, you can simply pick up the phone or jump on the Internet. It's no longer necessary to write a letter and wait three weeks for an answer just to find out if you can borrow an ox.

Because so few people write personal letters anymore, the pleasure in receiving one is all the greater. Which makes *your* heart beat faster? A fat envelope full of Valu-Coupons addressed to "Occupant" or a scented purple envelope with your name and address handwritten in ink? You should practice the art of letter writing for at least three reasons:

1. You'll please and impress people.

2. You'll bring joy to the recipients of your elegantly written epistles.

3. You'll get letters back.

There are as many different types of letters as there are human sentiments. There are love letters and thank-you letters; letters to say hello; letters to say good-bye; letters to lord over everyone else how great the past year was for you and your family; and letters of condolence, apology, inquiry, pleading, or complaint. No matter what the purpose of your letter may be, certain rules of etiquette come into play. Let's start with . . .

Letters to Your Parents

Writing home, whether from school, camp, or vacation, is a nonnegotiable tradition of the parent-child relationship. The parent who screams "I can't wait until you go back to school!" is the same parent who, two days after you've left, sits tearfully in your room stroking your trophies. Your letters, posts, emails, and text messages will provide your parents with a treasure chest of memories they can carry into their old age. They'll also provide you with a literary time capsule you can open in years to come whenever you feel like cringing at what you used to be like.

Every proper letter from a child to a parent should contain these three elements:

1. something to make your parents proud

2. something to make your parents worry

3. something to make your parents send you money

Mixed in with these essentials should be news, affection, chitchat, progress reports, social commentary, philosophical musings, and lots of questions that show you take an interest in your parents' lives. Everyday aspects of your existence—friends, teachers, outings, studies, grades, athletic competitions, intrigues, aspirations—are all grist for the quill. So are questions or issues raised in your parents' letters.

Think about what you would say in a phone call. Then just say it—on paper, or via email, text, or Facebook.

Dear Mom and Phil,

disguised affection →

What's happenin', dudes? Since I know how much you miss me, I thought I'd say hello. Guess what? I've joined the X-treme Club here at school. It's a

news —

group of students who go out every weekend to ride mountain bikes off cliffs.

something to make your parents worry

But don't worry. Our faculty advisor (he's this neat guy we call "The Torso" because he lost all his arms and legs trying to dive through a turbo engine) insists that we wear bungee cords. (He holds them.) So it's really perfectly safe.

something to make your parents proud

You know that French test? I aced it. I guess you guys were right when you said all I had to do to get good grades was put my derrière on the chair! I've volunteered to teach French to kids at the county juvenile detention center. But I have to learn some new words first, like "incarceration" and "probation."

something to make your parents send you money →

I've been going to the canteen a lot for serious snacking purposes. It's a little embarrassing because my friends always pay for me 'cause they know my funds are a bit tight. One day I hope to be able to treat them if I can manage to save some money. Or maybe next time I'm home I could bring back some of Mom's triple-fudge brownies to share with them.

hint, hint

How did Phil's speech go? Did Mom get the commission she was telling us about? How's the painting coming along? Tell Katie she can wear my shirt, but only if she promises not to drool on it.

Well, I gotta go study, so I'd better sign off.

Love,

Bentley

shows interest in your parents and kid sister

Try not to be self-conscious about your letters. Of course, you'll want to make them as presentable as possible. After all, they do indicate whether your parents are getting their money's worth from sending you away to school or camp. But what matters most is not *what* you say, but *that* you are saying it. Wise parents cherish any communication from their children. And they know that it's forbidden to make any comments regarding spelling or grammar.

Dear Alex

"My parents have said I can go to camp, but only if I promise to send them a letter twice a week. Isn't blackmail bad manners?"

This question calls for a lesson in life as well as etiquette. Many eons ago, a Stoic philosopher by the name of Epictetus said "Men are not disturbed by things, but by the view they take of them." Similarly, Shakespeare observed in *Hamlet* that "There's nothing either good or bad but thinking makes it so." In other words, our feelings are caused more by our *attitudes* toward life than by life itself.

You can see the truth of this if you imagine that you've been waiting over an hour for your mom to pick you up. If you *think* she's just been flaky and has forgotten about you, you'll feel angry. If you *think* she's had an accident, you'll feel worried or panicked. If you *think* the car broke down or she's caught in rush hour, you'll feel sympathetic. The attitude you take toward this or any event (being dumped, wanting friends, flunking a test) determines to a large extent how you'll feel about it. You can *choose* whether to have an attitude that is hopeful or despairing, understanding or intolerant, realistic or irrational—and your feelings will follow.

What does this have to do with your situation? You can call your parents' request for letters "blackmail"—or you can call it "fondness." Change your feelings by changing your thoughts. Instead of feeling angry, feel loved. Instead of thinking of letter writing as a chore, think of it as an opportunity to convey news, affection, and requests for food.

The duty to write letters home also gives you a great line to use when getting to know someone you like at camp. Simply approach your target, make a face, and groan. Then say "I HATE having to write letters. Do your parents make you do it, too?" If she says "I consider it a privilege to communicate with my beloved mater and pater," you're in a bit of trouble. But if she says "I know. I CAN'T STAND writing home either," you're in fat city. Say "I'm heading down to the lake to write one now. Do you want to write to your parents and we'll suffer together?"

Dear Alex

"I go to boarding school. I get emails from my parents almost every day, and I feel terrible because I don't respond very often. It isn't that I don't want to, it's just that I'm busy and never know what to say. Is it bad manners if I call instead of write?"

Phoning home is never rude as long as:

- you don't do it at 3:00 AM

- you disguise the request that's your main reason for calling

Failing to respond to the warm, written overtures of your nearest and dearest—whether by letter, email, text message, or phone call—is most certainly a breach of etiquette. It's like ignoring someone who's speaking to you. Not to mention paying your school bills.

Mail Manners

Courteous correspondents honor the following rites of writing:

Respect the recipient's privacy. No matter how curious you are, never open or peek at mail that isn't yours. This includes postcards. It's also improper to take note of who's gotten mail from whom. Thus, you would never ask your sister "What did your ex-boyfriend want?" as this suggests you know something that etiquette prevents you from knowing.

Respect the sender's privacy. If you get a letter from somebody, it's natural to want to share it with others. Before you do, think carefully about whether the writer would want you to. The letter may contain things that are very personal and were meant for your eyes only. If in doubt, err on the side of caution. Keep the letter to yourself until you can obtain permission to show it to others.

Be creative. Never begin a letter with "How are you? I'm fine." It's not that these aren't noble sentiments, it's just that they've been done before—about 896,443,221,909 times. Instead, try something like this:

Dear Grandma and Grandpa,

I just blew my nose into one of the beautiful handkerchiefs you gave me for my birthday, which got me thinking of you. How have you been? Is Grandpa over the flu? My hay fever has been real bad this season, but thanks to you I don't have to use my sleeve anymore. That was some tornado you had. Has anyone come yet to get the cow out of the pool?

Stationery

First things first: How can you remember that the stationery you write on is spelled with an "e" and the stationary that keeps you in your place is spelled with an "a"? The following mnemonic is offered as a public service:

Ask yourself "What do you do with stationery?"

Write letters.

"And what vowels are in the word 'letter'?"

Eeeeees.

Since eeeeees are in "letter," you use an "e" for the stationery you write on.

Class dismissed.

The kind of stationery you use depends on the kind of letter you're writing:

- For letters to your friends, you can use just about any stationery or writing implement you fancy—up to and including purple ink on lime-green paper with glow-in-the-dark pictures of bunny wabbits all over.

- For letters to businesses, schools, and representatives of the Real World, skip the wabbits and wainbows. These letters should be legibly handwritten or laser-printed on good-quality 8½" by 11" paper. No garish colors; just your basic white, cream, or very light gray.

- Personal letters to adults, relatives, and/or peers who aren't close friends should be handwritten in black ink on note-size paper or blank cards. (If your handwriting is illegible, you may type and print out a personal letter. The joy of getting your epistle will be diminished if the recipient can't read it.) Make sure that any artwork on the front of the card doesn't offend the recipient or clash with the purpose of your communication. For example, don't send a get-well card with a picture of food to someone in the hospital who's just had his stomach removed.

If you're prone to mistakes and changing your mind about what you want to say, you'll need to write a first draft. Once you've got your content, spelling, and grammar down, create your final draft.

Try not to get ink on your fingers, or you'll smudge the paper and people will start to call you Inky. Fold your letter only as much as necessary to get it into the envelope, which usually means into halves or thirds. A letter should not be folded until it's the size of a microchip.

Salutations

Virtually all letters begin with "Dear." What's next? That depends on the person you're writing to. Specifically:

- If you're writing to a man whose name you don't know, use "Dear Sir."

- If you're writing to a woman whose name you don't know, write "Dear Madam."

- If you're writing to someone of unknown gender, write "Dear Madam or Sir."

- If you wish to give old-world charm to your letters to loved ones and close friends, you may use "Dearest," as in "Dearest Mother."

For business correspondence, end your salutation with a colon (:). For personal correspondence, use a comma (,).

Love letters (more about those shortly) allow greater creativity, since it's assumed that no one but the beloved will be privy to your sappiness. Therefore, greetings like "My darling of delight," "Hunkie-wunkie," and "Honey bunny bear" fly below the radar of etiquette and, therefore, are off-limits for comment.

Dear Alex

"I just got an invitation addressed to 'Master' with my name after it. What's that supposed to mean?"

"Master" is used when addressing an envelope to a boy eight years old or younger. (Some people say it's okay to use it with boys as old as 10 or 12.) In the British educational system, a "Master" is a male teacher—think of the words "Headmaster" or "Housemaster."

Here's a rundown on how envelopes should be addressed:

For Boys and Men	For Girls and Women
Up to age 8:	*Up to high school:*
Master Jay Jehosophat	Miss Kay Kalamazoo
Ages 8–18:	*High school and beyond:*
Jay Jehosophat	Ms. Kay Kalamazoo
Ages 18 and up:	*Those who are married:*
Mr. Jay Jehosophat	Mrs. Kay Jehosophat

Exceptions: Some married women prefer to be addressed by their husband's first and last names—for example, "Mrs. Jay Jehosophat." If that's what they want, honor their wishes. Some women choose to keep their birth name (a.k.a. maiden name) rather than take their husband's name when they marry. Often this means that they retain the "Ms." rather than opting for "Mrs."

Closings

"Sincerely" is the all-purpose closing. Along with its cousins—"Sincerely yours," "Yours sincerely," "Yours truly," and "Very truly yours"—it's appropriate for both business and personal use. If the personal correspondence involves close ties and/or loving feelings, you may elect to close with "Love," "Affectionately," or "Fondly." If you're in junior high school, you may close with hearts, XXXOOO, and "Luv," but try not to.

For business correspondents with whom you have a prior relationship of trust, respect, friendship, and/or positive exchange, you may wish to employ a closing from the "regards" family:

Kind regards,
Warm regards,
Best regards,
Beauregards.

These breezy sign-offs split the difference between "Sincerely" and "Love." They're the literary equivalent of air kisses, halfway between a handshake and a smooch. You can use them with your agent, attorney, and/or stockbroker.

If you're going through a stage of Victorian formality, you may close letters to your parents with "Your devoted daughter" or "Your loving and affectionate son." Don't use "Your most humble and obedient servant" unless you want more chores to do.

Love Letters

Let's assume for a moment that there's a boy you really like and you want to write him a love letter. What's the best way to go about this?

V-e-r-y c-a-r-e-f-u-l-l-y. In fact, you might want to think twice about whether to write it at all.

It's admirable that you wish to convey your affection. The problem is, the minute you do so, you'll also convey it to half of the students at your school. This is because the young man, if he reciprocates your sentiments, will gleefully show your letter to all his friends. (If he can't stand your guts, he'll do the same—but with even greater relish, and what a pickle you'll be in then.) If this show-and-tell occurs at school, chances are someone will grab the letter from his hand and read it aloud to the assembled masses in the cafeteria. Emmm-barrassing!

Even though your love is undying and eternal, in adolescence "eternity" usually translates as "two weeks." Thus, it's possible that in less time than it takes to dissect a frog, your feelings may shift to a new object of affection. If this happens, will you want a chain of love letters in the public domain by which historians can trace your romantic evolution? Probably not.

Therefore, it's best that declarations of love be issued by mouth rather than by hand. *Tell* him how you feel. You can do this directly or indirectly. Directly means saying "I really like you." Indirectly means giving compliments, asking questions, spending time together, treating your beloved with kindness and respect—*behavior* that says "I really like you." This is far more romantic than sending a letter. And in the likely event that you'll break up, because nothing's in writing, you can deny having said all the mushy things you said.

Now that you know all of the above, you're still determined to write your love letter. Sigh. Here's how:

1. Choose romantic stationery.

Good	Bad
high-quality note paper and envelope	lined yellow legal paper folded and taped shut

If you choose a card with a photograph:

Good	Bad
snuggling puppies	chemical storage tanks

2. Use ink.

It's the proper thing to do, plus it prevents anyone from tampering with your words.

3. Convey the magnitude of your longing, but don't come across as a wussy, lovesick, protoplasmic mess.

You can see the difference:

Example #1: Lovesick

Sitting here in Chem Lab, I don't know how I can live without you. I can't concentrate. I feel hollow. My existence is as empty as a politician's promise. Without you, I am nothing.

The reaction to this is likely to be "Get a life, would ya."

Example #2: Lovely

Sitting here in Chem Lab, I watch the sulfur burn. And I think of how bright the flame of my love burns for you. It's hard to imagine I won't see you for 37 minutes and 14 seconds. But, with the vision of your soft smile and silky hair to sustain me, I shall endure.

The reaction to this is likely to be "Oh, my gentle little sweetie-poo." This is because your sensitive, empathetic, romantic soul is revealed in the context of your strength, courage, and stoicism. It's a highly attractive combination, *n'est-ce pas?*

Speaking of French, you can never go wrong with a touch of the Gallic (not to be confused with a touch of the garlic). This is because the French, having invented the French kiss, are properly associated with love. (Why do you think French is considered a Romance language?) Therefore, feel free to sneak a little French *(chéri, l'amour, je t'aime, moutarde)* into your love letters.

The Well-Mannered Conversation

Every relationship—whether between friends, lovers, or colleagues—begins with the people not knowing each other. They may meet by chance. They may be introduced by mutual friends or a task in common. But the way they get to know each other is invariably the same: through *communication*. Since conversation is a primary method for communicating, following are some tips and guidelines that will make you a talented talker.

How to Start a Conversation

Lots of people feel awkward or shy when starting a conversation. That's natural. But anyone can do it if they know the secret of successful small talk, which is . . . sorry, it's a secret.

Oh, all right, here it is: The secret is to *ask questions*. That's all you have to do to get a conversation going. The best questions are those with open-ended answers. Questions with yes-or-no answers are okay, but they make your work harder.

Here's what happens when someone trying to start a conversation offers personal opinions and yes-or-no questions:

"Great music."
"Yeah."
"Do you like the Empty Bladders?"
"Yeah."
"Cool party."
"Yeah."
"You a friend of Mike's?"
"Yeah."
"Cool."

Now watch how much better the conversation flows if the questions are more open-ended:

"What do you think of the music?"

"Rave totale. Compliments to the chef de musique. This DJ's waaaaay."

"Waaaaay?"

"Yeah, you know. Waaaaay. He was the spinologist at another festivity I went to last weekend. Total Empty Bladders freak, this guy."

"Where was the other party?"

"Lacey Kingman's abode of habitation. A sugary coming-of-automotivity party."

"Huh?"

"Sweet sixteen."

"What was it like?"

"Very waaaaay. Verrr-ry. A lot of the same revelers but the muncholinos tonight are mucho more magnifico."

"Knowing the way Mike eats, that doesn't surprise me. How do you know Mike?"

"Actually, it's his sibling of the female persuasion I am privileged to know. We were in the Convent of Our Lady of Parallel Parking together."

"Huh?"

"Driver's Ed, my man."

"I've got to take that next semester. What do they make you do?"

At this point, you're home free. You'll get a blow-by-blow description of Driver's Ed. Like it or not.

When meeting people your own age, there are a million things you can ask questions about: schools, teachers, classes, interests, current events, sports, video games, movies, TV shows, travel, music, people you know in common. Be alert to visual clues. You can ask someone wearing a Lakers cap about basketball, or someone with lift tickets dangling from his or her parka about skiing.

Talking with adults is no different. If you're visiting the home of a friend, you'll see things in the house that you can ask her parents about: curious objects, posters, books, hobbies, souvenirs from places they've visited. You can ask about the work they do or even their experiences when they were younger. As long as your questions are sincere and respectful—and you listen to the answers—people will be flattered by and appreciate your interest. After all, it takes a lot of pressure off of them. If they're good conversationalists, they'll ask *you* lots of questions. As the Q's and A's fly back and forth, you'll suddenly discover that you're having an easy, pleasant talk.

Now that you know the basics, here are a few conversation fine points:

Remember that good conversation is an art, not a science. Keeping a conversation going is a bit like driving a car. You don't just aim and floor it. You have to make constant adjustments in response to the route and driving conditions. The same holds true when you're chattering away. Be alert to body language and verbal cues you receive. You may discover that certain topics go nowhere; if that happens, slam on the brakes and try a new tack. Or, if someone really starts to bubble with enthusiasm, you've got a green light to put your pedal to the metal as far as that subject is concerned.

Stay away from gossip, badmouthing, and rumors. When you dish dirt, you get covered in it yourself. This happens because people think *Gee, if she says such mean things behind so-and-so's back, how do I know she won't do the same thing to me?* Backbiting can also get you into some very awkward positions.

Watch how easily this can happen:

You're at a party at Tim Devlin's house. You don't know him well, but since you're on the swim team together, you got an invite.

You notice Jill Banks standing on the opposite side of the room. She's generally regarded as the class airhead.

You start a conversation with Tim:

"Great party."

"Thanks."

"Hey, isn't that Jill Banks? Man, I can't believe she actually found your place. I mean, the directions you gave, you had to know left from right. I guess in this age of diversity, every party has to have a moron. I'm kind of surprised you invited her."

"I didn't."

"You mean she just crashed?"

"No. She lives here. She's my stepsister."

Oops.

Don't be nosy. When striking up a conversation, you want to show interest without sticking your nose where it doesn't belong. This can be a tricky tightrope to walk. You'd like to ask a question, but you're not sure if it's too personal. How do you know? Ask yourself how *you* would feel if someone asked the question of *you*—and *everyone in the room could hear your answer.* If you'd feel comfortable, chances are the question's okay.

In our culture, certain topics are considered off-limits by many people. You wouldn't ask someone you've just met about their religion or sexuality, or how much money they make, or if they've cheated on their spouse, or why they don't have children, or if their parents are divorced, or what their grade-point average is.

By the same token, it's a good idea to avoid questions that have an implied judgment or criticism. Examples:

"How can you drive such a gas guzzler?"

"Don't you think it's wrong to go out with Sanjit after telling Brad you'd go steady with him?"

Although these are reasonable questions for your little gray cells to ponder, it's bad form to ask them. Of course, the rules change if you're talking to a friend. Close relationships allow for more confiding and challenging—but you still should be kind and respectful.

Don't get drunk. Nothing ruins a good conversation faster or more permanently. Apart from being illegal and potentially dangerous for teenagers, getting drunk is one of the rudest things you can do to your host or social companions. One must remain in control of oneself in order to follow the Four Simple Rules of Polite Conversation:

1. Don't make speeches.

2. Don't say hurtful things.

3. Don't reveal secrets.

4. Tread very carefully when discussing controversial social, political, moral, and religious issues about which people have strongly held (and often irrational) views.

TRUE STORIES

FROM THE
MANNERS FRONTIER

Tanks for Nothing

Once upon a time, I went out to dinner with a small group of friends. The husband of one of them got tanked up and proceeded to rant and rave about anything and everything.

He violated just about every rule of polite social exchange: He monopolized the conversation so nobody else could speak; he shouted and swore so other diners stared at our table; he mortified and verbally abused his wife; he held forth on politics, the economy, money, welfare, and how everybody who wasn't pulling their weight should be blown off the planet.

It was ugly, embarrassing, and hurtful. I completely lost my appetite, and the sheep brains I was so looking forward to eating sat untouched.

Dear Alex

"My parents don't speak English. So at home we use our native language. I've never invited any friends over because I figure it would be rude if they don't know what anybody's saying. Is it impolite to speak a foreign language in front of guests?"

If that's all you did, it would be rude. Imagine the discomfort a guest would experience if everybody at the dinner table chattered away in a language he didn't understand. He'd feel excluded and might even think you were talking about him.

However, if you're willing to serve as a translator, this can be a wonderful experience for everybody. You can be an intermediary between your friend and your folks. You and your family can even teach your friend expressions and traditions from your native culture, and vice versa. Since a lot of communication occurs through facial expressions, gestures, and ritual, you can all have a fine old time even if you don't speak the same language. Just keep your hearts warm and your sense of humor engaged.

The Art of Polite Listening

Has this ever happened to you? You're talking away, only to realize that your so-called "listener" isn't paying any attention to what you're saying. You might as well be addressing a lamppost. This is very disconcerting, since very few people like to talk to lampposts.

Courteous conversationalists use many techniques to show that they're paying attention. Like what? Well, think of everything you *could* do if someone (like a parent or a teacher) gave you a Big Lecture: You could slouch, sigh extravagantly, roll your eyeballs, stare at the ceiling, doodle, tap your foot, drum your fingers, shift your position, and/or consult your watch. This is known as Communicating Total Indifference. Polite listeners do the opposite. They:

- sit or stand up straight
- look the speaker in the eye
- avoid tapping, squirming, or fidgeting
- grunt, nod, emit, and emote (all signs that show they're paying attention). Plus they cheer on people with expressions such as:
  "Hmmm."
  "No kidding?"
  "Wow!"
  "Really?"
  "And then?"
  "Cool!"
  "No way!"
  "Surely you jest."

The above attitudes, gestures, and responses show that you're *hearing* what the person is saying. But that's only part of courteous listening. You also want to show that you *understand*, that you *care*. You do this by pretending you're a mirror and reflecting the speaker's words back to him or her.

When engaged in talk "lite," it's generally most appropriate to reflect the *informational* content of the speaker's words:

Lou: *"Nice weather we're having."*

You: *"It's great to have some sun after all that rain."*

Lou: *"I'm not used to so much rain. I've been living in the Sahara."*

You: *"Wow! You lived in the desert? What was that like?"*

You show Lou that you're listening by making appropriate comments and asking relevant questions. If you respond to "Nice weather we're having" with "I prefer jelly donuts myself," Lou will rightly assume that you haven't been listening (and also that you have jelly for brains).

When engaged in "heavy" talk, it's best to reflect the *emotional* content of the speaker's words:

Sue: *"I HATE rain. The worst things in my life all happened on rainy days."*

You: *"Rain reminds you of a lot of bad memories?"*

Sue: *"My dog died. My gerbil died. My turtle died. My babysitter died. My uncle died."*

You: *"Rain must bring back a lot of sadness."*

You pick up on the fact that Sue isn't talking about the weather per se, but about some powerful associations she has with rain. You prove that you're listening by reflecting the feelings behind her words. Your show of empathy will keep Sue talking. She'll sense your support and understanding and feel safe about revealing herself.

You can see how inappropriate it would be to reply to Sue's statement as if it really were just about the weather:

Sue: *"I HATE rain. The worst things in my life all happened on rainy days."*

You: *"I don't mind the rain. But then again, my great-grandfather was a duck—quack, quack."*

When you clue in to what a speaker is saying and respond accordingly, you're using "active listening." This simple strategy says *I hear you, I understand how you feel, and I acknowledge your right to have those feelings.*

There will be times when you don't agree with the speaker's feelings, or you don't think those feelings are justified. Especially when you're the target of anger or hostility. Instead of arguing or lashing out, listen even more carefully. Try to uncover the feelings *behind* those the speaker is expressing. This is a great way to defuse potentially explosive situations and avoid conflict. Watch:

Your father says: *"Where have you been?! It's past midnight, and if you think you can just waltz in here—"*

You say: *"You must have been so worried about me."*

What was your father feeling? Anger, yes. But anger is usually a mask for some other feeling. In this case, your dad was worried sick. Just imagine all the horrible scenarios that flashed through his mind as he waited for you to come home.

Or consider this example:

Your friend says: *"How could you?! I told you that was a secret. Now everybody knows!"*

You say: *"I didn't mean to tell. It just slipped out. I know it was a terrible thing to do, and I can understand if you never trust me again."*

Here, too, there's a lot of anger. But underneath are feelings of hurt and betrayal. This is what you'll need to acknowledge in order to mend the broken faith between you and your friend.

In any conversation that seems to be heading for disaster, reflect the emotions *first* in order to calm things down. Then, if you think the problem stems from a misunderstanding, check the facts and assumptions behind the speaker's words. You can do this with statements like:

"It sounds as if you think I purposely disobeyed you."

"You believe I don't like your class because I'm late with my homework?"

"Since I went into your room, you assume I took your money?"

"You thought that I was going to give you a ride?"

Dear Alex

"Is it bad manners to listen in on other people's conversations as long as they don't know you're doing it?"

If the other people believe that they're speaking without being overheard, yes. This is a gross invasion of privacy called *snooping*. To understand the felonious nature of snooping, imagine how you'd feel if you learned that your parents rummaged through your text messages or read your journal.

Sometimes it's impossible not to overhear a conversation. Like when the couple at the next table is having an argument, or two kids on a bus are swapping the latest gossip. Listening in on such occasions isn't snooping, it's *eavesdropping*. This is how one learns about life and gathers material for a novel. Since eavesdroppees have no expectation of privacy in a public space, eavesdropping isn't bad manners so long as you hide the fact that you're doing it. This means keeping your nose in your book.

Concentrating on buttering your dinner roll. Adopting a meditative demeanor that suggests you're visiting a distant plane of consciousness.

Truly conscientious eavesdroppers make sure that their presence is known. For example, if your parents are having a private conversation in the kitchen, they may not realize you're in the dining room. Clear your throat. Bump a chair. You may lose your chance to eavesdrop, but you're doing the right thing. If you don't make any noise, you're snooping.

Corrections and Contradictions

What do you do when you're talking with someone and she says something you *know* is wrong? You can think *You blithering idiot! How can you be so stupid?* But you can't *say* it. Similarly, you can think *You clumsy oaf!* to the apologetic person who just stepped on your toe, but what you should *say* is "That's all right. No harm done."

Etiquette doesn't ask you to censor your thoughts. It asks you to resist the temptation to voice them. It's rude to correct or contradict someone in public—especially an adult. (And adults need to realize that it's equally rude to treat children this way.) Most of the errors people make in conversation are of little consequence. They are slips of the tongue, insignificant errors of fact, or minor mistakes of pronunciation or grammar. Someone may say "Alan Burr" instead of "Aaron," or get a date wrong, or confuse one event with another. It's not worth correcting the person because the matter is trivial. And if the person is profoundly wrong about something important, chances are her mind is closed to enlightenment. So it's usually best to let it go unless doing so will cause harm.

If you feel that you must issue a correction, here are some guidelines:

Do it in private. Spare the person from embarrassment by ensuring that no audience is present.

Do it with modesty. Approach the point in question as if *you* might be the one in error. You might say:

> *"Isn't that interesting. I was taught that George Washington was the father of our country. But maybe it's Dolly Madison. Now you've got me curious. I'll have to look it up."*

Often, if you're gentle and respectful in your correction, the person in error will say:

> *"You know, now that you mention it, I think you may be right."*

Siblings and close friends who disagree may simply say—
> *"Is."*
> *"Is not."*

"Is."

"Is not."

—for however long it takes until one of them gets tired and gives up.

Dear Alex

"My aunt tells the same stories over and over again. They're boring the first time and even more boring the fifth time. How can you shut people up when they do this?"

Your aunt doesn't mean to bore you. People often repeat themselves. For the elderly (anyone over 29), this is because they're down to their last three brain cells and have trouble remembering. For the young, it's because they have so many friends they can't remember to whom they've told what.

If someone starts to tell a story you've heard before, you have a window of about two seconds in which you can say:

"Oh, I remember that story. It was absolutely the most hilarious/sad/ touching thing I've ever heard."

The degree to which the story delighted or moved you must be stated extravagantly. This is so your enthusiasm will overwhelm any embarrassment the speaker might feel upon being unmasked as a twice-told taleteller. If others are present, you may follow your remark with:

"Wait 'til you hear this story. It's so great, you're going to love it. I'm just going to excuse myself for a moment while Auntie Alice tells it."

If you didn't manage to nip the story in the bud, you've lost your chance. You must now listen politely, giving no indication that you're bored to tears. Nod (but don't nod off), smile pleasantly, chuckle when others do, and use the time to meditate or put together a shopping list in your head. And if you're the one who is prone to repeat renditions of the same stories, you can always preface it by saying, "Stop me if I've told you this before." That gives permission to your listener to halt the recitation, sparing you both from embarrassment.

Dear Alex

"I have a friend who stutters. If I know what he means to say, is it okay to finish a sentence for him?"

No. In polite conversation, you wait for the other person to finish before speaking. In this case, you simply have to wait a little longer. Do nothing to indicate your awareness of his stuttering. Maintain eye contact. Refrain from twiddling your thumbs.

CONVERSATIONAL CONVENTIONS
THAT DON'T CROSS CULTURES

Every society develops conventions for addressing people, transacting business, negotiating, interacting socially, and so on. Here are some typical practices that may cause confusion or offense if practiced with people of different cultural backgrounds:

- In some cultures, it's increasingly common to call one's elders and total strangers by their first names. In other cultures, this is considered disrespectful. In fact, in some cultures, people avoid using names entirely. They refer to each other as "Sister" or "Brother" or "Lili's mother."

- In Western cultures, a person's family name (surname) goes last (e.g., Martin Luther King). In some Eastern cultures, the last name goes first (e.g., King Martin Luther). Thus, Park Young Sam would be Mr. Park, not Mr. Sam.

- In some cultures, people address married women as "Mrs." plus their husband's last name. In other cultures, wives retain their maiden names. Mr. Park's wife would not be addressed as Mrs. Park, but by her maiden name, Mrs. Kim.

- English slang in the United States such as "tied up at the moment," "having a cow," and "chill" are so common that locals don't realize that others may have no idea what they mean. Similarly, someone from the United States traveling to England—where they speak English!—would be confused if asked for a "fag" (a cigarette), shown to the "loo" (bathroom), or cautioned to "mind their head" (don't bump it).

- In some cultures, people are delighted to receive praise. But in other cultures, people are embarrassed and uncomfortable when someone praises them. Praise *now* suggests that their performance *before* might have lacked something. Also, being singled out for attention could alter relationships with work colleagues, possibly triggering jealousy or competition.

The Art of Polite Expression

If you wish to be a courteous and effective conversationalist, here are some rules you'll need to follow:

Use the magic words. The magic words are "Please," "Thank you," "You're welcome," and "Excuse me." They have the power to make people do your bidding; to help you escape from tight spots; to cause problems to disappear. In case you're a little rusty, here's how to work a little magic every time you open your mouth:

1. Include the word "Please" in any requests.

2. Always say "Thank you" when someone gives you something or does something for you.

3. If someone thanks *you*, respond with "You're welcome," or "My pleasure." Do not dismiss their gratitude by saying "Whatever" or "No problem."

4. Learn and master the many forms of "Excuse me."

"Excuse me!"	said with a bright lilt in your voice	means	*"Coming through!"*
"Oh, excuse me!"	accompanied by a sharp intake of breath, a look of mortification, and a hand placed over your heart	means	*"How clumsy/careless of me!"*
"Ex-cuuuse me?"	said sternly with raised eyebrows and ascending pitch	means	*"You'd better undo what you just did—fast!"*
"Excuse me."	said with demure matter-of-factness	means	*"Sorry about that there belch."*
"Excuse me . . ."	as the preface to a remark	means	*"Please forgive me for interrupting, but . . ."*

Choose your moment. You wouldn't have a heart-to-heart with someone during the bottom of the ninth with the score tied 3–3. And you wouldn't ask your parents for a new tablet an hour after denting your dad's car. Why not? Because timing is everything. If you want to be heard, if you want your requests to be granted, you have to speak up when your targets are in receptive listening mode. This means when they are relaxed, cheerful, and not in the middle of something.

Don't interrupt. If two people are having a conversation and you need to butt in—don't. Instead, wait for a pause or for one of them to turn to you. Then say "Excuse me" and whatever else you want or need to say. Of course, if it's an emergency, all bets are off and you're free to say, "Excuse me, but the house is on FIRE!"

Dear Alex

"What if you really need to interrupt a conversation, and you stand a few feet away waiting for a moment to interrupt, but they act as if you're not even there?"

Your body language is saying *I'm waiting for a chance to interrupt you.* Their body language (and perhaps also their facial expressions) are saying *We're not open to being interrupted.* Maybe they're being rude, but don't automatically assume that. Maybe they're involved in a heavy conversation and really can't be interrupted. Or maybe they're so engrossed in their conversation that they simply haven't noticed you.

Since you haven't been acknowledged, you could wander off and try again later. Or you could say:

> *"Forgive me for interrupting, but my carpool is leaving. Did you want that address now or should I call you with it later?"*

Then start to leave. If they need the information you're offering, they'll pause their conversation to get it.

Dear Alex

"What if you're talking and someone interrupts? There's a girl at school who does this all the time."

You have three choices:

1. Just keep talking. This is the equivalent of ignoring the rudeness. It can be a lot of fun, because you won't believe how hard it is to keep it up if the other person continues to talk. Sometimes, she'll get the point and yield to your right-of-way. Usually, she won't. So you'll end up giving her the floor, but spectators will be very aware of the rudeness committed and your graciousness in allowing the interruption.

2. Say "Just let me get out this one last thought" or "Please let me finish what I was saying."

3. Speak to the interrupter in private. Use the cardinal principles of correction: the assumption that the other person must not realize what she's doing, and the ownership of the issue as one of your sensitivity:

"Jill, I'm sure you're not aware of this, but sometimes you interrupt me when I'm talking. I'd really appreciate it if you could try not to. I'm such a scatterbrain at times that I need all the help I can get remembering what I want to say."

Bagging the Bragging

You're a person of many accomplishments, and you're right to think that everyone should know all about them. You may think that the best way to spread the news is to do it yourself.

Don't. Tooting one's own horn is never good form. It's much better to let your actions speak for themselves. There's no need to tell the world about your great save in the game or the prize you won at assembly. Other people were there. They saw it. And if it's something that didn't occur in the public eye, there's another way for word to get out—friends.

Yes, that's what friends are for. Any friend worth his salt will say "Did you hear? Bilbo bagged the bantamweight belt." Any friend *really* worth his salt will say it 10 times fast.

When people offer their hearty congratulations, respond with thanks and a bit of disbelief and demurral:

"I was so lucky."

"The others deserved it just as much as I did."

You cover yourself with modesty because people who say "Aw, shucks" are much more attractive than those who say "Ain't I grand!"

How do your friends find out about your successes? You tell them—in a way that reveals your surprise and appreciation:

"Guess what? You know that essay contest I entered? I actually won! I can't believe it!"

It's okay to do this because there's a difference between bragging (a form of conceit) and sharing one's joy (a form of giving). You owe the latter to your close friends and family.

Dear Alex

"There's this kid in my school who always brags. I like her, but it really gets boring, and I hate to be around my other friends when she's doing it. I don't want to give up being her friend, but sometimes I think I will."

It helps to understand that when people brag, it's often because they have a low opinion of themselves. They try to boost their self-esteem by telling other people how great they are. Of course, this has the effect of driving people away. Rejection then causes the braggart to feel even worse, leading to more bragging and more rejection. You can see the kind of nasty cycle this can turn into.

Etiquette doesn't require you to address the psychosocial problems of your classmates. You can ignore your friend's bragging and maintain the status quo, you can gently bow out of the relationship, or you can tackle the issue head-on by saying:

"I think you're a wonderful person—otherwise I wouldn't be friends with you. But I get the feeling it turns people off when you talk about yourself so much. I know it's kind of a habit because sometimes I do it myself. But I thought, if you wanted to do something about it, we can have a signal so that if I hear you bragging, I can let you know without anyone else knowing."

Your friend may feel a little hurt at first. But if you bring the subject up gently and follow through with humor and sensitivity, she'll know she's lucky to have you by her side.

How to End a Conversation

Now that you know how to get into a conversation and handle some of the fine points and rough spots, you need to know how to get out of one gracefully. This comes in handy when you have to talk to someone else, attend to a personal matter, or escape the clutches of the world's greatest bore.

There are many strategies you could employ. For instance:

- You could point to a distant spot in the room and say "Isn't that Bertie Wooster?" When the person goes to look, you disappear. By the time he or she turns back, you're long gone.

- If a very large person walks between you, you could slip away by using him or her for cover, in much the same way that cowboys used to ride out of town hidden behind the flanks of a horse.

The problem with these two techniques is that they're rude, rude, rude. In contrast, here are two socially acceptable methods for getting out of a conversation:

1. The Foist-'Em-Off Ploy. In one-on-one conversations at a social event, it's impolite to simply walk away from someone, even if there's a pause in the conversation. But it's permissible to hand her off to someone else. You do this by saying something like this:

"Oh, you just have to meet Clarence Darrow. Let me introduce you."

Approach Clarence, make a proper introduction, give good clues to get the new conversation started ("Clarence has just taken on a new case you may have read about"), and then excuse yourself and leave. Clarence may never speak to you again, but at least you're a free agent.

2. The "Please Excuse Me" Ploy. It's okay to abandon someone as long as you offer an excuse. The ideal excuse leaves the impression that, if it weren't for fate or duty, you'd love to spend the rest of your life talking to the person. Here are some tried-and-true excuse me's:

> *"Please excuse me, but . . .*
>
> *. . . I must catch Justin before he starts singing."*
>
> *. . . my ride is about to leave."*
>
> *. . . I have to make a call."* (This is preferable to "I have to go pee.")

Choose your excuse carefully, because you must follow it through (or at least give the appearance of doing so). It would hurt someone's feelings if you said you had to leave and then hung around the party for another two hours.

If you're on the receiving end of an excuse, accept it at face value. For example, if someone says "Excuse me, I'm going to step outside for some fresh air," don't say "Good idea. I think I'll join you." If he wanted your company, he'd say "Would you like to come outside for some fresh air?"

You can duck out of group conversations a lot more easily. Since the discussion will continue without you (although at nowhere near its former sparkle), you can just say "Excuse me" and depart. This form of "Excuse me" means "I wouldn't dream of interrupting, so you people should all just carry on without me."

Dear Alex

"How do you get out of a conversation with someone who doesn't give you a moment's breather to say anything?"

How do you extricate yourself from a conversation with a compulsive talker who for those of you who may be unfamiliar with the term is an individual who neither comes up for air when speaking nor speaks as most of us do in sentences punctuated with pauses the purpose of which is to invite the listener to reply but rather utilizes epic nonstop linguistic constructions that go on forever one idea following the next a sort of ceaseless drone a mind-numbing succession of verbal paragraphs that quickly lose meaning and induce feelings of sleepiness fantasies of escape and visions of violence on the part of the hapless listener trying to be polite but feeling more and more trapped by the minute?

Believe me, I know how difficult this can be.

Polite Ways to Get Away from Motormouths

Faint

Create a diversion

Disappear

If you're unable to find an opening, you must make one. Politely. While trapped as a listener, you'll have ample time to come up with an excuse (your bus is about to leave; you have to get to a shop before it closes; etc.). Decide whether you'll need visual or tactile assistance to accomplish your break-in (an expression of sudden surprise as if you just remembered something; a gentle hand placed on theirs). Then say:

"Mrs. Motormouth, I hate to interrupt because I do so enjoy our conversations, but I just remembered that I promised my mother I'd be home by four."

Get up, start walking away, and set your exit in inviolate motion.

What if she follows you, still talking? This is such an outrageous breach of etiquette that you have no choice but to do the only sensible thing under the circumstances: Run!

Dealing with Rude Adults

You wouldn't believe the things some adults say to kids. Then again, maybe you would:

"My, how you've grown."

"You're almost as pretty as your sister."

"Look at those freckles."

"You must be awfully nearsighted to have to wear those glasses."

"Aren't you a bit old to be in the 10th grade?"

"The camp you're going to—is it for overweight children?"

"How did you ever get to be so tall?"

It may take a whole village to raise a child, but some of the villagers should keep their mouths shut. Insensitive remarks aren't necessarily meant to be unkind. It's simply that most adults develop total amnesia about childhood once they leave it behind. They forget what it feels like to have adults scrutinizing your behavior and appearance 24 hours a day. Imagine what would happen if adults said to their peers the sorts of things they say to children:

"You're as pretty as Jim's last wife."

"Look at those stretch marks."

"My, I think you've put on at least 30 pounds since I last saw you."

"Aren't you a bit old to still be assistant manager?"

So what do you do when grown-ups make rude or intrusive remarks? You have three choices:

1. You can make a snappy comeback.

2. You can reply with patience, good humor, respect, and a smile.

3. You can assert yourself without being rude.

The second choice drives adults crazy. Watch:

EXAMPLE #1: An adult says "That's the third piece of cake you've had."

Snappy Comeback

You say: "It'll look a lot better on me than on you."

Analysis: The snappy comeback leaves the adult feeling that her intrusion was justified. Not only are you a pig, you're a *rude* pig. And the behavior of impolite children must be closely monitored and corrected.

Polite Reply

You say: "How kind of you to point that out. In all honesty, Ma'am, I was so busy enjoying it that I hadn't noticed."

Analysis: The polite reply leaves the adult scratching her head. You expressed appreciation for her kind attentiveness. You confessed to your own lapse in monitoring your food consumption. So how come she feels put in her place? Because your exemplary good manners reveal her remark for what it was—bad manners. Don't you love it?

EXAMPLE #2: An adult says "So tell me, is there a special little girlfriend in your life?"

Snappy Comeback

You say: "No, is there one in yours?"

Analysis: You might experience a moment of satisfaction as the adult turns red in the face and sputters off, wondering just how much you do know about his life. But all you've accomplished is to create an uncomfortable situation and establish yourself as disrespectful.

Polite Reply

You say: "I'm blessed with many friends, both girls and boys."

Analysis: With immaculate politeness, you slam the door in the face of this nosy question. Hidden within your reply, deep enough to shield you from accusations of disrespect but shallow enough to be felt by your questioner, is the message *None of your business.* Game, set, and match to politeness.

EXAMPLE #3: An adult says "I don't know why you young people do such things to your hair."

Snappy Comeback

You say: "At least we *have* hair."

Analysis: Nothing is gained or learned from such an exchange. The adult's stereotype of teenagers is reinforced.

Polite Reply

You say: "And I worked so hard to try to look nice tonight! I'd love to hear about the styles when you were my age."

Analysis: When delivered with a forlorn, injured expression, your reply will cause the adult to backpedal quickly, insisting that he never meant to imply that you don't look nice. And then, as he recounts the fashion fads of his youth, he'll recognize the folly of his comment. Your triumph will be complete.

When responding to ill-mannered questions and remarks, the basic principles are these:

- Rudeness returned is the least effective rejoinder to bad manners.

- Don't feel you have to answer a nosy question just because it was asked.

- Respond to rudeness by making a gracious, general statement:
  "You're very kind to tell me that."
  "Thank you for bringing that to my attention."
  "I'll give that some thought."
  "That's not something I'm comfortable discussing."
  "Do you really think so?"
  "I'm always interested in hearing another opinion."

Of course, you may need to modify these principles to fit the specifics of the situation. But you can see them at work in the following examples:

Adult: *"In today's world, you'll never make it as an artist."*
Child: *"Thank you for bringing that to my attention."*

Adult: *"You really should treat your parents with more respect."*
Child: *"Do you really think so? I'll give that some thought."*

Adult: *"In my opinion, you're much too young to travel by yourself."*
Child: *"I'm always interested in hearing another opinion."*

Now let's look at the third choice: asserting yourself without being rude. Maybe you've heard the old saw "It's not *what* you say, it's *how* you say it."* In fact, if you know *how* to say things, you can say almost anything without offending anyone. This comes in handy when you're dealing with boorish people. You can see from the following examples that polite phraseology is much more powerful than discourtesy:

*MAYBE YOU'VE HEARD IT A HUNDRED MILLION TIMES FROM YOUR PARENTS. EVEN SO, IT'S WORTH HEARING AGAIN, BECAUSE IT'S TRUE.

Rude	Politely Assertive
"You said no such thing."	"I must have heard you wrong."
"What an ignorant, bigoted thing to say."	"I beg your pardon?"
"You're a liar."	"I believe you're mistaken."
"Mind your own business."	"That's not something we discuss outside of the family."

Dear Alex

"I was adopted by an American family. Because there are obvious differences in appearance between my family and me, people can tell I'm adopted. I don't mind that, but I do mind all the questions they ask. Sometimes even waiters do it. What should I say? Is it considered rude in America to ask questions of this nature?"

Apparently not. Otherwise we wouldn't have so many ill-mannered people doing it. But it *is* rude. It is *so* rude, in fact, that you have very special latitude in dealing with such boorish busybodies:

To someone who says . . .	You may reply . . .
"Those can't be your real parents."	"Oh, they're very real to *me*."
"Why didn't your parents want you?"	"Isn't it interesting to speculate on why parents do the things they do? For example, did your parents want *you,* or were you an accident?"
"How come you were adopted?"	"Why do you wish to know?" OR "I prefer not to discuss personal matters with people I don't know well."

You may also, if you feel up to it, give the real reason—not because it's anybody's business, but because it reveals the inexcusable intrusiveness of the question:

"Why was I adopted? Because my parents were dragged from our house in the middle of the night, tortured, shot, and dumped in a shallow grave. After that, they were no longer able to care for me."

You may wish to consider the context in which the question is asked before deciding how to respond. For example, a classmate or teacher who inquires about your family may be trying to build a friendship. You may decide to speak openly about your feelings and history. A waiter, however, is more likely to be scratching the itch of curiosity. He deserves to be put in his place, politely but pointedly.

Responding in such a manner isn't rudeness. It's a public service. It may cause these people to hold their tongues the next time they're tempted to intrude into the personal lives of people they barely know.

When Parents Are Rude

Strangers, nonrelatives, and casual acquaintances aren't the only adults who are rude to kids and teens. Parents—perhaps including *yours*—can be shockingly rude. This may have to do with the confusion between "company manners" and "being real."* Or it may be linked to the mistaken belief that honesty is always the best policy.** Whatever the cause, parental impertinence is as much a breach of etiquette as teenage impudence.

When parents are rude, it's usually in the area of criticizing their children. Admittedly, some criticism is deserved and, when it's constructive, can even be welcome. But criticism is bad manners if the remark is unnecessarily harsh, unkind, or intrusive. For example, there's no excuse for saying "Can't you do anything right?" when the same idea could be expressed as "Let me show you how I learned to do that." Nothing in the parent-child contract excuses parents from showing the same degree of respect and politeness *toward* their offspring that they expect *from* their offspring.

Often the problem is one of definitions. As you can see from the following examples, parents and children use very different dictionaries when it comes to defining behavior:

What parents call . . .	Children call . . .
guidance	criticism
reminding	nagging
for your own good	unfair
ignoring	forgetting
slamming	shutting

The next time your parents call you on the carpet, say "You're absolutely right. I'm sorry. I'll try to do better." This stops criticism dead in its tracks. I guarantee it.

*THIS CONCEPT WAS DISCUSSED EARLIER IN CHAPTER 4.
**BE PATIENT. A THOROUGH EXAMINATION OF THIS ASSUMPTION LIES AHEAD.

THE SURVEY SAYS . . .

Here, according to my survey of *teenagers*, are 40 Rude Things Parents Say to Teens:

1. "How can you be so dumb?"
2. "You don't try hard enough."
3. "What's wrong with you?"
4. "You little @$#!%&!"
5. "Don't you ever think?"
6. "You'll never amount to anything."
7. "You should have known better."
8. "You're wearing that to school?!"
9. "Get over here."
10. "Get off the phone."
11. "Get out of my sight."
12. "Go to your room."
13. "Listen when I'm talking to you."
14. "Are you two years old?"
15. "Do what I say."
16. "No, and that's final."
17. "Don't you ever talk to me that way again."
18. "You're grounded."
19. "I don't know why I bother trying."
20. "I don't want to be around you for a while."
21. "I don't believe you."
22. "I don't love you."
23. "I don't care."
24. "It doesn't matter what you want."
25. "It's none of your business."
26. "You're such a brat."
27. "How can I ever trust you again?"
28. "I can't wait for you to leave home."
29. "I wish I'd never had you."
30. "I hate your friends."
31. "Why can't you be more like your brother or sister?"
32. "If so-and-so jumped off a bridge, would you?"
33. "Act your age."
34. "You're so immature."
35. "What do you know? You're just a child."
36. "You're too young to understand."
37. "Because I said so."
38. "Because I'm your mother/father."
39. "After all of the things I've done for you . . ."
40. "When I was your age . . ."

THE SURVEY SAYS . . .

Because fairness is my goal, here, according to my survey of *parents*, are 40 Rude Things Teenagers Say to Parents:

1. "Leave me alone."
2. "Mind your own business."
3. "Get out of my face."
4. "Get out of my life."
5. "Stay out of my room."
6. "Shut up."
7. "@$#!%&! you."
8. "You're the world's worst parent."
9. "I wish you weren't my mother/father."
10. "I wish I was never born."
11. "I wish you were dead."
12. "I hate being part of this family."
13. "I don't need you."
14. "You don't own me."
15. "I don't have to."
16. "I don't care."
17. "You can't tell me what to do."
18. "What about you?"
19. "YOU do it!"
20. "You have horrible taste."
21. "I'll do what I want."
22. "I'll do it when I feel like doing it."
23. "I don't need your help."
24. "You never do anything for me."
25. "You're so unfair."
26. "You're so mean."
27. "You're so stupid."
28. "You're too old to understand."
29. "I don't want to be seen with you in public."
30. "Give me money."
31. "It's my life."
32. "So?"
33. "Who says?"
34. "Fine!"
35. "Yeah, right."
36. "Big deal."
37. "This dinner is gross."
38. "I hate you."
39. "You don't care about me at all."
40. "Whatever."

Dear Alex

"My father says that all I do is complain and I don't appreciate what I have. That's not true. I do appreciate what I have. What am I supposed to do? Go around saying 'Gee, I'm so lucky, oh wow, this is great?'"

What we have here is the proverbial failure to communicate. You appreciate your good fortune, you take pleasure in the world, yet your dad isn't getting the message. This happens in a lot of families. For some reason, humans seem more readily disposed to complain than to praise, to express displeasure rather than delight. There's probably some evolutionary basis for this. After all, one is more likely to live to see tomorrow by saying "I hate it when you throw boulders at me" than "My, what a pretty dandelion."

What you need to do is let out all that appreciation. Politeness demands that you convey genuine pleasure when you feel it—as well as when you don't. Let's look at the three forms of pleasure:

1. **Pleasure in anticipation.** This is what you experience when you look forward to and/or are asked to participate in some future event. This brand of pleasure is expressed with comments such as:
   "Oh boy! That'd be great!"
   "I'd love to!"
   "I can't wait!"
   "Thank you for asking me."

2. **Pleasure in the moment.** This is what you feel when you're having a good time. A quick change of tense and we get:
   "Oh boy! This is fantastic!"
   "I love this!"
   "What fun!"
   "I'm so glad you asked me."

3. **Pleasure reflected upon.** This is what we experience in the afterglow of an enjoyable event. You convey this with comments such as:
   "That was super!"
   "I had a fabulous time!"
   "I hope we can do this again."
   "Thank you soooo much!"

Why should you communicate your delight? First, because it's the polite thing to do. Second, because it brings great joy to those who care about your welfare. And third, because a grateful, enthusiastic response increases the likelihood that the behavior that provoked it will be repeated.

Dear Alex

"My mother refuses to talk to me when I 'whine'—as she puts it. I think if someone is talking to you, it's impolite to ignore them."

Your mother isn't ignoring you. She's doing you a favor. "Whining" is the name we give to speech that's repetitive, singsongy, demanding, complaining, and selfish. Such language patterns are associated with small children who, through no fault of their own, haven't yet learned to consider their needs in fair balance with the needs of others. If your mother listened to you, she'd have to conclude that you were behaving in a childish manner. Therefore, you wouldn't stand a chance of getting or doing whatever it is you're whining about not being able to get or do. By refusing to acknowledge you, she's hoping that you'll adopt a more mature perspective and tone of voice so that she might accommodate your wishes. With that in mind, go give your mother a big kiss right now.

Is Honesty Always the Best Policy?

One of the first lessons parents teach their children is "You must never tell a lie." Invariably, a neighbor comes to visit shortly thereafter. Mommy says "Would you like to give Mrs. Sweetums a kiss?" And little Johnny, mindful of his parents' wise counsel, replies "No. She's ugly and smells bad."

As soon as Mrs. Sweetums is out the door, Johnny learns the second lesson parents teach their children: "You must never tell a lie, but you must not always tell the truth." The parent proceeds to explain that there's a difference between *lying to stay out of trouble* (which is bad) and *lying to avoid hurting someone's feelings* (which can be good).

Knowing when to tell the truth and when to take creative liberties is at the heart of good manners. Because this issue is so important, I wanted to learn what teenagers thought about it. So I asked them "Is honesty always the best policy?"

Here's what the teenagers I surveyed said:

Yes 39%

No 61%

And here are some reasons they gave:

"Honesty is always the best policy because . . ."

"If you're honest, your parents will trust you."

"People will like you."

"When you're honest, you never have to remember any lies. The truth always stays the same."

"If you're not honest, it will eventually come back to you in a bad way."

"Telling a lie will push your guilt button, and that's a yucky feeling."

"In my experience, if you lie you always get found out, and then you get in trouble for lying as well as for doing the thing you lied about."

One teenager put it this way:

"Honesty is the best policy. But it's not always the most convenient policy."

"Honesty isn't always the best policy because . . ."

The teenagers who responded this way to the survey fell into two camps. There were those who saw lying as a way of avoiding hassles:

"You can get away with things when you don't tell the truth."

"Honesty isn't the best policy—at least, not with parents."

"Honesty may get you into more trouble than you need."

"If the other person will never know the difference and the truth will hurt you, zip your lip."

"If someone offers you a drug, you might have to lie to get out of that situation."

And there were those who saw lying as a way of preventing hurt feelings:

"When giving opinions, lying is better than criticizing, but only because people are so damned sensitive!"

"I wouldn't want to tell someone they're ugly or look nasty."

"Honesty can sometimes make people commit suicide, cry, get hurt emotionally, or want revenge on you."

"If you're too honest, you can hurt a friend."

"Telling someone EXACTLY what you think is never good. You should use discretion."

So, is honesty always the best policy or not? The answer is "It depends."

The teenagers who said "Yes" realized that telling the truth leads to self-respect, a clear conscience, and the trust of others. They were aware that lies can trip you up and get you into trouble. They were looking at the issue from the *moral* angle.

Most of the teenagers who said "No" were looking at the issue from the *etiquette* angle. They recognized that there are situations where telling the truth can be cruel, antagonizing, and purposeless. This doesn't mean that it's okay to lie. It means that it's sometimes okay to substitute good manners for the literal truth. Here are a few examples:

- You're feeling lonely and depressed and you have a stomachache. A friend of your mother's drops by the house and asks "How are you?" You say "Fine, thanks." This isn't considered a lie, even though it's not the truth. You understood that the question was a social pleasantry rather than an earnest inquiry into your health.

- You have dinner at a friend's house. The food tastes so bad you can barely get it down. When it's time to leave, you say "Thank you so much for having me over for dinner. I really enjoyed it." You don't say "Your cooking was terrible and I almost threw up." This is because you're not a food critic. You're a sensitive human being who wishes to thank people for the social kindnesses they extend to you.

- A classmate invites you to a dance. What goes through your mind is *I think you're gross and dull, and I wouldn't be caught dead at a dance with you.* What you say is "I'm sorry, but I already have plans." Even if you don't. This is because the question being asked is "Will you go out with me?" and not "What do you think of me?" Thus, the relevant truth is most politely conveyed by using an untruth.

Dear Alex

"What are you supposed to say when someone asks you if they look fat?"

You say "Certainly not! Whatever gave you such an idea?" People who ask this question are seeking reassurance, not honesty. They're saying *Please help me feel okay about myself.*

It's important to be able to recognize questions like these when you hear them. Sometimes they're disguised as declarative statements ("I look so fat"). And sometimes they're introduced with "I want your honest opinion . . . ." But don't be fooled. The last thing the person wants is your honest opinion.

Since these questions are often asked by our closest friends and loved ones, you need to know how to respond when the trap is laid. Here are some practice questions. For each one, pick the answer you think is best:

"Do I look all right?"
   a) "That depends on what you consider all right."
   b) "You look terrific."

"Is my hair okay?"
   a) "It is if you're a bird looking for a nest."
   b) "Your hair is fine."

"I messed up so bad in my piano recital."
    a) "I'll say. Thirty people walked out."
    b) "Oh, no, it sounded wonderful."

In every example, the proper answer is b. But you knew that.

Are there ever times when it's okay to give an honest reply to a question about someone's looks or performance? Absolutely. So how do you know when to be honest and when to be, er, "reassuring"? Here's how:

Be honest when . . .

The statement or question seeks specific information.
"Is my tie on straight?" "Do I have bird doo-doo in my hair?"

The statement or question implies that the person wishes for, and is motivated to make, some change.
"Do you think I'd have more friends if I could control my temper better?"

The statement or question addresses an event in the future.
"How would I look if I shaved my head?"

An honest answer could lead to positive action or save the questioner from embarrassment, injury, or trouble.
"Yes, I *do* think you tend to bully people." "There *is* a huge rip in your bathing suit."

An honest answer, while hurtful, would serve a greater good.
"You weren't invited because you drink too much, and people are sick of having their parties ruined."

Be reassuring when . . .

The statement or question is vague or broad.
"Nobody likes me." "Do you think I'm a nice person?"

The statement or question refers to something the person can't easily change about herself.
"I hate being this tall. I look so dumb."

The statement or question addresses an event from the past.
"When I blew the final debate, everybody thought I was a total dork."

An honest answer could not be acted upon.
"Yes, girls *would* like you better if you were three years older."

An honest answer would be hurtful without doing any good.
"I think you're right. Nobody will ever want to go out with you."

It's especially important to follow these guidelines if the asker is a close friend. And even when honest input is appropriate, criticism should be expressed as positively as possible. This means, if you're out helping a friend buy a new outfit, you say "The green dress is very flattering" as opposed to "The blue dress makes you look like a cow."

Dear Alex

"What's the point of asking 'How are you?' Everybody just says 'Fine.' It's so fake."

Would you prefer "My hemorrhoids are killing me, thank you"?

You're right. It *is* fake. People who ask "How are you?" are no more interested in hearing your medical history than you are in reciting it. What they're really saying is *Hey, here we are, two human beings in this cold, cruel world. Let's share a few mindless pleasantries to acknowledge our encounter and leave each other feeling a little warmer than before.* Maybe an electric blanket could accomplish the same thing, but it wouldn't make for a very interesting lunch date.

Human beings have social rituals. So do animals. But humans, instead of sniffing or bleating upon greeting fellow members of the species, prefer to shake hands and say things like "How are you?" and "Nice to see you." It would be a mistake to take all of these phrases at face value. Their actual meaning is symbolic and may even be quite different from what the words literally say.

Polite Profanities

There's no such thing as a polite profanity. If you're prone to imprecations, maledictions, and naughty words, you may include them in the Great American Novel you're writing. But they have no place in polite conversation.

It's not that swearing is "bad" in the sense that if you do it, you'll go to H-E-double-toothpicks for eternity and never be able to watch TV again. But there are three reasons why it's a bad idea:

1. Excessive swearing makes your mind go soggy. People who swear all the time are tiresome to listen to:

> *"%#@&!-in'-A, man! I'm so %#@&!-in' mad. %#@&! him! I'm gonna %#@&! that &#@&!-er over, he won't know what the %#@&! hit him."*

A nine-word vocabulary doesn't allow for the expression of much insight, wit, intelligence, or empathy. If your speech is lazy, vague, and unimaginative, your mind is sure to follow.

2. Excessive swearing takes the shock value out of profanity. The whole purpose of swearing is to have a few words available for those occasions when all others are insufficient. If you say "&@#&!" when you drop a sandwich, what do you say when an airplane drops a 300-pound block of frozen waste on your foot?

3. Swearing in public is considered impolite because it's insensitive to the feelings of others. Many people find profanity offensive. It wasn't that long ago that nobody (except the most vulgar people imaginable) ever swore. To do so in the presence of a lady was unthinkable. Children had their mouths washed out with soap for saying "damn." Some of us learned very young that Dial tastes better than Ivory soap.

What's that you say? "But it's only words?" Yes, but the images those words conjure up—things one might be full of, or be asked to do to oneself or a close relative—aren't what most people want playing on their mental multiplexes.

Dear Alex

"Every time I swear, my parents make me give them 50 cents. Do you think this is fair?"

Certainly not. Your parents deserve at least a dollar.

Chapter Quiz

1. *You're home alone when the phone rings. You pick it up and discover that it's an obscene caller. Do you:*

   a) say "Excuse me, I have another call coming in" and put the person on hold

   b) ask the caller to pant a little louder

   c) hang up immediately

2. *You're having lunch with someone who keeps taking calls on his cell phone. You have every right to:*

   a) throw the phone in his soup

   b) do your impersonation of voicemail

   c) pull out your own cell phone, call him, and say you're going home

3. *A love letter meant for someone else ends up in your locker by mistake. Do you:*

a) open it, read it, and toss it in the trash

b) make a hundred copies and plaster them all over the school

c) hand it discreetly to the proper recipient and say "I found this in my locker. I think it's really for you."

4. *You're at a party where you don't know anybody. The best way to start a conversation with somebody is to:*

a) throw a drink in the person's face

b) start singing excerpts from *Lion King*

c) ask some open-ended questions

5. *Your father drags you up to his boss and says "Mr. Addlebury, I'd like you to meet my son, Ted." Mr. A. responds "My, aren't you a big boy!" Do you:*

a) punch him out

b) scowl and say nothing

c) smile and say "Healthy genes."

11

NETIQUETTE

Going Online Without Getting Out of Line

Billions of people are now online—texting, gaming, emailing, hacking, posting, blogging, tweeting, Skyping, Facebooking—with the number growing every day. Why, the possibilities for rudeness boggle the mind!

If you're out there surfing the salty cyberwaves, there is no Internet President, no central governing board, no manager, no bureaucracy, no single set of rules or laws. This, of course, explains why the Internet works so well. But it also means that the quality of your online life will be determined in large part by you, your fellow users, and the standards set (and enforced) by whatever communities you belong to.

The one constant online is change. Websites come and go. Today's trends become tomorrow's ancient history. Technological breakthroughs transform behavior, culture, and relationships. What used to take acres of computers and millions of dollars can now be done, better and faster, by a little device in your pocket. And, 10 years from now, that little device will have been replaced by something else.

Looking forward, some of the powerhouse websites you spend the most time on now will still be around. But others will have lost their popularity. For all you know, today's "Angry Birds" may become tomorrow's "Petulant Pigeons." "Facebook?" you'll say. "That's so last year."

When thinking about online etiquette, we need two approaches. One is to come up with specific guidelines for the websites, technologies, and online interactions that exist today—phones, Facebook, tweeting, texting, trolling, etc. The other is to recognize that in the years to come there will be brand-new Googles, goggles, gizmos, and gadgets invented by people who aren't even out of diapers yet. So we also need to come up with universal principles for polite, on- and offline behavior that can be adapted to whatever the future brings.

Let's start with these universal rules that apply to virtually any online or electronic interaction.

Be real. (Unless you're a total jerk in which case you'll have to work on that.) Don't impersonate anyone. Don't present yourself as someone or something you're not. Don't create a false identity (unless it's for a fantasy game). Anonymity breeds a lot of the nastiness you find online. When people can hide behind fake identities, there are no consequences for spreading rumors, telling lies, starting fights, issuing threats, spewing bigotry, and cyberbullying. This is why more and more sites are requiring users to verify their identity before allowing them to post comments. Good idea!

Use your devices at appropriate times. This is the #1 complaint of adults and teens: People who text, phone, browse, and/or game in a manner that disrespects those they are with or those they are watching. Make sure your use of electronic devices doesn't hurt others' feelings or interfere with the solemnity, silence, or serenity of an event or environment.

Be nice. Use the same courtesies online you would in a face-to-face exchange. Say "Please" when making requests; thank people for their insights and information; apologize if you commit a gaffe. If you disagree with someone's opinion, respond with respect and reason, not insult and tirade. If newcomers ask stupid questions, be kind. Either ignore them or gently point out the *faux pas* they're committing. You build a good reputation and reveal a winning personality online just as you would in person—by being thoughtful, reasonable, and considerate. First impressions count. Swearing online is considered unimaginative—the product of a lazy mind. People who brag, lie, and put down others are as unwelcome online as they would be in your living room.

Get the FAQs. Lurk before you leap. If you went to a new school, you'd probably keep a low profile for a while. You'd observe, read the rule book, and find out who's who and what's what in order to learn the customs and expectations of your new environment. The same thing applies online. FAQs (Frequently Asked Questions) will answer many, if not most, of your questions as a newcomer to a group. They also spare group members from having to answer the same questions over and over and over again. So don't put your foot in your mouse. Before you ask questions or post messages, scope out the content, behavior, and terms of use of communities you'd like to join.

Choose the right tool. Certain media and methods are better suited to some forms of communication than others. The more serious, emotional, or confrontational the issue, the less suited it is to electronic communication. Use face-to-face conversations for the most "heavy" or personal issues. Next best to that would be a phone conversation. For less serious but still important communications, emails and personal letters are appropriate. By the time you get to text messaging and IMs, you're looking at brief, casual, informative, fun communications that should never be used to convey sad or bad news, or issues with deep emotional content.

Watch what you say. You are what you post. Once your words or photos are out there, you can't get them back. They become public. They can be saved, reposted, and archived for however much longer the planet will be around. Even "disappearing" photos that only appear for a few seconds can be screen captured. So be prudent about what you say and how you say it. Don't post secrets. Don't spread rumors. Don't say anything you wouldn't feel comfortable saying to someone's face. Assume there is no privacy online, ever.

Don't blather. You know, like, how, um, someone will go, like, in real life I mean, like talking, you know, two people having a conversation, um, and it takes, like, so long, I mean, like so much time, um, you know, for the person who is talking, to like, um, get to the point, that it's been so long, getting there, you know, like, um, from the beginning, that by the time he gets there, it's like—ZZZZzzzz. Same thing online. If you want to be welcome as a conversationalist, be brief or you might get a message saying: TLDR (too long didn't read). If a question has been asked and answered by others, don't add your own two cents' worth unless it contains information or views not previously expressed.

Check your spelling and grammar. Have you seen some of the unreadable gibberish people tweet that masquerades as the English language? Typos. Misspellings. Abbreviations. Grammatical deformities. It's created a new species, Homo sapiens Twitter Illiterer. And you find the same thing in texts, emails, and messages. Do any of these people bother to read what they've typed before hitting send?! Granted, the Internet ain't no English test, but propper speling, punkchooashun, and grammer do make it ezier for peepel to reed and understand yor comunikashuns. As a mark of courtesy to your correspondents and your own reputation, check your writing for mistakes. Don't sweat it, though. We all make occasional errors. And whatever you do, don't chastise others for their mistakes. Blooper watchdogs quickly wear out their welcome.

Don't YELL! This just may be the most universal rule there is for digital communication across all media and methods. The sustained use of CAPITAL LETTERS FOR EMPHASIS is the electronic equivalent of SHOUTING and is therefore RUDE. As with face-to-face encounters, SHOUTING ESCALATES ANY CONFLICT INTO AN ARENA WHERE ARGUING, INSULTING, AND NAME-CALLING OBLITERATE THE POSSIBILITY OF REASON, **RESPECT, AND RESOLUTION!**

Ask permission. Don't forward or post other people's emails, texts, photos, or other content unless they've said it's okay, or you are absolutely 100 percent sure they wouldn't mind.

Give credit. If you reblog, retweet, or repost content—be it art, photos, quotations, tips, links, or other material—always try to give credit to the original source.

Give back. The online world is a grand and sometimes bizarre bazaar where people exchange all sorts of wares. It works best when there's a balance of give-and take. (Think Wikipedia.) Use it to get what you need, but give back so that others may get what *they* need. Answer questions. Steer people in the right direction. Do your part to make it a friendly place.

Be cautious and skeptical. You'll find treasures online in the way of people, information, education, and entertainment. But mixed among them will be the occasional scammer, imposter, or predator. The resources online are staggering in their breadth and depth; type a few words, click "search," and you'll come up with thousands of sites with information on your topic. While much of it will be valuable, accurate, and true, some of it may be misleading, malicious, and flat-out wrong. When you browse online, use your *skeptical* thinking cap. Don't take everyone or everything at face value. Question the source. Be vigilant. Be wary. Be safe.

Don't digitally distract yourself. This doesn't mean refrain from picking your nose when behind the wheel. It means that the *most* inappropriate and dangerous time to be using an electronic device is when driving or engaging in any activity where you need to pay attention to stay safe (e.g., crossing streets, riding bikes, wrestling alligators). This is why most states ban cell phone use by drivers under the age of 18, and texting for all drivers. Accident statistics show that the use of electronic devices while driving, regardless of whether you're texting, talking, typing, dialing, scrolling, or clicking, dramatically increases the likelihood of driving-related injuries and deaths. Phone company records reveal times and locations of phone use, often leading to the arrest and criminal prosecution of drivers found to have been texting or otherwise distracted while driving—if they're still alive.

To stay safe, never text while driving. If you're over 18 and must make or receive a call, only use hands-free, voice-activated phones. Better yet, pull over to make a call. Or give your phone to a friend who will take or make calls for you while you're at the wheel.

Don't break the law. Big brother IS watching. Things that would get you in trouble offline will get you in trouble online. Don't threaten the president, issue bomb threats, or harass anyone. Don't even joke about it as law enforcement doesn't have a sense of humor about these sorts of things. Don't violate copyright laws. Don't hack or spread viruses or worms. Don't engage in hate speech or illegal activities. Behaviors such as these could land you in juvie or jail—the ultimate downtime.

Don't be a compuholic. You probably know people who can't last a minute without their phones and tablets. They check 'em first thing in the morning and last thing at night. They take 'em to bed. They take 'em to the bathroom. They stay up all night gaming. They tweet, text, and update their status hundreds of times a day—during class and assemblies; at movies and parties; when walking, biking, and driving; when they're with *you*. While they may have magic thumbs when it comes to texting, they're *all thumbs* when it comes to face-to-face relationships. Their phone is their master, far more important than any live human being they're with. The mere thought of going an hour, let alone a whole day, without it causes them to break out in a cold sweat.

A number of experiments have been conducted to see if high school students could go tech-free, cold turkey, for a whole week. This meant no Facebook, no tweeting, no texting, no gaming, no calling—no nothing. Some students succeeded. Others experienced such profound "withdrawal" symptoms that they succumbed to temptation and jumped back online. No matter what happened, though, these teens reported learning a lot about the role these devices and interactions play in their lives.

Devices are great, but don't OD on yours. An online social life should be an enhancement to, rather than a replacement for, face-to-face interaction. You need to exercise more than just your brain and your fingers. If there's mold growing on your hair, it could be a sign you need to get out in the sun—and taking your tablet to a park doesn't count. Get a reality check from parents, siblings, or friends as to whether you're spending too much time online. If the answer is yes, you should think about cutting down.

Why? Because heavy computer use and video gaming has been associated with depression, lack of sleep, alcohol and other drug use, smoking, and lower grades. It's not rocket science; time spent gaming or social networking can mean less time spent on schoolwork or with friends (in person!). And, if you're glued to a screen for hours at a time, you're not physically active, and we all know how important physical activity is to your health! In fact, heavy computer use has been associated with increased neck/shoulder and lower back pain, and higher BMI (body mass index; in other words—*fat*). Now, don't get me wrong, we *LOVE* our phones, laptops, video games, and electronic devices. But, moderation is called for to ensure that your relationship with the digital world contributes to, rather than harms, your well-being.

You Know You're a Compuholic When . . .

Your friends take your keys away.

You wake up with a strange laptop and don't know how you got it.

You hide tablets all over the house and deny any knowledge of them.

If you think you may be overdosing on computer use or gaming, try to set some boundaries for yourself so that *you* control your phone, and not the other way around. Try turning it off at least once a day for a period of time—maybe to read a book, play sports, be with friends, go for a walk, or have dinner. How about once a week having a "no-Net" day? Well, how about a half day? A couple hours?! Try it. See what you feel and what you learn. It may be prudent to keep your phone with you—but promise yourself you'll only look at or use it in case of an emergency. A phone should be an "addition." Not an addiction.

If you've tried to cut back and can't, try to understand your relationship to these activities. Are you an online participant, or spectator? When do you go online? What do you do? What does it take the place of? How do you feel when you're using or not using it? Depending on what you discover, you may need to make new friends, get some counseling, or find new interests and activities. Connect with other kids who are recovering computer junkies—just don't do it online. It's easier to cut down if you have the support and empathy of like-minded individuals.

Dear Alex

"I'm the technologically gifted one in my family, and everyone (especially my parents) comes to me with their computer and Internet questions. They expect me to drop everything just because they deleted a file or got some error message that has them convinced their computer is going to self-destruct in 30 seconds. Is there anything I can do to discourage this dependence on me?"

Discourage it? You want to *encourage* it with every fiber of your being.

Look, the reason grown-ups have children is to ensure that somebody in the house will know how to sync phones with tablets, program the thermostat, and get back the TV channels that disappeared. Sure, more and more parents are getting up to speed with their techno-gadgets, but there's always something they can learn from their kids. Computer-savvy kids love to help their parents out. You can use your superior knowledge to get your parents to buy all sorts of stuff you've been dying to have. You can say to your dad:

> *"The only thing that will solve your problem once and for all is a Phantom X-Treme liquid neon color master 1350 watt gaming computer with 24X dual format drives, Rampage Ultra Quad Cards, 8 channel HD audio, Soundblaster X-Fi Titanium headset, and a Thunderbolt S23A950D Black 28" Full HD 3D LED LCD BackLight monitor."*

Dad might scratch his head and say:

"I need all that just because my phone is dead?"

To which you would confidently reply:

"Well, you could just charge your battery but I think this would work a lot better, Dad."

You also have a priceless opportunity to model proper teaching behavior for your parents. Adults tend to ask silly questions, rush ahead without reading directions, and get defensive when being corrected. Here are the best techniques for instructing adults without hurting their feelings or injuring their self-confidence:

Be tolerant. It's not your parents' fault if they're cybernetically challenged. Treat them with respect. Assume that they have the ability to learn. At all costs, avoid remarks such as "How could you be so dumb?" or "Can't you do anything right?"

Be patient. Experience is the best teacher—even if it means making mistakes. When you see your parents head off in the wrong direction, resist the temptation to jump in and take over. If they're about to nuke the hard drive or something equally irrevocable, you can usually prevent it by saying "Let's just consider this for a minute before proceeding." Then ask questions to help them think through their actions before taking them. Most adults will make responsible decisions if trusted to do so.

Be encouraging. In the face of their children's techno-brilliance, many parents lack confidence, feel stupid, and get easily discouraged. You must counter these feelings. Be a cheerleader for your folks. Say:

"You're doing great!"

"Keep up the good work!"

"Look out, Bill Gates!"

Be realistic. Your parents will want to come across as streetwise and cool when they text, message, and post online, which means they may try to use Internet slang in their communications. This is fraught with danger if they don't know what they're doing. For example, did you hear about the mom who texted her son with bad news?

You can see the trouble parents can get into if they text beyond their abilities. Caution your parents about the downside of abbreviations and

> Grandma Sadie passed away last night. LOL.

> Why are you laughing, Mom? That's not funny.

> What do you mean? I'm not laughing.

> LOL means Laughing Out Loud.

> Oh no! I thought it meant Lots of Love. And I sent that to all your relatives!

acronyms. Encourage them to consult online slang dictionaries *before* attempting any fancy texting tricks.

If you practice these teaching methods diligently, you'll find that your parents' computer, social media, and online skills will increase to the point where they'll be less dependent on you for help. And, given your shining example, they may start to use these methods of instruction with you.

Textiquette

Texting is a miraculous way of communicating with friends, family, teachers, and anyone else who has pointy thumbs. But when teens text in class, during meals, or in social settings it becomes a major gripe of parents and teachers. And, if you want to know a secret, many teenagers feel the same way. They, too, want the full attention of their friends. As one teen who filled out my survey advised her peers, "Don't text while we're together. I want to be with *you*, so put down your phone and reciprocate."

So you can text without others getting vexed, here are some guidelines:

Match the medium to the message. Texting is meant for brief, informal communications among friends and family (and sometimes for business purposes such as arranging a meeting). Never use texting or instant messaging to convey bad or sad news, issue formal invitations, send condolences, or break up with somebody. For that, pick up the phone or go see the person face-to-face.

Watch your slanguage. BTW JLUK IRL many PEEPS and RENTS n eVeN ur BF FRM SKL DK C or 1337 & WLD B :? by NET SPAG. If YDK 4SHO IIWY I WLD UZ PRPR EnGliSh or ThEy MiGhT teLL U 2 GJOAC. K?*

Be with the ones you're with. Just because your phone is hidden on your lap doesn't mean people don't know what you're doing. They'll see you looking down and think that you are either inordinately interested in your crotch or sending a text. If you're eating with others, sitting at your desk in class, or participating in a meeting, put away your phone.

Double-check the number. It's easy to misdial or select the wrong phone number from your contact list. To avoid embarrassment—or worse—always make sure you're texting to the right phone number.

*TRANSLATION: BY THE WAY, JUST LETTING YOU KNOW, IN REAL LIFE MANY PEOPLE AND PARENTS AND EVEN YOUR BEST FRIEND FROM SCHOOL DON'T KNOW COMPUTER LANGUAGE OR LEET, AND WOULD BE CONFUSED BY NET SPELLING, PUNCTUATION, AND GRAMMAR. IF YOU DON'T KNOW FOR SURE, IF I WERE YOU I WOULD USE PROPER ENGLISH OR THEY MIGHT TELL YOU TO GO JUMP OFF A CLIFF. OK?

Identify yourself. Someone who doesn't have you in his or her contact list may not recognize your number and know who the message is from. If you're not sure someone will know who the text is from, begin your message by introducing yourself: *Hi. It's Marcy ur lab partner.*

Be patient. You never know when somebody will get around to reading your text message. Not everyone eats, sleeps, and breathes with a phone in hand. Don't feel hurt or insulted if you don't get an immediate response. And don't feel you have to respond instantly to every message you receive. Unlike telephone calls, text messages will wait patiently until you're ready to answer them. Unless your phone spontaneously combusts, the message will still be there in 30 minutes, an hour, or a whole afternoon. Wait until you're alone or your attention is not required, and then respond.

Get with the plan. Not everyone's service plan includes unlimited text messages. Before you bombard a friend with texts, it's polite to ask if she has to pay for individual messages she sends and receives.

Stay toned. The tone of brief messages—be they emails, texts, or IMs—can be hard to discern. Someone might take offense at or misinterpret what you thought was an innocuous statement. To avoid awkward or ugly situations, be careful what you write. If you must, use smileys to signal your intention.

Be discreet. Remember that text messages can be traced, stored, and forwarded. Once sent, you can't take them back. Never text anything that's confidential or that could embarrass you or get you into trouble.

Watch out for autocorrect. The nerve of your phone! Thinking it knows more than you do about what you are typing. Well, sometimes it does and the autocorrect feature is a handy, time-saving device. But other times, it can get you in trouble if it replaces your typo or misspelling with a word you didn't intend. This can lead, if you're *lucky*, to some pretty weird or hilarious messages. If you're not so lucky, you could end up sending a confusing, vulgar, or obscene text.

And now, on page 393, straight from the minds of texting teenagers who took my survey, are 20 Do's and Don'ts of Texting Etiquette.

Dear Alex

"My parents are always telling me to stop texting and put my phone away. What's so wrong with texting?"

Nothing's wrong with texting. Texting is grand! It's a wonderful way to stay in touch with friends, take care of the business of life, and wear out your fingers. With texting, it's not *what* you do, it's *when* you do it.

20 DO'S AND DON'TS OF TEXTING ETIQUETTE

DO

- try to use correct or at least understandable grammar and spelling.
- double-check the recipient before sending.
- tell people when you have to stop rather than just leave them hanging.
- respect the limits your plan has on texting.
- refrain from spreading gossip or rumors.
- keep private messages private—no forwarding.
- set the phone aside when you have company.
- text your parents so they know where you are.
- watch out for autocorrect.
- call your friends from time to time.

DON'T

- become text obsessed.
- text in class, at the movies, or anywhere else where people are trying to concentrate on something other than your annoying beeps and blue light.
- text rude or hurtful messages. Those are forever.
- say anything you wouldn't say in person.
- pester the recipient with multiple texts.
- use so many abbreviations you forget what the actual spelling is supposed to be.
- text while eating dinner or at a social gathering.
- text people in the same room as you while excluding other people.
- let texting come between you and your responsibilities.
- text and drive.

That's what your parents are objecting to. A basic principle of good manners is to give people your full attention when you're in a social setting. If you're having a conversation or are in a group, you wouldn't suddenly pull out a book and read. It's not *texting* your parents are objecting to. It's that you're not participating in the social interaction. This could be dinner with your family or sitting in the living room with company. So, when your parents say nix on the texting, what they're really saying is they want your jolly company and full attention.

Dear Alex

"My teacher told the class that we can't use ABBR in our papers. What's up with that?"

Polite behavior always has to do with context. With spoken language, you and your friends converse in a manner—slang, contractions, slurred words, grossities—that you wouldn't use in a formal setting with adults. Similarly, texting and tweeting have spawned a new language—one with ABBR (abbreviations), smileys, purposeful misspellings, and the use of numbers as stand-ins for phonetic sounds (SK8). Within the context of sending brief, informal electronic messages on microscopic keyboards, this language, within reason, makes sense.

But it doesn't make sense for schoolwork. One of your teacher's responsibilities is to help students master the English language. Texting mangles the language—which is okay if you're texting—but you need to know and use proper English spelling, punctuation, and grammar for more formal occasions such as writing papers, taking exams, sending letters, and corresponding with businesses. If you're not careful, repeated use of improper language can dumb down your use of English in general. For example, much of spelling is based on knowing whether a word "looks right" or not. If you're used to seeing gurl, cuz, luv, wut, and kewt, it's easy to forget how the real words are spelled. So, when you're texting, enjoy the new slanguage, but when you're at skool, leave it behind.

Dear Alex

"My bf texts me constantly. Like hundreds of times a day. How do I tell him to stop?"

Assuming the problem is just one of your boyfriend being overly fond and hyperactively fingered, the best thing is to talk to him. He may not realize that he's a textaholic and that it bothers you. Explain that, while you love to stay in touch with him, what he's doing is way too much. It distracts you and you don't have time to reply. Tell him he's going to have to cut back to X times a day (whatever you're comfortable with). You may have to keep after him at first. But if you stick to your guns, and don't reply to more frequent texts, he should come around.

There's a possibility, though, that such constant messaging means your boyfriend is jealous and controlling. He wants to know what you're doing and who you're with at all times. That's not normal or healthy. How do you know if he's trying to control you? Look at the nature of his messages. Are they loving, supportive, humorous, and friendly? Or are they angry, mean, and abusive? Do his messages make you feel bad or scared? Watched and stalked? If so, the best thing to do is still to talk to him. Let him know that his messages are hurtful and out-of-line and that he has to stop sending them to you. You'll learn a lot from his reaction about the motivation behind his constant messaging. If he doesn't stop, you're in an emotionally abusive relationship that you need to break off. Call your phone company or get an app that lets you block his calls and texts. Save or make a record of his messages for documentation. If he continues to stalk you, tell an adult you trust.

Dear Alex

"Is sexting okay if both people agree to it?"

"Sexting," a combination of the words "sex" and "texting," is the practice of electronically sending lewd remarks or sexually revealing photos of oneself or others, usually by cell phone. Because of the risks involved, while it isn't necessarily bad manners, it is almost always bad judgment to send such photos and texts, even if both people—the sender and the receiver—agree. Here's why.

Let's look at the most "innocent" circumstance in which sexting might occur. Two teens are dating. One of them takes a revealing selfie and sends it to the other. After all, they trust each other. It's possible that the photo will go no further and no harm will be done.

But what if the person who received the photo forwards it to a few close friends? What if each of them sends it on to a few more people? What if the couple breaks up, and one of them is hurt and angry and for revenge sends the photo to as many people as possible? Before you know it, the photo could be on thousands of cell phones or even up on the Internet.

Think of the embarrassment and humiliation the person in the photo would feel. Think of the damaged reputation. Think of the taunts and wisecracks. If either of the teens were under the age of 18, it's even possible that one or both of them could be charged with distributing child pornography. That's a federal crime that can lead to imprisonment and having to register as a sex offender. This could affect their getting into college, getting a job, and even where they are permitted to live. It could affect their relationships, self-esteem, and health. And this could all happen from the most "innocent" circumstance. Now imagine if the subject of the photo was forced into being photographed. Or photographed when drunk. Or the photo was secretly taken. A bad situation becomes even worse.

Sexting may seem like harmless fun, but once you hit "send," you lose control of where the photo goes. Anytime you're thinking of taking, or having someone take, a picture of yourself, ask if you would be comfortable with everyone you know seeing it, or having it posted on the Internet. If the answer is no, don't take the photo, don't take the risk. After all, even if both people are "okay" with sending the photo, it's bad manners to knowingly put someone in a position where their behavior might have devastating consequences down the road for themselves or others.

Facebook Etiquette

If you're like a lot of people, you spend time every day on Facebook. It's where you go to chat, see what's new, listen to music, play games, share photos, and find out what your friends had for lunch. Naturally, this offers new opportunities for bad manners and rude behavior. Since your Facebook is your online presence, you'll want to look and act your very best. Here's how.

Keep your status up-to-date. Your friends want to know how you are, where you are, and what you're up to. But they don't need to know every time you blow your nose, scarf a sandwich, or go wee-wee. Show some restraint and your updates will be much more valued.

Decide relationship status together. It takes two people to have a relationship and it should take two to decide how to describe that relationship. Unless you're a confirmed bachelor or bachelorette where your status is never in doubt, check with your boyfriend or girlfriend before posting your relationship status. Otherwise you risk coming across as too uncommitted or too forward, or, worse, committing the sin of dumping someone on Facebook.

Don't be snarky. If Facebook were meant for airing grievances, getting even, and starting fights, they would have called it Macebook. Social networking should be fun and uplifting. Save the grousing and verbal fisticuffs for private, personal, or face-to-face communications.

Avoid soap operas. You know how quickly drama spreads at school. News of a big breakup or blow-up races from one end of the building to the other like a fast-moving tornado. Facebook isn't group therapy. Psychoanalyze your friends and their dramas offline.

Don't be "like"-happy. Liking everything can make you look insincere and open the floodgates to you and your friends' News Feeds. If you "like" selectively, it will mean much more to you and others and you won't be barraged with updates.

Learn the culture. If you're new to Facebook, check out the pages of friends and people you like and respect. See what they're doing and what their pages look like. That way you'll learn the ropes without being knotty.

Play tag. Carefully. It's great to tag friends in photos. But make sure it's a photo they're okay with your having posted. And never use a tagline to put people down. If someone has tagged you in a photo you don't like, you can untag yourself to remove it from your profile. If it's really bugging you, ask whoever posted it to take it down from his or her page.

Don't gossip or spread rumors. With so many friends and mutual friends, you can't always know to whose News Feed your comments might travel. If you refrain from making malicious or catty remarks, you never have to worry about where they might end up.

Don't be a spoiler. People often use Facebook to announce big news: births, deaths, awards, parties, victories, college acceptances, engagements, etc. If you're in the know, there's a great temptation to spread the news about someone else yourself. Don't. Let your friends be the first to make their announcements. If you beat them to the punch you're stealing their thunder (this, grammar groupies, is what's known as a mixed metaphor).

Use your settings. If you're not careful, you can be swept away by a tsunami of likes, comments, statuses, chat requests, and notifications. Don't be afraid to use privacy and other settings to control the inflow and outflow. If someone asks about it, just breezily say, "I just have to do that so I don't O.D. on Facebook."

Don't be a downer. We all have bad days. But we don't all have to mourn our rotten existence on Facebook. Avoid sharing your misery in search of attention and sympathy: "I'm so bummed out! Worst day ever!! I hate my life!!! I hate everything!!!!" People don't want to read that and they don't know how to deal with it. By all means, don't bottle up those feelings. Tell a friend. See a counselor. Make a phone call. Just don't use Facebook as your shrink.

Be a cautious befriender. Facebook isn't a competition to see who has the most friends. Better to have 50 friends who mean everything to you than 5,000 you've never met. To keep your Facebook friendships meaningful, only friend people you know. If someone asks to friend you and you don't know who that person is, it's perfectly fine to say, "Have we met?" or "How do you know me?" If you want to friend someone you've never met, don't just send a request. Ask a mutual friend to introduce you, or send a message introducing yourself and why you'd like to become friends. Maybe you have a lot in common, or friends in common. Let the person know and you're more likely to have your request accepted.

Be careful what you post. You've probably heard that employers and college admissions officers check out applicants' Facebook profiles. It's true. Well, you think, I've got everything under lock and key with my privacy settings. They can't get to the really wild stuff. Maybe not, but what you have on your Facebook is only as private as your least discreet friend. Photos and comments and chats can be copied and saved elsewhere. What if a good friend this year becomes an angry friend next year? So that you never have to worry, don't post anything online that you wouldn't want an employer or a college admissions officer to see. (This is also why some teens create Facebook profiles under names that don't identify them.)

Reply to comments. Not every single one, but just enough to show people posting on your timeline that you're reading and appreciating what they write. Otherwise they'll feel like they're talking to a wall.

Think carefully about your profile. This is you. Online. Be yourself.

Use in moderation. Don't live through Facebook. Live your life and let Facebook be a fun and useful part of it. Nobody wants to end up being a Facebook addict and having to attend NA—Networks Anonymous.

And now, from the inquiring minds of genuine teenagers I surveyed . . .

20 DO'S AND DON'TS OF FACEBOOK ETIQUETTE

DO

- be positive, brief, and careful with what you post.
- say things that uplift people.
- use Facebook to stay connected to your friends.
- manage your profile and keep it clean.
- update your status (but don't write down your every step).
- write on your friends' timelines (but don't overpost).
- always be respectful—this is a public website.
- get someone's permission before you post or tag a questionable picture of him or her.
- be careful who you friend.
- avoid drama.

DON'T

- embarrass anyone with words or pictures.
- say things you wouldn't say face-to-face.
- write anything negative, mean, or sarcastic.
- spread gossip or rumors.
- harass or bully anyone.
- get into big fights with friends and make it public through the Internet.
- post desperate or depressed statuses (but be sure to talk to someone if you're upset!).
- post anything that might embarrass you later.
- let these sites define your social image.
- become obsessed with Facebook.

Parents and Facebook

Oh, nooooooooooooo. Your parents have asked to friend you. If you're okay with that, no problem. But if you're not, what should you do? Easy. Thank them for the friend request and then say something like, "You know I love you guys. But I'd like to have Facebook just for my friends and me. I'm sure you understand." And then be extra friendly and communicative in real life. If they say *Either you friend us or no Facebook for you, young lady,* they have you over a barrel. So friend them, and leave the *How Rude!* Code of Facebook Etiquette for Parents of Teens somewhere they will be sure to find it.

Dear Alex

"If someone sends you a friend request, do you have to accept?"

If the friendster-to-be is somebody you don't like or don't have a clue about, it's okay to ignore or delete the request. If it's someone you know a little bit, there's nothing wrong with accepting the request. No harm done and you might even make a new friend this way. Many people take a rather broad definition of "friend" on Facebook, so accepting a request doesn't have to mean you're best friends forever with the person. Just don't be phony about accepting requests for the sole purpose of upping your "friends number."

Dear Alex

"What do you do if you ignore someone who wants to friend you and they ask 'How come you haven't friended me?'"

This situation is similar to being asked out by somebody you don't want to go out with. Your best bet is to give a general, non-shaming reason. So you can say something like "I've decided to keep my friend list small." This may be problematic if you have 500 friends. So you could say "My friend list has gotten so big that I'm not adding anyone to it at this time." Or, "I'm trying to wean myself off of Facebook," or "I'm only adding my closest, closest friends," or "I like to restrict my friend list to people my own age." If there is a particular reason why you don't want to friend someone with whom you have an offline relationship, it's fine to explain your reasons (e.g., "I enjoy being your friend but your posts are too crude for my timeline").

THE HOW RUDE! CODE OF FACEBOOK ETIQUETTE FOR PARENTS OF TEENS

Dear Parents,

There are two types of offspring. Those who would welcome you as a Facebook friend, and those who would not. If your child belongs to the first category, take it as a great compliment and repay the kindness by minding your Facebook manners. If your child belongs to the second category, can I convince you not to send a friend request to your child? No? Can I convince you to respect your child's desire for privacy, to accept that older teens may want and need to close their Facebook door to you? No? You mean it's nonnegotiable? They must friend you if they're going to be on Facebook? Okay. Got it. But please follow the Code of Facebook Etiquette for Parents of Teens.

- Rejoice in this opportunity to enter your child's world. But remember that it is his world and you are there as an invited (or begrudgingly accepted) guest.

- Don't post on your child's timeline. No. Stop. Resist. Desist.

- Be a silent witness. Kids reach an age where they are very sensitive to being seen "in public" with you. Nothing is more public to your child than the Internet. Stay hidden. Think carpool. Sit back and read, listen, and learn. Let your child and her friends chatter away as if you weren't there.

- If you must post, be discreet. Remember that anything you post on his timeline will be seen by all of your child's friends.

- Talk with your child about the types of things she is okay with you posting.

- Never post a photo of your child on his page without asking permission.

- Never post a photo of your child on *your* page without asking permission.

➡

THE HOW RUDE! CODE OF FACEBOOK ETIQUETTE FOR PARENTS OF TEENS (CONTINUED)

- Don't use your child's timeline to post reminders. This is not the place to bug her about flossing her teeth after lunch.

- Hold your tongue. On your child's Facebook you will come across the good, the bad, and the OUTRAGEOUS. If it's something you can't overlook, something dangerous or hurtful, bring it up with your child in private at an appropriate time.

- Talk with your child about good judgment, online safety, consequences, and consideration.

- Google your child by name and screen name. This is a good way to discover what the public can see.

- Be the parent. While your child may privilege you with Facebook "friendship," you are not his "pal."

- Never send a friend request to your child's friends. Let them ask you.

- Don't comment on your child's friends' postings. Your child knows your values and will only get defensive. Unless you feel that a moral or legal line has been crossed, or your child or her friends are targets or perpetrators of bullying, let it go.

- Be a role model. Watch what you post on your own Facebook. Your children and their friends may have access to it. Make sure it reflects the values and good judgment you wish for in your children.

- Don't freak out if your child unfriends *you*. You trust your child to be out on his own in the real world. Just think of Facebook as another environment your child visits where you trust him to stay safe and make good decisions.

Dear Alex

"Is it okay to unfriend my ex-bf on Facebook?"

If it was an ugly, hurtful breakup, it's a natural thing to want to do and you'll get no argument from me. But if it was mutual, or just something that evolved without leaving a legacy of bad feeling, why not keep him as a friend? You may, indeed, still be friends. And, whatever happens, it sends a message to your other friends that you are a mature person who moves on in life without the need for payback. And, besides, if your ex remains a friend, he'll be sure to notice when you have a *new* boyfriend.

Dear Alex

"How many status updates a day should you make?"

Just enough so that your friends know the highlights, but not the minutia of your life. That could be a few times a day, or a few times a week. There's no set rule. If you're one of those folks who issues bulletins every two minutes ("Gonna make a sandwich"; "Feels like a whole wheat kind of day"; "Spreading the mayonnaise"; "A layer of ham, a layer of swiss, slather the mustard"; "Yum, yum"), get yourself a Twitter account.

Dear Alex

"Is it okay to say happy birthday on someone's Facebook?"

Sure. If it's someone you know really well, it's much more meaningful, though, to send them a card, give them a call, or take them out to do something special.

Atwitter About Twitter

In addition to providing the world with an amazing way to connect and communicate, Twitter's main accomplishment may be to demonstrate how much rudeness can be contained in 140 characters or less. You look at some of the things people tweet and you wonder *are they crazy?!* (Or, *are they drunk?!*) And then you've got people who think they're sending a private tweet that ends up going to 421,583 followers. YIKES!

If you don't want people to titter about you on Twitter, here's a tweet cheat sheet for proper behavior in the Twitter-sphere.

40 DO'S AND DON'TS FOR BEING
A POLITE TWITTER CRITTER

DO

- lurk until you get the hang of things.
- show interest in others.
- respond promptly to tweets and direct messages.
- use your tweets to show the best side of human nature.
- #hashtag with #care. #More than #2–#3 in a #tweet #makes #reading #difficult.
- proofread your tweets before posting them.
- tweet enough to let people know what you're up to, but not so much that people wish they *didn't* know what you're up to.
- fill in your profile and post a photo or avatar.
- feel free to block whomever you want.
- be aware that if you use somebody's Twitter handle in a tweet they will see that tweet.
- be positive—people don't like downers.
- beware of Too Much Information—nobody needs to know that you've had diarrhea all day.
- tweet things that make people think.
- tweet things that make people laugh.
- tweet interesting pics, reviews, news, blog posts, links.
- tweet catchy quotes: "I can resist everything except temptation"; "Be yourself. Everyone else is already taken" (Oscar Wilde).
- remember who can see your tweets.
- give credit where credit is due. If it wasn't your well-turned phrase, fabulous tip, hilarious comment, or insightful observation, it's polite to let people know where you got it from.
- be careful with abbreviations. Use them but make sure your tweet is easy to read and understand.
- be generous to your followers. Feature their ideas and tweets and encourage others to follow them.

DON'T

- be a narcissist: For every tweet about yourself, send 10 about something or someone else.
- overtweet. If you're witnessing dinosaurs stampeding down Main Street, by all means keep us in the loop. Otherwise, nobody needs constant updates on your every thought or activity.
- get into wars of words.
- tweet personal info (phone numbers, addresses, party dates/locations)
- feel you have to follow everyone who follows you. While it's polite to reciprocate, not all of your followers will be tweeting things of interest to you.
- feel your Twitter worth is measured by the number of followers you have. It's not a popularity contest.
- ask people to retweet you—unless it's for an important reason or charitable cause.
- clog the universe with airhead tweets like "Good morning, world."
- tweet in the company of others—most tweets can wait.
- retweet praise about yourself.
- share private information about others.
- share stuff about yourself you might later regret.
- feel you have to thank everyone who retweets or follows you. If someone has really done something special, thank them. Otherwise, use a group thank you to show gratitude to all those who retweeted your brilliant words or signed up as new followers.
- tweet others' news if you think they might want to be the first to announce it.
- tweet spoilers about the latest books, movies, or TV shows.
- tweet because you feel you have to. If it seems like a chore, maybe it's time to become a Twitter quitter and retreat from the tweet.
- tweet when angry—you can't undo a rant (even a short one).
- forget to provide relevant links that point followers toward more context or information.
- be rude or nasty.
- send a public reply to a direct message. Use direct messages to keep private things private.

IM Etiquette

Until people can have conversations with each other simply by reading minds, how handy to be able to talk back and forth in real time with a friend, or, if you're a gifted multitasker, with 47 friends! Naturally, so we can all IM as one big happy family, here are some etiquette guidelines IM going to tell you:

Knock, knock. It's always a good idea to "knock" first before starting a conversation. Ask, "Can you talk?" or "Is this a good time?" That way you'll know if someone's available.

Mind your own busy-ness. You can hang out a shingle that says "busy" or "away from keyboard" (AFK), or you can make up your own status message. If you're not available, say so and let the person know when you'll be free. And if someone else says he's busy, respect that and catch him later.

Say good-bye. If you have to go, don't leave someone hanging, not knowing whether the conversation is over or not. Wrap things up with a "sayonara" or G2G/GTG (got to go). If you're just disappearing for a short time, don't leave your IM buddies wondering if you've been eaten by a shark. Let everyone know that you'll BRB (be right back), or pick another acronym from the "BB" family: BBIAB (be back in a bit); BBIAS (be back in a sec); BBAIGTAP (be back after I go take a pee).

Give 'em time. Not everyone holds a land speed record in typing. Be patient. Conversations get confusing if you've fired off five thoughts before your friend has responded to the first. So give her time to respond.

Keep it short. It's not called *instant* messaging for nothing. Respect the medium. Keep your messages brief.

Be careful. As with emails and text messages, what you IM can be saved and sent around. Don't ever put anything in an IM that you wouldn't say in person or be comfortable with others seeing.

Don't sound off. You never know where your buddy is. He could be in school, or sitting on the toilet in a public restroom (why he'd have his tablet out is a good question, but you never know with some kids). To avoid embarrassment—both yours and his—don't ever send audio-enabled graphics without getting an "okay" first. Same goes for "buzz" features that make a sound to get somebody's attention.

ARLABMPWKWYTA. Not familiar with that one? It stands for "Avoid Ridiculously Long Acronyms Because Many People Won't Know What You're Talking About." If you're IM'ing adults or strangers, use proper grammar, punctuation, capitalization, and spelling. It's best, at least initially, to avoid emoticons, abbreviations, and acronyms. When the person replies, you can see what style he or she employs for IM communications, and adapt yours accordingly.

There's no font for sarcasm. Certain types of humor and tone don't come across well in written communications. It's too easy to misinterpret the meaning. If you need a smiley to make sure people catch your drift, well, then, you have my permission to use them—sparingly. But here's another idea: How about rewriting the sentence so you don't need a smiley or frowney or winkey or blinkey?

Be professional. You may want to create an IM screen ID just for messaging with adults, relatives, teachers, employers, etc. After all, "Pottymouth16" doesn't quite have the formality required for those types of communications.

Mind your multitasking. Some people can wash their hair, fix a sandwich, darn a sock, talk on the phone, write a term paper, put on makeup, shoot baskets, and carry on 12 IM conversations at the same time without missing a beat. If you're not one of the multiply gifted, consider limiting your multitasking so you can give each person the attention he or she deserves. IM conversations aren't fun if you have a long wait between each message. People know they're not getting your full attention and that can hurt feelings.

Is this the person to whom I am speaking? Keep in mind that the person you are messaging may not be the person using that device at that moment. Always begin an IM with something safe and harmless. Confirm the identity of the recipient before you get into anything personal.

Email Manners

No more postage or envelopes. Yay! No paper cuts on your tongue. Yay! No wondering where the flap has been before you lick its backside. Yay! No more yicchy glue aftertaste. Yay! While most of your online communicating may occur via texts, tweets, posts, private messages, or chat, there will be times when email is the way to go. So here's the lowdown for sending and receiving e-missives:

Protect addresses. Many people don't want their email address broadcast to the world. If you're sending an email to a long list of recipients, use the BCC (blind copy) feature (or whatever convention your email provider has for keeping addresses private).

Don't be too forward. In general, it's not polite to forward emails with personal content without permission from the sender. If somebody sends you something that you'd like to share with others, always get their okay before doing so.

Put a meaningful topic in the subject line. People often need to find old emails they've sent or received. If there's no subject or a vague one (e.g., Hi! Greetings!), you may have to wade through hundreds of emails until you find the one you're looking for. You can avoid that both for yourself and your recipients by putting specific, descriptive titles in the subject line (e.g., Biology 4 Lab Assignment).

Openings and closings. It's polite to start an email with a salutation. For formal correspondence, use "Dear." For more casual occasions, you can start with "Hello" or "Hi." If you're writing to several people, you can include all of their names in the greeting: "Hi, Curly, Larry, and Moe." For closings, you have many choices: "Love," "Sincerely," "Yours truly," "Regards," "Kind regards," "Kindest regards," "Best," "Best wishes," "Thanks," "Warmly," "Take care," "Ciao," "Cheers," "Hugs," "XOXO"; it all depends on your relationship to the person and the nature of the correspondence. Once an email thread has been established and you're writing back and forth, you can dispense with the salutations and closings. After all, now you're in a conversation.

Don't be an emoti-conman. With over 600,000 words available to all of us free of charge, can't we say what we mean without burping little bug-eyed faces all over the screen? Do we need to dumb down the language even more than it already has been? Shakespeare didn't write:

For never was a story of more woe, than this of Juliet and her Romeo :(

He didn't need little pixel-pusses to convey emotion. He did it with *words*.

Sometimes you may want to use emoticons to be sure your message is received as you intended. But relying too much on emoticons encourages lazy thinking and lazy writing. It's like sending someone a greeting card with a ready-made message instead of your own carefully chosen words. Which would you rather get from your true love?

Proofread your message. When using their phone to send email, more and more people are adding a message that says "Please excuse any mistakes in this message. It was sent from my phone." Among friends, you may agree to overlook typos, misspellings, sloppy grammar, and other errors. But for more formal correspondence, take the time to proofread your message. Otherwise the real message you're sending is: "I didn't think you were important enough to receive a perfect email from me."

Don't assume your message has gotten through. Systems crash. And, believe it or not, there are bozo-brains who send mail to the wrong address or forget to click "send" in the first place. If you don't get a response to one of your emails, check to see that your message was received *before* you assume that the intended recipient is an inconsiderate, slothful, procrastinating blockhead.

Count to 10. You get an email or text from a friend. You read it. You're furious and upset. You whip off a hurtful, accusatory reply and click "send." Later that day, you wonder if maybe you took what she wrote the wrong way, and maybe you were partly to blame, and maybe she didn't mean it the way you thought she did, and maybe what you wrote is only going to make things worse, and if only you could take it back. TOO LATE! Your message is long gone, the damage done. It's easy to hit "send" before you comprehend. Count to 10, or 100, or 10,000 before replying to an email or text message that upsets you.

Give people adequate time to respond. Email is so convenient that it's natural to expect people to drop whatever they're doing to reply to your missives. Be patient. If days pass without a response, send a polite follow-up query to be sure they got your message. If they did, they'll get your message.

Urban legends. A lot of urban legends get spread via email: Teens who park on Lover's Lane, hear a news bulletin on the radio about an escaped one-armed serial killer—and find a hook on their car door handle when they get home; people who wake up in a bathtub full of ice and discover a kidney has been removed; Internet companies that give away $5,000 to anyone who clicks on a Facebook link. Be suspicious. Fact-check before forwarding. Consider the source or you'll end up with egg on your face if you spread these around to friends.

TRUE STORIES

FROM THE MANNERS FRONTIER

Memail

It's easy to send email to the wrong person. Just the other day, I accidentally sent a message meant for Paula to myself! Imagine my surprise when I checked my email later in the day and discovered that I had new mail from—ME!

At least no harm was done. But if I had sent Paula's message to Pegeen by mistake—oh, boy, I'd be in big trouble. So be extra careful about what you write—and to whom you send it.

TRUE STORIES

MANNERS FRONTIER

Patience, Please

I once had a house that I wanted to rent out. I put a notice online. One morning I got an inquiry. Two hours later, when I hadn't yet responded, I got another email from the same person asking whether I had received his first email. Hmmm, I thought, a rather impatient fellow. Another two hours went by and, lo and behold, in came yet another email. In six hours' time I ended up getting four emails from this demanding, entitled person. When, later on the same day, I finally had a minute to answer his email(s), my response was, "Sorry, the place is not available." No way was I going to rent to such a pushy person. So, the moral of the story is, the nagging bird doesn't get the worm, er, lease.

"What do you say to a friend who always forwards dumb stuff to you?"

What you want to say is, "Stop forwarding such dumb stuff to me!" But no can do. Instead, explain that you're trying to cut back on your online time, and even though he is sending you funny and interesting things, could he please help you out by removing you from his mailing list. Making it seem like he's doing a favor for you softens any feelings of rejection he might have.

The Safety Net

As long as there are people, there will always be jerks. And if you go online, you may encounter the occasional Bad Apple—and by that I don't mean a Macintosh with a personality disorder.

There's no need to be paranoid, or to imagine that behind every pixel lurks a candy-bearing pervert who wants to entice you into an oven in his house in the woods. But you need to exercise the same caution online that you would in the "real" world.

Your parents have probably admonished you not to talk to strangers from the time you were old enough to understand. If, however, you're active on the Internet, you'll "talk" to strangers every day via email, blogs, social media, gaming, etc. The thing to keep in mind is that these people aren't necessarily who or what they say they are. Sometimes this is part of the fun—for example, in simulation games where players are encouraged to create characters for themselves. Occasionally, though, someone you meet online may be hiding behind a false front in order to scam, harass, or harm you. You can easily protect yourself if you follow a few basic rules:

Beware of false intimacy. The anonymity of online communication makes it very easy to share personal information that you would never reveal in a face-to-face conversation. While this has its rewards, it also has its risks. Watch out for PC-pals who get very friendly very quickly—people

410

who want to know what you look like, who want to meet you right away, who ask questions about your age, sexual interests, fantasies, or experiences, or who share theirs.

These are perfectly reasonable topics, and you might want to talk about them online. And there are certainly many kind, trustworthy, empathetic individuals—peers and adults—with whom you could safely share your thoughts, questions, or concerns. What you need to do is follow your instincts, just as you would in "real" life. If it feels weird, it probably is. And if it feels okay, it probably is. But just in case it isn't . . .

Never go alone to meet someone in person you've met online. Let's say you've met a fellow robotics enthusiast and he invites you over to his place to look at his robots. This could be a great opportunity and the start of a true friendship. Google him. Even if everything seems to check out, you can't be 100 percent sure who this person is. So, if you go to meet him, go with a friend. Go with several friends. Go with several BIG friends. Be sure your parents know where you're going and have contact information for the person you're meeting. Be sure the roboguy knows that your parents know where you're going. Good people won't be offended by your caution in checking them out. They'll understand and be impressed.

This doesn't mean you have to approach everyone as if he (or she) is a serial ax murderer. You may chat up someone through a school network, and it'll be obvious from her knowledge of teachers and fellow classmates that she's on the level. Or a friend may orchestrate an online introduction between you and someone they think you might like. In cases where you can check with someone you trust, or confirm that somebody is who he says he is, it's fine to arrange to meet in a public place without a phalanx of bodyguards.

Play your cards close to your chest. Sad to say, but wherever humans congregate, there are low-life weasels out to steal your money, identity, or innocence. You can avoid these sharks by keeping your address, phone number, school, birthday, and social security or other identification numbers to yourself. Don't give out credit card numbers unless you're buying something from a safe, known, encrypted site. Never tell anyone your passwords. Even friends. Change them often. (Your passwords, not your friends!)

Be alert to phishing scams and emails or pop-ups that say there's "fraudulent activity on your account," or "we're checking to confirm passwords," or "your computer is infected," and then ask you to click on a link to "verify" your details or eradicate the virus. If anyone asks for your password, report it to your system administrator.

Remember that your friends' address books and accounts can get hacked. You may get a communication purporting to be from a friend, which turns out to be bogus. If you're not sure, check with your friends to see if they actually sent the message before you click on any links or download any files.

Back up your files. In fact, make *two* sets of backups for important files. Keep one set at home. Keep the other set off premises—in your school locker, at a friend's house, or in cloud storage. This way, if there's ever a fire, burglary, or earthquake, or your house gets swallowed by a sinkhole, you'll still have your work safe and sound. Paranoid? Perhaps. But for the few seconds and few pennies this extra protection costs, isn't it worth it?

Use antivirus software. If your modem operandi is that of an active downloader, sooner or later you're going to get blasted with a virus. How rude! While more and more websites and email providers take protective measures to guard against viruses, phishing, scams, and spam, if you're not sure about, or comfortable with, the safeguards provided, protect your devices and files with appropriate software, passwords, and encryption.

Trolling for Trouble

Have you ever heard the term "flaming"? It doesn't mean setting some-one's computer on fire. Rather, flaming is the intentional posting to a public forum of aggressive, hostile, racist, bigoted, hateful, offensive, or inflammatory messages for the sole purpose of causing harm or pro-voking arguments. Such postings are known as flame-bait or trolls. The flamer then enjoys the malicious mayhem that results as more and more people take the bait and the flame war escalates into an online barroom brawl, an ugly digital duke-out of name-calling, accusations, insults, and attacks. And once the conflagration ignites it's difficult to put out the fire.

Another term for "flaming" is "trolling." The person who does it is a "troll." This makes sense as the formal definition of "trolling" is: *A style of fishing in which one trails a baited line through a likely spot hoping for a bite.*

For Internet trolls, "likely spots" for getting a "bite" would be discus-sion forums, blogs, news sites, hobbyist communities, Facebook, game chat, or video-sharing websites such as YouTube—anyplace where they can make public comments.

While some flame wars erupt from serious debates about controver-sial topics and remain grounded in some semblance of reason and civility, the typical troll is not invested in facts or logic. Hiding behind a mask of anonymity, these online arsonists get a rush from dominating or destroy-ing a discussion. So they toss verbal grenades by making extreme com-ments about politics, gender, religion, immigration, sexual orientation, women, celebrities, sports teams, n00bs, video games, operating systems, spelling, grammar—whatever they think will cause the most hurt, disruption, and ill will on that particular site.

You've probably seen this yourself. There could be a tragic news story about a child who drowns in a backyard pool. The first few posts will express sympathy, wish the family peace and healing, and offer reassurance that the child is dancing with angels. But mark my words, within a few more posts, some troll will say that God is punishing the parents for being atheists, or gay, or anti-gun, or pro-marijuana, or looking for insurance money—and a wild free-for-all will consume everyone and everything in its path.

So, here's how to respond to trolls:

Ignore them. There's no more powerful reply. Trolls want to start a fight. Don't give it to them. They won't respond to logic, reason, or etiquette. They won't let facts get in the way of their opinions. You can't appeal to their better nature because they don't have one. Some trolls may increase their nastiness if they realize they are being ignored. No problem. Just increase your ignoring!

"Do not feed the trolls." Not everyone recognizes the menacing nature of trolls. They don't realize that if you feed trolls, they grow stronger. Warn people so they won't let trolls lure them into their trap. If you don't rise to their bait, it's likely that the troll will get bored and look elsewhere for prey.

Block the troll. Depending on where the troll trails his line, you may be able to block messages from reaching you or other members of that community.

Rat the troll out. Online services and communities usually have procedures for reporting people who are violating that site's standards of civility or terms of use. If you encounter a troll who refuses to shut up or slink away, inform the moderator or follow the process for reporting inappropriate content or behavior. The site administrators will investigate and take action. This usually means blocking the troll's IP address, kicking him off of the system, or "muting" his posts so that they don't appear on the site.

Give the "maybe-he's-not-a-troll" the benefit of the doubt. Generally speaking, if someone looks and acts like a troll, he is a troll. But there's always the possibility that a participant is simply rude rather than rabid. Perhaps his comments were sincere but tactless. Perhaps English isn't his first language. Simply being wrong, boorish, or offensive doesn't automatically mean that someone has bad intentions.

If you think this might be the case, and you're feeling charitable, respond calmly to the offensive post. Restate or clarify your position if you think the person may have simply misunderstood you. Offer a correction. Point him toward earlier postings or a resource that addresses the issue. Explain why his message was inappropriate, inaccurate, and unwelcome. Be a model for respectful, reasoned debate that focuses on the issue and not someone's personality or intelligence. You'll find out soon enough from his response whether the person's intent was constructive or destructive.

But...

Don't get caught in the middle. Sometimes the person who tries to stop a flame war becomes everyone's target. If you advise flamers to take their dispute out of the group, you may end up with a plague from both their houses.

Gaming Without Flaming, Shaming, or Blaming

Takes place online? ✓
Allows anonymity? ✓
Encourages competition? ✓
Provides weapons? ✓
Promotes violence? ✓
Produces adrenaline? ✓
Spikes testosterone? ✓

Add it all up and you get online gaming. Rudeness, trash talk, profanity, and poor sportsmanship. Now, I suppose you can find that on a polo field, too. (Those horses sometimes have NO manners.) But, chances are you're going to see many more examples of rude behavior in the world of multiplayer online gaming. So here are some guidelines you can use to game without shame or blame:

Choose a good gamertag. A good one is easy to read and pronounce. Pick a name that you'll enjoy being known by. Some of you may want to choose gamertags that do not reveal your gender. Names that are obscene or offensive, or that relate to hate speech, drugs, illegal activities, or sexual topics are likely to get reported, or zapped by game enforcers, so don't bother with those. Many people find names written in leetspeak annoying. ("Leet" is an alternative online alphabet that uses symbols as substitutes for letters. For example, 1337 would be leet for "leet." @$$ would be leet for, well, figure it out.)

Be a good sport. Video gaming can be frustrating, challenging, and ego shattering. But nobody likes complainers who are always griping about weapons, kills, tactics, features, players, etc. And nobody likes sore losers. You've probably played with people who disconnect ("rage quit") from the game if they're losing, go around ganking novice players, make bigoted comments, laugh at defeated opponents, and brag about their own victories. Be a force for fun. Uplift the play. Don't take things personally. Forgive team members when they mess up.

Gloat not. If you've watched football, you know that there's a big difference between spiking the ball after a touchdown, and celebrating with cartwheels, fist pumps, climbing into the stands, free hot dogs, skywriting, and jigs that look like a cross between Irish line dancing and professional wrestling. The NFL even has a name for these over-the-top end-zone antics: "excessive celebration." When you or your team win, enjoy! But don't brag about it or trash talk your opponents for losing.

gg. You could spend the rest of your life reading what gamers believe about when or whether to say "good game" to their opponents at the end of a match. There's general agreement that it's bad manners to say gg to a losing player or team *before* they have lost. Many gamers believe the losing team should make the first move when it comes to saying gg. For the winning team to say it first could be considered smug. And if the losing team does say gg, it would be bad manners for the winning team not to reply in kind.

Many gamers think it's just good manners to say gg when the game is over, sort of like an Internet version of shaking hands after a game. It's a courtesy, not to be taken as a literal evaluation of the gaming experience and results. Other gamers take it very seriously. They will not say gg if it wasn't. And if someone has the nerve to say gg to them, they will respond by saying "no" or bg (bad game). Given the strong feelings gamers have about this issue, the best thing to do is: check out every game's culture and rules to see what the gg protocol is; and find your own comfort level with how you'd like to use gg.

Check out the rules. While etiquette can vary from one gaming community to another, most codes of conduct are pretty similar. Basically, be nice. Don't say anything or create content that discriminates, offends, or promotes violence based on race, gender, age, ethnicity, disability, religion, or sexual orientation. Don't encourage anyone to harm individuals, groups, or animals. Don't impersonate, bully, or defame anyone. Don't do or discuss anything illegal, obscene, or pornographic. Don't do or say anything that promotes terrorism, genocide, torture, illegal drugs, bomb making, identity theft, copyright infringement, fraud, tampering with hardware or software, etc. I know. There goes all the fun.

Be on time. Imagine a tennis match where you show up 30 minutes late. Same thing applies to gaming. Players have arranged their schedules to participate. Everyone being on time makes for the best teamwork and morale.

Be a team player. If you're on a team, cooperate with your teammates. Winning the game is more important than maxing your personal score. While a polite suggestion may be welcome, don't tell fellow gamers how to play. Everyone brings different skills and strategies to the game, and as long as your teammates are engaged, being polite, and trying hard, let them follow their own gut and learning curve. What you can do, though, is . . .

Be nice to n00bs. And even nicer to n00blets (*very* young n00bs). Whether it's spin the bottle or Monopoly, it takes a while to learn the ropes of a game you've never played before. Every game has its own rules, slang, acronyms, score-keeping, tactics, traditions, and nuances. Of course some n00bs can be obnoxious, attention-seeking know-it-alls who know nothing. And that can be annoying. Other n00bs will be polite and well-intentioned, but still mess up their play and your team's efforts. And *that* can be annoying. But shaming and ranting isn't going to solve the problem or help them become better players. So don't call them n00bs, b00bs, or rubes. Don't criticize or attack them. Mentor them. Say "I see that you're new to this game. Let me help you." If they're in way over their head, there's also nothing wrong with gently steering them to another game or encouraging them to play with friends at the same skill level.

n00bs, mind your manners. If you, young sir or mademoiselle, are a newbie, you've got a world of excitement awaiting. But be aware that newcomers can influence the play and enjoyment of their teammates and opponents. Any beginner, whether on a court, ski slope, or race track, will have an effect on more experienced competitors. So, look for gaming groups with players at your skill level. Keep an online gaming dictionary handy for the game you're playing. Get friends who are also newbies to play with you. And, if you're in with the big boys and girls, make an extra effort to be modest, polite, and grateful for advice you receive.

Camp with care. This doesn't mean bring your tent and sleeping bag to video games. Rather, it means that "camping"—a tactic most often used in first-person shooter games where a player hides in a safe location to ambush enemies without revealing his position—is a controversial strategy that often leads to ugly conflicts among players. Some players feel that camping is cheating and bad manners. Other players believe that camping is a perfectly legitimate and intelligent strategy that rewards players who have invested a lot of time in the game to learn the best defensive positions. Of course, if every player camps, there'll be no conflicts, which means there'll be no game. So, before you camp, try to get a sense of that game's culture and whether it is considered a respectable tactic or not.

Don't cheat. Of course you already know that. Any victories you achieve will be hollow and your legitimate game-playing skills will never improve. So this advice is really meant for all those flaming, gaming idiots who are so intent on winning that they'll do anything, no matter how unfair or dishonest, to vanquish their opponents. But they're not reading this book, so I guess this advice won't get to the people who need it the most. But, speaking of idiots . . .

Report griefers to service enforcers. Griefers are trolls who game. Ignore or block them. As with garden-variety trolls, griefers will not respond to penalties, rules, or reason since they play for the sole enjoyment of ruining the game for everyone else. Most games have guides and/or enforcers and a procedure for reporting serial griefers. The enforcers will look into that person's play and reviews and then take action. Since the response can include suspension or banning from the site, be sure you're reporting serious bullies and bigots, not someone who lost his cool for a few minutes.

Mute thyself. Don't you hate it when you're at the movies and someone right behind you is smacking his lips, sucking soda, unwrapping candy bars, and chomping on corn chips while you're trying to concentrate on the movie? Same thing applies when gaming. If you're playing a game with voice chat, mute your microphone when not speaking. Your fellow gamers do not want to hear your phone calls; screaming little sister; barking dog; mom asking about homework; loud music; sneezing; humming; temper tantrums; or potato chips.

Don't be a quitter. Since when, whether, and how you should leave a game before it has ended can vary from game to game, know the protocols for the game you're playing. In most games (although not all), it's considered bad manners to quit before the game is over or a clear victor has been declared. A premature disconnect can leave your team at a disadvantage. While there may be situations where you have to temporarily leave the game, try not to. And if you must absent yourself, don't just stop playing. Let teammates know you're about to step away so they can adjust their play or replace you with another player. And whatever you do, don't storm away from a game just because you're losing.

Protect your rep. Gamers debate whether player review systems are fair and/or effective. For example, you can review people you've played with based on such things as their language, game behavior, sportsmanship, and playing skill. You can keep track of those players you "prefer" and would like to play with again, and those you'd like to avoid. This supposedly influences who you might be matched with in future games. If you enjoyed playing with someone, give him positive feedback and send a friend request. And if you came across a creep, give him negative feedback and list him as a player you want to avoid. Be aware that player review features are different from complaint systems. If you simply want to register a thumbs up or thumbs down for people you've played with, use the review feature. If you want to report truly horrible behavior, follow the complaint procedures.

Of course, player review systems work both ways, and people with whom you play can leave reviews about you. If you follow a game's code of conduct, if you're friendly and polite, if you're a good sport and a good team player, you should be able to build an excellent reputation.

Cyberbullying

Cyberbullying is when someone uses technology—emails, IMs, texts, blogs, chat rooms, social media—to insult, harass, humiliate, and/or threaten someone else. It is the ultimate in bad manners and cowardice. While you can't get a broken nose from cyberbullying, you can get a broken heart. You can lose your confidence, your motivation, your sense of safety, your friends, and your belief in a bright and hopeful future.

Kids who cyberbully do it for different reasons. Some don't think they're bullying at all. In their minds, they are rightly getting back at someone for some real or perceived wrong they think was committed. Other kids who bully online do it for more typical reasons. They want to show their power, control others, and/or extort money or valuable objects from the target. They're looking for a reaction. They like an audience, and may brag about what they're doing. Still other kids who cyberbully may be bullied and picked on offline themselves. But if their Internet and computer skills are highly developed, they can get back *online* at the person bullying them *offline* in effective and anonymous ways. Sometimes kids who bully online work as a group—a clique of mean girls or boys who, egging each other on, go after somebody.

To know how to deal with cyberbullying, you need to ask a number of questions.

- What is the nature of the communication? Is it lewd language? An insult ("You're fat and ugly")? A vague threat ("You better watch out"; "You better not come to school tomorrow")? A serious threat of bodily injury or death ("You're going to DIE!" "You should kill yourself")?

- How frequent is the bullying? Did it occur once? More than once? Is it getting worse? Are more and more people participating in the bullying?

- Who's doing the bullying? One person? Several people? Do you know or think you know who is doing it?

- What form is the bullying taking? For example:

  - stealing your passwords

  - breaking into your accounts

  - posting mean comments on your blog

  - sending insulting, hateful, hurtful, or threatening texts, emails, or IMs

  - making death threats

  - encouraging you to harm yourself

  - sending or posting real or fake embarrassing/revealing photos of you online

  - creating a website to harm/shame you

  - revealing personal, private, and/or secret information about you

  - revealing your contact information so others can bully you

  - hacking into your computer and spreading viruses or worms

  - registering you with porn sites or email lists

  - impersonating you to send mean or insulting communications that provoke others into attacking you

  - creating fake profiles, blogs, or websites under your name

  - setting up a voting site with questions designed to humiliate you

  - provoking you into saying something rude or hateful and then reporting *you* as a bully

Your best initial response to a mild act of cyberbullying—a prank or teasing—is to ignore it. As with offline bullying, someone bullying online is often just looking for a reaction. If he doesn't get one, he'll eventually lose interest. And it's possible that the act, while hurtful, was stupid rather than malicious behavior, and won't be repeated.

If you respond with anger or threats of your own, *you* risk being accused of cyberbullying. And once you're in a cyberwar, who started it becomes irrelevant. You could even be reported to your Internet service provider for violating its terms of service.

If you continue to get unwanted and abusive communications, block the senders on your email and IM accounts. Block their phone calls and text messages. Make yourself invisible to buddy lists. Be sure you save or record the abusive texts, tweets, photos, messages, blog entries, etc., for documentation. You want to preserve the electronic evidence. It's also smart to Google your name and screen names. This will give you a better idea of the extent to which you are being talked about online.

At this point you should definitely tell an adult about the bullying. Talk to your parents; a teacher, advisor, or counselor at school; or another trusted adult. The school should know that this bullying is taking place. While more and more states are passing anti-bullying legislation, if it is all happening outside of the school day and off school grounds, the school may not have the legal authority to discipline a student who is cyberbullying. But it is important that they be informed as there may be other things they can do to help, such as talk with the student's parents, offer awareness campaigns, and/or provide counseling.

Report cyberbullying to service providers and site administrators. Many social networking sites are now taking an active stance against cyberbullying by introducing anti-bullying tools and filters, clear procedures for reporting offenders, and "safety centers" with resources, support, and guidance to help kids respond to cyberbullying.

If the cyberbullying is serious and/or escalating, you should report it to the police. Taking legal action is another option, especially if you know who is behind the bullying. Lawsuits, though, can take years and cost many thousands of dollars. It's an expensive and stressful approach, but just the threat of it may be enough to get the bullying to stop.

If you're being cyberbullied:

- Trust yourself. If it feels wrong, hurtful, or threatening, it is cyberbullying and it must stop.

- Don't ever respond to the person bullying you. That just starts a war and opens you up to charges of bullying or making threats.

- Tell someone. A friend, sibling, parent, or trusted adult needs to know.

- Get support. This is a time for your friends to rally round you.

- Report the bullying. Tell your school. Tell a website host or site administrator that someone has created a website or page about you or is using your name. They may be able to remove it.

- Protect your information and accounts. Use all the privacy and blocking settings at your disposal.

- Protect your identity. Never reveal your name, address, phone number, date of birth, school, or other personal information unless it is to someone you know well and you are in a protected and private online area. Don't post photos with a license plate number, school hoodie, or identifiable landmarks that might provide clues to where you live or go to school.

- Save everything. You want to have documentation for evidence should school officials, police, or attorneys get involved.

- Get a fresh start. Close your accounts. Open new ones with new screen names, IDs, email addresses, and phone numbers.

Dear Alex

"A good friend of mine is getting cyberbullied. We think we know who's doing it. How can I help her?"

Your friend is lucky to have you looking after her. There are a number of things you can do:

1. Listen to your friend. Give her a warm shoulder to cry on.

2. Show your concern. Let your friend know that she doesn't have to go through this alone.

3. Recruit backup. Get other friends to step up. You don't want your friend to feel alone with the bullying.

4. Resist the urge to respond to the bullying emails, texts, or IMs. This will only inflame the situation.

5. If the bullying has just started, might be unintended, and/or is mild, consider talking to the kid doing the bullying. Go with your friend or in a group. Tell the person that you know she is doing it and if it doesn't stop you'll report her.

6. Report the person if the behavior continues. Tell a parent or other trusted adult; tell the school; tell the person's Internet service provider.

7. Make sure your friend is doing everything on the list on pages 420–421: telling an adult; getting support; reporting the bullying; protecting her accounts and identity; saving everything; and opening new accounts if necessary.

8. Keep checking in. If the bullying continues, you need to continue to support your friend.

Chapter Quiz

What do these emoticons mean?

1. { : - - - - - - - - -

   a) My nose is running.

   b) I told a fib.

   c) I was a lollipop in a previous life.

2. { : -
   |

   a) I love to pump iron.

   b) I was born with a pole through my head.

   c) I have *very* large ears.

3. { : >>>>>

   a) I'm gonna hurl lunch.

   b) Each of my five chins has a goatee.

   c) I just swallowed a V-chip.

4. (: -)

   a) I have two ping pong balls stuffed in my cheeks.

   b) I'm going to huff and puff and blow your house down.

   c) Do you like my earrings?

5. : (l)

   a) Don't call me monkey face.

   b) My lips are sealed.

   c) My tongue got run over by a steamroller.

CLOTHES-MINDED

You Are What You Wear

Each day, when you wander to your closet, dresser, or Everest-size heap of clothes on the floor, you're not just deciding what to wear. You're deciding what you want to tell the world about yourself. When you walk out the door, your clothes will say:

"I'm cool" or *"I'm trying to be cool."*
"I take pride in my appearance" or *"I'm a slob."*
"I spend a lot of money on clothes" or *"I'm a wardrobe cheapskate."*
"I want to be noticed" or *"I want to blend in."*
"I'm trying to look older" or *"I'm trying to look younger."*
"I respect social traditions" or *"I thumb my nose at society."*

Of course, your clothes might also say:

University of Chicago
Camp Crystal Lake
Fruit of the Loom
My parents went to Tobago and all I got was this lousy T-shirt.

Clothes can tell you whether someone is a police officer, Girl Scout, aging hippie, soldier, flight attendant, nurse, convict, businessperson, or baseball player. And because clothes make such powerful statements, the way you dress can be a source of conflict with your parents, teachers, peers, or employers. So let's take a look at some of the issues involved.

Why Clothes Matter

Why does everybody make such a big deal about clothes? If you wear certain things, it's because you like them, right? Not because you're angry or rebelling or making a statement. As long as you're not going around naked, why does it matter what you wear?

It matters because clothes are symbolic. They make a statement about your attitudes, status, and self-image, even if that's not your intent. When you say that you "like" certain clothes, what do you like about them? Probably the way they look and feel. Which means that you like the way they make *you* look and feel. Consciously or not, you're attracted to the associations those clothes trigger in your mind: *I'm artistic; I'm tough; I'm laid back; I'm sexy; I'm politically correct; I'm totally uninterested in clothes.*

Because clothing is an external, visual representation, there's no way you can avoid being judged by what you wear. Before the first word pops out of your mouth, your clothes and appearance have already said quite a bit about you. The problem is, what they say may not be true. For example, you could go out this afternoon, shave your head, get a swastika tattoo, put on boots and camouflage gear, and the world would think you're a neo-Nazi skinhead. You'd still be

Fashion Tip for Teens #1:

Always wear an apron while barbecuing in gym class.

Fashion Tip for Teens #2:

Beachwear should never be worn in church.

Fashion Tip for Teens #3:

Remove all piercings before stepping through airport security.

your same sweet self, but your image would say otherwise—and people would react accordingly. This is why the first thing a defense attorney does is a client makeover. The serial murderer who, when arrested, looked like a cross between Bigfoot and the Big Bad Wolf will enter the courtroom looking like a choir boy on his way to church.

You have the right to dress any way you like. But if you defy social standards, as is your privilege, people will make judgments accordingly, as is their privilege. It's up to you to determine whether what you wear will hurt you or help you.

Dear Alex

"I wear nice clothes, but I never feel that I look good. It's not like I'm ugly. I just don't like the way I feel."

You probably look wonderful. But what can you do to help yourself feel that way?

First, you need to recognize that the way people feel involves much more than the clothes they wear. Feeling smart and snazzy is a function of self-confidence, personal hygiene, and overall mental and physical health. To get a handle on the source of your malaise, write down as many words as you can to describe how you feel. Then analyze them.

Do the words suggest that your problem is one of *attitude* (you feel "uncool," "dumb," "ugly," "self-conscious")? Or one of *grooming* (you feel "sticky," "itchy," "frizzy," "smelly")? Or that the problem may be *physical* or *health-related* (you feel "uncoordinated," "tired," "depressed," "achy")?

If the problem seems to originate in your head, that's where you should go to look for a solution. You don't feel you look good because you don't feel good about *yourself*. Teenagers often get down on themselves because of the pressures of measuring up. Get a reality check from a close friend, a sibling, a parent, or an adult you trust. Talk to your school counselor. Explain how you've been feeling. Find out why you're so hard on yourself, then work to improve your self-esteem.[*]

If the problem seems to be one of grooming, you may need to wash, shower, and clean your hair more often. Try new body gels, lotions, powders, and scents. Take a toothbrush to school and brush after lunch.

If you think the way you feel has to do with your overall health, see a doctor. You may have a physical problem that's sapping your energy and making you feel dull. You may have mono or a low-grade infection. You may be depressed and need some counseling or medication. You may need to work on your posture, exercise more, or change your

*SEE PAGE 469 FOR IDEAS ON HOW TO BUILD SELF-ESTEEM.

eating habits. Get your eyes checked. See a dentist. All of these things can affect the way you feel.

Finally, experiment with the clothes you wear. Different clothes have different "feels." For example, heavy boots may be in, but you might feel snappier if you don't clunk around in 20 pounds of footwear. Try being dressier. Or more casual. Try looser clothes or tighter clothes. Try fabrics that are softer or starchier. You may discover that a change in look will create a change in the way you feel.

Dear Alex

"There's a girl at school who wants to be friends with me. I'm popular and I like her, but she wears the most uncool clothes. People tease her a lot, and I'm afraid if I hang out with her they'll tease me, too. How can I tell her without being rude that she has to change the way she dresses if she wants to have friends?"

Assuming that the girl you describe is neat and clean in her grooming, and that her clothes, while not in keeping with prevailing fashion fads, are presentable and appropriate for school, the dilemma you face presents you with a choice—one that you're likely to encounter repeatedly throughout life:

1. Do you allow the snobbish, intolerant standards of a peer group, in combination with the fashion industry's self-appointed arbiters of taste, in cahoots with greedy clothing manufacturers using child slave labor, to dictate what's important to you and who your friends are?

OR:

2. Do you stand up for the right of people to be judged on who they are and what they do rather than on how they look?

As you can see, this isn't about clothes. It's about *values*.

There's no polite way to tell someone you don't like the way she dresses. What you *can* do, though, is work both sides of the issue. You can tell your friends that the girl is really a lovely person and they shouldn't judge her because of her clothes. If you're popular, your opinion should carry some weight. At the same time, as you get to know the girl, you can find out more about how she feels about her dress and image.

The next time you go shopping for yourself, invite her along. The conversation will naturally include talk about clothing likes and dislikes, and you'll get a better understanding of her situation. Maybe her family can't afford to buy her the latest clothes. Maybe she feels perfectly fine about what she wears. Maybe she's clueless about how to create a look.

Depending on what you learn about her, you may want to suggest a makeover—gently, discreetly, and politely. This could build a friendship and help a friend. Or you might find yourself back at square one, having to decide between friendship and fashion.

The Age of Entitlement: Choosing Your Own Clothes

When should children be able to choose their own clothes? Generally, they should be given some say when they're old enough to dress themselves. At this tender age, they'll be malleable to their parents' definitions of practicality and good taste. Parents should take advantage of this opportunity to imprint proper standards of dress on their offspring, who can usually be satisfied with being allowed to decide whether they want choo-choo trains or dancing bears on their pajamas. It's only when they get older that they'll question whether they want pajamas at all.

Children old enough to go shopping by themselves come under a different set of rules: those of the Parent-Child Dominant Peer Group Appropriate Dress Treaty. Briefly stated, this pact stipulates the following:

1. When in the company of peers, the child may dress any way he or she likes (within some semblance of reason).

2. When in the company of parents, the child must conform to adult interpretations of appropriateness.

3. When in the company of both peers and adults, the decision goes to whichever generation can make a better claim for ownership of the event.

In other words, a child accompanied by parents to a school basketball game would be permitted to dress as he wishes. A child accompanying her parents to an office picnic would have to dress in accordance with their wishes.

Dear Alex

"My mother insists on going clothes shopping with me. (I'm 15.) We have these big arguments because she won't let me get any clothes with designer names or company logos. I don't think this is fair."

You're right. It isn't fair. Calvin Klein has to pay through the nose when he puts a 12-story underwear billboard on Times Square. Why should teenagers provide advertising space for free?

But fairness isn't the issue here, and it's not a good argument to pose to parents (who are likely to reply "So what? Life isn't fair"). Your goals for any clothes-buying trip with your mother should be to:

- avoid needless argument
- show that you're willing to be financially aware and responsible
- end up with a wardrobe that makes you both happy

As a first step, take an inventory of your closet. Determine the articles and outfits you'll need to purchase for the next six months or year. Divide these into two categories:

1. those you'll wear primarily in the company of your peers
2. those you'll wear primarily in the company of adults

Next, establish with your mother a budget for each category. Then approach her with this proposal:

As long as you stay within budget and reason, Category #1 items are yours to buy without your mother's approval, and Category #2 items are to be selected jointly, with your mother's wishes given priority.

In addition, you're free to use your allowance or earnings to buy clothing of your own choosing.

This solution is likely to work because:

- it respects both viewpoints (yours and your mom's)
- it recognizes that teenagers and adults have different tastes and operate in different worlds
- it requires maturity, compromise, and generosity of spirit on everybody's part

In other words, *it's fair.*

Dear Alex

"How much should a clothing allowance be?"

Let's acknowledge that not all parents wish to give their children clothing allowances or can afford to do so. If your parents do and can, your clothing allowance should be enough to buy everything you need, but not everything you want, with a little left over for something you'd really like.

Dear Alex

"Do you see anything wrong with boys wearing an earring?"

I see absolutely nothing wrong with boys wearing a discreet earring—as long as it doesn't look like a Calder mobile and is worn according to the terms of the Parent-Child Dominant Peer Group Appropriate Dress Treaty (see page 428).

In fact, I've often thought it unfair that women can adorn themselves with any number of rings, necklaces, baubles, pearls, diamonds, earrings, and brooches while men must make do with a lousy tie tack.

The Big Three Clothing Categories

You probably have a regular uniform of jeans, hoodie, and sneakers. Or cutoffs, T-shirt, and sandals. Or khakis, polo shirt, and boat shoes. Or mini skirt, graphic tee, and flip-flops. But the day will come before too long (if it hasn't already) when you'll be required to wear something else.* For example, you might receive an invitation in the mail with the words "Black tie," "White tie," or "Black tie optional." Rather than stand before your closet in quiet desperation, read on.

Most people recognize three categories of clothing: *casual, semiformal,* and *formal.* Trying to define them is a bit like trying to define *inexpensive, moderate,* and *expensive* in relation to restaurant prices. The boundaries are fuzzy and constantly subject to debate. In fact, one could argue that there are really 14 categories, which, in descending order of dressiness, are:

*PRUDENT POINTERS ON PROPER ATTIRE HAVE ALSO BEEN PROVIDED IN PREVIOUS CHAPTERS. YOU MAY WISH TO PERUSE PAGES 51–52, 166, AND 229.

14. coronation stuffy formal

13. inaugural populist formal

12. white-tie ultraformal

11. black tie

10. lowbrow formal

9. Hollywood formal

8. high semiformal

7. traditional semiformal

6. nontraditional warm-climate semiformal

5. dressy casual

4. standard casual

3. grungy casual

2. grungy

1. "Where do you think you're going dressed like that?"

But we'll stick to the Big Three.

Casual

Generally speaking, *casual* refers to your nicer everyday clothes—the types of things you'd wear to school, the dentist, a recital, and your mom's office. These include khakis, sport shirts, sweaters, slacks, blouses, and skirts. I'd even include jeans if they're not torn, frayed, or worn.

Most people allow themselves one or more categories of dress below casual—the kinds of things you'd wear to clean out the basement, mow the lawn, or hang around the house or the beach, including T-shirts, shorts, scruffy jeans, cutoffs, and tank tops.

Parents are usually satisfied to be seen at the supermarket or the doctor's office with children in casual dress. Casual clothes don't have to mean casual manners.

Semiformal

To most people, *semiformal* means dresses for girls, suits and ties for boys. (The arguments begin when someone asks "Well, then, what do you call it when a boy wears a navy blue blazer, a white shirt, a tie, gray flannel slacks, and dress shoes?" Call it "spiffy" and leave it at that.) Thus, teenagers would wear semiformal clothes to school dances, fancy dinners out, job interviews in the business world, etc.

Parents may require semiformal dress when taking their children to a concert, an office holiday party, a worship service, or to meet their friends.

Formal

Formal refers to long dresses for girls and black tie for boys. Formal is harder to define for girls than for boys. This is because the fashion industry changes the lengths, colors, fabrics, and styles of women's clothing almost daily. For men, *black tie* means formal evening wear—black dinner jackets with the shiny lapels, white shirts with studs instead of buttons, black pants with zippy stripes running down the sides, cummerbunds, black bow ties, shiny black shoes—you know the look. One would never, ever wear this during the daytime (with the possible exception of attending the Academy Awards).

Even more formal for evening wear is *white tie.* This is the outfit that makes you look like a butler. You trade in the black tie for a white one and wear a long jacket with tails.

Formal wear during the day is called *morning dress.* This doesn't mean you have to put on a dress. It means wearing a *cutaway*—a long coat with striped gray trousers. This is what you'd wear if you were an usher at a formal daytime wedding.

Black tie optional indicates that the hosts couldn't make up their minds what they wanted. This shouldn't be confused with Clothing Optional.

In general, formal wear isn't considered appropriate for young men under the age of 18, so why are we even discussing it?

The Three Categories of Dress

| Casual | Semiformal | Formal |

Dear Alex

"I hate wearing ties. Does etiquette say I have to wear them? What purpose do they serve?"

Historically, etiquette has said a great deal about clothing, most of which may be summarized by one simple statement: *The more uncomfortable, the better.* This has been demonstrated down through the ages by such bizarre inventions as powdered wigs, corsets, suits of armor, wool underwear, lederhosen, thongs, bustles, high-heeled shoes with pointy toes—and neckties.

Ties serve absolutely no purpose.* So how did they come about? In the 1660s, Croatian soldiers wore scarves around their necks. Nobody seems to know why. The French thought this a delightful touch, and soon began to sport long, knotted-at-the-neck scarves themselves. The fad spread to England, where Charles II made it a fashion staple of the court. The citizens of London, who had just endured a great plague and fire, needed something to take their minds off of death and destruction. Neckties provided it, and the rest, as they say, is history.

*ALTHOUGH IN A HURRICANE YOU COULD ALWAYS USE ONE TO LASH YOURSELF TO A TREE.

Men began wearing neckties for formal, ceremonial, and business-oriented occasions. As a result, ties came to symbolize respect and professionalism. Of course, this was all arbitrary. If history had gone a little differently, wearing a dollop of molasses on your nose could just as easily have been the means of conveying such a message.

Today, etiquette doesn't require you to dress up in stiff formal clothes and be uncomfortable. It requires you to dress appropriately. And that means making sure that the symbolism of your clothes is in keeping with the occasion. Thus, it's just as much an error to wear a jacket and tie to a swim class as it is to wear a bathing suit to church or temple.

Formality doesn't have to be boring or uncomfortable. You can always add a dash of your own individuality to any outfit. Try a splash of color or reinterpret an old symbol in a new and unique way. For example, I once wore a white, double-breasted linen suit with a delicate green pinstripe to an outdoor summer wedding. Only instead of a conventional shirt and tie, I wore a white, open-collared shirt with a light orange knit tie loosely knotted around my neck like an ascot. I can't tell you how many marriage proposals this generated.

School Uniforms

Should children and teenagers be required to wear uniforms in school? (That is, other than jeans, hoodies, T-shirts, and baseball caps?) Depends on who you ask. Some school authorities have decided that the only thing wrong with our educational system is the way kids dress. So, instead of dealing with crumbling buildings, overworked teachers, inadequate resources, and parental apathy; instead of demanding that communities and politicians address the relationship between poverty, crime, drugs, dysfunctional families, and the discipline and learning problems of kids, what do they do? They send parents and kids on a shopping spree to the mall.

Proponents of uniforms claim that academic performance increases, and disciplinary problems decrease, when schools make kids dress alike. This may be true. *But it's not because of the uniforms.* It's because schools that require standardized dress are likely to be schools where teachers and administrators respect students and expect them to behave responsibly, where parents are involved in their children's education, where conflict resolution, peer mediation, and anti-bullying programs are in place, and where community values are articulated and enforced—in short, where the school climate is based on the highest principles of good manners.

If you took away the flannel pants, those schools would function just as well (although kids might complain about their legs being cold).

Children and teens opposed to school uniforms claim that they infringe upon their inalienable rights to life, liberty, and the pursuit of designer labels. Fashion, they say, is a means of self-expression—it's their very individuality. What some of these libertarians overlook is that freedom of dress, like other freedoms, must be exercised responsibly. The role of fashion in determining school pecking orders can be so extreme that kids spend more time each day choosing outfits than doing homework. Families that can barely put food on their table buy $150 sneakers so their child won't be a social outcast. When the symbolism of clothing is used to convey disrespect, promote snobbery, exclude, and embarrass, this is neither well-mannered nor conducive to a positive school climate.

Ultimately, the issue of school uniforms is one of politics, pedagogy, and power, not etiquette. If students don't want to be dressed alike, they should stop shooting each other over their clothes and stop judging each other by the price of their jeans. And if school authorities want to do a makeover, let them do it on the school rather than on the student.

Hats in School

You may have heard that a number of schools are banning baseball caps inside the building. Your own school might be among them. Some students are asking "Does this violate our rights? Should we take the school board to court?" These students are missing the point. This isn't a legal issue, it's an *etiquette* issue.

Baseball caps are grand. They're functional, jaunty, and, when worn with the visor to the rear, they make you look like your head's on backwards. Personally, I'm all for them—just not in school.

Why not? *Because etiquette demands that gentlemen remove their hats when they are indoors.* This makes sense. Hats were designed to:

1. keep your head warm

2. protect you from sun and precipitation

3. keep your hair from blowing all over creation

4. hide baldness

Since you're not yet follicularly challenged, your only justification for wearing a hat would be to protect you from the elements. Unless your school has no roof, it would be inappropriate to wear a hat in the classroom.

Your school may have additional reasons for not wanting students to wear hats indoors. For one thing, a hat prevents teachers from seeing your eager little face. It's not very rewarding to teach a class of visors.

Caps also make it hard for teachers to identify students when they raise their hands. It depersonalizes the learning environment if students are referred to as Bulls, CAT, John Deere, and Red Sox.

Your school may also be concerned about gang warfare. The color or tilt of a cap can be used to identify oneself as a member of a particular gang, or to challenge someone in another gang. Wear the wrong cap and you could end up getting beaten or shot. This is disruptive to the educational process. If nobody is allowed to wear caps, it eliminates the problem—at least within the school building.

The final reason for banning baseball caps in schools is a practical one: As your head fills with knowledge, it must have room to expand.

Dear Alex

"I know you're not supposed to wear hats at church or inside someone's house, but is it okay to wear them inside stores and other public places where nobody knows you?"

Once and for all, here are the rules about hats:

A gentleman, regardless of his age, is expected to take off his hat indoors. Indoors means houses, places of worship, restaurants, stores, elevators, theaters, schools, airports, trains, tanning salons, etc. This is considered a sign of respect. The only exceptions are:

- A gentleman may wear his hat at indoor sporting events such as hockey games or wrestling matches, even while brawling.

- A gentleman may keep his hat on in spaces which, while indoors, serve "outdoor" functions (e.g., a shopping mall concourse, train station platform, or glass-sheltered bus stop).

- A gentleman may keep his head covered indoors if the traditions of his religion require it.

A lady may keep her hat on indoors (even in churches, restaurants, and private homes) provided she is dressed up in formal daytime clothes. Hats worn on these occasions usually look like fruit baskets or nesting birds. Ladies may also wear hats during dressy evening events. These hats are more elegant. The exceptions for women are:

- A lady may not wear a hat indoors at her own home.

- A lady may not wear a baseball cap indoors. This is because baseball caps are considered unisex and women wearing them must abide by the same rules that apply to men.

Well-Mannered Warnings

How do you tell someone that his fly is open? Or that her skirt is caught in her underwear? Or that a friend has unwittingly committed some other sartorial slip-up?

Carefully and discreetly, as follows.

If you know the person very well, you can say (mix-and-match as appropriate):

"Sweetums,		fly		full of lint."
"Honeybunch,		zipper		undone."
"Darling,	your	bellybutton	is	falling off."
"Dogface,		slip		showing."
"Dad,		strap		coming apart."

If you don't know the person well (or at all) and the problem is non-embarrassing, you can tell him or her regardless of your sex. This would apply to things like buttons about to fall off, belts caught in car doors, labels showing, etc.

If the problem is of an intimate or personal nature (i.e., involving clothing or body parts considered "private"), it's best to have someone of the same sex deliver the news. This lessens the embarrassment quotient. Thus, a male could approach another male on a subway and say:

"Excuse me, sir, in case you weren't aware of it, I thought you might like to know that your fly is open."

If, however, you're a male and you see a woman in need of a private word, you can go up to an approachable-looking female and say:

"Excuse me, Ma'am, I wondered if you'd feel comfortable letting that woman know that her skirt is caught in her undergarments."

Braces

If you wear braces, you've probably already been the butt of jokes. Your friends make fun of you because exhibiting extreme cruelty toward peers is one of the favorite leisure activities of the young and the restless.*

It's only natural that braces draw a certain amount of attention. Adults are famous for such stunning observations as "Oh, you got braces." This is not said out of rudeness, it's said out of shock. They see the bulk of a family's financial assets in a child's mouth and think *There but for the grace of an overbite go I.*

*IT'S MY SINCERE HOPE THAT THIS BOOK WILL CUT DOWN ON THAT DEPLORABLE PRACTICE.

When your peers call you "tinsel teeth" or hum the *Jaws* theme in your honor, don't take the bait. Flash a sparkling smile and say "Yes, I'm so glad I've gotten braces. My teeth will be beautiful." By placing subtle emphasis on the word "my," you can suggest the obvious implication without being rude.

As a wearer of braces, however, you have certain responsibilities. You must conduct all maintenance tasks in private. This means never removing or installing retainers at the dinner table, in the classroom, or anyplace else where spectators are present. Equipment should be kept out of sight and therefore out of mind. Would you want to have your grandfather's false teeth staring at you from his butter plate all through dinner?

Dear Alex

"Is it okay to ask someone about their braces? Or is that like asking someone about a disability?"

Wearing braces isn't considered a disability, except in the presence of saltwater taffy. Polite inquiries ("Who's your orthodontist?" "How long do you have to wear them?") are perfectly appropriate for casual conversation among peers and/or fellow sufferers, er, wearers.

Umbrellas

Teenagers don't seem to use umbrellas much. Maybe it's because they're more rain-resistant than adults. Or maybe it's because they figure *Why bother? When I take one it never rains. And when I don't, it does! So I can't win either way.* True, true. But just in case you do find yourself with an umbrella in the middle of a downpour, here are some *parapluie* pointers:

Try not to poke anyone's eye out. If you're carrying an umbrella, particularly on a crowded sidewalk, you need to constantly adjust its height, tilt, and wind expansion vector so you don't gouge an eyeball or collide with another umbrella. Watching a procession of hundreds of bobbing umbrellas on a crowded sidewalk can be quite inspiring, as it reminds the viewer of what humans can accomplish through cooperation. It's also an excellent exercise for developing hand-eye coordination.

Unfurl your umbrella *after* you step outside. Most buildings have awnings or overhangs that permit you to do this without getting wet. You've probably heard that it's unlucky to open an umbrella indoors. This has nothing to do with superstition. Rather, it has to do with the reaction you'll incur from the innocent bystander whose cheek you stab. When carrying an umbrella indoors, keep it close to you.

Know how to share. When the umbrella is used to shield more than one person, it should be held by the taller of the two, unless one person enjoys walking with his or her arm extended at full mast. It's perfectly fine to offer shelter to a stranger. Particularly one you hope to know better.

Know how to shake. Humans shaking water off of their umbrellas should follow the same rules as dogs shaking water off of their coats, namely:

1. Do it away from people.

2. Do it outside. When approaching a building or residence that has an overhang, shake the umbrella before entering. In a public building such as a mall or a bank, you may also shake it indoors if the building has an entry vestibule or rubber-floored area clearly intended as a transition between outside and inside. Umbrellas shouldn't be shaken once you've stepped into a private residence or restaurant. Instead, look for an umbrella stand or ask your host or maitre d' where it would be best to berth your bumbershoot.

Chapter Quiz

1. *Tight clothes shouldn't be worn by teenagers because:*

a) they cut off circulation

b) they take too long to wiggle in and out of

c) they make parents insanely jealous

2. *You have a clothing allowance of $100 a month. The best way to spend it is on:*

a) candy

b) a pair of sequined underwear

c) overpriced designer items that will be out of fashion in three weeks

3. *You arrive at a school dance to discover that you are waaaay overdressed. Your best bet is to:*

a) crawl under the refreshments table

b) grab the school banner and turn it into a toga

c) find a kid wearing VERY baggy pants and ask if you can jump in

4. *The purpose of a tie is to:*

a) make you late for dressy occasions

b) keep your Adam's Apple from dropping down your throat

c) secure your head to your body in the event of high winds

5. *Your school has just announced that all students must wear a uniform. The proper response is to:*

a) refuse to wash yours

b) wear your Spiderman pajamas underneath it

c) dye it pink and say your dog did it

6. *Your friend's family has invited you to spend a weekend with them at a nudist camp. As a first-time guest, it's best to bring:*

a) a bathing suit

b) a bathrobe

c) the bare minimum

13

AHH, AHH, AHH— CHOOOOOO!!!!

Body Talk, Hygiene, and Disgusting Habits

The body is a marvelous, miraculous invention. For centuries, it has inspired great works of art, dance, literature, and Spandex. It's capable of breathtaking feats of skill and endurance. Is there anything else on the planet that can do a three-and-a-half double-reverse gainer, leap across a stage while singing Italian, scarf down 14 cheeseburgers at a sitting—and then go home to reproduce itself? Yes, bodies should be celebrated and well cared for. They are nature's finest work.

Some people feel that because bodily functions are "natural," it's okay to exhibit them in public. Well, earthquakes, monsoons, and eating one's offspring are natural occurrences, too. But that doesn't mean we want to witness them in our daily lives. If ever.

There's no reason to feel embarrassed or ashamed about the natural noises and emissions of your body. But, as the old saying reminds us, there's a time and a place for everything. Knowing when and where is the key to keeping a well-mannered body.

Bodily functions tend to fall into two categories:

1. **Things you do to your body.** Usually these are things you can control (picking your nose, cracking your knuckles, going to the bathroom), although your ability to do so may vary with your age and how many sodas you've had to drink.

2. **Things your body does to you.** These are events and occurrences (sneezing, yawning, hiccupping) over which you have little or no control.

Etiquette divides these categories further. There are things that befall people in public that, while natural, are considered socially unacceptable. Farts, for example, Do Not Exist as far as society is concerned.*

They are acknowledged by neither perpetrator nor bystander. Burps, on the other hand, are acknowledged by the burper ("Excuse me") but not the burpee. Other bodily trumpetings, such as sneezes, are acknowledged by sneezee and sneezer alike ("Gesundheit." "Thank you.")

Bodily functions carried out in the privacy of one's bedroom or bathroom are just that—private. Therefore, in the eyes of society, they Do Not Exist. As such, they are nobody's business.

If this seems a bit confusing, don't be alarmed. We'll take (almost) all of the things bodies do and consider them one by one. But please, let's try to be mature about it. Hee, hee, hoo, ha, ha.

*THE WORD "FART" IS TODAY CONSIDERED VULGAR BY MANY PEOPLE. BUT IT WASN'T ALWAYS SO. CHAUCER AND OTHER EARLY ENGLISH WRITERS USED THE WORD OFTEN AND WITHOUT SHAME. IT EVEN APPEARED IN THE RESPECTED *OXFORD ENGLISH DICTIONARY* UNTIL THE ONSET OF THE VICTORIAN ERA.

Things You Do to Your Body
Nose Picking

Digital roto-rooting is a natural, necessary maintenance task one must perform to keep the breathing apparatus in tip-top form. In fact, archaeologists (people who like to dig) have established that nose picking began in ancient Egypt during the Pharocious Period, which occurred approximately 3000 BC (Before Cable).

All that sand blowing across Egyptian mucous membranes led to major booger production. This was a problem for the workers who were building the pyramids, since they had to stop every few minutes to excavate the Nubian nostrils. It also upset the Pharaohs, since the mucous mining was putting pyramid construction waaaay behind schedule.

So Queen Nasaltiti, the wife of King Toot-and-Come-In, decreed that people picking their noses in public would have a 2,000-ton pyramid stone dropped on their proboscises. As a result of this edict, the citizens of Egypt learned that it was neither polite nor healthy to pick their noses in public. (This is why so many Egyptians are depicted with flattened noses on ancient vases.)

It's practically and aesthetically wise to navigate one's nasal passages in private. Etiquette demands the use of a handkerchief, which is later washed, or a tissue, which is subsequently discarded in an official waste receptacle. Because so few people today carry handkerchiefs or tissues, avoid running your hands along the undersides of desks, chairs, and car seats.

Teeth Flossing

Let's now turn to flossing conventions. No, these are not large gatherings where people discuss the relative merits of waxed vs. unwaxed dental tape. Rather, they're rules that govern the use of said tape for the purpose of removing chow crumbs from between one's teeth. Here are all the dental dictums you need to know:

1. Never pick your teeth or floss your fangs in public.

2. If you floss your teeth as a guest in someone's home, be kind and clean the mirror if you have sprayed it with tooth boogers.

3. Don't floss your teeth before having sex. This is not a joke. This is a genuine Safer Sex Health Bulletin. It's meant neither to encourage you to engage in sex nor to abstain from flossing, but simply to apprise you of the facts. HIV, the virus that causes AIDS, is transmitted via the exchange of bodily fluids. Flossing often results in small cuts to and bleeding from the gums, which may put you and/or your partner at risk.

Zit Popping

Pimples are properly popped in private.* Squeeze with eeze, but pleeze, keep it a secret between you and your mirror. And wipe said mirror off when you're done.

Spitting

It used to be perfectly acceptable to spit in public. Back in the 17th century, when floors were made of dirt or stone or rushes, people even spit indoors. But as furnishings and floor coverings became fancier, anyone with a hankering for hawking was expected to hang on to a hankie.

Samuel Pepys, who kept a diary during that time,** wrote on January 28, 1661, of an experience he had while attending the theater. He was sitting in a dark corner when a "lady spit backwards upon me by mistake, not seeing me; but after seeing her to be a very pretty lady, I was not troubled at all."

*SOME PEOPLE SAY THAT THEY SHOULDN'T BE POPPED AT ALL. BUT I HAVE YET TO MEET ANYONE WHO HAS EVER FOLLOWED THAT ADVICE. **THIS IS A FAMOUS DIARY. IF YOU ASK FOR IT AT THE LIBRARY, DON'T SAY "DO YOU HAVE A COPY OF *THE DIARY OF SAMUEL PEPISS?*" INSTEAD, SAY "DO YOU HAVE A COPY OF *THE DIARY OF SAMUEL PEEPS?*" THE LIBRARIAN WILL BE IMPRESSED THAT YOU'VE PRONOUNCED THE NAME CORRECTLY.

AHH, AHH, AHH— CHOOOOOO!!!!

Times have changed. Most people today would be deeply troubled if they were spat upon, no matter how pretty the lady. If you need to spit and a spittoon isn't available, your best bet is to go to a private spot such as a bathroom and spit into the toilet. If privacy isn't an option, your next best bet is to spit (when no one is looking) into a handkerchief or someplace where others won't have to see it or come into contact with it. This doesn't mean behind the bookshelf. It means in the gutter, down a storm drain, or onto the grass.

In an emergency, such as an open-mouthed head-on collision with a fly, you may either swallow the tasty little critter for extra protein or spit it out. The edicts of etiquette are waived as long as you're outdoors and you aim away from people.

Never spit into a water fountain. And if you ever spit out the window of a moving vehicle, make sure the car behind you isn't a convertible.

On occasion, you may be asked to spit. People who issue these requests are called *dentists*. It would be rude and leave a bad taste in your mouth to reject their kind invitation. So spit away. Just do it in the shiny round sink with the funny noises and water swirling round—not on the dentist.

Finally, if you should need help remembering these rules, here's a song from my childhood, sung to the tune of that great refrain from the opera *Carmen:*

Tor-e-a-dor,

Don't spit on the floor,

Use a cus-pi-dor.

That's what it's for.

Scratching

If the itch is on your arm, leg, shoulder, or back, go ahead and scratch. Just try not to look like a monkey. But if the itch is in a more private area, front or rear, you may not scratch in public.* Times like these call for covert scratching techniques.

*THIS RULE IS SUSPENDED FOR BASEBALL PLAYERS, WHO ARE PAID LARGE SUMS OF MONEY TO SCRATCH THEIR PRIVATES IN PUBLIC.

TRUE STORIES
FROM THE MANNERS FRONTIER

Great Expectorations

For some people, spitting is a nervous habit. They have a windup longer than a major league pitcher's as they dredge the spittle up from their toes. HAGGGGHHHHKKKK, HAGGGGHHHHKKKK, HAGGGGHHHHKKKK, PTOOOEY. A projectile wings through the air and lands splat on the sidewalk, where it waits for somebody to step in it.

You can't possibly win friends and influence people if you spit in public. Just the other day, when I was riding the bus, the rear door opened. A fellow passenger poked his head out and dribbled a stream of drool onto the sidewalk. I suppose I should have been grateful that he didn't do it inside the bus. But I'd rather he hadn't done it at all.

Covert Scratching, Posterior Itch

Going to the Bathroom

Every human being is allotted three years during which his or her bathroom goings-on are a matter of public record. Ideally, these should be the first three years. After that, your activities in this domain should be a matter of no one's concern but your own.

Schools are the biggest violators of this rule. Children shouldn't be forced to reveal the status of their bladder to the entire class by having to ask the teacher for permission to go to the bathroom. They should be allowed to slip out of the room discreetly, take care of their need, and come right back. Since they aren't, is it any wonder that so many adults feel compelled to announce their bathroom comings and goings to anyone who will listen?

"Nature calls, heh, heh."

"I'm going to the john."

"I gotta take a whiz."

Here's how to be on your best bathroom behavior:

If you're in a group of people and you need to relieve yourself, don't declare your intentions. Simply get up, say "Excuse me," and leave. Most people are imaginative enough to figure out where you've gone. If you're not sure where the bathroom is, ask your host, a friend, or a waiter. When you return, make sure your hands are dry in case you have to shake hands with anybody.

Put the toilet seat up, boys. (Unless you have to sit down.) In case the logic behind this has never been explained to you, it's because if you don't, the seat is likely to get wet. The next person to use the bathroom will either get a wet behind or be required to clean up after you. When you're through, put the seat back down. If you're in a public bathroom and don't want to touch the seat, you can use the side of your shoe to lift it. This is an excellent exercise for improving one's balance, overall body tone, and hamstrings.

AHH,
AHH, AHH—
CHOOOOOO!!!!

Protect your seat. If you're in a public bathroom and need to sit down and there's no toilet seat protector dispenser at hand, you can tear off three strips of toilet tissue to place on the seat. If the toilet paper is of the single-sheet variety, you'd better not be in a hurry, because you're going to have to balance about 20 pieces.

Wash your hands. Something like 94 percent of all Americans claim to wash their hands after going to the bathroom. But scientists have discovered that only 60 to 70 percent actually do wash their hands. And many of them don't use soap. How, you might ask, did scientists discover this? By stationing someone in the bathroom to count.*

*THIS, CURIOUS READER, IS CALLED *RESEARCH.* NEXT QUESTION: HOW MANY OF THE PEOPLE OBSERVED TOLD BUILDING SECURITY ABOUT THE WEIRDO HANGING AROUND THE BATHROOM WITH A CLIPBOARD?

These fascinating facts aside, *not* washing your hands is a prime means of contracting various diseases that can make you very ill or even very dead. No joke! So, for your own health as well as that of your fellow planeteers, give your hands the old scrub-a-dub after you go to the bathroom. This doesn't mean waving them in the vicinity of a faucet. It means energetic rubbing with soap and water for 15 to 20 seconds. (The CDC recommends that you time it by singing "Happy Birthday" twice. If you're in a public bathroom you may want to do this silently.)

As you leave the bathroom, ponder this: What's the point of washing your hands if, as you open the door, you have to grab the door pull that the slob before you who didn't wash his hands just touched? You see the problem. And here's the solution: Public restrooms should be required to have little towelette dispensers right by the door. Upon exiting, you'd grab a towelette and use it to open the door. And when you were through, you'd deposit the used towelette in the receptacle provided for that purpose right outside the door. As these devices become ubiquitous throughout the land, just remember where you first heard about the idea. Of course, you could just dispense with doors entirely, as many public bathrooms do.

Never pee in a pool. It's rude to litter. Besides, some people put a chemical in their pools that turns the water dark if it comes into contact with urine. "Oh, that's just a legend," you say. Are you willing to put it to the test?

If you're traveling and you come across a bathroom, always use it. You never know when you'll see one again.

If, before you go out with your family, your parents ask "Do you have to use the bathroom?" always say "No." To do otherwise would violate one of the most sacred parent-child covenants.

Flush. Unless you're a guest in a home with sewer problems and your host has specifically instructed you otherwise.

Dear Alex

"What do you do if you use the bathroom at somebody's house and really stink it up?"

Hold your nose? Americans are so finicky when it comes to odors associated with the body. If God hadn't meant us to smell each other, he wouldn't have issued schnozzolas. Still, you'd like to leave the bathroom in the same olfactory condition in which you found it. That's because you're a considerate guest.

Since going to the bathroom is a private activity that falls into the Does Not Exist category, so would taking a discreet look under the sink to see if there's a can of air freshener available. If so, a quick spray should do the trick. If there's no can in the can, there's not much you can do except leave the fan on or otherwise ensure maximum air flow.

Don't be embarrassed. There's no such thing as immaculate evacuation. And, with any luck, someone else will use the bathroom after you, thus lengthening the list of suspects.

Incidentally, it's silly to run water to mask the sounds you make. Good manners already prevent anyone from hearing them. And all it does is make people think *He's running the water to try to cover up those noises he's making*.

Knuckle Cracking

Cracking your knuckles is the same as scraping your fingernails across a blackboard. It sends shivers down the spine. Therefore, it's to be done only when you're alone or in the company of like-minded individuals. But if your knuckles swell to the size of golf balls or your fingers fall off someday, don't say you weren't warned.

Gum Chewing

Smack, chomp, clop, POP! How attractive. Gum chewing offers the imaginative teen endless opportunities for grossing people out. You can chew so loudly that it sounds like a regiment of soldiers marching through mud. You can pull out long strands and swing them to and fro like a pendulum. You can fill the air with sweet, noxious fumes. You can blow bubbles that burst in your face and adhere to your nose and cheeks. Of course, this is what makes gum chewing so much fun. Feel free to indulge whenever you're in the company of fellow masticators.

AHH,
AHH, AHH–
CH0000000!!!!

But if you don't want to gum up your reputation for good manners, here are some suggestions to chew on:

Be discreet. While some arbiters of etiquette insist that gum chewing is never acceptable in public, I say it is—*if* others in the vicinity can't tell you're doing it. Clandestine gum chewing falls into the realm of etiquette offenses that Do Not Exist.

To accomplish this deception, don't actually *chew* your gum. Instead, fondle it with your tongue. Wedge it in your cheek. Turn it over with your teeth. But no smacking, blowing, pulling, or popping allowed. If you find it impossible to restrain yourself, it may mean that you were a cow in a previous life. Seek professional help.

Never spit out or drop your gum on the ground. The reason for this is obvious: In today's ecology-conscious world, gum should be recycled. Do you think someone else is going to want to chew it if it's been on the ground? Also, people are liable to step on it, and we all know what a pain that can be.

Never dispose of gum by sticking it under a seat or desk. This is very rude because when other people drop off *their* boogers and gum, they'll get *yours* all over their fingers. Gum that has expired should be placed in a wastebasket or trash barrel. If the container isn't lined with a plastic bag, wrap the gum in paper or tissue first.

Nail Biting

In a perfect world, there would be no nail biting. People would be serene, life's pressures would be manageable, and children wouldn't labor under a crush of anxiety and unrealistic expectations.

If nail biting must be done at all, it should be relegated to the private realm. The problem, of course, is that nail biting (and its cousin, cuticle picking) is a nervous habit. You may be several minutes into the activity before you even realize you're doing it.

Since it's rude to mutilate oneself, you should try to break the habit. If you're a chronic nail biter, there are many things you can do to help yourself stop. Wear gloves. Try hypnosis. Put bandages around your fingertips. Sit on your hands. Join a 12-step support group like Cuticles Anonymous. Keep your mouth busy by chewing gum. Keep your hands busy with a hand squeezer or those silver Chinese anti-stress balls. Apply that foul-tasting chemical that's supposed to discourage nail biting (check with your pharmacist). Put lotion on your hands to keep them smooth; this minimizes the little dried skin flaps that are so appealing for picking. Or, better yet, look for the sources of stress in your life and see what you might do to reduce or eliminate them.

Combing Hair and Applying Makeup

The brushing of hair and applying of makeup should be done in private or semiprivate settings. Private settings include your bathroom, bedroom, or boudoir; semiprivate settings include public restrooms and cars. Lipstick may be applied discreetly at the table in a restaurant if you are with relatives or close friends. Never comb or brush your hair in the vicinity of food. Locks in the lox spoil the appetite.

Producing French Horn–Like Sounds from Under One's Arms

This should only be done during band practice. People who make popping sounds by placing a finger in their mouth may join in if invited.

Things Your Body Does to You

Some of these involuntary events should be acknowledged by perpetrators and bystanders alike. Others should be acknowledged by perpetrators only. Still others should be ignored by all. Read on to learn which is which and why.

AHH, AHH, AHH– CHOOOOOO!!!!

Sneezing

"Ahh, ahhh, ahhhhh—CHOOOOOOO!!!!"

The responsibility of the sneezer is to cover his nose with a handkerchief. (It never hurts to include the mouth, too.) Don't study what you've produced, no matter how proud you feel. If you don't have a handkerchief or tissue, or the sneeze comes on so quickly you don't have time to get one out, germologists (people who study germs), recommend that you turn away from others and sneeze into your upper sleeve or the crook of your arm (the joint opposite your elbow). This is because you're not likely to spread germs by touching things with the crook of your arm. The science of sneezology has developed to the point that we now know that the old-fashioned technique of putting your fingertips together over your nose and mouth like a gas mask, and sneezing into that, is unhygienic since chances are you will then go and touch something with your mucus-y hands.

The sneeze observer's responsibility is to convey sympathy. This is done by saying "God bless you," "Gesundheit," "Que Dieu te benisse," and the like. The sneezer may then respond "Thank you," "Danke," or "Merci."

Serial sneezes. It's not unusual for hay fever sufferers to sneeze dozens of times in a row. If you witness a display such as this, don't acknowledge more than two or three sneezes. Otherwise, the hapless hayseed will feel self-conscious, and you and she will spend the day saying:

"Ah-choo!!!"

"Gesundheit."

"Thank you."

"Ah-choo!!!"

"Gesundheit."

"Thank you."

"Ah-choo!!!"

"Gesundheit."

"Thank you."

Instead, smile sympathetically after your first or second "Gesundheit" and say "Hay fever, huh?" The sufferer will nod gratefully and continue to sneeze.

Advanced Body Etiquette Tip #1: If you must sneeze in the vicinity of a buffet, always turn your head.

Nose Blowing*

When you blow your nose in public (which you should try not to do), do so into a handkerchief or tissue. Try not to honk. Refrain from strenuous wiping during the final cleanup. Otherwise, it looks as though you're unscrewing your nose. If you're discreet about carrying out this perfectly normal function, others will respond by not noticing.

Throwing Up

Throwing up is like growing up. Both activities, through no fault of your own, sometimes create messes that others have to clean up for you. An unscheduled upchuck presents well-mannered persons with a unique paradox. On the one hand, etiquette insists that a ralph-a-rama be ignored. On the other hand, it's impossible to ignore.

Here's how these seemingly irreconcilable demands may be met:

- If you make it to the bathroom in time, the entire event is overlooked. It took place offscreen and therefore Did Not Exist in any social sense. Concerned parents, hosts, and/or close friends may inquire discreetly "Are you all right? Is there anything I can do?" either through the door or afterward. No such remarks are permitted of others. Unless you're too sick to do so, you must remove any telltale traces from chin and bathroom before rejoining society.

- If you don't make it to the bathroom on time, you must appear wretched and allow yourself to be ushered to more comfortable and less vulnerable quarters. If possible, utter in deathbed tones "I'm sorry. I don't know what came over me. I feel just terrible about it." Meanwhile, any onlookers should act as if nothing happened. The host, relative, or concerned friend who must mop up the mess focuses on consoling you by saying:

"Don't you worry."

"It happens to everybody."

TRUE STORIES

FROM THE
MANNERS FRONTIER

He Blew It

Once upon a time, I had a farm. And on that farm there was a—well, that's beside the point.

The point is that I was sitting on the veranda one afternoon, surveying the rolling hills and pastoral beauty, when a guest walked to the edge of the porch, placed his index fingers on both sides of his nose, and blew. Two streams of you-know-what cascaded to the ground.

I suppose he was overcome by all the natural splendor. I was overcome by nausea.

---

*ALTHOUGH NOSE BLOWING IS A VOLUNTARY ACTION, IT'S DONE IN RESPONSE TO SOMETHING YOUR BODY HAS DONE TO YOU. HENCE ITS PLACEMENT IN THIS PART OF THE CHAPTER. IN CASE YOU WERE WONDERING.

AHH, AHH, AHH– CHOOOOOO!!!!

"You just lie down."

"I had 14 children, so this doesn't bother me a bit."

The bottom line is: No rebuking for puking, unless your vomit comet was the result of alcohol consumption, in which case you deserve maximum discomfort, inconvenience, and humiliation.

Coughing

The lone cough, along with the minimal multiple cough, need not be recognized by cougher or coughee. The cougher must, however, follow the same guidelines as sneezers by coughing into the crook of his or her arm.

Extended coughing fits may be acknowledged by asking the cougher if she's okay. Any inability on the cougher's part to answer indicates that she's not. At this point, you might want to consider the possibility that she may be . . .

Choking

Chokers not at risk of death (i.e., the soda went down the wrong way) should say "Excuse me," once they have recovered. Observers need not say anything.

Chokers turning blue in the face (i.e., those with chicken bones stuck in their windpipe) should point to their throat and hope that someone nearby knows the Heimlich maneuver. When breathing resumes, they should say "Thank you for saving my life."

The response "It was nothing" might be misconstrued. Therefore, it's better to simply say "You're welcome."

Burping and Belching

We are referring here to the involuntary burp. Those talented souls who can belch on command should do so in the barn and only in the company of like-minded individuals.

If you're the perpetrator of an accidental burp, place your hand to your mouth. (This confuses inattentive listeners into thinking they may have heard a cough, which is considered more socially acceptable than a burp.) Then say "Excuse me."

Advanced Body Etiquette Tip #2: Belching contests are not permitted during the cadenza.

Yawning

People yawn for one of three reasons:

1. They're tired.

2. They're bored.

3. They see someone else yawn.

Yawning is highly contagious. If you don't think this is true, watch someone yawn. I guarantee you'll soon be yawning yourself.

Cover your mouth when you yawn. Interesting as your uvula is, most people would just as soon not see it. It's also impolite to indicate your boredom with present company or proceedings. Your hand helps disguise what the mouth cannot deny.

Yawners and yawnees alike need never comment on the event. However, if you're a guest and your host exhibits chronic yawning syndrome, you should say "My goodness, I had no idea it was so late. I really must be going." Then go.

Stomach Rumblings

The human digestive system was designed to growl during tests and other periods of silent prayer. Should your stomach ever attempt such a communication, adopt a tranquil, meditative expression. This suggests that the noise was either a figment of the listener's imagination or a paranormal acoustical phenomenon involving the ozone layer. Whatever it was, it clearly had nothing to do with you.

Passing Wind

It sounds so lovely. The perfect thing to do on a summer day. You can just imagine a friend returning from an outing to the beach:

"Oh, we had a great time. Dale and I spent the afternoon surfing, listening to the waves, enjoying the breeze, and passing wind."

In case you didn't know it, "passing wind" is a euphemism for farting.* The release of bodily gas is nothing to be ashamed or embarrassed about. Chimneys smoke, kettles steam, and humans fart. In fact, humans fart an average of 14 times a day, expelling approximately one-half liter of gas. How much you fart and how much your farts stink depends on such things as what you eat, the bacteria in your intestines, how much air you swallow, and how long you keep the fart in. (I think there's an interesting science project in all this.)

*BECAUSE IT PAYS TO BUILD AN EXTENSIVE VOCABULARY, OTHER EUPHEMISMS FOR FARTING INCLUDE "BREAKING WIND," "PASSING GAS," AND "CUTTING THE CHEESE."

AHH,
AHH, AHH—
CHOOOOOO!!!!

Anyway, farting is the natural order of things.

Teenagers often see possibilities for humor, creativity, and social sanction in farts that would go right over the heads of most adults. One properly consummated fart is good for at least 10 minutes of distraction in the average classroom. At a sleepover, one good fart deserves another, and hours of entertainment can be derived from the production, analysis, and, believe it or not, lighting of farts—however the latter should only be attempted by professional drivers on a closed course.

What does etiquette say about farting?

Speak no evil. Hear no evil. Smell no evil.

Perpetrators of, and witnesses to, vacated vapor must convey the following in their body language and facial expressions:

Perpetrator: *I didn't do that.*

Bystander 1: *I didn't hear that.*

Bystander 2: *I didn't smell that.*

This rules out behaviors such as giggling, groaning, fainting, fanning, and saying "EEEEE-yoooooo" while looking at the dog. Furthermore, it's absolutely forbidden to engage in conversations such as:

"Oooo-ooo, Brandon cut one."

"He who smelt it, dealt it."

"Oooo Brandon."

"I DIDN'T DO IT!"

"Did too."

"Did not."

"Did too."

"Did not."

Advanced Body Etiquette Tip #3: Deny everything.

Thus, the only reaction anyone can have when a butt bomb goes off is: None. The first few seconds are the hardest. During this time, the perpetrator tries not to blush, and the bystanders try not to breathe. Once this initial period has passed, it's fine to roll down a window, make an unscheduled exit from the elevator, or suddenly remember an errand you have to run.

Hiccupping

The hiccup is a practical joke the body likes to play. You never get the hiccups when it's fourth-down-goal-to-go in the last 10 seconds of the Super

Bowl and everybody's yelling their heads off. You always get them right after the teacher says "Class, I don't want to hear a peep out of anyone."

"Hic.
　　Hic.
　　　Hic.
　　　　　　Hic."

The proper response for anyone in the presence of a hiccup is to ignore it. This is difficult, since hiccups are timed to go off just after you've forgotten about the last one. Nonetheless, the etiquette is to forgetiquette.

The hiccupper shall do nothing to draw attention to herself. If you wish to stand on your head, gargle, drink water upside down from a glass, eat a spoonful of sugar, hold your breath until you turn blue, and/or sing the National Anthem while a friend smacks you on the back, take it someplace private. Upon your return, be prepared for the assembled masses to be eagerly awaiting your next hiccup.

The hiccuppee shall do nothing to focus attention on the hiccupper. This means no laughing, no fake hiccup echoes, and no trying to scare the hiccupper out of her wits.

"Hic."

Hormonal Happenings

The male organ, especially during its owner's adolescence, often elects to stand up for itself at the most inconvenient times. Such "elections" should never be remarked upon or pointed out by witnesses. Other than for the embarrassed one, they Do Not Exist.

If you're of the gender for which the words "rise and shine" have special meaning in the morning, you may wish to avail yourself of those fashion styles designed as protective covering for adolescent boys, such as baggy pants and long flannel shirts that go down to your knees. One hopes that your parents and teachers will have the sensitivity not to insist that you tuck in your shirt.

Dear Alex

"How do you tell someone they have body odor or bad breath?"

From upwind.

First, you should know the person or at least have a vested interest in his or her ability to go through life without offending those who are near or dear. This category includes friends, relatives, and people you must sit next to on a regular basis. It doesn't include strangers on the bus.

Second, the problem should be ongoing. If the whiff you sniff is situational—i.e., the person just finished cutting the lawn on a 110-degree day—don't say anything unless he's about to go on a date or you're really hard up for conversation.

AHH,
AHH, AHH–
CHOOOOOO!!!!

Once you decide to break the news that someone's body or breath has the bouquet of swamp gas, keep in mind that few people enjoy being told that they stink. Therefore, you need to exercise utmost tact. Bring up the subject in private. There are several approaches you can take:

Direct: *"I hope you don't mind my saying this, but your breath is very strong."*

Indirect: *"You might want to get that jacket cleaned. I think it's picked up a very strong odor."*

Confidential: *"I sometimes have a problem with this myself, so I thought I'd let you know that you have body odor. There's this great new anti-perspirant I've been using that lasts all day and is strong enough for a woman yet gentle enough for today's sensitive guy."*

TRUE STORIES

The Price Is Right

Recently, I was waiting in the checkout line in a store. The woman in front of me was wearing a beautiful silk scarf from Neiman-Marcus that cost $295. How did I know that? From the price tag. Good Samaritan that I am, I said "Excuse me, Ma'am. I wasn't sure if you knew, but the sales tag is still on your scarf." She gave me an icy stare and replied through pursed lips "Thank you."

Although it's pleasing when virtue is rewarded, I remained undaunted by the rebuff and set off to do another good deed. After all, the world is full of people with their flies open.

Dear Alex

"Should you tell someone they have something stuck between their teeth?"

This question has plagued humankind since the dawn of time. Is it *our* responsibility to apprise others that they have spinach in their teeth, milk in their mustache, and boogers dangling from their nose? I say "Yes!"—for otherwise we are no different from the lowest animal.

If you're polite and discreet in pointing these things out, most people will be grateful, preferring a moment of embarrassment to a day of humiliation. If a bright-eyed, respectful youth came up to me and said "Excuse me, Sir, but you have a roll of toilet paper trailing from your pants," I'd reply "Thank you for telling me, young sir" and hand him a gold coin.

So, by all means, if it shows, tell. Before you do, though, make sure it's correctable. There's no point in alerting someone to something they can't do anything about at the time—like a run in their stocking or a stain on their shirt. Also, for certain really personal or embarrassing things, you might, if you're not of the same gender as the target, ask someone who is to break the news.

Here's how to handle your garden-variety spinach-on-the-chin dilemma:

Let's say you're at Taco Bell with your 11-year-old brother and he's eating rather messily. It's fine to say "Excuse me, Ivan, but you have some salsa in your beard." You can use this *Excuse me, but you have . . .* technique for just about anything. Sometimes it's helpful to point to the location of the offense on yourself. This way, instead of saying "Excuse me, but you have a dried booger hanging out of your left nostril," you can say "Excuse me, but you have a little something here" while gently touching your own left nostril.

Taking this one step further, many couples, through years of intimacy, develop sign language for alerting each other to errant dribbles. I can remember sitting at the dinner table as a child on occasions when we had company. Once in a while, a little bead of gravy would squat on my father's chin. I would watch with fascination, wondering how long it might remain in residence. But invariably, if I turned toward my mother, I would see her catch his eye and subtly brush her chin twice with a finger. My father would take his napkin and dab at the corresponding location on his face. Thus I learned the benefits of being in a relationship.

Chapter Quiz

1. *It's okay to pick your nose in public as long as you:*

   a) wear white gloves

   b) raise your pinky

   c) do it one nostril at a time

2. *You're paying rapt attention as your English teacher recites a poem by Emily Dickinson. An unpleasant odor wafts across your nasal radar screen, suggesting that one of your nearby classmates has passed wind. Do you:*

   a) jump out of your seat, fling open the windows, and shriek "AIR RAID!!"

   b) point at your neighbor and yell "Billy cut the cheese, Billy cut the cheese!"

   c) ignore it, silently reminding yourself that "There but for the grace of baked beans go I."

AHH,
AHH, AHH—
CHOOOOOO!!!!

3. *Your mother asks you to pass some hors d'oeuvres at a party she's giving. You're standing in the hallway, conversing with a guest, the tray in your hands, when suddenly you get this wicked itch on your backside. Do you:*

a) drop the tray, make gorilla sounds, and scratch energetically

b) turn around, bend over, and say to the person "Excuse me, could you please scratch my butt?"

c) surreptitiously use the banister to massage your behind

4. *You're at a family picnic in the park. Your cousin Cindy sits across from you and a couple of seats down. You notice that she has a big kernel of corn clinging to her chin. Do you:*

a) say "Hey, everyone, look at the corn booger on Cindy's chin!"

b) take out your slingshot and try to knock the kernel off with a pea

c) catch Cindy's eye and discreetly point to your own chin

14

I BEG MY PARDON

Being Polite to Yourself

Here we've spent a whole book talking about how important it is to be polite to your family and friends, to teachers and employers, even to total strangers you'll never see again. But we've left out the one person for whom you should always be on your best behavior: *Yourself.*

What does it mean to be polite to yourself? Certainly it means saying "Excuse me" if you accidentally step on your toe. And getting up to give yourself a seat on a bus. But it also means being kind to yourself. Taking good care of yourself. Treating yourself with the same tolerance and understanding you extend toward others.

How do you know if you're treating yourself with respect and consideration? When you make a mistake, do you think *I'm such an idiot. How can I be so dumb? I can't do anything right!* If so, how rude! Do you ever look in a mirror and say *I'm so ugly. I hate the way I look!* If so, how rude! Do you ever do things that could get you into serious trouble or harm your health or body? If so, how rude!

Why should you be polite to yourself? For the same reasons you're polite to others: Because it feels good. Because it demonstrates respect. And because people will enjoy your company. (You *do* want to enjoy your own company, don't you?)

Many teenagers don't treat themselves with the kindness they deserve. If you're one of them, if you're constantly dissing and dismissing yourself, you need to stop being so rude and start being more courteous.

How can you do this? To find out, I surveyed hundreds of teenagers across the land. Except for one boy who said "I don't get offended, so it isn't necessary to be polite to myself," most teens who responded offered sensible suggestions for self-courtesy:

"I keep myself looking good."

"I take care of my hair."

"I brush my teeth."

"I do my nails."

"I wear nice clothes."

"I take showers."

"I exercise."

"I meditate."

"I eat good food once in a while."

"I don't smoke or do drugs."

"I give my body and mind rest."

"I compliment my looks."

"I set aside time to relax and think."

"I look both ways when crossing the street."

When you're frazzled and hassled, it's easy to let your most basic needs slide. Not sneakers and tunes, but exercise, proper nutrition, good hygiene, and plenty of rest. All of which help you feel, be, and do your best.

There's a famous Latin saying: *mens sana in corpore sano*. It means *a sound mind in a sound body.* The early Romans recognized the importance of mental and physical hardiness. In fact, their system of educating the young—cold showers and lessons with Nero—was based on this concept. It's no wonder the Romans left so many lasting contributions to the world, such as togas and marinara sauce.

If you mean to leave your mark on the world, you must keep your mind and body in tip-top condition *(mens tiptopa in corpore tiptopo).* Here's how.

Exercise

It's a well-known fact that today's teenagers are in poorer physical condition than their parents and grandparents were when they were children. This is because prior generations had to get up to change channels. Advances in technology have made it easier for today's teens to be less physically active. Exertion to them means texting. But the more energetic you are, the more energy you'll have. (This is called a *paradox*, which is Latin for *two ducks*.)

So unless you're already playing on a school team or working out or swimming laps, it's time to get the ticker ticking and the endorphins flowing.

As long as your doctor gives you the okay, get a strenuous aerobic workout for at least 20–30 minutes three times a week or more. Do some heavy-duty bike riding or inline skating. Jog. Run up and down a flight of stairs 40 times. Go to a gym. In addition to your aerobic workout, take up a sport. Play basketball or tennis. Join a soccer or baseball league. Challenge your parents or siblings to a game of badminton or base running. And if you hate sports, go dancing (which counts as exercise as long as you're not just slow dancing). Or take long walks. If you make several nonstop window-shopping circuits of a major mall, that's a couple of miles right there.

The physical benefits of exercise are obvious, especially to those admiring your finely toned bod. But there are other benefits as well. Research shows that exercise reduces depression, generates feelings of well-being, promotes sound sleep, and enhances one's sex life. What more could you ask for?

Eat Right

This means making sure that your daily diet includes all four basic food groups: pizza, candy, nachos, and soda.

Ha, ha. Just kidding. Machines need proper fuel in order to run properly. If you fill up on ice cream, or don't fill up at all, you're not going to have the energy you need to get through the day.

Check online or with your parents, physician, school nurse, or local library for the lowdown on healthy eating habits. There are four reasons why you should consume regular, balanced, nutritious meals:

1. You'll look good.

2. You'll feel good.

3. You'll live longer.

4. You'll be able to cheat occasionally with junk food.

Keep It Clean

The problem with hygiene is the word itself. It sounds so . . . sanitary. Like something you'd have to do with a clothespin on your nose and tweezers when no one's looking. So let's come up with a new concept: *self-detailing.* Surely you deserve as much care as the family car. Before you set off for the day, pull in for a pit stop and run through your checklist:

- ☐ **BODY:** Washed? Sweet-smelling?
- ☐ **FACE:** Scrubbed? Shaved? Made-up?
- ☐ **HAIR:** Cleaned? Moussed? Conditioned? Combed?
- ☐ **TEETH:** Brushed? Flossed? De-bugged?
- ☐ **FINGERNAILS:** Trimmed? Filed? Painted? Polished?
- ☐ **NOSTRILS:** Emptied?
- ☐ **EARS:** De-waxed?
- ☐ **SKIN:** Oiled? Lotioned? Perfumed? Sunblocked? Stridexed?
- ☐ **CLOTHES:** Laundered? Ironed? Ripped only where intended?

If you treat yourself to this sort of daily detailing, you'll run better, last longer, and turn heads when you drive, er, walk by.

Do Nothing

A lot of teenagers feel pressured to do things that will help them get into college: lessons, dance, music, sports, extra courses, school clubs, student councils, mentoring, volunteering, etc. These activities are great if you love what you're doing and don't feel overextended, exhausted, and stressed.

But there's no law that says you have to spend every waking moment being productive. Make sure you leave some time to do nothing. I'm not talking about being lazy, irresponsible, or slothful; I'm talking about being *idle.* Relaxed. Laid back. Carefree. Cool (if not chill).

Take a moment to smell the roses. Be still. Meditate. Lie on your bed and stare at the dead flies in the ceiling light fixture. Sit on a bench and watch the people go by. Enjoy the sunset. Look at the stars. Listen to the wind. Let your mind wander.

Why is it so important to do this from time to time? Because, as a teenager I know once said, "If you don't daydream, you'll never get anywhere in life."

Do Something

Some teenagers find that instead of having too much to do, they have too little. Time wears heavily. So they hang out at malls, cruise in cars, drink, use drugs, and get into trouble. And, chances are, they don't feel very good about themselves.

This is because humans were designed to learn and love and grow and give. Teenagers who keep busy, who open themselves up to new people and adventures, tend to feel self-confident, happy, and hopeful. Teenagers who use only a fraction of their capabilities, who get into ruts, who don't try new things, tend to feel aimless and unhappy.

While it's important to schedule some downtime into your week, most people feel best about themselves and their lives when they're connected and creative. So discover your passions. Learn a musical instrument. Shoot a film. Take up a sport and experience the joy of total physical exhaustion. Read. Paint. Draw. Make models. Get active with a cause. Take a stand. Volunteer. Build connections to old people, young people, homeless people, people who are doing things you want to do; open yourself up to nature, to spirituality, to the mysteries of the universe, to love. You'll find that the more you get outside of yourself and the more you give to others, the richer you'll feel. And that's a very nice thing to do for yourself.

Do Unto Others

Popular teenagers tend to be friendly, outgoing, and empathetic. They're upbeat, considerate, and involved. No wonder other kids like to be around them. Here's what the teenagers I surveyed said about themselves:

"I try to be nice to people so I can have friends."

"I help others."

"I ignore a fight waiting to happen."

"I'm polite to others so others are polite to me."

Now that you've read this book,* you know almost everything you need to know about treating others well. Etiquette is all about doing unto others. Keep that in mind and you can't go wrong.

*YOU *HAVE* READ IT, HAVEN'T YOU?

Plan Ahead

Treating yourself with respect also means thinking about tomorrow, and the next day, and the next several years of your life. As the teenagers I surveyed said:

"I work hard for my future."

"I take in knowledge."

"I stay in school."

"I do my homework."

"I try to get good grades."

"I keep myself well organized."

"I carry myself in a professional manner."

Do yourself a favor and learn the basics of goal setting (if you haven't already). Spend some quiet time thinking about what's important to you. Then follow these steps:

1. Write down all of the things you'd like to accomplish during the next 10 years. These are your *long-range* goals. Be specific and thorough.

2. When you complete your list of long-range goals, prioritize them. Select the three to four that are most important to you.

3. Write down all of the things you'd like to accomplish during the next three to five years. These are your *intermediate* (medium-range) goals. Prioritize them and select the top three to four. **Tip:** Some of your intermediate goals should help you achieve your long-range goals.

4. Write down all of the things you'd like to accomplish within the next year or so. These are your *short-range goals.* Prioritize them and select the top few. **Tip:** Here, too, some of your short-range goals should relate directly to your intermediate goals.

5. Write down all the things you'd like to accomplish within the next week. These are your *immediate* goals. To achieve your weekly goals, for example, writing a history paper, you may want to break it down even further into daily goals (e.g., Day 1: Internet research; Day 2: Interview subjects; Day 3: Begin first draft; Day 4: Finish first draft; Day 5: Rest and goof off; Day 6: Write final draft; Day 7: Proofread and email to teacher.

6. Consult your lists regularly—once a day (best) or once a week (minimum). When you reach a goal, write down that date in your log.

7. Revise your lists as needed. Some of the goals you have today will stay the same for years to come; others will change as you change.

This system will help get you on track and keep you on track. Make a promise to yourself to try it for at least three weeks.

Give Yourself Presents

Giving yourself presents is a very polite thing to do. The teenagers I surveyed reported that they often use incentives to pat themselves on the back or get through a difficult time:

"If I've had a good week, I try to reward myself by going out."

"I treat myself to candy."

"I go on trips."

"I take myself shopping."

"I hang out with my friends."

"I have fun."

Just remember that if you give yourself a present, you have to write a thank-you note.

Think Well of Yourself and the World

How would you feel if someone criticized you nonstop 24 hours a day?

"You're such a loser! You're so stupid! Look at you. What a mess! Nobody's ever going to like you. You're a total failure."

You'd feel sad, hopeless, and hurt. It would be a struggle to get through each day.

Fortunately, most teenagers aren't exposed to relentless criticism of this sort. At least, not from the outside. But a lot of kids have an *inner* voice they can't shut off. Their mind blabbers on incessantly:

"I HATE myself. I'll never have any friends. I HAVE to be popular. Nobody likes me. I can't stand school. I'm going to flunk. Nothing will ever change. It's not fair. If I don't get invited to the dance, I'll die. I'm never going to amount to anything. I'm a rotten, terrible kid. I HATE my life. I HATE it! I HATE it!"

Imagine what life would be like if your mind was your best friend instead of your worst enemy. Imagine if it functioned as your personal

---

TRUE STORIES
FROM THE MANNERS FRONTIER

In Record Time

When I was in high school and all stressed out because of, say, some upcoming tumbling exam in gym class, I used to tell myself *All right, Alex, if you practice hard and don't roll off the mat in the middle of a somersault, you can buy yourself a record when it's all over.* (Records were these primitive round disks that played music.)

Of course, if I flunked the test and was totally depressed, then I'd buy a record to cheer myself up.

All told, it was an excellent system.

cheering squad. A conscience that prevented you from hurting yourself or others. A rudder that kept you steady and on course. A source of dreams, fantasies, and comfort. Here's what a mind like that would say:

"Take it easy. Stay calm. Deep breaths. Worrying won't help. You don't have to prove anything. You're a good person. You've come through things like this before. You have a lot going for you. Even if you blow it, it's not the end of the world. Believe in yourself. You can do it!"

It should be easy to get your mind on your side. But your mind has a mind of its own. And it's been barraged with messages ever since you were a little kid. These messages—from the media, television, advertising, family, friends, organized religion, and other societal institutions—can lead you to create expectations for yourself and others that are unrealistic and nearly impossible to meet.

From television, for example, your mind learns to expect instant solutions and rewards. (After all, people in sitcoms solve their problems in 30 minutes, with time off for commercials.) The message from movies and ads is that there's something wrong with you if you don't have a fancy car and 5 million bucks by the time you're 25, or that sex is always spectacular and without consequences. Some religions lay down such rigid absolutes for behavior that the internal conflict kids experience when they don't "measure up" can create deep feelings of guilt and shame.

These irrational and unhealthy attitudes lay the foundation for driving yourself crazy. How? By filling your mind with "musts":

1. I must do well.

2. I must have the approval of others.

3. Others must do right by me.

4. The conditions of the world must be fair and easy.

When we're driven by "musts," we take reasonable desires—for success, approval, love, money, pleasure, friendship—and turn them into absolute needs: *I MUST be liked by everybody. I MUST be thin. I MUST be rich.** And then, when we don't get what we want, when our needs are thwarted by reality, we view this as the worst calamity that could possibly happen. We become angry, resentful, and depressed. We "awfulize"** the consequences of having our needs unmet:

I'll die if I don't get the part.

Everybody will hate me if I don't break the record.

I won't be able to stand it if we move to another town.

*CLINICAL PSYCHOLOGIST ALBERT ELLIS CALLED THIS "MUSTURBATING."
**HE COINED THIS TERM AS WELL.

When we have unrealistic needs and awfulize the consequences of their being unmet, we worry endlessly about getting what we want, about not getting what we want, and about keeping what we get if we *do* get what we want. And that's not all. When we can't fulfill all of our (irrational) desires, we conclude that *we're* at fault. We must be dumb, worthless, undeserving. And we blame the world, which must be cruel, unfair, and out to get us. This three-part process—being driven by "musts," awfulizing, and dumping on oneself—is one of the things minds do to drive their owners crazy.

You can tell your mind to shape up and stop being silly. This is what kids who are polite to themselves do. In fact, the teenagers who responded to my survey reported all sorts of strategies for keeping their mind on their side:

"I compliment myself."

"I trust my feelings."

"I value myself for who I am."

"I encourage myself."

"I respect myself."

"I keep my confidence and self-esteem high."

"I judge myself fairly."

"I try to be calm and take things step-by-step, because if I do things in a hurry I'll mess up."

"I don't hurt myself."

"I try not to swear in my thoughts."

"I think positive."

"It's a pleasure to see you again."

"I try not to believe in things I know aren't true [about me]."

"I avoid putting myself down."

"I tell myself not to listen when people tease me."

"I love myself."

"I smile at myself in the mirror."

You might want to borrow some of these techniques and try them in your own life. Or come up with ideas of your own. Put your mind to it!

More Ways to Be Polite to Yourself

Watch out for "shoulds." Like "musts," "shoulds" can turn reasonable desires into unrealistic needs: *I should be able to do this; I should know this; I should understand this; I should be this kind of person or that kind of person.* Certainly, there are some "shoulds" that are worth following through on:

I should be kind and civil to others; I should keep my promises; I should behave responsibly. But don't be guided by demands that lead to guilt, shame, and feelings of failure.

Hold realistic expectations. Don't torture yourself because you can't live up to impossibly high standards. You're a human being, not a machine. You're going to discover that you have strengths and weaknesses, and you're going to make mistakes.

Give yourself credit. You know those things you "can't stand"? The things that "drive you crazy"? Guess what? You're standing them and you're not crazy. In other words, you're a lot stronger than you think.

Thank yourself. When other people extend themselves on your behalf, you thank them. Do the same for yourself:

> *"I just wanted to thank me for the way I stuck up for myself today. I gave myself that extra effort. Good going!"*

Develop your special talents. Pursue your passions. Schools teach many things. If you're lucky, you'll get turned on by a lot of them. But it's also possible that your interests and gifts lie outside the classroom. There are a lot of valuable things to learn that never find their way into the typical school curriculum. Make room in your life for the things you enjoy.

Surround yourself with positive people. Hang with friends who are doing things and going places. Their positive outlook will help you excel and handle the obstacles and bummers life throws your way.

Avoid people who are going nowhere fast. This doesn't mean shunning friends who sometimes get into trouble. It doesn't mean snubbing those who are unpopular, hurt, or underachieving. Everybody has problems, and it's important to be there for your friends when they need a helping hand. But some kids are going down, and they want to take you with them. They're proud of their attitude and lack of motivation. Misery loves company, and people who smoke, get drunk, use drugs, shoplift, tease, bully, and join gangs need to find others who will validate their behavior. Don't be duped into thinking it's cool to destroy your life or the lives of others.

Dispute negative thinking. Critiquing the errors and incidents of your life is one of the best ways to learn and grow. But don't let your own mind put you down. Don't let one event define your self-image. When your inner voice starts working overtime with negative blather, shout it down with some positive pepping up. Examples:

Negative Self-Talk	Positive Self-Talk
"Everybody hates me!"	"That's not true. Terry likes me. My parents like me. Grandma likes me. Mr. Reed likes me. It sure would be nice to have more friends, though."
"I can't do anything right!"	"That's not true. I'm good at lots of things. Just because I didn't make the team doesn't mean I'm a failure. I can try again next year."
"I can't stand it when people tease me!"	"But it happens to a lot of kids. I guess it's just part of life. I *can* stand it. I'll just ignore it and stay strong."

Don't let other people's opinions get to you. Sometimes, other people can offer valuable feedback that will help you solve a problem or work on yourself. But often, other people's opinions are pretty worthless. Think of all the people who once swore that the earth was flat. That humans could never fly. That individuals would never want computers in their homes. The people who are most successful and creative are those who believe in themselves, who forge ahead despite the so-called wisdom of others.

Don't give other people and events the power to control your feelings. Most people believe that feelings are the result of what happens to us. We feel good or bad based on events, on what others do or say. A teacher who praises us makes us feel proud; a parent who grounds us makes us feel angry. You can see these beliefs at work every time you hear statements like "You kids are driving me crazy" or "She made me so mad!"

If someone you love dies, or a friend dumps you, or a roommate loses your jacket, it's normal and healthy to feel sad, hurt, or annoyed. But often we let others push our buttons. We get consumed with anger or other self-defeating emotions because of the way we choose to look at the things that happen to us. We turn our confidence and serenity over to things we can't control.

Why give other people and events such power over you? Instead, control your *feelings* by controlling your *thoughts*.* Negative thoughts lead to negative feelings; positive thoughts lead to positive feelings. Examples:

*THE IDEA THAT FEELINGS ARE CAUSED MORE BY OUR THOUGHTS ABOUT LIFE THAN BY LIFE ITSELF LIES AT THE HEART OF A METHOD OF PSYCHOTHERAPY DEVELOPED BY ALBERT ELLIS CALLED *RATIONAL-EMOTIVE THERAPY (RET)*. ALBERT IS THE GUY WHO COINED THE TERMS "MUSTURBATION" AND "AWFULIZING." TO LEARN MORE, PICK UP HIS BOOKS OR CHECK HIM OUT ONLINE.

The Event	Ways to Look at It	Likely Results
Your teacher catches you passing a note and sends you to detention. Meanwhile, other kids get away with it.	**1.** *I hate him. He has no right to do that. He's the worst teacher in the world. Why should I have to go to detention when no one else does? It's not fair.*	**1.** Fury. Frustration. Resentment.
	2. *I did pass the note. I wish I hadn't been caught. Oh, well, it's just one afternoon. I guess I can use the time to do homework.*	**2.** Acceptance. Less stress. Most of your homework done by 4:30 PM.
There's someone in school you really like. You ask her out on a date—and she turns you down.	**1.** *This is awful. I can't stand being rejected like this. What's wrong with me? Nobody will ever want to go out with me.*	**1.** Hurt. Shame. Isolation. Self-doubt.
	2. *Man, that hurts. I really like her. Too bad I can't make her like me. But there are 878 other kids in this school. I'll hang in there. If Mortimer Snerdhopper can get dates, so can I!*	**2.** Disappointment— but you'll get over it. Courage to try again. A date next weekend.

Ask yourself a question. When you're worried about something, it's often because you're projecting dire consequences into the future. Next time this happens, ask yourself *What's the worst thing that could happen?* You'll probably discover it's nowhere near as bad as you imagined.

Solve the problem. Many people let their problems simmer and stew instead of trying to solve them. When you have a personal problem or a conflict with somebody in your life, sit down with yourself. Instead of worrying, take action. Grab a piece of paper and a pencil. Go through the five-step problem-solving strategy.[*] It will help you solve almost any problem you encounter—and understand which ones really *can't* be solved, which is a good thing to know.

*SEE PAGES 136–138.

Build your self-esteem. Some adults believe that the way to do this is by looking in a mirror and repeating self-congratulatory mantras. They teach kids to tell themselves *I'm great at math. I'm lovable and good.* This can, in fact, raise self-esteem—to the point at which many nasty, selfish kids who are flunking math start to feel good about themselves. But this is just a mind trick. *The way to build genuine self-esteem is by doing esteemable things.* Care, give, treat others with kindness and tolerance, be honest but gentle with yourself, do the best you can in the things that really matter. You'll build your self-esteem—and it will be genuine and deserved.

Admit when you're wrong. People spend enormous amounts of time and energy protecting their pride. If you make a mistake, 'fess up. Do what you can to repair the damage. You'll be amazed by how liberating it can be to assume responsibility for your actions.

Keep a diary, blog, or journal. Many teenagers like to record their thoughts and feelings. Keeping a diary or journal or writing a blog is an excellent way to catch your breath and reflect on the people, events, and moods you experience. It's also a way to release feelings that might otherwise stay bottled up inside. In fact, studies suggest that daily expressive writing can reduce stress, boost the immune system, improve memory and academic performance, and help people recover faster from traumatic events.

Use good manners. By being grateful, appreciative, courteous, tolerant, and polite, you can create an aura of goodness that will allow you to observe the selfishness and thoughtlessness of others with philosophical acceptance rather than anxious outrage. This is much better for your blood pressure.

Each day, you make choices. Some are small and inconsequential: Vanilla or chocolate? Seven-thirty or nine-thirty? Gray or black? Others can affect the rest of your life (or end it): How hard should I work in school? Should I try cocaine? Should I wear my bicycle helmet? Should I have sex without a condom?

How do you know what to decide?

It usually comes down to this: Do you want to be polite or rude? Do you want to respect yourself or disdain yourself? Forgive yourself or berate yourself? Protect yourself or harm yourself?

There's only one person in the world whose behavior you can control. And that's you. So why not treat yourself with the courtesy and respect you deserve?

Dear Alex

***"Does using good manners always work? I want to know—is this 100
percent positive?"***

There are no guarantees in life other than death, taxes, and being called
on when you're daydreaming. But in most situations, with most people,
good manners are definitely the way to go. People with good manners
are far more likely than those with bad manners to like themselves,
have friends, and live to see tomorrow. And they're far more likely to
get others to stop being rude.

Think of manners as you would seat belts. Sometimes they take
a little getting used to. Sometimes you forget to use them. Sometimes
they confine you more than you'd like. But they're the best system we
have for keeping you in the driver's seat and out of trouble.

Chapter Quiz

1. *If other people put you down, the best response is to:*

    a) call out the custard pies

    b) give them a wedgie

    c) ignore them

2. *One builds self-esteem by:*

    a) hiring a good carpenter

    b) repeating "I'm so great!" 10,000 times

    c) behaving honorably and giving to others

3. *Keeping a journal is a good idea because you can:*

    a) give your fingers a workout

    b) leave it where your parents will find it

    c) record your thoughts, feelings, and experiences

4. *Which of the following are unhealthy "musts"?*

    a) I must be thin

    b) I must be rich

    c) I must my hair

5. *When negative self-talk threatens, you should:*

    a) gag yourself

    b) scream "Shut up!"

    c) seek a rational, balanced perspective

6. *Being polite to yourself means:*

    a) getting up when you enter a room

    b) looking yourself in the eye when you speak

    c) treating yourself with kindness, patience, and understanding

Answers to the Chapter Quizzes

Chapter 1: Minding Manners (page 24)

1. d. Although it's never permissible to bolt upright in your coffin during the funeral. (For more on funeral etiquette, see pages 314–319.)

2. a, b, and c are all correct, unless someone is having a *really* bad hair day, in which case d would also be correct.

3. d.

4. None of the answers is correct. It's okay to be rude back ONLY if it's the third Tuesday of the month.

Chapter 2: Social Interactions 101 (page 63)

1. c.

2. c.

3. c.

4. c. As long as the owner doesn't hear you, you may ask the parrot directly if it knows any swear words.

5. c.

Chapter 3: Uncommon Courtesies (page 115)

1. c. If the elderly woman says "Yes" when you ask her if she would like a seat, don't say "Well, I hope someone offers you one."

2. c.

3. None of the answers is correct. Only *foreign* cars may be frontside bluntsided if you are to remain within the bounds of propriety.

4. c.

5. None of the answers is correct. Oranges must be *two* for a dollar.

Chapter 4: Family Life and Strife (page 158)

1. c. *Then* you may laugh.

2. c. If the problem-solving session doesn't work, you may run his underwear up the flagpole as long as it's clean (the underwear, that is).

3. c.

4. c. As an alternative, you may drench the bathroom with Lilac Fresh-Hint-of-Spring Air Freshener. Just don't announce it to everyone.

Chapter 5: Artful Lodgers (page 184)

1. All of the answers are correct.

2. All of the answers are correct. (Just checking to see if you're awake. Of course, *none* of the answers is correct. The only acceptable response would be to respectfully decline the invitation.)

3. Either c or a—if you use a frozen *egg roll.*

4. None of the answers is correct. You may only bring your pet to someone's house if his or her *pet* extends an invitation.

5. The proper response is to spit immediately at the kid who asked and say "I won."

6. Every written invitation should include the nature of the event, the date and time, and a crisp $50 bill.

Chapter 6: School Rules (pages 230–231)

1. c. You may add Red Dye #9 to your specimen.

2. c. Or, as an alternative, write *wrong* answers in big handwriting, let him copy, and then change your answers just before the bell rings.

3. c. You may then throw Styrofoam peanuts at him.

4. c.

5. c.

Chapter 7: Friends, Romance, Countrymen (pages 274–275)

1. c. Answer a is close, but still incorrect. You need to hand out *counterfeit* $20 bills. That way you won't go broke.

2. c.

3. c.

4. c. Alternately, you may place the tarantula on his head.

5. c. Although you may stand up during assembly and ask the *other* half of the boys in school what's wrong with them.

6. c. If that doesn't work, do a striptease on the stairs.

7. c. If you *must* pin the corsage to a tan line, always disinfect the area first.

8. None of the answers is correct. You must keep *five* feet on the ground.

Chapter 8: Eat, Drink, and Be Wary (pages 312–313)

1. c. Whatever you do, don't spit it out *on* your hostess.

2. c.

3. c. You may hum the "Rice-a-Roni" theme song under your breath.

4. c.

5. c. However, it's forbidden to read aloud from cereal boxes, as severe brain damage may result.

6. c. If this doesn't work, call the restaurant a dump, the waiter a jerk, and run for your life.

Chapter 9: On Your Best Behavior (pages 332–333)

1. c.

2. c.

3. c. Bonus points if you wear platform shoes.

4. c. You may also make goofy faces at him.

5. c. If you really, really don't like the bride, you may step on the cake.

6. c. Then try to remember to bring it.

Chapter 10: Talking Headiquette (pages 381–382)

1. c.

2. None of the answers is correct. Instead, throw the person in his soup.

3. c. If the recipient opens it, reads it, and tosses it in the trash, you may retrieve it and peruse it at your leisure.

4. c. If the person fails to respond, you may answer the questions yourself.

5. c.

Chapter 11: Netiquette (page 422)

1. c.

2. None of the answers is correct. The emoticon means *I was born with a pole through my very large ears.*

3. None of the answers is correct. The emoticon means *Has anyone seen my Siamese twin? He looks like this: <<<<<:}.*

4. None of the answers is correct. The emoticon means *My ears just came loose from my head.*

5. None of the answers is correct. It means *Me Cheetah.*

Chapter 12: Clothes-Minded (pages 437–438)

1. c.

2. c. Although if you can find items that will be out of fashion in two weeks, so much the better.

3. c is close. Find a kid wearing VERY baggy pants and turn him into a toga.

4. b and c are both correct.

5. None of the answers is correct. The proper response is to dye your dog pink and say Spiderman did it. This way, you'll probably get sent to another school.

6. None of the answers is correct. First-time guests traditionally bring the volleyball.

Chapter 13: Ahh, Ahh, Ahh—Choooooo!!!! (pages 455–456)

1. a.

2. c. Alternately, you may point at your book and yell "EMILY did it!"

3. c. For *really* nasty itches, you may slide down the banister.

4. c. If Cindy doesn't get it, you may want to stick a large kernel of corn to your own chin and point to that.

Chapter 14: I Beg My Pardon (page 471)

1. c. And then eat a custard pie.

2. c. Or, for *really* high self-esteem, say "I'm so great!" 1,000,000 times.

3. c. In which case it's fine to blackmail yourself.

4. a, b, and c are all correct.

5. c. Although eating a half gallon of rocky road ice cream sometimes helps.

6. c. But the supreme act of politeness would be to turn to page 1 and read this book all over again.

Index

Page numbers in **bold** refer to reproducible pages.

About the Author

Alex J. Packer (but you may call him "Alex") is a very polite educator, psychologist, screenwriter, and award-winning author. Alex's books have been translated into many languages including Spanish, German, Korean, Japanese, Thai, Mandarin, Romanian, Serbian, and Greek—the last of which Alex says "is all Greek to me." Alex is sought after by the media for his provocative commentary on manners, child-rearing, and substance abuse prevention, not to mention his recipe for key lime pie. He lectures widely across the United States and around the world. Recent talks have taken him to such far-flung locations as Caracas, Bangkok, Buenos Aires, Paris, Hamburg, Shanghai, Bogota, Beijing, Tokyo, and Mexico City. It takes all his concentration to remember where he is and whether he's supposed to bow or curtsy when being introduced.

Alex prepped at Phillips Exeter Academy, where he never once referred to kitchen personnel as "wombats" (although he *was* told to get a haircut by his dorm master). He then went to Harvard, where he pursued a joint major in social relations and finger bowls. A specialist in adolescence, parent education, and substance abuse (prevention, that is), Alex received a master's degree in education from the Harvard Graduate School of (duh) Education, and a Ph.D. in educational and developmental psychology from Boston College, where he always held doors for his professors.

For eight years, Alex was headmaster of an alternative school for children ages 11–15 in Washington, D.C. He has since served as director of education for the Capital Children's Museum and president of FCD Educational Services, Inc., a leading Boston-based provider of substance abuse prevention programs for schools worldwide. When asking kids not to use drugs, Alex always says "please."

Although it's rude to talk behind someone's back, reliable sources report that Alex has flown ultralight aircraft without crashing, spends several months a year in France, loves vintage sports cars, and chews with his mouth closed.

When asked to supply a photograph, Alex refused, saying "What?! And never be able to go out to a restaurant again without hordes of adoring teenagers asking me which fork to use?"

Do you have lots of ideas and opinions? Have you ever seen a book or website and thought, "I'd do that differently"? Then we want to hear from you! We're looking for teens to be part of the **Free Spirit Teen Advisory Council.** You'll help us keep our books and other products current and relevant by letting us know what you think about things like design, art, and content. Go to **www.freespirit.com/teens** to learn more and get an application.

Other Great Books from Free Spirit

Words Wound
Delete Cyberbullying and Make Kindness Go Viral
by Justin W. Patchin, Ph.D., and Sameer Hinduja, Ph.D.

Written by experts in cyberbullying prevention and reviewed by teens, this book provides strategies for dealing with teenage bullying happening online as well as for those who have taken part in bullying others. It also presents ways for teens to make their schools and their communities kinder places that are free from online cruelty. This book gives teens the tools they need to keep themselves and others safe. For ages 13 & up. *200 pp.; softcover, 2-color; 6" x 7½"*

Heart of a Warrior
7 Ancient Secrets to a Great Life
by Jim Langlas

Seven principles, rooted in the long tradition of Taekwondo and tied to courtesy, integrity, perseverance, self-control, indomitable spirit, community service, and love, are explored through a mix of storytelling from the Hwarang and writings from the author's former students. For ages 12 & up. *160 pp.; softcover; 2-color; 6" x 9"*

What Do You Really Want?
How to Set a Goal and Go for It! A Guide for Teens
by Beverly K. Bachel

This book is a step-by-step guide to goal setting, written especially for teens. Each chapter includes fun, creative exercises, practical tips, words of wisdom from famous "goalgetters," real-life examples from teens, and success stories. Includes reproducibles. For ages 11 & up. *144 pp.; softcover; illust.; 6" x 9"*

Interested in purchasing multiple quantities and receiving volume discounts?
Contact edsales@freespirit.com or call 1.800.735.7323 and ask for Education Sales.

Many Free Spirit authors are available for speaking engagements, workshops, and keynotes. Contact speakers@freespirit.com or call 1.800.735.7323.

For pricing information, to place an order, or to request a free catalog, contact:

Free Spirit Publishing Inc.
217 Fifth Avenue North • Suite 200 • Minneapolis, MN 55401-1299
toll-free 800.735.7323 • local 612.338.2068 • fax 612.337.5050
help4kids@freespirit.com • www.freespirit.com